THE
FAITH OF A MORALIST

MACMILLAN AND CO., LIMITED
LONDON · BOMBAY · CALCUTTA · MADRAS
MELBOURNE

THE MACMILLAN COMPANY
NEW YORK · BOSTON · CHICAGO
DALLAS · ATLANTA · SAN FRANCISCO

THE MACMILLAN COMPANY
OF CANADA, LIMITED
TORONTO

THE FAITH OF A MORALIST

GIFFORD LECTURES DELIVERED IN THE UNIVERSITY OF ST. ANDREWS, 1926–1928

BY

A. E. TAYLOR

SERIES II

NATURAL THEOLOGY AND THE POSITIVE RELIGIONS

Not where the wheeling systems darken,
  And our benumbed conceiving soars!—
The drift of pinions, would we harken,
  Beats at our own clay-shuttered doors.
FRANCIS THOMPSON.

MACMILLAN AND CO., LIMITED
ST. MARTIN'S STREET, LONDON
1931

First Edition 1930
Reprinted 1931

PRINTED IN GREAT BRITAIN
BY R. & R. CLARK, LIMITED, EDINBURGH

PREFATORY NOTE

I HAVE nothing to add here to what has already been said in the Preface to the first volume of these Lectures, further than to request the reader's particular indulgence for such oversights of the Press as he may discover in the last third of the text, which has unavoidably been "corrected" in great haste and at a distance from books. I have done my best to detect and remove errors, but it is only too possible that I have not been wholly successful.

A. E. TAYLOR

GOATHLAND, *August* 1930

Dr. Gore has called my attention to what I regretfully admit to be a double injustice to himself—though an unintentional injustice—on pp. 113 and 142. It is apparently implied in what is said there that Dr. Gore would "exclude from active participation in the devotional life of the Christian community" all who are not prepared to pledge themselves to the historical fact of the 'Virgin Birth'. I ought to have remembered that in other writings than the book from which I was quoting, Dr. Gore had expressly explained that he proposes only to exclude such persons from the ministry of the Church. And I ought also to have known that Dr. Gore has equally expressly defined his attitude on the matters referred to in the footnote on the same page. I should therefore have raised the point there dealt with but without mentioning Dr. Gore's name. In the reprint I have made what changes I can in this sense in the wording of the footnote and of the reference on p. 113. I trust that this sincere expression of my deep regrets will be accepted.

A. E. T.

EDINBURGH, *June* 1931

CONTENTS

NATURAL THEOLOGY AND THE POSITIVE RELIGIONS

We have so far discovered three great "supernatural" implications of the moral life, God, grace, and eternal life. These may be called the central "themes" of the great historical world-religions; an historical religion which should present them all adequately and preserve the right balance between them would be the "absolute" religion for mankind. In actual fact, no historical religion presents these themes in their pure metaphysical abstractness; each has what we may call its contingent side. It claims (1) to trace its origin back to a definite historical founder: (2) to bring men a message which could not have been discovered by demonstration or probable argumentation, but to be "revealed" through an historical founder: (3) to present this message in the name and with the authority of God, the source of all truths, and to possess an authoritative tradition of the right interpretation of the message: (4) and to prescribe a common rule of life and worship for the community. "Natural" religion and theology themselves have been the products of the meditation of thinkers brought up as members of societies with such specific religious traditions, and have never flourished except in a soil and atmosphere of historical religion. This can be illustrated by considering the case of influential teachers who have been personally in revolt against the prevailing tradition, *e.g.* Plato, Spinoza, George Fox. We have, then, to ask what is the right attitude for the individual man who accepts our general position to adopt towards positive institutional religions? Are the "historical" and contingent elements in them related to their permanent content as "husk" to "kernel", or rather as the skin of the living animal to its flesh? Ought a religiously minded philosopher to cultivate an attitude of detachment from the positive religious life of the community, as was often held in the nineteenth century? "Anti-clericalism" has its historical explanation, but the explanation is not an adequate justification of religious individualism, nor is the "Church" the only, or the most presently dangerous, claimant to excessive authority. Piety, like any other activity of life, is not likely to flourish vigorously in the individual unless it is sustained by a corresponding organised activity on the part of the community. "Saints" presuppose a community which cares for sanctity, as artists a society which cares for art. Yet it may be asked how we can be justified in finding any "authority" in religious matters for the individual but that of his own reason and "common sense".

On the other side all reference to the community involves the acknowledgement of some authority which is not the individual's reason and yet has a right to his allegiance. This may be illustrated by considerations taken from the fields of scholarship, science, art, morals. Even the man who effects a "Copernican revolution" is revolutionary only in respect of this or that principle; the whole body of his convictions is not a merely personal construction. It would be a paradox if religion and theology were the one sphere of human life in which authority had no place. But there is the difficulty that elsewhere the authority recognised is admittedly human and therefore limited in its range and relative, whereas the authority appealed to in the great religions is asserted to be that of God and consequently to be absolute and to be unlimited. An honest thinker, it may be argued, cannot recognise this kind of authority, and hence must practise complete detachment from the life of an historical "church".

There is a real and difficult problem here which must not be met by a crude over-simplification. We are not entitled to assume that authority in religion can only be secondary and subordinate, since it is conceivable, until the opposite has been proved, that there have been special critical contacts between the divine and the human, of special significance for the spiritual life of mankind, in fact, "revelations" through historical persons. If this is so, that which is communicated to the recipient will come to him with the character of an immediate given disclosure from the side of God, and his message will be believed in by others primarily as something which has the absolute authority of God behind it, not because it is supposed rational evidence of its truth may or might be produced. There will be a real justification for distinguishing between religious truths which can be discovered by the "natural light" and those only known on the strength of a specific "revelation". The acceptance of such a view makes the practice of an historical religion hard for the thinking man, since it raises the difficult problem of distinguishing the substance of the "revelation" from its accidents. But the power and value of a purely non-historical religion may be immeasurably inferior.

Each of the historical world-religions professes to be in possession of truth about the unseen order which could not be discovered by reflection on the features common to human experience but originates in a specific self-disclosure from the side of the unseen, and is therefore, in some sense, final, not provisional. Is it disloyalty to intelligence to concede that there is a sense in which religious truth is unprogressive? If it is, no historical religion can be universal, the only universal religion will be "religion within the limits of mere reason". There is a practical side to this issue. Each great historical religion has actually claimed to be *the* universal world-religion; hence their mutual exclusiveness. God cannot have spoken with equal finality through Moses, through Jesus, and through Mohammed, for their witness does not agree.

Against the claim of any historical religion to be the universal religion it may be argued (1) that a specific revelation is antecedently very improbable, if not impossible. Its content is either false or superfluous: (2) that no self-disclosure of God can be final, since, to be intelligible at all, it must be adapted to the peculiar "mentality" of the man through whom and the society to which it is made, and the "mental" outfit of men varies indefinitely with time and place: (3) that, in fact, the element of permanent value in all the religions has proved to be their insistence on a high moral standard which is much the same for worthy professors of them all: (4) that every such religion has included as part of its "revelation" assertions about nature and human history which are irrelevant to the spiritual life, and, in some cases, can be shown to be false. But one may reply that as to (4) it is a stricture on the incidental errors of theologians and no more. As to (3) the argument forgets that the highly virtuous outsider has regularly got his moral inspiration in the first instance from the social traditions of the believing community. Kant's "categorical imperative", for example, only yields moral direction which would satisfy Kant when it is applied by a person who has first absorbed the general moral tradition of European Protestant Christianity, as Kant himself had done. And it could not be replied that the morality characteristic of a world-religion and its other contents are "conjoined, not connected". These religions have been the most potent forces in producing moral reform, though none has ever aimed at moral reform as its chief objective. All are concerned primarily with God; the moral change follows as the effect of a new disclosure about God. Their moral effects depend on the relations with God into which they bring their adherents. In this respect religion presents an analogy with science and art; they, too, have a moral effect on those who are devoted to them, but an indirect effect. They "do us good", but not by directly, in the first instance, improving our discharge of our duties to our families and neighbours. So religion has a much more powerful influence on the discharge of social duties and yet is primarily worship, something quite different from a moral rule of life.

As to (2), it is true that any truth must be a truth for its own particular time and place, and this holds of the truths of natural science as much as of those of theology. So a great work of art, or a great philosophy, is always instinct with the spirit of its "age", and has to be understood "historically". But the question is whether because every truth must be a truth for *its* time, no truth can be a truth for *all* time. We cannot decide the issue by appealing to the propositions of pure mathematics as the type of "eternal verity". For even in mathematics there are limits to the possibility of stereotyped "symbolism". And again, mathematics at best only amounts to the construction of a formal abstract type of pattern inadequate to describe the simplest piece of concrete fact.

A more fruitful analogy is offered if we consider the works of art and imagination which are found to have permanent significance. Their "universal appeal" seems to be due to the depth with which they are rooted in the special life of the society from which they spring (*e.g. Hamlet*). The same thing is true of systems of scientific or philosophical thought, and there is no reason why it should not be true of a "revelation". Even the recipient, however, can only put the content received into words in an inadequate fashion, and he has again to communicate it to others in the language *they* understand best. Hence there is always for the theologian the problem of distinguishing the permanent substance of the "revelation" from its imperfect expression. Also, it is only tentatively that we discover what is the substance, by experience of the spiritual life of the community. This may be illustrated by consideration of the question, *e.g.*, of the value of prayer, and the objections urged against it by Kant and others.

As to (1) the objection might equally be raised against all that we call "genius". Genius has the same "intrusive" character as revelation, and a "materialistic" age is commonly sceptical about both, exactly as it is sceptical about the objectivity of the world of sensible qualities. In the life of the "genius" also we have the startling and sudden self-disclosure of realities not equally disclosed to all men and at all times, which may be called "natural revelation". The world at large only learns to apprehend the reality disclosed to the man of genius by beginning with an "act of faith", and it is reasonable to anticipate that the same thing will be true of the self-disclosure of God. In neither case does this mean that the reality

PAGE

disclosed is created by the recipient, nor yet that it could have been reached, without him, by the "unaided" natural light. The "surprises of Shakespeare" are an illustration of this. It is quite rational to hold that there is this revelational element in all the world-religions and yet to hold that some one of them may be the "final" revelation of God in any sense in which we can speak of a "final" revelation. The visible sign of the finality of a religion would be its success as a universal missionary religion (*e.g.* whether it could produce British, French, Indian, Chinese followers who could make it "native" to themselves).

The difficulty of distinguishing between a permanent "deposit of faith" and the always progressive theological formulation of it. This cannot be overcome by identifying "religion" with mere emotion, nor by the distinction between believing a statement and believing *in* a person. I cannot believe *in* a man without believing some statement about him, or share in another's faith without having some intellectual conviction in common with him. A complete divorce between religion and "dogmatic" theology is as impossible as a complete dissociation of the "physicist's world" from the "real" world of everyday life. In physics a theory which involves consequences to which our senses give the lie is thoroughly discredited. So a theological doctrine is discredited if its truth would require that the religious life of the soul should be fostered by conditions which in fact thwart it, or checked by conditions which in fact further it. Refutation of this kind, when obtainable, is final. And the attempt to dispense with intellectual formulations of faith is as real a danger to religious life as the premature stereotyping of formulae. It is not well done to leave all doors indiscriminately open.

III. Religion and the Historical 109

What has been said so far would leave it an open possibility that the *contents* of a "revelation" should all be truths of a strictly super-temporal order disclosed through historical persons and on historical occasions. But among the *credenda* propounded for belief by the great positive religions there are, in every case, some which are assertions about historical facts, past or future, and this is especially the case with Christianity. The historical religions treat these assertions about historical fact as essential, and it might be said that this, rather than the concept of revelation, is the *crux* for the philosophic mind. How can a statement about historical fact have the value of "saving truth"? Can convictions about alleged "events" have any real bearing on the spiritual life? The difficulty is increased by the considerations (1) that every great religion has, at one time or another, been forced to modify its list of such *credenda*,

(2) that many of the events propounded for belief are "miraculous" and without parallel in the ordinary course of nature, and may thus be said to be incompatible with the intelligible unity of the world. It is thus tempting to look for the fuller spiritualisation of religion by frank elimination of the historical from the contents of its creeds. But is such an attitude really justifiable? If it is, it should follow that the spiritual value, *e.g.*, of Christianity would persist undiminished if the theories of the *Christ-myth* speculations became the universally accepted tradition of mankind. But this seems incredible. The cultivation of the specifically Christian life would be destroyed by the reduction of the story of Christ to myth or allegory; a mythical Christ would no longer be evidence to the character of God. In a lesser degree other religions would suffer in the same way from the discrediting of their historical *credenda*. We might, in fact, fairly anticipate that the religion which grapples most successfully with the practical task of the reorganisation of life with God as its centre would be the religion which brings God most intimately down into the historical story of the creatures. The exceptional prominence of the historical in its *credenda* may be a proof of strength rather than a source of weakness. The completest "revelation" conceivable would be an actual temporal life, subject as such to the contingency characteristic of the temporal, which should be also, in all its detail, the complete and adequate vehicle of the eternal. That such a life has been lived in actual fact is the conviction which gives Christianity its distinctive character. Acceptance of the conviction as true demands a specific act of "faith", and cannot be fully justified by appeal to empirical evidences, a consideration too often forgotten in popular apologetics. It has to be admitted that the impartial historian must regard very few facts of the life of Christ as known with certainty, and that the Gospel narratives must not be treated as beyond the range of critical scrutiny, and again that the Gospel contains no formulated complete rule of life for all times and places. Appeal to the records at best avails to show that it is *possible* to interpret the narrative of Christ's life in a way consistent with the claims made by Christianity for his person. And it seems clear that the first historians did not base their faith either on detailed acquaintance with their Lord's biography or reflection on the excellence of his moral teaching, but on the direct impression of contact with a "numinous" personality. What facts they knew they saw in the light of Pentecost. There is, indeed, a real appeal to history by which a religion may be judged, the raising of the question whether its founder has brought a new spiritual quality into human life. The historian who is to try this issue must himself have the gift of genuine spiritual vision. His verdict will thus always involve a personal factor, as, in

PAGE

fact, all serious historical appreciation always does. It cannot be given on the strength of mere erudition and critical acumen. In the case of Christianity the verdict on the attempt to retain the specifically Christian spiritual life while reducing the person of Christ to a symbol is not really in doubt. Such attempts are as old as the dawn of Christian speculative theology. The struggle with Docetism and Gnosticism was already beginning before the latest New Testament documents were composed. Though, in some ways, the Church suffered in the conflict, it is historically undeniable that the victory of the heretics would have killed its spiritual life. At bottom the attempt to divest religion of attachments to historical persons and events is an attempt to manufacture the supreme reality out of mere "universals", or to make an "is" out of a mere "ought", and ends by degrading religion into theosophy. The presence of statements about historical facts among the *credenda* of the great religions is thus no mere accident. But it is not possible to say with finality just how much in the tradition is historical fact. Consensus as to the historical character of the central fact is compatible with wide divergence in the estimation of details. On the other side it is dangerous to dismiss such a *credendum* summarily on the ground that it has no "spiritual value", and is therefore irrelevant to religion. The *presumption* is that the proposition asserted was asserted because it was taken to have such a value, and my personal inability to discover the value is not sufficient proof that it no longer exists. Private judgement needs here to be tempered by docile humility. It may be urged that the authority of the spiritually-minded should not be taken into account in these matters on the ground that spirituality and sound historical judgement are not *in pari materia*. This would be conclusive but for one consideration, viz., that the point on which the appeal is made is not a point of naked fact. But it remains true that the rights of spiritual intuition are narrowly circumscribed. There is also an equal need for humility and docility on the part of the representatives of an official tradition.

IV. THE SUPERNATURAL AND THE MIRACULOUS . . 150

A special difficulty is created by the "miraculous" character of some of the historical facts included in the *credenda* of the positive religions. Apart from the old *a priori* rejection of such events as impossible, they are attacked either on the ground that increasing acquaintance with natural science leads one to believe that such events do not happen, or on the ground that anthropology can account for the belief in them without admitting its truth. Why should we desert in one case the anthropological explanation we accept in all other similar

cases? This is really the most powerful of the current arguments against "miracles", though it probably exaggerates the degree of resemblance between the "miracles" asserted by the great religions and the tales of folk-lore. The question for us is whether the conception of the relation of the world to God implied by "miracle" is unphilosophical. It is important to distinguish clearly between the notions of the supernatural and of the miraculous. There can be no religion without belief in the supernatural, but there may well be religion without belief in the miraculous. It may be held that the "supernatural", just because it is present everywhere, must not be looked for in any special unusual or startling events, and that the tendency to look for it in that quarter is a "survival" from primitive superstition. Yet the belief in the great miracles of, *e.g.*, Christianity did not arise in a society with the supposed "mentality" of the primitive savage, unaware of the existence of a "routine of nature". What the belief really illustrates is the persistent tendency of minds to which that conception is familiar to expect that the unexpected will attend the doings of men through whom God discloses himself, as a "sign". The persistence of the tendency is no proof of its soundness, but does suggest the question whether it is merely mistaken. We might conceive of an eternal purpose either as quietly pervading the whole course of history or as also revealing itself specially by "intrusions", and antecedently neither conception seems more reasonable than the other. Such analogies as are afforded by the relations between novelty and routine in a well-lived life or a work of art cut both ways. The saint or hero or genius is neither an "eccentric" nor a creature of routine. We can "count on" him, and yet he does surprise us by his "originality", though, after the event, we find the "surprise" eminently rational. The success of such theories as that of "emergent evolution" seems to show that something very much like "miracle", an element of the abrupt and discontinuous, meets us in all fields and cannot be "rationalised" away, since the historical and individual cannot be analysed completely into universals. And in human life the reality of what are called "miracles" of genius or of grace is indisputable. Refusal to allow the occurrence of anything analogous in the course of "nature" seems to be due to mere prejudice. The historical is really one, not divided into two water-tight compartments, the physical and the mental. This does not mean that reality is irrational but merely that we never succeed in completely rationalising it; the rationality of the whole is a "postulate of the practical reason", and it is never a final argument against the reality of a fact to say that it cannot be harmonised with the "laws of nature" as at present known. Nor is the reality of miracle disposed of by the true contention

PAGE

that the vast majority of "miraculous" narratives are untrustworthy. We may say in general of "nature-miracles": (1) that to call an event a miracle means that it is at once startling, a "portent " and also a "sign", a special disclosure of the divine purpose; (2) that the event belongs to the *sensible* order. An event might be startling without being a "sign", or might be a "sign" without being startling, but such events would not be called miracles. Hence there are two distinguishable questions about an alleged miraculous event—(1) Did it occur? (2) Has it the religious value of a "sign"? (*e.g.* it would be possible to hold that Christ rose from the dead and yet to deny that this event has any significance). "Historical evidence" only goes to establish (1), and leaves (2) untouched. The event can only be recognised as a "sign" by an act of faith. This suggests that "miraculous" is a relative term, like "probable", and that what is "miraculous" relatively to one "standard of reference" may not be so relatively to another. This view would be incompatible with the traditional distinction between events produced "immediately" by God and those produced "through second causes", but this distinction itself is difficult to sustain. A miracle, then, would be an event recognised as having a "numinous" character. That this character is often wrongly ascribed is no sufficient reason for holding that the description is always incorrect. Right recognition of the "numinous" may be as hard as right recognition of beauty. The conception of the miraculous is only in place in a *rationalist* philosophy. In an irrationalism like Hume's, where anything is possible and nothing is significant, the problem does not really arise. A theist and a non-theist will necessarily differ about the kind of "singularity" which may be expected in the course of events, and this makes it reasonable that they should estimate the "evidence" for an alleged miracle differently.

V. The Meaning and Place of Authority . . 197

Somewhere, in every great positive religion, appeal is made to an authority which claims to be that of God and therefore absolute. What comes to us with this authority, it is claimed, must be accepted, whether it commends itself to our judgement or not, with a *foi du charbonnier*. But it is also maintained that to recognise any such absolute authority is treason to reason. It is held that there ought to be no initial acceptance by faith of that which is unexamined; that there is no more absolute and divine authority than the individual human reason and conscience. Yet it is clear that individualism of this kind must logically be fatal to the claim of any religion to be universal or supremely directive of life. Historically, religious movements which guide and deepen spiritual life seem to be regularly

accompanied by revival of insistence on authority of some kind. All attempts to locate authority in a definite seat seem to fail, and yet it seems also impossible to conceive of an adequate religion without an element of mystery and a consequent note of authority. The presence of mystery is, in fact, a direct consequence of the individuality of the real. The function of intelligence is always to transubstantiate immediate apprehension into recognition, and this function can never be completely achieved. Authority is the assertion of the reality of an experience which contains more than the individual experient can analyse out for himself. This may be illustrated analogically by the authoritativeness of sense-perception for our knowledge of physical reality. If there are undeniable facts received on the testimony of sense which will not square with our intellectual constructions, it is always these constructions which have to give way, and sense-perception thus has a position analogous to that claimed by the theologian for his authority. The appeal to authority thus means that the object of religion is not constructed or postulated by the intellect but found as given in a context which contains something more than mere thinking. It should be noted that in neither case can we demonstrate that "givenness" is not an illusion, and in neither can we come upon any primitive experience which consists purely of the "given" without any element of intellectual interpretation. The simplest attempt to say what is given already involves interpretation. This is why the "infallibility of sense" does not guarantee the inerrancy of any single "judgement of sense". There is a sense in which sense is authoritative, or even "infallible", and yet no record of observation is beyond criticism. Similarly in respect of human knowledge of God, if it is to be genuine knowledge and not mere personal opinion, there must be authoritative control of my convictions by a reality not "constructed" but "given", and impressive contacts with such a reality, not being indispensable to the mere maintenance of the organism, are not given to all of us. This is why we cannot find our authority in the "common sense" of the average man, any more than we can make the musical perceptions of the average man an authority. In all these cases the individual experience at once invites and defies intellectual analysis. The rightful demand of the intellect for freedom to think and for protection against the vagaries of pure subjectivity are only to be harmonised by the cultivation at once of docility and adventurousness. The docility must not be confined to one section of the community and the adventurousness to another. Official custodians of truth who lose the spirit of docility proportionately forfeit their claim to authority. And it is imperative to recognise that rightful authority is not the same thing as inerrancy, and that the permanence of truth is compatible with the obsolescence of the formulae in which we seek to convey it. True docility on the part of the official representatives of theology would have as a consequence a salutary advance on the part of philosophical thinkers from religiosity to religion and an increased respect for the dogmatic formulae of the great religions. It would be increasingly understood that in no field where there is a genuine "given" for the intellect to work on can the fruit of the protracted elaboration of this "given" be neglected.

Is it a valid objection to this distinction between authoritativeness and infallibility to urge that it may hold good when the authority appealed to is that of accumulated human thought or experience, but not in theology, where the authority appealed to is divine? When we remember (1) that the self-communication of the divine is always conditioned by the creatureliness of the recipient and (2) that nature and supernature have the same source, the objection seems to lose its force. The real worth of an authority which is not tantamount to formal infallibility may be well illustrated by considering the authority of conscience. Conscience is not infallible; yet its authority constitutes a strict obligation.

The history of any of the great religions will illustrate the universality both of the tendency of religions to create an elaborate system of institutional and ceremonial worships and of the opposition that tendency awakens. We find everywhere both the drift towards conventionalising the expressions of the religious life and the rebellion against this tendency as "unspiritual". ("Ritual" not to be confused with pomp. The antithesis is not so much between splendour and simplicity as between convention and spontaneity.) The tendency to conventionalism and the tension against it are equally to be found in connection with other characteristic human activities. Every social activity tends to create its ritual, and the ritual tends to provoke a reaction against itself. Neither the tendency to ritual nor that away from it is wholly good or wholly bad. Every social activity, if it is to be preserved from debasement, needs to find worthy outward expression, and if it is to be kept alive, needs to have its occasions of special prominence, and it is here that "ritual" has its justification; the most adequate "ritual" is always in danger of becoming merely external; hence the necessity for a perpetual tension against it. The antithesis is the same which we meet everywhere between the devotees of significant form and the enthusiasts for a vitality which bursts all bounds. The absolute rejection of "ritual" would mean complete quietism, and a complete quietism would

PAGE

be fatal to vitality itself. We may illustrate from a consideration of the results of neglect of the "ritual", *e.g.*, of family or national life. Some "ritual" is demanded for the simple reasons that men are forgetful creatures, and the extemporised expression is always liable to be inadequate. These considerations apply to the activity of the community in worship, and here the tension is naturally felt at its keenest. Ritual form seems to be specially necessary for the activities in which the community is to be most completely lifted above the level of worldly transactions, and yet the very intimacy of the relation of the worshipper to God makes him resentful of confinement to special occasions and modes of approach. Hence the modern tendency to imagine a sharp contrast between a "prophetic" and a "priestly" type of religion, and to regard the latter as unspiritual. On a lower level, the opposition to institutionalism may be prompted by worldliness and indifferentism, or again by the view that the whole value of religion lies in its perceptible results in the promotion of good morals. But it is a bad mistake to value religion solely as instrumental to morality. To degrade worship into a mere means to moral reforms is like degrading art into a mere vehicle of instruction. Both religion and art owe most of their moralising and reforming influence to the fact that they aim primarily at something else. And religion is degraded again when it is regarded as merely a private transaction between the individual and God. The object experienced, which gives the experience its significance, is not private. Hence it is no valid objection against the forms of an institutional religion that many of them have no direct connection with moral improvement, and again it is unreasonable to demand that the community's forms of worship shall always be those sensibly beneficial to myself in particular. Neither religion nor art is the speciality of a small *intelligentsia*, and to overcome our personal repugnance to that which appeals to cruder minds is a reasonable exercise in humility. Nor is it really true that even the most artificial "institutional" worships exclude the spontaneous lifting up of the heart. Still the attainment of the right balance in devotion between freedom and prescribed form is always a "costing" thing, and it might be well if communities, and even individual congregations, took more care to avoid becoming slaves to a single "use".

VII. SACRAMENTALISM 289

A special difficulty is often felt about the sacramentalism characteristic of historical religion. A sacrament is a ritual act which besides being a ritual act is held to be a channel of grace, an *efficacious* sign or "instrumental cause" through which the Creator acts on the created spirit. It is said that belief in such sacraments is irrational, a survival of "materialistic magic". This language, however, obscures the real issue. Some acts which originated in savage "magic" may perhaps have been continued into the sacramentalism of the historic religions, but they owe their place there as sacraments to their having received a significance which takes them out of the category of the magical (*e.g.* circumcision in Judaism, the Lord's Supper in Christianity). The act is regarded as sacramental because it is believed to be of divine appointment and to have specific consequences attached to it in virtue of this appointment. It does not produce the effect, as a magical act does, automatically. Magic is, like its descendant natural science, a strictly "this-world" affair; a sacrament is an occasion of activity coming from the "other-world". The problem is whether it is irrational to hold that specific bodily things and acts may become by divine appointment the usual vehicles of a specific contact between the divine and the human spirit. The prejudice on this point is only one form of the more genuine prejudice of a false spirituality against the body. In fact it is the general rule that the physical is everywhere instrumental to the spiritual. If we take the word sacrament in a wider sense to mean any physical occasion which normally ministers to the soul's life, there are natural sacraments and the physical world is pervaded by them. (A man's thinking and conduct are normally influenced for the better if he is properly fed, gets proper sleep, air, and exercise.) Here, as in the sacraments of religion, the dependence of the effect on the instrument is usual, not universal, and the benefit presupposes the co-operation of the right disposition in the recipient. The possibility of a "nature-miracle" does not justify negligence of the regular "means". Again specific intellectual, artistic, moral achievements are normally dependent on the awakening of interest by features of the physical environment. Normally genius gets its opportunity from occasions furnished by specific surroundings. We might thus expect that if there is a still higher level of spiritual life concerned with conscious relation to the eternal, the body and its occasions would have an analogous place to fill at that level. It is true that in the cases we have considered the instrumentality of the bodily is part of the *cursus ordinarius* of nature, and does not depend on a special historic divine appointment, but this difference cannot be regarded as ultimate by a theist. Or it might be said that if the bestowal of grace is a supernatural transaction between Creator and created, there should be no instrumentality at all. Logically, perhaps, this view is tenable, but it would be as fatal to belief in the "ministry of the word" as to belief in sacraments. The true question, however, is not

PAGE

how God must act but how He does act. Hostility to sacramentalism largely arises from the inability to think historically characteristic of philosophies which regard mathematics as the one type of true knowledge. The true question, then, is whether if there is a quality of life which is specifically religious, life with that quality is normally exhibited at its highest in connection with definite practice of sacramental acts or in detachment from them. The appeal requires to be made to the history of whole communities if it is to receive a definite answer, and attention should not even be confined to the history of a single great religion. Thus it is desirable to compare the spiritual effects of a highly sacramental religion like Christianity with those of a non-sacramental religion like Mohammedanism, and the comparison should be a double one, of the saints of one religion with those of the other and also of the average sinners of both. The effects to be considered, again, should be those which are fruits of the specifically religious life.

VIII. The Ultimate Tension 320

The source of the apparent incompatibility of so many of the leading characteristics of the great positive religions with a rationalistic metaphysic seems to lie in a rooted prejudice of the metaphysical mind against ascribing reality and significance to the historical. The positive religions ascribe so much more reality to the temporal than is conceded by many metaphysicians. (The same prejudice has shown itself in Christian theology in the traditional doctrine of the divine impassivity.) It is significant that there seems good reason to hold that it has been the permeation of Western European thought by a positive religion which has taught us to think historically in a way not possible to the ancient world. (*Cf.* the objection of Celsus that the Christians "believe in a myth which does not admit an allegorical explanation.") Our own outlook in physical science itself is historical in a sense in which that of the Greek philosophers was not. What the influence of Christianity brought into the world was an adequate sense of the significance of individuality, and the present trend in the philosophy of the sciences towards an "historicising" of the physical sciences is itself an effect of this. Hence it would be a strange paradox to hold that in religion and theology reversion from a historical to a "geometrical" way of thinking could be an advance. The distinction between "historical" and "geometrical" illustrated by reference to the contrast between Time as described in the *Timaeus* of Plato and the *durée réelle* of Bergson, or the space-time of later thinkers. The important point is that *real* duration is "local" time, and that every different type of con-

PAGE

tinuant in the cosmic "becoming" has its own characteristic intrinsic *tempo*, and its own "biography". For the philosophy of History this means that the conviction that history is a drama with a meaning and an author does not furnish us with any means of anticipating the actual movement of events on the strength of a formula, or of saying in advance where we may expect the incidents which unveil the purpose of the drama. Contingency requires to be recognised as more intimately ingrained in the historical than philosophers have been willing to admit. The attempt to reach the deepest truth about the world, after the fashion of Spinoza, by contemplating the historical "under a form of eternity", *i.e.* as not really historical, is necessarily illusory, a mere deindividualising of a reality which is through and through individual. Spinoza himself should have been led logically to the conclusion that the "attributes of God" are totally unknown to us. In the actual world we never come upon anything which has no more individuality than consists merely in being located here and now in a framework of reference; we do come upon endless degrees of wealth of individual character. The richer the individuality, the less are its adventures prescribed for it by relation with individuals of an inferior type. Completed individuality, such as could only be found in the *ens realissimum* would mean that the intrinsic character of the individual is the sole determinant of its life. What we see in "historical" individuals is neither such stabilised "being", nor mere "becoming", but "becoming" tending to the establishment and maintenance of stable activity of self-expression. The bearing of this on (*a*) the practice of an institutional religion, (*b*) the difficulties connected with the conception of divine immobility and impassivity.

IX. Review and Conclusion 373

Final words on the degree of autonomy which may rightly be claimed for the sciences in general and for ethics in particular. This autonomy is real and genuine, in the sense that every science is entitled to pursue its own problems by its own methods without dictation from either metaphysics or theology as to the results it shall arrive at. But the principle itself also incidentally justifies theology in refusing to be made into a mere instrument of ethics. And it is a consequence of the unity of life and experience that the bearings of the conclusions of any science on morality and religion are relevant to the truth of those conclusions. "Autonomy" must not be confused with a supposed right to dictate. Nor must it be forgotten that knowledge is more extensive than science, and life than both.

I

THE PROBLEM STATED

Καὶ ἔχομεν βεβαιότερον τὸν προφητικὸν λόγον, ᾧ καλῶς ποιεῖτε προσέχοντες.—2 Pet. i. 19.

In the first series of these lectures we have been concerned to argue that whole-hearted acceptance of the postulates of the moral life itself involves an outlook on the world and on man's place in it which is more than merely moralistic. The good man who thinks out to the end the implications of his loyalty to the moral good, we urged, will find that he is pledged to something more than simple recognition of an ideal of conduct as entitled to his unqualified respect. He is committed, we held, to a belief in the final coincidence of the "ought" and the "is", in virtue of their common source in a transcendent living and personal Good—one, complete, eternal—the only belief which rightfully deserves to be called belief in God. He is also committed to the recognition that whatever is, other than God Himself, is a creature of God, having the token of its creatureliness stamped upon it by its temporality and "passage"; that for a reasonable creature, such as man, the fundamental concern of life is a reorganisation of personality, only possible as a response to an initial movement manwards on the part of the Eternal itself, by which reorganisation the creature comes to seek and find its own intimate felicity not in the temporal, but in the abiding; that the very imperativeness of this quest makes it only reasonable to anticipate ultimate attainment in a life no longer condemned to failure by its inherent successiveness. In a word, we tried to show that the moral life of man, rightly studied, bears impressive testimony to three great strictly *supernatural* or *other-world* realities—God, grace, eternal life. An attitude to life and the world dominated by these recognitions is clearly entitled to be called definitely religious, since it is they which are the mainsprings of what we know in history as the great positive religions of mankind, and can be seen to be so with increasing clearness in the proportion in which each of these religions has proved able to control the type not of some one minor social group, with special local, racial, or other characteristics, but of humanity at large.

God, grace, eternal life, we may say, are the three interconnected themes from which all the great religions have been built up, much as a whole series of musicians, from Nicolai to Mendelssohn, have left us their different versions of the melody known, I believe, as the *deutsche Gloria*. Or, to express the same thought in a different terminology, they might be called the "arguments" of which the great positive religions are "functions", or the "determinables" of which these religions are "determinants". One religion may, indeed, give special prominence to one of these "themes" or "arguments" at the cost of others, with consequent loss to itself in wealth of contents. Thus, I take it, it would not be wholly unjust to say that in Mohammedanism—I speak as a mere outsider and always subject to the correction of those who know from within—the themes of "grace", as something distinct from a mere condonation of offences, and "eternal life", as other than mere unending continuance of a life of strictly temporal quality, are very much in the background. In some modern versions of Christianity,[1] and, again, I should suppose —speaking again as a very ill-informed outsider—in Buddhism, it is God, the most fundamental theme of all, that is relatively obscured. To preserve the right balance between all three is no easy matter, and the faith which can do this effectively may fairly be said to have made out its superior claim to be the "absolute" or final religion for man. But all three, I should say, are to be discerned in any religion which has proved on the large scale its power to govern the hearts and minds of humanity. The mere absence of any is, as it seems to me, just what makes the difference between a religion and a, possibly splendid, speculation. Spinozism, for example—I mean the convictions to which Spinoza is strictly entitled if his professed premisses are true and his conclusions validly inferred from them—remains a speculative metaphysic and nothing more, just because there is no room in the scheme for "grace", the outgoing movement of God towards man. "Theosophy" and "spiritualism", again, are speculations, and at bottom I think we must say irreligious speculations, because both make God really superfluous and know nothing of a genuine sense of "creatureliness".

If we turn from our three great themes to the actual religions in which they have been embodied, we are at once struck by the fact that the three great "determinables" are never found actually operative as dominating human life in their pure metaphysical abstractness. They actually dominate only as further specified in all sorts of ways by particular "determinants". Every religion which has ever achieved anything of moment towards lifting men above mere worldliness has been

[1] I am thinking of the kind of religion which von Hügel had in view in his warnings against undue "Christo-centricism". F. H. Bradley once remarked to me years ago, in the same spirit, that "the modern Christian really worships Jesus Christ, not the Father".

more than a metaphysic of God, grace, and eternal life. All have their *philosophical* side, but all have also another side, which we may call the *contingent*, or, in a sufficiently wide sense, the *historical*. For one thing, unlike tribal cults and nature-religions, all claim not to have sprung up no one knows how or when, but to trace their origins back to definite historical "founders" —Our Lord, Moses, Mohammed son of Abdullah, Zoroaster, Gautama, Orpheus.[1] Each insists on at least one fact of the historical order as vital to itself, the alleged fact that its characteristic teaching, rule of life, or worship, goes back to a founder who was a genuine man among men. In each, again, this founder is held to have brought men a message of some kind not attainable, independently of his personality, by any process of demonstration, or weighing of probable arguments. The founder is always believed to have spoken with immediate knowledge of matters which the rest of mankind could never have known except as mediated by his direct apprehension. Each of these religions thus claims to be a *revelation*, a disclosing, through an historical personage, of some truth of the supra-historical order which we should not have learned but for that specific disclosure. In almost all cases the founder is held to have received the disclosure which constitutes his message, or mission, immediately from God. Buddhism, indeed, standing as it does on the border-line between a religion and a metaphysic, may be said to be an exception, but it is an exception of the kind which is said to "prove the rule". Even in the Buddha's case, his message to men, though not supposed apparently to come from God—of whom Buddhism origin-

[1] I would add that the "historicity" of the founder seems to be a *genuine* historical fact in all the cases mentioned except the last, and that even "Orpheus" is quite likely to be no real exception. The name probably does conceal some actual "prophet" of whose personal history we know nothing.

ally apparently knew nothing—retains the significant appellation of the "great *illumination*". That is, I presume, it is regarded as a *sudden immediate* disclosure of truth, following on, but not inferred from, the intensely concentrated meditation said in the legend to have prepared the way for its reception. In some form or other, immediate revelation, to and through a particular historical person, seems regularly to appear as the asserted origin of all the great religions which in any way lift man above mere "nature". It is surely significant that it should be only the nature-religions that do not claim to have begun with a *revelation*, an *intrusion* of the "other" and supra-historical into the ordinary historical routine of "becoming".

A further direct consequence of this abruptness and intrusiveness of origin is that in all the great positive religions there is a sheer *authoritarian* element. For the followers of any of them, there are things of the first importance to be believed, or to be done, which must, in the first instance at least, be accepted, not because their reasonableness is self-evidently or demonstrably established, nor yet because these things have been believed or done through an immemorial past, and so are a part of the "customs of our ancestors", but because they have been asserted or commanded by an infallible voice from the "other" world. Normally, the voice is, in the last resort, that of God, the eternal source of all truths, directly disclosing truth to the founder—Moses, or Zoroaster, or Mohammed,[1] or, as in the case of Christianity, speaking more directly still

[1] I do not forget here that, to be precise, the Mohammedan tradition is that the Prophet's revelations were brought to him through the medium of the angel Gabriel, but this is a matter of detail which does not seriously affect the statement of the text. It might be urged that, according to the general view of scholars, *written* "scripture" is a relatively late thing in Hebrew religion, unknown to the earlier prophets. But my point is that Judaism only became a world-religion when it had come to appeal to a *written* "Law of Moses" as its basis.

through the mouth of a person who is actually God as well as man. Usually, again, the authoritative revelation is not confined to a single short message; it has an extended compass and is embodied in *scriptures*, sacred writings of considerable magnitude, and these have consequently an authority derived from their transcendent source. An extreme example is the well-known doctrine of Mohammedan theologians that the actual vocables of the Koran are uncreated and eternal.[1] The Christian scriptures have rarely, if ever, been exalted by theologians to quite this position; yet the Vatican Council was only declaring what was, until less than a century ago, the general conviction of Christians, and is still the conviction of great numbers of Christians, when it laid down that the Holy Spirit is the *author* of the whole of the canonical writings of the two Testaments, that is, that every statement in them is made on His authority and with His guarantee of its truth.[2]

Commonly, again, perhaps universally, a religion which claims to possess an authoritative Scripture claims also to enjoy a more or less ample authoritative tradition, supplying the key to the interpretation of this Scripture, and to have, by consequence, a permanent authority, vested in its officials, to determine controversies, speculative and practical, as they arise. The bitter disputes about tradition which have marked the internal history of more than one of the great religions have rarely been disputes about the existence or non-existence of such an authoritative tradition. The rejectors of the prevalent tradition have regularly challenged it in the name of some older and purer tradition of which they have claimed to be the restorers. Thus

[1] See the article "Qur'an" in *Encyclopaedia of Religion and Ethics*, x. 538 ff.

[2] "Spiritu Sancto inspirante conscripti (*sc.* libri canonici) *Deum habent auctorem.*" See the explanation of the formula (by E. L. van Becelaere) in art. "Inspiration" (Roman Catholic doctrine), *E.R.E.* vii. 350 ff.

the original Protestant reformers of the sixteenth century, in general, professed not to be rejecting tradition in principle, but to be restoring the genuine apostolic tradition which had been corrupted in the course of the dark and middle ages of "Papistry", just as, it was held, the first Christians had rescued the truer tradition of the meaning of the Old Testament from the perversions of the "Scribes and Pharisees".

Finally, the great organised positive religions have always been expressions of the convictions and aspirations of whole societies, and have inevitably exhibited themselves as features of the social life of communities with a common core of belief and a common worship and rule of life. They have therefore regularly found embodiment in institutions and institutional churches. So, if we try to construct a *type* of positive world-religion from consideration of the various actual religions which a reasonable classification would recognise as falling under the type, we may, I think, fairly say that historical origin, revelational character, authority, tradition, institutionalism, are all features of the type.

The point, then, to which I would call attention is a twofold one. In the first place, there never has been an actual religion, with real power over men's hearts, which has had no content beyond that of such a natural, or philosophical, theology as we have been hitherto considering. There has never been a society of men with a living religion whose religion has made no appeal to the contingent, known of no historical founder, no revelation, no tradition, claimed no authority, or embodied itself in no institutions. Every great religion which has done much for the spiritual regeneration of mankind has done the work just in proportion as it has made God, grace, eternal life, realities to its followers, but none has ever made them real except through and in dependence on the contingent, insistence on historical persons and happenings, specific revelations, authoritative traditions, venerated institutions. Men have never been regenerated by a faith like that of Rousseau's Savoyard Vicar, never been trained for eternity by the cult of Robespierre's *Être suprême*. Moreover, "natural" religion and theology themselves have regularly made their appearance as products of the meditation of men brought up as members of a community with a specific religious tradition of its own; and, further, the quality of the philosophic theology and devotion of the thinkers who have been historically important in this field is found on examination to be deeply coloured by the positive religious tradition of the society in which such a thinker has been brought up, even when he happens to be personally in marked rebellion against that tradition. There seems to be little ground to believe that philosophical theology itself would flourish, except in a soil and atmosphere saturated with historical religion.

Thus in Plato we have—in the tenth book of the *Laws*—a resolute attempt to *demonstrate* the main tenets of a philosophical or natural theology, the existence of God, the moral government of the world, the eternal abidingness of the issues of human conduct, independently of any appeal to history, revelation, or authority; but if we seek to discover the source of these passionately held convictions, we surely must go back to the influence of the example of the life and death of Socrates, and the *Apology* of itself makes it abundantly clear that the personal faith which inspired the life of Socrates had been fed by the revelational religion of the Orphics.[1] Spinoza is perhaps the most striking case

[1] I may be allowed, since the point is important, to quote my own words in another place. "The specific allusions of [*Apol.*] 41 A to Hesiod, Musaeus, Orpheus and the Orphic judges of the dead . . . make it clear that Socrates' convictions are not meant as simply inferences from 'natural theology'; we have to see in

among modern thinkers of a man who makes the impression of having a purely natural or philosophical religion of his own, wholly unindebted to the doctrine or practice of an historical religious community, as its author, in fact, lived an outcast from the Synagogue, without either receiving or seeking admission into the Church. If we could look anywhere for religion wholly independent of history, revelation, authority, institutions, it is hard to see where we might look with better prospect of success than in Spinoza's *Ethics*. Yet, when we come to the one specifically religious element in Spinoza's great book, the element which was manifestly more precious than any other to the philosopher himself, the doctrine of that "intellectual love" of man for God which is one with God's "infinite" and eternal love for Himself, and, for that reason, is man's only way of escape from slavery to paltry vanities and passions into freedom, we see at once that the whole conception of this way of salvation is at variance with the naturalistic foundations of Spinoza's metaphysic and psychology. If "God" is only an honorific name for nature, conceived as a simple, everlastingly selfsame, "conservative system"; if love is "delight accompanied by an idea of the cause of the same", and delight the "transition from a less to a greater perfection"—all assertions formally made in the *Ethics*[1]—

---

them the influence of the Orphic religion, though the *Euthyphro* and the second book of the *Republic* show that Socrates thought very poorly of the ordinary run of 'professing' Orphics in his own time" (*Plato, the Man and His Work*, p. 167).

[1] *Ethica* i. def. 6, props. 14, 29, 33; ii. 44; iii. affectuum definitiones 2, 6. The drift of the whole is that there can be no *amor* where there is no *laetitia*, no *laetitia* where there is no *transitio* to a higher level of "perfection". But God, or nature, the one really existing substance, is once and for all completely perfect and experiences no *transitio*. We cannot even say of Spinoza's *substantia*, *plus ça change, plus c'est la même chose*, since, in fact, *ça ne change point*. Indeed, in rigour it is inconsistent with Spinoza's nominalism about "universals" to admit that "Peter or Paul", or anything else, can really become more or less "perfect". In strictness all *amor* should be the effect of an illusion which adequate thinking dissipates.

to say that "God loves himself with an infinite intellectual love", and that man can enter into that love, is to utter a meaningless contradiction in set terms. Clearly we must look for the true source of the very doctrine which has won for Spinoza the reverence of so many fine natures, distracted by the warfare of creeds and confessions, outside the four corners of his own system. The God who thus loves Himself is not really the "substance" of the *First Part* of the *Ethics*; He is the "Blessed One" of the devout Jewish home in which the philosopher had been brought up.[1]

We may fairly apply to the philosophical theologian who fancies that he has cut his religion and theology loose from all attachments to the historical and contingent what von Hügel has excellently said of the type of Christian who, like George Fox,[2] sets himself in violent opposition to all that is recognisably authoritarian or traditional in Christianity. The individualist is anxious to acknowledge no source of his inspiration except a strictly personal and incommunicable "inner light"; yet, since he is, after all, a man born of woman, not a solitary of nature like the fabled phoenix, he invariably reveals his own dependence on tradition and the community in the very act of defiance, as Fox did, when he announced as his own particular illumination doctrine actually to be found in set words in the Fourth Gospel, the most authoritarian and sacramentarian of the New Testament documents. Or as Descartes did, in a different sphere, when he reproduced Proclus' doctrine of causation as a thing "immediately evident by the natural light".[3] An impressive example on the

[1] Kant's "moral theology", again, is all through really moulded by the evangelical Pietism against which Kant himself is in such violent revolt, as is manifest to the reader of *Religion innerhalb der Grenzen der blossen Vernunft*.

[2] *Essays and Addresses*, first series, pp. 92, 293.

[3] *Med.* iii. lumine naturali manifestum est tantundem ad minimum esse debere in causa efficiente et totali, quantum in eiusdem causae effectu, etc. The *causa*

other side, illustrative of the way in which a "natural religion", deliberately cut loose and kept loose from attachments in the historical community's tradition of belief and worship, soon degenerates into a naturalism with nothing religious about it, is afforded by the history of English Deism in the eighteenth century, with its rapid descent from a genuine, if thin and sentimental, devoutness into coarse and commonplace worldliness.[1]

Reflection on these familiar facts seems to force on the thoughtful mind the question, What is the right attitude for one who agrees with the main conclusions we have so far reached to adopt towards positive institutional religion? Is the quintessence of true piety to be looked for in a purely philosophic religion, wholly detached from all the revelational, historical, authoritarian, institutional elements of the existing faiths of mankind? Is all this "contingent" factor in those faiths no more than an accidental husk of disfiguring accretions, of which we may expect to see "true" religion divest itself more and more to its own great advantage, as its spiritual and abiding significance is more clearly understood?[2] Or may it possibly be that these elements of the contingent and particular are not irrelevant

---

efficiens is simply the παρακτικὸν ἄλλου of Proclus, and the principle assumed is equivalent to *Inst. Theol.* 7 πᾶν τὸ παρακτικὸν ἄλλου κρεῖττόν ἐστι τῆς τοῦ παραγομένου φύσεως. The distinction of *formaliter*, *obiective*, *eminenter*, on which Descartes' subsequent reasoning turns, is just Proclus' distinction of καθ' ὕπαρξιν, κατὰ μέθεξιν, καθ' αἰτίαν.

[1] Contrast the temper of Shaftesbury, for example, or, for the matter of that, of Locke's *Reasonableness of Christianity*, with that of Collins or Toland (if, that is, the historians of philosophy, on whom I am here dependent, have not misrepresented the latter two).

[2] Cf. the tone of Pope's *Universal Prayer*, or, to take an example from a different quarter, of the quatrain numbered 34 in Whinfield's text of Omar Khayyám. (I quote Whinfield's version of the lines.)

> "Pagodas" [the text says bluntly "idol-houses"], "just as mosques,
> are homes of prayer,
> 'Tis prayer that church-bells chime into the air,
> Yea, Church and Ka'ba, Rosary and Cross
> Are all but divers tongues of world-wide prayer."

trappings, but themselves an integral and indispensable factor in a living religion? Possibly the very metaphor of the "husk" should serve to remind us that though the husk is not the kernel, the kernel will certainly not ripen without any protective husk, and still less can an animal thrive without its skin. When we dream of a "true" religion without creed, church, or institutions, we may be making the same mistake as those physicists of the last century who supposed themselves to be getting down to the "reality behind appearances" by converting the physical world into a vast apparatus of differential equations. This is the issue to which I propose to devote the remainder of our inquiry.

It has, indeed, been suggested to me that in even raising the question I am travelling outside the bounds set to the treatment of my subject by Lord Gifford's directions. I cannot see that the suggestion is justified. Certainly, Lord Gifford's expressed intentions would make it improper to convert these lectures into a simple apologetic for the specific *credenda* or *facienda* of a particular historical religion, a thing I have no desire to do. But I do not see how the instruction that the subject of religion is to be treated "from the point of view of natural reason" can in any way preclude us from raising the question whether natural reason does, or does not, demand from those who would be loyal to it an attitude of hostility to, or at least detachment from, the organised life of the religious community. Whether it is irrational to believe in the possibility or the fact of a "revelation", to profess a creed, to join in the *cultus* of a specific community, are questions of vital concern for the whole future of religion among mankind, questions which the very necessity of ordering our own personal life on some definite plan forces upon each of us, and natural reason may fairly be presumed to have something to say in the matter. We cannot, even if we would, debar the intellect from asking the question whether "philosophic theology" is to be regarded as one theology among others, competing with the rest for the exclusive allegiance of mankind, or rather as an element all-pervasive in every faith worthy of respect, but incapable of constituting by itself the whole of a reasonable man's faith. We might as well deny the right of the intellect to raise the question whether the truth about the natural world can be reached by exclusive reliance on *a priori* rational mechanics or not. It would, no doubt, be a violation of Lord Gifford's instructions to make consideration of this broad issue of the relations between Faith and Reason into a polemic in favour of the distinctive *credenda* or practices of a particular historical religion, such as Christianity or Judaism, and against those of others, and a still worse violation of them to conduct the polemic by appeal to any extra-rational authority. I must not, for example, tell you that you are to believe or do this or that, *because* Scripture, or the General Councils or the Pope, has commanded so. But I see no ground for objection to discussing the question whether it is or is not reasonable to recognise the claims of an authority of some kind in matters of faith and practice, and on what grounds or within what limits such recognition of authority is reasonable, if at all. There can surely be no impropriety in illustrating a discussion of so general an issue by reference to beliefs and practices in which all of us were probably brought up, with which we are familiar, and which most of us, in some degree, presumably continue to share, or at any rate to respect.

I know, of course, that there is a certain weight of accumulated prejudice to be encountered by one who, speaking in the name of philosophy, ventures to suggest that there are reasonable grounds for doubting the satisfactoriness of a "religion within the limits of mere reason". All through the last century, there was in the best minds a certain ingrained prejudice in favour of the view ascribed by Bishop Burnet to Algernon Sidney, that "religion ought to be a sort of divine philosophy in the mind",[1] without scriptures, creeds, or visible institutions, and that whatever in the historical religions is more than this can at most be tolerated for a time on the score of human weakness. The philosopher was commonly expected to prove his own exemption from such weakness by sitting in solitary majesty

> Like God, holding no form of creed,
> But contemplating all,

and consequently to withdraw himself from all active participation in the specifically religious life of his society.

Oddly enough, this distrust of historical attachments was often markedly characteristic of philosophers of the very school who made it their boast that they had learned from Hegel to think historically. I well remember the warmth with which the eminent Professor Josiah Royce explained to me that he held it a point of conscience, as a metaphysician, never to set foot in a church; yet Royce regarded himself as anything but an enemy to Christianity. An equally distinguished philosopher, well known in St. Andrews, Professor Bosanquet, exhibited the same prejudice no less unambiguously. He has laid it down in express words, in an essay reprinted very recently (1929) in the collected volume of his

[1] *History of My Own Times*(Oxford, 1833), ii. 351: "He seemed to be a Christian, but in a particular form of his own; he thought it was to be like a divine philosophy in the mind; but he was against all public worship, and everything that looked like a church."

scattered papers called *Science and Philosophy*,[1] that the whole historical element in the religions of the world is "mere accident", and belongs to the "childhood of humanity", that revelation is a word which is only harmless if it means "nothing in the world but our own common sense and reason", and that "authority", whether of Church or of Scripture, is a "very mischievous doctrine", because books and men cannot have any rightful authority—"except by convincing our own minds".[2] Religion, it should seem, is a purely individualistic affair, and the Church, the Synagogue, or whatever other name man has given to the religious community, is only to be tolerated on the understanding that it is reduced to the *status* of an ethical society. Strangely enough, Bosanquet seems to have fancied that in saying these things he was reproducing for a perverse generation the thought of St. Paul!

Now, one understands quite well the historical *causes* of this attitude of ultra-individualism. No one, with the history of Europe before his eyes, can dispute the

[1] See the essay, "The Kingdom of God on Earth", in *Science and Philosophy*, p. 333 ff.

[2] To be "convinced" that the circle cannot be "squared", one needs to be satisfied that it has been proved that neither π nor π^2 can be the root of an algebraical equation with rational coefficients. To understand the proof one needs a fair acquaintance with a considerable amount of mathematics. It cannot "convince the mind" of a man whose mathematical knowledge, like that of most circle-squarers, is confined to the "four rules" of arithmetic. Does it follow that the *consensus* of mathematicians should have no weight with the mathematically uneducated circle-squarers? One has only to read the contemptuous anonymous refutations of Darwin, or the "higher criticism", with which the correspondence columns of our evening papers abound, to see that their authors have no conception of the kind of evidence which is relevant in biological or historical study, and are therefore incapable of being "convinced". Are we to say that their contempt is justified? Would Bosanquet himself have claimed the authority attaching to an expert pronouncement in some science with which he was personally unacquainted? I should say myself that it is an important mark of the educated man that he can judge soundly when he must be content with authority, precisely because *he* is not in a position to be "convinced by the evidence". It is deplorable to find a really eminent philosopher holding out so much encouragement to the self-confident ignorance which denies that there is justification for a statement merely because it is not itself capable of seeing the justification.

enormous spiritual evil which has been done by illegitimate insistence on the principle of authority, though it would be only fair to observe that priests and preachers have not been the only offenders in this kind. Possibly the State may have done as much harm to mankind as the Church by claims to an unlimited authority, though Bosanquet, all through his life, seems to have been in theory as favourable to the absolutism of the political *Leviathan* as hostile to the absolutism of the ecclesiastical *civitas Dei*, as anxious to maintain that the citizen has *no* rights against the State as to deny that the Church has *any* rights against its individual members.[1] We have also known something of the effects of the same authoritarian temper in ecclesiastics in retarding the progress of medicine, and even of theoretical natural science, though fortunately not with the same addition to the sum of human misery. But one might suggest that there is, after all, a real difference between psychological explanation and rational justification. Memories of the fires of Smithfield, the "horrors of the Spanish Inquisition", the fanatical opposition of misguided pietists of a later date to the introduction of anaesthetics into medicine, even of the rather farcical "persecution" of Galileo and the foolish squabbles about Darwin and Bishop Colenso, may explain a religious individualism like Bosanquet's; they certainly do not justify it.

In our lifetime the serious dangers to reasonable

[1] Cf. the trenchant language of Prof. Hobhouse about the Hegelian theory of the State as expounded by Bosanquet. "This theory is commonly spoken of as idealism, but it is in point of fact a much more subtle and dangerous enemy to the ideal than any brute denial of idealism emanating from a one-sided science" (*Metaphysical Theory of the State*, p. 18); "this theory . . . by which, in the judgement of so many able men, the state assumes in the modern world a position which earlier ages might have given to the church or to the Deity Himself" (*ib.* p. 25). (Prof. Hobhouse, indeed, in my opinion, errs by going to the opposite extreme of assuming that there is an antecedent probability that *any* "rebel" is in the right against the institutional State.)

personal liberty of speech and action have not in the main came from that much-abused body "the clergy"; at the present moment one might rather be tempted to accuse "the cloth" of over-eagerness to divest themselves of all vestiges of a claim to authority. There is point in the complaint I have read somewhere that the first question the modern working "parson" asks himself about everything is not "Is this true?" but "Can I induce Mr. Jones to look at the matter in this light?" I cannot help suspecting that the anti-clericalism of many philosophers, which makes them so prone to see an "obscurantist", and possibly a concealed Torquemada, in anyone who ventures to hint that authority has its place in religion, and that the historical may be of some importance, is little more than a belated survival of the diatribes of eighteenth-century free-thinkers against "priestcraft", and as much out of relation to the realities of life as the diatribes of the same century, which our Hegelians do not repeat, against the "barbarism" of Shakespearian drama and Gothic architecture.[1] We have long enough taken a complacent pride in our possession of the historical mind; I fear there is still too much of the "old Adam" of the deistic "enlightenment" persisting unsubdued in too many of us.

It may be a suitable preparation for the balanced consideration of our problem to start from a penetrating observation made by von Hügel.[2] We all remember the famous epilogue of the three rings in

[1] "I would observe that in this charge of Lysicles there is something right and something wrong. It seems right to assert, as he doth, that the real belief of natural religion will lead a man to approve of revealed; but it is as wrong to assert that Inquisitions, tyranny, and ruin must follow from thence. Your free-thinkers, without offence be it said, seem to mistake their talent. They imagine strongly, but reason weakly; mighty at exaggeration, and jejune in argument! Can no method be found to relieve them from the terror of that fierce and bloody animal an English parson?"—Berkeley, *Alciphron*, v.

[2] *Essays and Addresses* (second series), pp. 122-3.

Lessing's *Nathan der Weise*, and the complaint there suggested, that it should be so impossible to find a man content to be just a man, without further qualification as Moslem, Jew, or Christian.[1] Manifestly the complaint carries its own answer with it. A man who is a religious man without having any religion in particular is hard to come by for the same reason that it would be hard to find a man who is a good citizen, but a citizen of no city in particular, or a man who is a human being without being European, Asiatic, Negro, American Indian, or anything more specific than just a member of the genus *homo sapiens*. The curious thing is that, except in this one matter of religion, we are all so familiar with the principle that the determinable is only to be found specified by determinants (ἐν τοῖς εἴδεσιν τοῖς αἰσθητοῖς τὰ νοητά ἐστι), and yet so obstinately prone to make an exception for this one case. We have long ago learned that it is no way to promote the spirit of devotion, to the public good of mankind, to make ourselves, like Aristippus, "aliens wherever we go",[2] that the man who sits loose to the duties of family life cannot be trusted to be a dutiful citizen, or the man who is "agin the government", wherever he happens to find himself, to be a self-sacrificing servant of the brotherhood of man. We fully understand the point, whether or not we admit the justice, of Swinburne's charge against Byron, that he fancied himself to be writing like a good European when he was only writing like a villainously bad Englishman. It is only of religion we tend to think as a spirit living most vigorously when denuded of the last vestige of a body.

I say this partly, though not wholly, simply to remind

[1] *Nathan*, iii. 7.

[2] Xenophon, *Memorab*. ii. i. 13 οὐδ' εἰς πολιτείαν ἐμαυτὸν κατακλείω, ἀλλὰ ξένος πανταχοῦ εἰμι.

you that piety, like art, or science, or any other activity of life, is an affair of the community, as well as of the individual. None, I imagine, is likely to deny that intense spiritual vitality of any kind can hardly flourish in individuals unless it is nourished by a corresponding activity on the part of the community at large. No one counts on a succession of great scientific men in a society grossly indifferent to science and preoccupied with war or money-getting, nor a succession of great painters or composers in a community whose interest in painting and music are not well-developed and widely diffused.[1] The society which produces great artists need not, indeed, be one in which all men, or even most men, are themselves artists. Much nonsense has been talked about the supposed passion of the "average Athenian" for art from simple neglect of this consideration. There were plenty of "Philistines" at Athens—they furnish Aristophanes with such figures as Dicaeopolis, Strepsiades, Trygaeus—just as in our "nation of shopkeepers" there are plenty of persons who could not keep shop for a month without having to put up their shutters. But though every Athenian was not a Phidias or Polyclitus, a succession of men like Phidias and Polyclitus could not have existed at Athens unless a large number of Athenians had been enough interested in their art to feel proud of it and to desire that it should be encouraged. But for this the artists would have starved for want of support, or gone elsewhere. So it will presumably be conceded that a succession of saints is only reasonably probable in a society which, at least, appreciates and admires sanctity; sanctity,

[1] A striking example is furnished by the history of philosophy. We are all accustomed to talk loosely of Athens as the very home of philosophy, and yet, as Professor Burnet has more than once remarked, there are only two philosophers of real eminence in the whole history of Athens, Socrates and his immediate disciple, Plato. The reason is that philosophy never was one of the "communal interests" of Athenian society.

like everything human, must meet with some measure of sympathetic response if it is to be kept alive. But where is the relevance of this consideration, which may be readily admitted, to the notion of *authority*? Greatly religious persons, when they are not the rarest of exceptions, may presuppose a religious community. How does this justify us in holding that there can be any *authority* in religion for the individual except that of his own "common sense and reason"?

I must not anticipate here the detailed discussion of the notion of authority in religion, which I am reserving for special treatment later. But I would at once make some remarks on a matter of general principle. Reference to the community at once carries with it acknowledgement of authority *of some kind* which is independent of the "common sense and reason" of the individual, and may yet properly claim a right on his allegiance and submission. Nowhere, when we are dealing with a supra-individual manifestation of rational and spiritual life, can the personal judgement of the individual be taken as the single and sufficient rule for his direction. It is constantly a problem—often a difficult, sometimes a well-nigh insoluble, problem—to decide when "private judgement" is entitled to take the lead, and when it is a positive duty to subject it to an authority external to the individual. Anyone who has tried to work at an historical or philological subject knows perfectly well that it is his business to form opinions for himself about the true sequence of events related in conflicting ways, the genuineness of a document, the soundness of a "reading"; he knows also that though he may sometimes be right in preferring his personal judgement to any consensus on the other side, he would often go wrong in doing so. There are cases in which a judicious man would think it no more than right to leave some disputed point undecided in deference to the "weight of authorities", or to retain an MS. reading in his text of an author, though he knows that his own personal judgement all the time is that the disputed point is not really an open question, or the MS. reading not really defensible. Indeed, I believe we might say that in this field authority has so much weight that a man will at times do right to defer to it when his own individual opinion is not merely wavering, but definitely made up in a different sense. There is, for example, an amount of authority which would make it impossible for a scholar of any modesty to make a change in the reading in a classical text, even though his own definite private conviction were that the *textus receptus* is "not Greek", or "not Latin", as the case may be. The consensus of great scholars who are at issue with the individual judgement of the particular editor may be such that it is the decided probability that his strong personal conviction is mistaken after all. There are few qualities more valuable to the scholar than the *flair* which tells him instinctively when he should adhere to his own judgement in the face of formidable agreement against him, and when even a strong personal judgement should give way to opposing "authority". It is chiefly because this *flair* is so difficult to acquire, and presupposes such delicacy of perception, that truly great scholars are as few as they are, and that mere industry, or mere brilliance, does not give a man a place among them.

The same considerations apply to "authority" in the various sciences still more obviously. The field of the sciences is so vast that no man can be personally completely at home in more than a tiny region of it. The schoolmen were therefore right in the main when they laid down the rule that the "artist", that is, the specialist, must be believed in his own speciality, and right for two reasons. For one thing, the man who will admit the actuality of no facts which he has not ascertained by his own personal observation or experimentation, and the validity of no methods which he cannot personally follow with comprehension, is plainly likely more often to be wrong than to be right; the appeal to our *own* "common sense and reason", if the phrase means, as it should, what a given person can see for himself to be rational, is notoriously the favourite controversial weapon, not of men of science conducting a scientific argument, but of the uninformed, and obstinate "faddists", the "flat-earth men, anti-gravitationists", fundamentalists, and their likes.[1] I clearly must not deny that a proposition in the *Principia* is rationally demonstrated on the ground that I, who have perhaps never given an hour's study to the elements of geometry in my life, cannot see for myself the compelling force of the proof, and that, even among the "educated", it is only a small minority who profess to be able to see it. Moreover, in the sciences, as in the practical affairs of life, so much depends on the soundness of *immediate* judgements, and for this no general criterion can be laid down. Only the specialist, habitually familiar with

[1] For a beautiful illustration of the point compare Whewell's crushing refutation of the circle-squarer James Smith recorded in De Morgan's *Budget of Paradoxes* (ed. 2, ii. 24). The refutation consists in a single sentence, "In the whole course of the proof, though the word cycle [? circle] occurs, there is no property of the circle employed". To anyone who understands the elements of mathematical reasoning this is final, but it made no impression on Mr. Smith's "common sense and reason". It is not uncommon to find it urged, even by men who are good reasoners in some quite different sphere, as a fatal objection to analysis of a work like the Pentateuch into its component parts, that no one can produce the alleged earlier documents, there is no extant copy of "D" or "JE". An argument of this kind which, if valid, would prove that there has *never* been any such thing as a "composite document" of which the separate components have perished, is frequently treated as a triumphant appeal to "common sense" against the vagaries of pedantic scholars. If, however, by "common sense and reason" Bosanquet meant, as he presumably did, something *not* peculiar to the individual, his remark is the emptiest of truisms, and only means that "authority" cannot establish what can be shown to be false. No one, I take it, disputes that.

the careful observation of facts and the weighing of evidence *of a specific kind*, is really competent to say with any confidence what the precise bearing of a well-established but complicated set of observations, or the probative force of an intricate piece of scientific reasoning, really is. The specialist's judgement on such a question is a *reasonable* judgement, an interpretation of data by intelligence, though it would often be impossible for him to exhibit the whole of his "reasons" for his decision in a form which would carry conviction to the acutest logician not at home in this particular province of scientific work.[1] It is thus intelligence itself we respect when we properly defer to a weighty "consensus" of the experts in a case where our own personal "reason and common sense", left to themselves, might leave us in suspense, or even lead us to decide in a contrary sense.

It is also clear that, in the application of science to practice, we should often be doing grievous wrong if we did not *act* on such respect for authority. Thus a medical man who should insist on always following his own personal judgement exclusively in diagnosis, or in treatment, against that of colleagues or the profession at large, would often do serious harm to his patients, and I conceive that in some cases, where death had ensued, he might properly be severely censured by the coroner. There are times when the physician would be justified in taking the risk of such complete defiance of authority, as there are times when the individual

[1] Cf. Burnet, *Greek Philosophy, Pt. I.*, i. p. 1: "A man who tries to spend his life in sympathy with the ancient philosophers will sometimes find a direct conviction forcing itself upon him, the grounds of which can only be represented very imperfectly by a number of references in a foot-note. Unless the enumeration of passages is complete—and it never can be complete—and unless each passage tells in exactly the same way . . . the so-called proofs will not produce the same effect on any two minds. That is the sense in which philological inquiry, like every other inquiry, requires an act of faith."

scientific man does right to stand alone in rejecting an unanimously supported established theory, but it requires the nicest judgement to know when this is right and when one would be merely perverse in taking such a line, and it is always blameable to take it without a grave sense of responsibility.

The same problem meets us in questions of art or moral conduct. As Dr. Edwyn Bevan observes, in an admirable essay dealing with this very question of authority,[1] a man would often be justified in saying, "Though I cannot myself see that this painting is admirable, though, in fact, I neither like nor admire it, I know it is highly admired by others whose taste in such matters is entitled to respect, and I suspect therefore that my dislike, or my inability to admire, is due to some personal defect in myself", and a man charged with the duty of recommending the purchase of pictures for a public collection would be acting improperly if his recommendations were not influenced by this kind of deference to authority. So in difficult questions of moral conduct, it is manifest that personal inability to see the reasonableness or unreasonableness of a certain course of action may often be due to want of fine ethical discrimination, or to inability to keep all the relevant features of an unfamiliar or complicated situation clearly before the mind. This is the reason why all but the criminally rash, when they have to make a decision in such cases, are careful to allow great weight to the accepted ethical traditions of a society with which they are in general moral sympathy, and, again, to the counsels of persons for whose uprightness and clearness of moral insight they have what they believe to be a well-founded respect. It is also the reason why in dealing with situations of an unfamiliar kind—as

[1] *Christianity and Hellenism*, p. 245 ff.

when a retired student has to deal with a problem of investments—we do wisely not to torment ourselves with scruples which are in all probability fantastic and due to our own unfamiliarity with the kind of details in question. If I, for example had to act as trustee for a minor, I should do well to act on the principle that an investment recommended to me as morally above suspicion by a business man whom I know to be both at home with such matters and personally honest is above reproach. In practice, I believe, we all recognise that it may often be no less than a bounden duty to follow a moral judgement which is not our own, but comes to us primarily on the authority of the community, or an individual "spiritual adviser", even though the adviser may not have been able to formulate the grounds for his counsel in a way which compels assent, or even to formulate them at all. For my own part, I confess that there are some persons whose mere declaration, "I feel sure you will be acting wrongly if you do that, though I cannot prove the point", would, in some matters, be decisive, and I do not suppose that I stand in the least alone.

The same thing is true about issues of public morality. A modest man, for example, would not, as I think, lightly refuse services demanded by the government in war-time on the ground of his inability to convince himself personally of the justice of the national cause. He would, at least, take into account the presumption that a cause seriously regarded as just by the bulk of the responsible members of the nation, and by a reasonably honest ministry, probably is just, and that his difficulty in seeing the point for himself arises from his inevitable ignorance of many of the relevant facts, or his inability to keep the facts as a whole, and in their due proportions, before his mind. This presumption, of course, would not hold if he antecedently believed the bulk of his community to be morally corrupt, or the ministry to be a set of knaves, and it is, in any case, one which consideration *might* destroy, but a man of modesty would, at least, recognise its existence and allow very fully for it. He might be prepared to be a "conscientious objector", if he felt the call of duty imperative, *after* due consideration, but not *before* consideration; he would not fall into the strange mistake of supposing that loyalty to "conscience" can take only one form—that of *dissent* from the "general conscience" of the community.[1]

The same considerations probably explain the hostility of most highly conscientious men to casuistical discussion of moral situations which are merely theoretical. They have a deep, and I should say a generally reasonable, distrust of their own verdicts of right and wrong in unfamiliar and complex situations, where there is no clear social tradition with recognised authority, and a decision, if reached at all, must be reached by the individual wholly for himself. It is because casuistry, if used as a direct guide to action, threatens to make right and wrong a purely individualistic affair that it is widely felt to be destructive of the genuine spirit of morality. (At bottom, it is this same distrust which explains Hegel's exaltation of *Sittlichkeit* at the expense of *Moralität*.)

Perhaps I am unnecessarily labouring a point which should be obvious when we consider the history of the formation of our convictions. It is surely beyond ques-

[1] It may be true that, as the "born dissenter "is fond of saying,

"He's a slave, who dares not be
In the right with two or three";

but (*a*) Is there any special virtue in being in the *wrong* with a small minority? (*b*) and Is the mere fact that I am in a small minority sufficient presumption that I am "in the right"?

tion that everywhere, alike in science, in art, in matters of conduct, the bulk of any man's convictions are never reached in a way independent of *some* authority external to the individual. In all these matters we begin as *learners*, taking our beliefs on the authority of a scientific, artistic, or moral tradition, which we have done nothing to create, and have, in the first instance, simply to receive and assimilate.[1] As we advance in discernment of the principles underlying the tradition, the case is altered. We learn, though we learn only if we begin with the docility which submits to learn before it attempts to teach, to see for ourselves the justification of much that we took at first on trust. It is but a further step in the same process by which we discover the defects in the tradition of the "elders". No man can criticise or reform a great tradition effectively, except from within; the traditions of the "authorities" are only remoulded by those who have first proved them in use. And, again, the convictions even of the outstanding "rebels" against tradition, the eminently "original" thinkers, artists, men of action, for the most part and in most matters remain convictions which they have not originated for themselves, but taken over from the community of their fellows. Even the man who effects a "Copernican revolution" in some department of thought or life is a revolutionary only in respect of this or that principle; the *body* of his convictions is

[1] This seems to me the truth which Professor Wm. James and others misrepresent when they talk about our "passional nature" as the source of our beliefs. The average man believes that God exists, that one must tell the truth, that the earth is round, all for much the same reason, that he has been taught all these things in early life. He could not give any very convincing reasons for any of these beliefs, but, because he has been *taught* to hold them when his mind was most plastic, he looks on the atheist and the earth-flattener alike as uttering absurdities. He is impatient with both for their "unreasonableness"; his "passional nature", if it is the source of his theism, ought also to be called the source of his geography. His *reason* for impatience with the atheist is that he regards him as denying what is "plain" to common sense and reason.

not a purely individualistic construction, as subsequent generations regularly discover in due course.[1]

It would thus be at least singular if the pure individualism of regard for nothing but what approves itself to my own personal judgement, so impossible in every other department of human thought and life, could be the one right rule in religion. Life and the human spirit are, after all, one in all their manifestations, and for that reason we may fairly expect to find that tradition and authority have their place in religion and theology, no less than in science, art, and practice. It would be really paradoxical, were it the fact, that there should be just one realm where a man is justified in refusing to acknowledge any truth but that which he has reached by his own personal efforts, or, indeed, where profitable intellectual ability is possible, except on the basis of antecedent receptivity. In principle this should be a sufficient reply to the extreme zealots of individualism who treat the very recognition of any kind of authority in matters of religion as a merely "mischievous" disloyalty to reason.

No doubt there is an important further *special* problem arising from the special nature of the authority which has been claimed in matters of religion for Scriptures and Churches. It may be said that in all other matters the authority for which deference is claimed is admittedly that of the body of acknowledged experts in the field in question; it is therefore never

[1] Copernicus himself may serve as an example. In essentials his doctrine was a *revival* of the tradition of the heliocentric astronomers of antiquity, Aristarchus and Seleucus. He took from them both the fruitful part of their ideas, the ascription of the "annual" and "diurnal" motions to the earth, and the unfruitful and erroneous conception of the sun as "at rest" in the centre of an outermost "sphere" with the stars all equidistant at the outer surface. What was *personal* and specifically "Copernican" in this hypothesis was its weakest feature, the superfluous "third motion" intended to explain the parallelism of the earth's axis to itself, and this is just the one feature of the "Copernican hypothesis" which had to be most promptly suppressed.

supposed to be absolute, and it is always allowed to be confined to some particular realm of knowledge or practice. But the authority claimed for Scriptures or Churches professes to be that of God, and consequently to be final and to extend to all questions whatsoever. When we respect human authority, it is thus to "reason" itself, as embodied in the accumulated tradition of the community, that our respect is paid, and therefore the respect is always qualified; our regard for the gathered wisdom achieved in the living tradition in no way precludes us from revision and purification of the tradition in the light of growing knowledge. But in every historical religion we meet with the notion of a *depositum fidei* which claims to be final truth, permitting of no revision. Again, since authority in the non-religious sense is always understood to be restricted in its sphere, the claim advanced for the "consensus of experts" is limited by the principle *ne sutor ultra crepidam*, the "artist" is only to be believed "in his own art". There is never in theory, whatever may be the case in practice, any question of a right of the moralist to prescribe, in virtue of his authority as a moralist, what we shall receive as true in physics or physiology, or of the physicist or physiologist to prescribe what we shall believe about right and wrong, or of the historian to dictate to either moralist, physiologist, or physicist. But experience has abundantly proved that the theologian, who claims to speak with the authority of God, the source of all truth, will recognise no limitations on the scope of his competence. At any moment he may demand, in the name of God, that propositions shall be regarded as true in natural science, or in history, which the specialist in those spheres, who adheres loyally to his own canons and methods, is bound to pronounce doubtful, or actually false, or the rejection as false of propositions which the specialist in history or the sciences is bound to accept as true. What Newman said of the Christian Church might be said to be historically borne out by the procedure of every religion professing to be based upon a revelation. "It claims to know its own limits, and to decide what it can determine absolutely and what it cannot. It claims, moreover, to have a hold upon statements not directly religious, so far as this, to determine whether they indirectly relate to religion, and according to its own definitive judgement, to pronounce whether or not, in a particular case, they are consistent with revealed truth . . . and to allow them, or condemn and forbid them, accordingly. It claims to impose silence at will on any matters, or controversies of doctrine, which on its own *ipse dixit* it pronounces to be dangerous, or inexpedient, or inopportune. . . . And, lastly, it claims to have the right of inflicting spiritual punishment, of cutting off from the ordinary channels of the divine life, and of simply excommunicating, those who refuse to submit themselves to its formal declarations."[1]

It is true that not all organised religious communities make such frequent use of this authority as that to which Newman belonged when he wrote these words, or possess the same formidable machinery for exerting it, but it is also true that if most of them refrain from making much use of this tremendous authority, and are careful not to remind us very often of its existence, the claim to possess it is still there, in the background, it may be, but ready to assert itself whenever it is felt to be challenged. Hence it may be said that the claim to authority *of this kind* inevitably creates a problem which can never arise in connection with the narrowly established claim of the "expert" to authority within

[1] *Apologia*, pt. vii.

the limits of his own competence, the problem of the legitimacy of "faith" as an independent source of knowledge. Here, it may be urged, we find real justification for such language as that of Bosanquet about the purely "mischievous" character of the claims of Churches and Scriptures to authority. What the honest philosophical thinker must not admit, we shall be told, is authority in this absolute sense, and with this unrestricted range, and his quarrel with all the positive religions is that all of them, some more and some less explicitly, lay claim to this kind of authority. And, in the last resort, it is precisely because they are all *historical* that they cannot avoid making the claim. The appeal to the final and imprescriptible authority of God cannot consistently be absent from a religion which professes to have originated in a direct revelation from God. Consequently in rejecting absolute authority, a philosophic, or natural, theology must inevitably reject the claim of any religious community to possess such an historical revelation. We can understand, therefore, why a metaphysician like Professor Royce should have thought it a duty to refuse the sanction of his presence to the worship of an historical Church.

The problem is undeniably a very grave one and will call for careful special discussion in a later lecture of our course. For the present I would content myself with a few preliminary remarks intended to urge the point that it is a real problem and to plead against any attempt, from the side either of "churchman" or of metaphysician, to get rid of it by a facile solution. It is easy to dismiss the whole question *ab initio* in either of two ways. There is the way of the pure Fideist, which is to invalidate all opposition to the extreme authoritarian position by rhetoric about the uncertainty of science and the deficiencies of human reason. Absolute and blind dependence on authority may be justified by a metaphysic of complete scepticism. We are, to put it bluntly, to take the Pope's word, or the word of the Wesleyan Conference, or that of our favourite biblical commentary, or our favourite preacher, for everything, *because* there is never adequate rational ground for believing anyone's word about anything, and where everything is so utterly uncertain, the Pope's word—or that of any other of the "authorities" just mentioned—is in no worse case than the word of another. This, I hardly need say, is not the position of sober theologians of the Pope's, or any other, persuasion, nor do I suppose it likely to commend itself to many of my hearers. Yet some such theory has had its defenders, and not all of them are intellectually negligible. I suppose we might say that Tertullian and Pascal, in certain moods, come near it, and we all remember the line taken by Montaigne in his *Apology for Sebundus*,[1] and by Philo in Hume's *Dialogues concerning Natural Religion*, who, at least, pretends—though one may reasonably doubt his entire sincerity—that his universal scepticism is adopted as the surest way to Christianity.[2] Even in our own days Lord Balfour has been, in my own opinion most unjustly, represented by hostile critics as arguing that in a world where everything is entirely uncertain we may as well

[1] "Voulez-vous un homme sain, le voulez-vous reglé, et en ferme et seure posture? affublez-le de tenebres d'oysivité et de pesanteur: il nous faut abestir, pour nous assagir; et nous esblouir, pour nous guider" (*Essais*, ii. 12). This is presumably the source of Pascal's famous *cela vous abêtira et vous fera croire*.

[2] Hume, *Philosophical Works* (Green and Grose), ii. 467: "A person, seasoned with a just sense of the imperfections of natural reason, will fly to revealed truth with the greatest avidity: while the haughty Dogmatist, persuaded that he can erect a complete system of Theology by the mere help of philosophy, disdains any further aid, and rejects this adventitious instructor. To be a philosophical Sceptic is, in a man of letters, the first and most essential step towards being a sound, believing Christian."

acquiesce in what is put forward on authority by the established Church of our country as in anything else.

My only concern, at this moment, with this extreme Fideism is to remark that, impossible as it is for men who mean to think seriously, it reaches its conclusion by the exaggeration of what is, after all, true. It is true, and no one knows this better than the men of science themselves, that the actual achievements of science, great as they are, are much more modest than they are supposed to be by the "man in the street" and the literary representatives of his point of view. There are no specific scientific laws or theorems, not tautological, which are not provisional, and, in theory at least, subject to modifications of unknown extent, as the recent overhauling from within of the "classical" Newtonian scheme has forcibly reminded us. It is true, again, that, as Dr. Whitehead puts it, the whole body of philosophical principles of natural science, which not a hundred years ago seemed so sure and certain, has now gone into the melting-pot. (You may remember that in our first series I quoted Dr. Whitehead's epigrammatic statement, that what seems to-day the sheerest nonsense may be the accepted scientific truth of to-morrow.[1]) It is true, again, that the whole theory of inductive method, without which a rational natural science cannot advance a single step, seems to have been riddled through and through by the destructive criticism of the scientific workers themselves. No one to-day seems able to give any tolerable answer to the

[1] *Science and the Modern World*, pp. 24, 80, 166. Since this lecture was delivered, Professor Eddington has told us much more to the same effect, in sparklingly epigrammatic language, in *The Nature of the Physical World*: "The law of gravitation is—a put-up job" (p. 143); Sir W. Bragg "was not overstating the case when he said that we [the physicists] use the classical theory on Mondays, Wednesdays, and Fridays, and the quantum theory on Tuesdays, Thursdays, and Saturdays" (p. 194).

two questions which Mill disposed of so jauntily in his famous *Logic*, what exactly are the methods the experimental worker follows in eliciting his scientific theories from his elaborately established records of data, and what guarantee has he that the postulates about the structure of nature which those methods presuppose may not be radically false. The writers of the text-books of logic, for the most part propound a version of the matter which is openly inadequate, even where it is not manifestly untrue; the working men of science go on their way without asking themselves whether their methods have a rational justification or not, exactly as the Fideist in religion acquiesces passively in the declarations of *his* authority.[1] And I understand that it it also true that, in many cases, our accepted special hypotheses are under the disadvantage of being inconsistent with some part of the very facts they are devised to explain. Men who ought to know tell us, for instance, that in the theory of light at the present moment, there seem to be only two options, to explain the facts by a theory of undulation or by a theory of emission, and that there is one group of facts which obstinately refuses to be explained by the former, a second which cannot be explained by the latter.[2]

[1] Whitehead, *Science and the Modern World*, p. 35: "The theory of Induction is the despair of philosophy—and yet all our activities are based upon it". Mill comes face to face with the central difficulty once (*Logic*, bk. iii. c. 3, § 3) when he asks "Why is a single instance, in some cases, sufficient for a complete induction, while in others myriads of concurring instances, without a single exception known or presumed, go such a very little way towards establishing a universal proposition?" That is the problem Mill ought to solve, but he finds no more to say than that the man who can solve it "knows more of the philosophy of logic than the wisest of the ancients". As Dr. Broad remarks (The *Philosophy of Francis Bacon*, p. 67), Mill "closed the door of the cupboard" on the skeleton and tactfully "turned the conversation into more cheerful channels".

[2] Whitehead, *Science and the Modern World*, p. 264: "To-day there is one large group of phenomena which can be explained only on the wave theory, and another large group which can be explained only on the corpuscular theory. Scientists have to leave it at that, and wait for the future . . ." Cf. Eddington, *Nature of the Physical World*, p. 201: "We can scarcely describe such an entity [as light]

Amid all these difficulties, one thing seems to be clear. Scientific theories only retain unqualified convincing force so long as we keep them strictly *abstract*;[1] so long, that is, as the theory aims at being no more than a logical exposition of the consequences entailed by a set of initial assumptions, artificially made precise and simple. As soon as we bring a theory into connection with the "unfaked" facts of the real world, the peculiar certainty so often claimed for science as a way of knowing begins to vanish. Science, in fact, may give us our best examples of clear and transparent connection between the various consequences of a set of assumed principles, but scientific theories, if taken to be propositions asserted about the "actual facts", are very far from being our best examples of certainty. Our existence would be far from happy, if we could not be much more sure of the truth of the propositions which matter most for the conduct of life than we can be about our scientific and philosophical theories. He would be an unfortunate man who had no more certainty of the loyalty of his friend or the fidelity of his wife than he is warranted in feeling about his metaphysical speculations, or his theories in chemistry. So much, by way of a general caution, against over-simplification of our problem by the assumption that, in a conflict between "science" and "authority", should

---

as a wave or as a particle: perhaps as a compromise we had better call it a 'wavicle' ".

[1] Cf. Whitehead, *Science and the Modern World*, p. 36: "If we confine ourselves to certain types of facts, abstracted from the complete circumstances in which they occur, the materialistic assumption expresses these facts to perfection. But when we pass beyond the abstraction . . . the scheme at once breaks down. The narrow efficiency of the scheme was the very cause of its methodological success." Eddington, *Nature of the Physical World*, p. 53: "To think of a man without his duration is just as abstract as to think of a man without his inside. Abstractions are useful, and a man without his inside (that is to say, a *surface*) is a well-known geometrical conception. But we ought to realise what is an abstraction and what is not." And on the whole subject see the third lecture in J. Ward, *Naturalism and Agnosticism*, vol. i.

such a conflict arise, we may safely assume *a priori* that authority is a mere impostor, because "science" is the one source of assured truth and is infallible. It is the perception that this claim for "science", that it is co-extensive with knowledge, will not really stand examination which is the grain of truth contained in the wild diatribes of the Fideist.

The rival over-simplification is that of the "rationalist" of the type who understands by the "rational" that of which I have been personally convinced by arguments, or which I at least believe to be capable of being established by arguments, decisive for those who are in a position to follow them. When it is denied from this point of view that there can be any real conflict between "authority" and reason, since authority has no rightful claim upon the intellect, we must be careful to draw some necessary distinctions, if we would appreciate the force of the "rationalist's" contention. It is not, of course, seriously meant that any proposition which is, as a matter of fact, asserted by me "on authority" must be false. It may quite well be a true proposition, but, if it is true, either there are, or there will some day be, or, at the very least, there *might* be, adequate *grounds* on which it may be justified, independently of the authority on the strength of which I am, in point of fact, advancing it. So long as this justification is not forthcoming, the authority of the person, or the body of persons, making the assertion must not be alleged as a "motive of credibility". (Thus a statement contained in one of the books of the Bible may be true—as the extremest "rationalist", if he is sane, will allow that hundreds of such statements are—even though there may happen to be no means of proving its truth—as, *e.g.*, we have no means of *proving* that the name of King David's father was Jesse, though no one doubts that it

I

was so;[1] but the mere fact that the work in which such a statement appears is a canonical Christian "scripture" must not be put forward as *proof* that the statement is true, any more than the occurrence of a statement in the works of Aristotle may be regarded as proof of its truth.)

If we take this to be the last word that can be said on the question, authority is obviously relegated to a purely subordinate place in religion. A clear-cut rationalism of this kind can, of course, afford to recognise the practical *usefulness*, or even the practical *necessity*, of some kind of *administrative* authority, prescribing what may be said or done publicly in the name and with the sanction of a given society. Administrative, or executive, authority is indeed the only protection of any society against the merest anarchy of individual caprice, and does not go beyond the limits of the kind of practical regulation which is exercised by a University, or an Education Department, when it has to decide what works may be used as text-books. But there is an end of all pretence that authority, as such, has any place in the determination of what is true. A

[1] An interesting parallel may be adduced from so severely "rational" a discipline as pure mathematics. Some of Fermat's most fascinating propositions in the Theory of Numbers were enunciated without proof, and were still unproved, as one sees by Legendre's treatment of them, at the opening of the nineteenth century. For all that a non-mathematician like myself knows, some of these theorems may still be undemonstrated. But it would not be *irrational* to believe them true, on the ground that Fermat may have had demonstrations of some of them, which he never published, or that, even if he had not, such demonstrations may yet be discovered, since it is not probable that a Fermat should have enunciated false propositions in the Theory of Numbers. Thus Fermat enunciated the proposition that the sum of the nth powers of two integers is never itself an nth power of an integer, if n be greater than 2. The proposition is given as a truth in the relevant section of Peano's *Formulaire Mathématique*, but, in vol. 4, with the observation that, though it can now be demonstrated for values of n up to 100, "la demonstration complète est encore inconnue." (This remark no longer appears in the subsequent edition (vol. 5) of the *Formulaire*). It is implied, of course, that we may hope that the "complete demonstration" will not always be "unknown"; this is what differentiates the case of such a theorem from that of a truth accepted "on the authority of revelation", according to the traditional view of the matter.

University, or an Education Department, would not merely be within its rights, it would be doing no more than its plain duty, in refusing to prescribe as a text-book some work in which views were freely advanced at variance with the general body of "expert" opinion. It would, I conceive, have been unjustifiable to prescribe the *Origin of Species* as an "authoritative" educational text-book at a time when Darwin's central theory was a novelty still awaiting the judgement of biologists and naturalists at large. But no one imagines that the truth of a theory is in any way affected by the fact that the "educational authority" has not yet seen fit to enjoin the teaching of it. Statements are not true because they are to be found in the standard text-books; they are found there—if the "authorities" have made their selection wisely—because there is ground for believing them to be true. Thus in matters of science there would seem to be no place for any real conflict between "reason" and authority. The issue between the scientific "paradoxist" and his opponents is, or ought to be, simply, on whose side "reason" lies.

It is naturally tempting to extend this view of the functions of authority as secondary and purely administrative to the field of religion and theology, and all the more tempting that history has striking examples to show of the mischief or futility of attempts to hold up the advance of knowledge by appeal to an authority asserted to be divine, and therefore infallible. Yet it should be clear, apart from all that we have said about the fallibility of science itself, that we are not really entitled to deal with the problem in quite this summary fashion. It is at least *conceivable*, until the opposite has been proved, that there may be, and actually have been, special critical contacts between the divine and the human, charged with a peculiar significance for the spiritual life of mankind. Since such contacts, if real, would be directly due to the outgoing activity of the divine and transcendent, to us they would inevitably wear the appearance of sudden and inexplicable "irruptions" into the familiar course of human life. We could not say theoretically when they may be expected, nor devise any kind of formula connecting them with "antecedent circumstances". We could, at best, recognise their significance after the event, and note their occurrence as significant, and, from our point of view, wholly contingent matter of historical fact. "The spirit bloweth whither it listeth, and thou canst not say whence it cometh, nor whither it goeth." Such a sudden intrusive contact, originating on the side of the transcendent, would be exactly what has always been meant by a specific historical "revelation"; its occurrence is no more to be ruled out of the scheme of things on purely *a priori* grounds than the similarly apparently sudden and inexplicable appearance of genius of the highest order in thought or in art. Whether this is or is not God's way of communicating religious insight to man, we could determine only by consideration of the history of the spiritual growth of our race, not from principles of metaphysics. If it is, then revelation through definite historical persons is as much a fact as the disclosure of the meaning and resources of art through specific persons and in specific environments. Thus, for example, the old cavil that it is unreasonable to ascribe to the great succession of the Hebrew prophets a spiritual enlightenment significant for all time and strictly *sui generis*, mediated to the rest of mankind through this channel and no other, will lose its apparent force; the fact, if it is a fact, will be really analogous with the fact that it happened, once and only once, at a particular juncture in Attic history, that there arose a philosophical genius of the first order, Socrates, and that he exercised a dominant intellectual and moral influence on the life of a second genius of the same order, Plato; or, again, that there should have been a Beethoven just once in history, and that Beethoven should have lived just where and when he did, and have done and suffered just what he actually did and had done to him.

If these things are facts, it is also clear that the experiences of the recipient of such an enlightenment will be for himself unmediated, direct disclosures from the "wholly other" and supernatural, not reached by inference and reflection, but *seen*, as in everyday life the wealth and riot of colour is *seen*, not inferred. It will be a distinctive feature of them that the "seer" has an overwhelming sense of their *givenness*, comparable with our familiar sense that, when the neo-Kantian from Marburg has said all he has to say, the sensible world remains something we do not construct, but find given to us. The seer will be unable to give any grounds for this conviction of his except that it comes to him from God, *haec dicit Dominus*, *factum est verbum Domini ad me*, and his message will be believed and received by others, to whom such a direct vision has not been granted, on the strength of their conviction that it had this origin, and that the authority behind it is the authority of God. Thus, in the fact of the reality of special direct spiritual insight enjoyed by specific historical persons, if it is a fact, we should find reasonable ground for belief in divine authority as a basis for convictions in matters of religion.

In that case, such authority really would be different in kind from the secondary authority we ascribe to "experts" of all types in their own speciality. All that we mean by such secondary authority is that the expert presumably has good reasons for his conclusions, which could be convincingly presented to any second person with sufficient special training to estimate them correctly, though not to the untrained "layman". But the *givenness* of the religious revelation means that the recipient *cannot* present compelling evidence of this kind to a second person, as he might if he were dealing with inferences of his own, any more than I can produce such evidence for the veracity of the "revelations" of my senses. If I, not being myself the recipient of the revelation, believe in its content, I am not simply accepting "for the time" a belief which I expect to find, in process of time, converted into a demonstrated conclusion, simply seeing with another man's eyes until I have learned to see with my own. To see the same thing with my own eyes, I should need to receive the same revelation a second time in my own person; unless, or until, this happens I am believing on the word of another something for which I can have only his word. And this, of itself, means that no historical religion can be sublimated without remainder into a philosophy, however true or exalted, without destroying its peculiar character. If revelation is a fact, there must be an historical element in a true religion which cannot be eliminated, and there will be a genuine justification for the theologians who have distinguished between those truths about God and the eternal order which are cognisable by the "unaided light of natural reason", and others, vitally significant for the spiritual life, which are not so cognisable, however hard it may be to draw the dividing line with precision.

It is plain, no doubt, that acceptance of the view that a complete religion involves this element of the historical, revelational, and authoritative makes the practice of such a religion hard for the thinking man. It confronts him at once with the difficult problem of distinguishing, in the revelation he accepts, between the divine content and the accidental and temporary form due to the personal temperament and situation of the immediate recipient, of judging how much of the always largely traditionary, "sacred story" is inseparable from the reality of the revelation, and how much is legendary accretion, of saying where the legitimate assertion of authority passes into the abuse of it. It is much easier to have a religion, like that of Plotinus or Kant, with no historical attachments, than it is to believe *ex animo* in any version of historical Christianity. In a critical age, like our own, the "option" for Christianity, or any other historical religion, must bring a perpetual tension into one's intellectual life from which acquiescence in a "religion within the limits of mere reason" would leave us free. But it would be unsafe to assume that in matters of religion, or in any others, the option which makes things easiest must be the wisest. "How the world is managed, and why it was created", says a great living scholar, "I cannot tell; but it is no feather-bed for the repose of sluggards".[1] We could get rid of the tension equally readily by blind acquiescence in tradition and authority, or by a cheap and easy rejection of both. But it may well be that the sort of religion with which either simplification would leave us would be immeasurably inferior in strength and renewing power to that we may have if we are willing to pay its price. It may be, as von Hügel held it is, that the *costingness* of a faith which will sacrifice neither history nor metaphysics, the torment of mind, if you like to call it so, by which such a faith is won, or held fast, is itself evidence of its worth.

[1] A. E. Housman, *Manilius I.* p. xxxii. Cf. Ward, *Naturalism and Agnosticism*[1], i. 108: "Dangerous as teleological arguments in general may be, we may at least safely say the world was not designed to make science easy".

II

REASON AND REVELATION

If my puffed life be out, give leave to tine
My shameless snuff at that bright lamp of thine:
Oh what's thy light the less for lighting mine?

F. QUARLES.

IT is characteristic, as we have said, of all the great religions which have claimed to be universal, that is, to have a right to the allegiance of mankind, irrespective of distinctions of race, nationality, local history, on the ground of their intrinsic truth, that each of them professes to rest, in the last resort, on a *revelation*. Each claims to be in the possession of truths of moment about the unseen which have not been, and could not have been, found out by any process of reflection upon the common features of all human experience, but contain an element derived from an immediate self-disclosure, an irruption of the unseen order itself into the visible and familiar, an element which is accepted as *given*, not discovered by man's own activity. It is a consequence of this givenness of the central content of the revelation that it also regularly claims, at least in respect of what is essential to it, to be, in some sense, *final*. The disclosure, because coming spontaneously from the side of the divine itself, is not subject, like the results of scientific inquiry, to unlimited revision and restatement. There is something in it which is not *provisional*, but once for all, and yet cannot be, and never will be, established like the so-called "immutable" laws of pure science. Hence the unending difficulties in which the divines of the various universal religions have found themselves involved when they begin to discriminate between the elements in their own teaching, as formulated at a given time, which really belong to this unchanging "deposit" or "core", and those which are only part of its accidental setting, and admit of legitimate accommodation to the changing intellectual "environment" of successive generations. Hence also the question, inevitable for any really critical age, whether it is in principle legitimate to admit the possibility of *any* "deposit" with this unchanging character. Is it disloyalty to intelligence itself to concede that there is some sense in which "religious truth" is *un*-progressive? If it is, it must also be an equal disloyalty to believe seriously in such self-disclosures of the divine as we have contemplated, and there will really be an unbridgeable gulf between the theology possible to a thinking man and that of any of the historical universal religions. There will, in fact, be *de iure* only one universal religion and theology, one confined rigidly "within the limits of pure reason", and we ought to anticipate, and do all we can to forward, the arrival of a day when all the historical religions shall have purged themselves of what is specific to each, and are indistinguishably merged in such a pure natural religion, just as there are those who would have us work for a future in which national loyalties will have lost themselves in a common attachment to a "commonweal of mankind".

The problem thus has its very practical side. Just as it is a practical question for each of us whether we serve mankind best by sitting loose to ties of nation and race, or by setting ourselves to be good Britons, or Frenchmen, or Germans, so it is a practical question whether we serve God best by owning no allegiance to a particular faith or Church, or by doing our best to be good Christians, or good Jews, as the case may be. It is true, to be sure, that the parallelism between the two situations is not complete. For no man, as I take it, seriously supposes that the universal brotherhood of man, if it is to be achieved, will be achieved by the expansion of the British Empire, or the French or American Republic, over the whole globe. But the good Christian, or good Jew, in proportion as he deserves the name, does look for the ultimate achievement of unity in religion, if it is ever to be attained, by the conversion of mankind to Christianity or to Judaism. Religions which claim to be universal claim also, in virtue of the element of finality in them, to be permanent, in a way in which states do not: there is a real exclusiveness about them, and it is inevitable that there should be. A brotherhood of all mankind would be consistent with the retention of separate local loyalties, so long as these latter were kept subordinate and secondary. In a "federated" religion for mankind, Christianity, Islam, and the rest of the universal religions would simply have lost their being. The "missionary" spirit is inseparable from all of them, because none can regard itself as a mere temporary precursor of the world-religion yet to come, without abandoning its pretension to be the self-disclosure of the divine. God cannot have spoken with equal finality to men through Moses, through Christ, and through Mohammed, for their witness does not agree; if God has spoken with finality through one of these messengers, then the claims of the faiths which treat the messages of the other two as the full self-disclosure of God must be surrendered. And what makes a man an adherent of the religion of Moses, Mohammed, or

Christ is precisely the consideration that through this one channel God has spoken finally, as through no other, and that to identify the self-disclosure of God with the general features in which several competing faiths are alike to the exclusion of all that is specific to any one of them, would be to rob that "revelation" of what is richest in it.

We can readily understand, then, why, when reflective men who profess one of the universal religions come to discover that societies not demonstrably inferior to their own in intelligence and virtue, possibly in some respects even superior, profess another, a distinction comes to be made between convictions in which several such religions are found to agree and those specific to each; why the former, inasmuch as they are seen to be independent of any one particular historical "revelation", should be assumed to be capable of demonstration by "natural reason", but the latter to be knowable only in virtue of special revelation; why, also, in each of the great religions it should be the latter, the specific "truths of revelation", which are regarded as of supreme importance.[1] It is equally easy to understand the reaction of the critical intelligence against this point of view. Some such reaction, indeed, might have been expected to show itself, even if history has presented us with no more than one single revelational religion, with no competitors. Even in such

[1] Cf. C. C. J. Webb, *Studies in the History of Natural Theology*, p. 158-9: "We shall not find in Anselm a sharp distinction . . . drawn between the spheres of Natural and Revealed Theology. Modern Roman Catholic writers, for whom the distinction established by St. Thomas Aquinas is authoritative, sometimes find themselves obliged to apologise for Anselm's inattention to it. No doubt the reason for it is to some extent historical. The intimacy of the later schoolmen with the doctrines of Aristotle least capable of reconciliation with Christian dogma . . . as also with the writings of the Mohammedan commentators, forced upon their attention the fact of the diversity of creeds, and the consequent question whether there was not a common stock of knowledge concerning things divine independent of this diversity." [I should suspect the study of Maimonides had most to do with calling the attention of St. Thomas to the point.]

a case it would seem inevitable that the religion should be lived and practised before it could be reflected upon, and an attempt made to say precisely what are the "doctrines" about the unseen implied by this life and practice. And the first attempts to answer the question would be bound to take account of what was most obvious. In course of time the answers would need reconsideration, in view of constantly emerging divergences of speculation and practice within the growing religious community, of new situations calling for fresh adaptations, of collisions between the earliest formulations of the community's belief and subsequently discovered facts of the temporal and secular order. The necessity of taking account of competing theologies only accentuates this process a little more acutely; even apart from that necessity, theology, the intellectual formulation of the implications of a religion, is clearly largely tentative and progressive, and this is enough to raise the problem whether the religion itself may also be considered, in the end, to be wholly provisional and tentative—a view which would make real revelation superfluous.

If we consider the problem, as I hold that Lord Gifford's instructions compel us to do—in its complete generality, without any suggestion of an *apologia* for the claims of a particular world-religion to be *the* revelation of God to man—I believe we may fairly summarise the main arguments against the reality of "special" revelation as follows:

(1) A revelation, if not impossible, is at least antecedently highly improbable.[1] For either the statements

[1] I am of Professor Eddington's opinion that it is a much more damaging objection to a thesis to call it "highly improbable" than to call it "impossible". The "impossible" commonly only means that which an opponent has ruled out of consideration by an *arbitrary* initial postulate. (*Nature of the Physical World*, pp. 74-7.) It is a trivial objection against the causal efficacy of human volitions that

alleged to be revealed are in conflict with truths ascertained by the "natural use of reason",[1] or they are not. In the second case, they are attainable in due time by the unaided patient employment of human intelligence, and so a revelation of them is, at best, superfluous; in the first, they are not even genuine truths, and therefore, *a fortiori*, not revelations.

(2) If God discloses Himself to us at all, it should be in a way intelligible and convincing to men in all times, and at all places; otherwise there can be no finality about the disclosure. But from the nature of the case, *such* disclosure is impossible.[2] A revelation made through a particular person, to particular persons, in particular circumstances, will not be intelligible—much less convincing—unless it is adapted to the "mentality"—*sit venia verbo*—of the man through whom it comes and the men to whom it comes. All truths, to be received and understood, must be thus adapted to the whole state of mind of the specific recipients, as a spoken message, to be apprehended, must be conveyed in a determinate idiom. You cannot speak without speaking some particular language—Latin, French, English, or some other—and if you are to be understood by speakers of English, you must speak not only

---

it is an "impossibility" (*i.e.* will not fit into the wholly arbitrary "determinist" metaphysical scheme); it is a grave—I should say an insuperable—objection to all theories of "parallelism" that, as James Ward urges, invariable concomitance *without* causal connection is infinitely improbable.

[1] I mean, of course, by "use of reason", the employment of reason upon data supplied to it by perception. I am not suggesting that reason can function *in vacuo*. I fully concede that, if reference to data is excluded, "reason" condemns nothing but violation of the formal "laws of thought".

[2] I must not be charged with inconsistency on the ground that I am now urging "impossibility" as a grave objection to revelation, in spite of what has been said in n. 1 to p. 47. The reasoning given here is not my own, but that of certain σοφοί whose view I am stating for purposes of examination. Cf. d'Holbach's question "s'il (viz. God) a parlé, pourquoi l'univers n'est-il pas convaincu?" and Shelley's employment of the passage in the note to *Queen Mab*, vii. 13. I am trying to make the best argumentative case I can for d'Holbach and Shelley; their own exposition contains much more bad rhetoric than tolerable reasoning.

English, but the English of a definite period, the English of the contemporaries of Cynewulf, or Chaucer, or Milton, or Tennyson, as the case may be. Now the mental outfit of men varies with place and time, like their speech, being moulded in much the same fashion by the traditions of their historical past. The very thoughts which were true and significant to a Galilean of two thousand years ago have lost their truth and significance for us, to whom they are as foreign as the Aramaic vocables in which they were originally uttered. What is the highest and most vital truth for us may similarly be unmeaning for men of the fortieth century, whose whole intellectual outlook on the world will presumably be as unlike ours as their speech. There are, in fact, no "truths for all time"; every truth, to be genuine truth, must be the truth for *its* time.[1] Revelation, then, as it has been conceived by the world-religions is not merely superfluous, but actually impossible.

(3) If we consider what has been the really valuable element in the various world-religions, we shall be led to the same conclusion. They have been of value just so far as they have been an elevating influence in life, and they have made for the elevation of life in proportion as they have taught and enforced a high standard of moral conduct, and no further. In a society which has reached a sufficiently high level of reflective moral civilisation, a variety of religions may be professed, but the recognised rules of conduct are much the same for the adherents of all, as we see, in our own society; the serious-minded men, whether they are Christians, or Jews, or stand outside all the great historical religious communities, have much the same ideal of good conduct, and conform to it about equally

[1] Remember, once more, that οὐκ ἐμὸς ὁ μῦθος.

well. It is reasonable, then, to look for the final and divine element in the various religions in a moral ideal and rule of life, just the characteristic in respect of which they tend to merge into one another; unreasonable to attach significance to the features which discriminate them. Thus the element of true and abiding religion in all the religions is a purely moral one, independent of revelations alleged to be made to particular persons and at particular times. At most, we might perhaps include in it, along with the moral ideal and rule themselves, whatever implications about the unseen order a genuine morality demands. But these implications will constitute only a "natural" or "philosophical" theology, "within the limits of mere reason".

(4) It might be added that there is not one of these revelational religions which has not included, as an integral part of its professedly divine revelation, assertions of fact about the course of nature and of human history. But it is difficult to believe that, in a rational universe, any man's attainment or non-attainment of his final good can be contingent on the accident of his acquaintance with events of which he may never have had the opportunity to hear. Moreover, in the case of every such religion, the assertions of fact about nature and human history which have been made on the strength of revelation have included some which have proved to be false.

This, I believe, is the main substance of such a case as a fair-minded man might make out against admitting the possibility of recognising divine self-disclosures, made at specific times and places, as a real source of knowledge about God and about man's beatitude. With more special polemical objections against the genuineness of a particular revelation, the Christian or another, we are not now concerned. I propose to offer some reflections on the cogency of such a destructive *Kritik aller Theologie, die als Offenbarung auftreten will.*

It has, no doubt, to be admitted that there is point in much of what has been urged, and that the discredit into which the notion of revelation has fallen with, perhaps, a majority of reflective men has, in large measure, been due to the fault of the representatives of revelational religion themselves. Even when, as in the case of the Christian Church, they have professedly limited the sphere of revelation to faith and morals, they have been apt to bring a great many assertions of natural and historical fact under this rubric, on the plea that they are indirectly necessary for religion and morality, and have often shown a levity in advancing this claim which has recoiled on themselves, as the assertions in question have been more and more completely shown to be mistaken. They have failed signally to distinguish, as they should have done, between the content of the primary revelation upon which they rest, the actual self-disclosures of God made through their founders and prophets, and the whole contents of the sacred writings which profess to record the circumstances of those self-disclosures, or to comment upon and expound their significance. It is a more serious matter that they have often revolted the sensitive conscience, as some of them still continue to revolt it, by making the eternal welfare of men depend on the historical accident of acquaintance with, and appreciation of, their own special revelation. Ignorance, even when wholly unavoidable, has been put, in this respect, on a level with deliberate and obstinate rejection of the truth. Thus the traditional Moslem belief has been, and presumably still is, that "idolaters", Jews, Christians, all go to "the fire", even those who have never heard of the Prophet and his "perspicuous book"; and Christians, on their side, have only too often maintained the same thing of all the millions of the human race who have never known of the Gospel and its contents. The claim to the exclusive possession of the final revelation has naturally and directly led to the dictum *extra ecclesiam nulla salus*, and it is instructive to note the devices to which the sensitive and thoughtful have been driven, in order to reconcile themselves to such a principle. Thus we have in the Middle Ages the examples of the attempts of men like Roger Bacon and St. Thomas to exempt the great Gentiles from the sentence, either by forced exegeses which discover the special doctrines of the Church's theology in the text of Plato and Aristotle,[1] or, more modestly, by falling back, with St. Thomas,[2] on the double possibility that the

[1] This view commended itself to Roger Bacon, from its coherence with his "illuminationist" conception of philosophy as originating in a revelation to the patriarchs. Cf. what is said of Aristotle in c. 1 of Bacon's "edition" of the *Secretum Secretorum* (*Opera inedita*, fasc. v. p. 36): "erat vir magni consilii et sani et literature magne, penetrabilis intellectus, vigilans in legalibus studiis, in gratuitis moribus et spiritualibus scienciis, contemplativus, caritativus, discretus, humilis, amator justicie, relator veritatis. Et propter hoc multi philosophorum reputabant ipsum de numero prophetarum. Invenitur etiam in antiquis codicibus Grecorum quod Deus excelsus suum angelum destinavit ad eum dicens: Pocius nominabo te angelum quam hominem . . . de morte sua diverse sunt opiniones. Quedam enim secta que dicitur peripathetica asserit ipsum ascendisse ad empeireum celum in columpna ignis." Bacon's own comment on these statements of his (Arabic) author is (p. 37) that the philosophers had certain "preludia fidei, set quod sufficientem fidem habuerunt non debemus ponere, nec tamen debemus affirmare dampnacionem aliquorum dignissimorum virorum, quia nescimus quid fecerit eis Deus."

[2] *S. Th.* ii.^{a} ii.^{ae} q. 2, art. 7 ad tertium. "Multis Gentilium facta fuit revelatio de Christo, ut patet per ea quae praedixerunt. . . . Si qui tamen salvati fuerunt quibus revelatio non fuit facta, non fuerunt salvati absque fide Mediatoris: quia etsi non habuerunt fidem explicitam, habuerunt tamen fidem implicitam in divina providentia, credentes Deum esse liberatorem hominum secundum modos sibi placitos." The case under consideration is that of the Gentiles of pre-Christian time. It is not clear to a non-specialist whether Thomas would extend the principle to meet the case of Gentiles in Christian times, living remote from Christendom. Possibly they might get the benefit of the doctrine of the "baptism of desire", which Dante introduces to explain the presence of Rhipeus in Paradise (*Par.* xx. 127-8). Dante's own treatment of the problem *seems* singular. The great Gentiles in general are placed in a Limbo which is technically in Hell, but where there is no *poena sensus*. It should seem to follow that they are excluded from Paradise neither by mortal, nor by venial, sin, but solely by the *peccatum originis*, like unbaptized

righteous man, living remote from the society which possesses the saving revelation, may either receive a strictly personal revelation, or, at any rate, may attain to an "implicit" faith in a redemption which God will effect by ways known to Himself.

With all this, however, we are not specially concerned now. Whatever may be the best solution of the question of God's dealings with those who, from no fault of their own, have been beyond the reach of an historical revelation, it is irrelevant to make difficulties of this kind a ground for denying *in limine* the possibility, or the worth, of such a revelation. If the possibility of a real specific self-disclosure of the divine be granted, the problem raised by the fact that it is not bestowed equally on men in all times and at all places becomes, in principle, identical with the more general problem, why men everywhere and at all times are not equally favoured with other good gifts; why one man has endowments and opportunities which are denied to another. That problem admits of no solution, except that of Uncle Toby[1]—and St. Paul—that God in His wisdom has disposed it so. The alleged moral difficulty only arises when we go on needlessly to complicate the problem by the assumption that a God of infinite wisdom and goodness penalises His creatures for not possessing what He has not seen fit to bestow on them; and this assumption, we may fairly say, is

---

infants. And this seems to be actually implied in the case of Virgil, of whom we are told that only Baptism is wanting to him (*Inferno*, iv. 39). Yet Dante can hardly have supposed that the most excellent Gentiles were wholly free from venial sins, and his Limbo contains persons like Julius Caesar, whom he cannot have thought clear of some mortal sins.

[1] Sterne, *Tristram Shandy*, iii. 41: "There is no cause but one, replied my Uncle Toby, why one man's nose is longer than another's, but because that God pleases to have it so. . . . That is Grangousier's solution, said my father. 'Tis he, continued my Uncle Toby . . . who makes us all, and frames and puts us together in such forms and proportions, and for such ends, as is agreeable to his infinite wisdom."

obsolete in any form of historical religion which is a "live option" for educated Europeans to-day.[1]

The other three considerations demand less summary treatment, and it may be convenient to deal with them in the reverse order from that in which we stated them. Is revelation shown to be superfluous, and therefore not reasonably to be reckoned with, as a source of knowledge of the divine by the contention that knowledge of our moral duties is sufficient for us, and on them there is agreement? For one thing, I am not myself clear that the agreement is as complete as the argument assumes. What is meant seems to be that the precepts of such a code as the Ten Commandments are, in the main, accepted and followed equally by Christians, Jews, Moslems, persons without any special religious "profession". In our own society a decent man who is theoretically a complete "Agnostic", or even an avowed Atheist, is usually about as "moral", in the way of paying his debts, abstaining from violence and fraud, and leading a wholesome family life, as the man who is a regular Church-goer. So much, no doubt, is happily true: we have long ago discovered that the man who professes no religion at all is not, as a rule, the more likely to cut our throats, corrupt our daughters, or cheat us of our property; he is not neces-

[1] The Anglican Church formally anathematises, in its 18th Article, those who "presume to say, that every man shall be saved by the law or sect which he professeth, so that he be diligent to frame his life according to that law, and the light of nature", on the ground that "holy Scripture doth set out to us only the name of Jesus Christ, whereby men must be saved". But nothing is said, or implied here, as to the destiny of the non-Christian. All that is denied is that the "virtuous unbeliever" will be saved *by* his unbelief. That no "virtuous unbeliever" will, in fact, be saved, has never, so far as I know, been the teaching of the Anglican Church, and is certainly not the belief of any responsible Anglican teacher to-day. I am surprised that a philosopher of the distinction of James Ward should have gone wrong on so simple a point. (*The Realm of Ends*, p. 424, "There is one doctrine of the theology now in vogue which gives special point to the objection we have considered—the doctrine that those who die outside the pale of Christianity are "lost eternally". I do not know where this theology is "in vogue"; certainly not in any Christian community with which I am acquainted.)

sarily a would-be criminal only restrained by fear of the police, as eighteenth-century apologists were too ready to contend, forgetful perhaps of the vehement assertions of thinkers of the so-called "ages of faith" about the inferiority of the moral practice of their contemporary Christians to that of classical Paganism in its flourishing days. But when it is further assumed, on the strength of this general uniformity of moral standard and practice within our own community, that religion, as an inspiration to practical good living, is independent of all historical revelation, certain relevant facts seem to be overlooked. It is forgotten, that whatever may be the theological tenets of the individual among us, the morality by which he lives is one which he has learned from the tradition of his community, and that this tradition has been formed under the direct influence of a great revelational religion. Even where a rule of conduct has not been directly inspired by the specifically Christian tradition, the interpretation put on the rule, often a far more important thing than the formula itself, has come direct from that tradition.

It might, no doubt, be said that when once the interpretation has been reached, its reasonableness, and the unreasonableness of any other, can be discerned without reference to its origin, and, in principle, I would not dispute this. But, as Aristotle should have convinced us long ago, in moral matters there are no postulates which are self-evident *ex vi terminorum*; it is only the man who has begun by accepting the postulates by an act of faith, and thus acquired "moral insight" *pari passu* with the acquisition of virtuous habit, who comes in the end to see that the ἀρχαί of "practical philosophy" *are* true and rational. Thus the fact that men of to-day who have been trained in doing good to those who hate them and persecute them pronounce the principle of meeting hatred by love rational, even though they may no longer accept the Gospel as "revelation", is not sufficient proof either that such action would ever have come to be recognised as "conformable to right reason" without the Gospel, nor that it will continue to be regarded as reasonable in a society which has been emancipated from the influences of Christian theology long enough to be able to treat the Gospels as a mere interesting historical monument.[1]

The point can perhaps be made still clearer if we consider the most famous modern attempt to construct an exceptionally high and austere morality in complete independence of history and revelation—the attempt of Kant. There is no principle upon which Kant is more anxious to insist than the strict "autonomy" of ethics. According to him all that is valuable in religions is their *enforcement* of a right rule of conduct on the "heart" and the imagination; the rule itself is discoverable by metaphysical analysis, without any reference to historical social tradition, much more without any reference to revelation; we discover it by *analysing* the implications of the concept "reasonable action". Ethics must thus be built up from the first without any reference to God, either as the *source* of obligation or the object *towards* which we have obligations. It is only by subsequent reflection on the ultimate presuppositions of an

[1] The argument becomes much stronger when we compare the moral standard of persons, whether "believers" or not, who have been brought up under the influence of the Christian tradition, with that of those who have been untouched by it. Christian morality, for example, and Moslem morality, both forbid adultery. But the Moslem tradition, with its permission of polygamy, concubinage, and divorce, recognises as morally unobjectionable a great deal of conduct which, by Christian standards, is deliberate and persistent adultery. The individual Moslem, as we know, may often conform in practice to the demands of the Christian standard in this matter, but the fact remains that behaviour which to the Christian is obligatory, on pain of mortal sin, is to the Moslem a "counsel of perfection".

already constituted and recognised true morality that we discover justification for believing in God as the monarch of the "kingdom of ends". For ethics itself it has to be kept an open question whether the commonwealth of ends may not be a pure democracy. It is consequently vital to Kant's unqualified "rationalism" to maintain, as he notoriously does, that the "Categorical Imperative" which enjoins reasonableness, and forbids unreason in our every action, has a twofold character. It is not only merely a general formula under which all specific right action can be brought, as the *dictum de omni et nullo* is a general formula under which all valid syllogisms can be represented; it is also an infallible direct *criterion* of the rightness or wrongness of any specific act proposed to be done.[1] We can guarantee ourselves against the commission of moral wrong-doing if we will only take care to ensure that there is no latent contradiction in the principle of the act we are proposing to perform, and that the act is, in consequence, formally reasonable. (In Kant's theory there can be no question of a *material* wrongness which would be compatible with merely *formal* rightness. If the act is formally right, it is right *simpliciter*, and the worst you can say of it is that it has had "unwelcome" consequences, an extra-ethical consideration.) Kant thus holds out to anyone who will apply the proposed criticism to his contemplated acts a moral inerrancy, which may remind us of the intellectual inerrancy promised by Descartes to those who will suspend their judgement whenever their ideas are not "clear and distinct".

Now it is notorious that the chief difficulty found by later critics in Kant's doctrine arises, not from his treatment of the Categorical Imperative as a correct

[1] *Werke* (Hartenstein[2]), iv. 251.

general formula for right action, but from this insistence on its further applicability as an immediate practical criterion. As is often said, it is a defect of the criterion that the only results Kant can get from it are purely negative. At best, it only stamps acts of certain kinds, like the deliberate making of fraudulent promises, as wrong. It gives no positive guidance whatever, as Kant might have seen if he had asked himself how the test is to be applied to a really difficult moral problem, like, for example, the choice a young man may have to make between the career which will immediately qualify him to contribute most efficiently to the support of his mother and sisters and that in which he can make the most valuable contribution to art or science; or the problem whether a specific man, in specific circumstances, would do right to make a specific offer of marriage, or, again, to break off an engagement to marry. Kant's criterion, that the unreasonable course is the morally wrong course, will only apply in such cases if one has already discovered, in some unexplained way, what is the *reasonable* course. If that is still uncertain, the application of the test leaves the uncertainty where it was.

What is worse, but even more illuminating, the failure of the criterion is not confined to these cases of special decisions in highly complex situations, where no sane moralist would expect to be able to lay down any rule of general applicability. The test equally fails in cases where moralists in general would agree that there is a recognisable rule. For example, it obviously rules out adultery, since adultery—breach of bed-vow—is only possible where marriage, as a status with definite rights and duties, exists, and thus he who wills to permit himself an act of adultery is willing at once that there shall and shall not be respect for the rule of marriage. But the advocate, or practiser, of complete sexual promiscuity would come out unscathed from the application of the test. *His* "maxim" is simply that the sexual side of human life should be, like many other sides of it, left unregulated to the "inclination" of the parties concerned, and there is no more *logical* absurdity in such a maxim than there is in the proposal to leave men to please themselves at which end they will break their breakfast-eggs, or whether they will starch their collars. Yet we may feel fairly sure that Kant would have agreed with the common verdict that, though adultery is morally bad, universal promiscuous "free love" would be worse.[1] How, then, comes he never to have reflected that his highly extolled criterion of right and wrong cannot well be sound, since it fails in so obvious a case? The only answer I can find is that Kant all along tacitly assumes that he *already* knows what sort of acts are right, before he resorts to his criterion. He takes it unconsciously for granted that the traditional moral rules recognised by educated German Protestants of his own time are known to be the right rules, and may therefore—since his analysis has yielded the equation *right* = *rational*—be presumed to be rational. If you

[1] Cf. the singular argument by which Kant attempts to prove in the *Metaphysik der Sitten* (*Werke*, Hartenstein[2], vi. 76 ff.) the immorality of all sexual relations outside the limits of lifelong monogamous marriage. Strict fidelity to monogamy is demanded on the ground that an act of sexual intercourse is one in which a human being "converts himself into a thing, conduct which conflicts with the right of humanity in its own person". This, says Kant, can only be legitimated if *each* party to the act adopts the same attitude; each must "convert its personality into thinghood", *i.e.* each must assume the position of *instrument* to the pleasures of the other. This really seems to amount to no more than a certain well-known sentiment of Ovid. If Kant's description of the sexual relation were truly an adequate one, it should surely follow that it conflicts with the rights and duties of personality in a way not to be made good, and is therefore simply vicious. And, at any rate, if the conflict is removed by reciprocity, it should follow that simple fornication to which both parties are freely consenting is as unobjectionable as marriage. The artificial reasoning by which Kant tries to evade this consequence, if valid, would seem equally to prove that morality is outraged by a cricketer who employs different "professionals" to bowl to him on different occasions.

grant this, it is not very hard for him to prove plausibly that various ways of acting, which conflict with this tradition, being in conflict with what is *ex hypothesi* rational, must be irrational, and therefore wrong.

But to justify his own claims for his criterion, Kant ought to have done something very different. He ought to have shown that by applying it we can work out an unambiguous moral legislation *in vacuo* for a community of human beings[1] destitute of all tradition. If we recognise that *this* task is insoluble in principle, and that consequently pure "rationalism" in the strict Cartesian sense, rigid deduction of conclusions, through a chain of "clear and distinct ideas", from principles "evident by the natural light", is as impossible in ethics as in other fields of thought, we must admit that it is a matter of moment for morality itself what the unproved "synthetic" postulates of a moral tradition are. In point of fact, these postulates which give a moral tradition its distinctive individual quality are not found, in the history of civilisation, existing apart from the religious tradition of the community; they are part and parcel of it. Christian religious tradition is not, indeed, the only source of the moral ideal current in our own country and our own age; we have also to take into account the influence of racial and national temperament, of our inheritance from the classical moral civilisation of Greece and Rome, and, no doubt, of other factors not so easy to trace. But the influence of the specifically religious Christian tradition is *all-pervasive* in our accepted scheme of values. Even when some particular feature in our moral scheme seems at first sight most obviously due to the historical in-

[1] I say "*human* beings" because in their case only we may presume empirical acquaintance with the great fundamental "inclinations" common to the kind, and this empirical knowledge is necessary for "applied" ethics.

fluence of Greece or Rome, the lesson *we* learn from classical antiquity is, commonly, profoundly modified for us by the Christian medium through which we have received it;[1] it is just this which makes it difficult for the historically minded student of morals to understand the ethical thought of a Socrates or an Aristotle, "objectively", without unconsciously Christianising it in all sorts of more or less subtle ways. We have, I submit, no right to say that our moral tradition of conduct could have come to us in any way except that in which such tradition has historically come to every society with whose moral tradition we are acquainted, that is, as connected by relations of reciprocal interdependence with a religious tradition.

It might be possible to admit the fact of this complication of the morality characteristic of a world-religion with its specifically religious element, and yet to dispute the importance of the fact. For, it might be said, though, in fact, we never find the religious and the ethical isolated from one another in an historical tradition, we may isolate them for ourselves by a *Denkexperiment*. Noetic analysis will enable us to get each loose from the other, though in actual fact they are regularly presented together. In fact, that is, they are always "conjoined", not, in any real sense, "connected"; why then should we make the conjunction any reason for doubting that the one may be the precious ore, the other merely so much dross? I should

[1] To give a single illustration out of many which might be adduced: In one of the most impressive of recent books on Plato, I read that "conscience" is a characteristically "religious" and "Christian" concept which is meaningless from the moral standpoint of Plato (Stenzel, *Platon der Erzieher*, p. 278). To my own mind such a statement makes nonsense of the *Apology*, the *Crito*, the *Gorgias*, and I can only account for its presence in a valuable book by the reflection that whereas I see Plato through a tradition shaped by Augustine, Cudworth, Butler, Richard Price, the German author views him through a different medium, just as inevitably as an Englishman sees the great Attic tragedians in the light, so to say, of Shakespeare, a Frenchman, presumably, in that of Racine.

reply that, if we take that line, we lay ourselves directly open to a rejoinder which I find unanswerable. Each of the great world-religions has been, for good or for evil, a most potent force in transforming the whole scheme of moral "valuations"; each has produced a moral *reform*—not necessarily a salutary one—on the grand scale, and it would be hard to point to any other influence in history which has had the same effect on such a scale. But it is equally true that no great historical religion has ever aimed, first and foremost, at a moral reform as its main objective. Each has always rested its claim on mankind primarily not on the improved morality it enjoins, but on the new light it throws on God and man's relation to God. Mohammed is credited with improving the morals of the Arabs of the "ignorance" in various ways, notably by the prohibition of infanticide. Islam has also been called the greatest of all "temperance societies". But the main business of Mohammed, as declared by himself, was not to prohibit infanticide, to limit polygamy, or to abolish intoxication; it was to proclaim the unity of God. No one, I imagine, doubts that St. Paul improved the morals of his converts (though it is to be observed that he seems usually to assume that what was wrong with them in their unregenerate days was not theoretical ignorance of the moral law, but practical disregard of it; he does not claim to be the prophet of a "new" morality of any kind). But his immediate concern was not the improvement of manners and morals; it was the preaching of "Jesus and resurrection".[1] The all-important thing with him is that men should accept his message about God and what God has done for them; moral improvement follows, or ought to follow,

[1] *Acts* xvii. 18 *οἱ δὲ (ἔλεγον). Ξένων δαιμονίων δοκεῖ καταγγελεὺς εἶναι· ὅτι τὸν Ἰησοῦν καὶ τὴν ἀνάστασιν εὐηγγελίζετο.*

as a matter of course from the consciousness of a new relation to God.

I think we may say two things about all the great religions which have proved their power, in varying degree, to mould the life of men as men, not as men of this or that stock or speech: all owe their origin to individual founders, and in no case has the founder conceived himself, or been conceived by his followers, in the first instance, as a moral reformer. A religion of this kind is the most potent of all forces in transforming moral ideals and practice, but it owes it potency to the very fact that it is something other than a project of moral reformation. Indeed, it is often urged by unfavourable critics in depreciation of the founders of such religions, as it has been urged against Our Lord, that they are wanting in ethical originality; their precepts, it is said, are not found, on careful scrutiny, to contain anything which had not been said, more or less explicitly, before them. The criticism would be largely just, but for the fact that the founders of religions do not announce themselves as moral reformers, except incidentally and in the second place.

The consideration I would urge, then, is this. Even from the standpoint of those who, like Kant, judge religions by their value as instruments of moral reform, it would be a bad mistake to suppose that we can estimate the worth of a religion by artificially isolating the expressly ethical deliverances of its founder or its prophets. The real moral effects of a religion depend primarily on its new and characteristic declarations about God, and the relations into which it brings the worshipper with God. Moral improvements effected by a religion are consequences, and very largely indirect and half-unconscious consequences, of the changed attitude towards God into which the convert believes himself to have been brought. We should be misconceiving the facts if we thought of the founders of the great religions simply as men of remarkable moral insight, and consequently conceded that their directly ethical precepts, being reached by an immediate intuition of the morally right which is beyond the range of more ordinary men, may properly be regarded as a "revelation" or self-disclosure of the supreme moral personality, God, but persisted in confining the concession to these merely ethical utterances, as Kant would like us to do.[1] From the standpoint of the Kantian philosophy of religion, it would be justifiable to find a revelation from God in such sayings as "Love your enemies", "Resist not evil"; but such utterances as "No man knoweth the Father but the Son", or "Hereafter ye shall see the Son of Man coming on the right hand of the Power", would have to be dismissed as the pardonable excesses of an exuberant imagination. But in point of fact, so far as Christianity has been really operative to moral renewal, it has been so precisely through these not directly ethical utterances, with the new vistas they open on the strictly transcendent and eternal. It is they, much more than any specific moral precepts of the Gospel, which are at the roots of the Christian conception of the practical life itself, and furnish it with its "dynamic". Either the claim of Our Lord to special direct intuitive apprehension of the divine must be surrendered, or it is to these "otherworldly" utterances that we must look for the evidence of a first-hand disclosure from the supernatural. So, even from the point of view which measures the worth and estimates the truth of religions exclusively by their influence on morals, it is reasonable to attach weight

[1] Cf. Kant, *Werke* (Hartenstein²), vi. 209, on the *oberstes Kriterium aller Schriftauslegung*.

not merely to the ethical precepts of the *Religions-stifter*, but to their intuitions concerning God and the eternal world. They too will have weight, just so far as we are justified in regarding them as genuine disclosures of a reality which is there in its own right, not creations of human fantasy. And we must certainly add that it seems a bad mistake to regard religion in this fashion, as merely a useful instrument of morality, as Kant, for example, wished to do.

No doubt, we should be justified in saying that a religion which did nothing to make the standard of morality at once more elevated and more inward, still more a religion which actually debased the moral standard, must be a false, as well as a bad, religion. The indignant eloquence of Adimantus in the *Republic*,[1] when he denounces the moral corruption chargeable on the Orphic pardon-mongers and vendors of "sacraments", rightly carries us away with it, as we read. Nor should we, I conceive, feel inclined to dispute the verdict of the aged Plato, that the worst kind of "infidel" is the hypocritical trafficker for private ends in the credulity of mankind.[2] But this is no more than might also be said, with the same sort of truth, about science, or art. It may be the case that, in particular instances, this man or that man has suffered morally from his interest in science or in art, that he would have been a morally better man, in some important respects, if he had not been so good an artist, or man of science. There are undeniably men whose devotion to scientific research has made them, in some respects, inhumane, and others whose absorption in art has led them to neglect their duties to wife and children. But I think we should all deny that devotion to art or science, as such, has any inherent tendency to make men cruel,

[1] Plato, *Republic*, 363.

[2] Plato, *Laws*, 908 B ff.

or indifferent to family affections; we should be ready to admit that if, in particular societies, the practice of art, or the following of science as a vocation, has really tended generally to deprave the moral standard, the art and science in question have been debased art and false science. I believe we should go further, and might fairly say that, in the main, devotion to the highest art and to rightly conceived science tend, on the whole, to the *all-round* elevation of moral character. There are bad men among artists and men of science, and some of them rise to eminence in their vocations; but among the very greatest, in science and in art, the greatly good do not seem, to say the least of it, to be more uncommon than in any other walk of life. If we hear more of the moral frailties of famous artists than we do of the shortcomings of shopkeepers, or attorneys, or labourers, the reason is, perhaps, partly that our curiosity about the artist leads to the collection of gossip about him which is not forthcoming for the shopkeeper; partly that most of us are more like the shopkeeper than we are like the artist, and are prone to indulge the "all-too-human" habit of confining our reprobation to the vices to which we are personally least addicted.

The very unity of human personality would seem to make it impossible that courage, sincerity, self-denial, loyalty to the best one can conceive, untiring reaching out from the good to the better, should be regularly characteristic of a man in one great part of his activity, and merely wanting in another. And, on the other side, if a man is generally slack, indolent, readily satisfied with the second-best, fitful, backboneless, in the conduct of his life, we should hardly expect to find these qualities regularly replaced by their opposites in his vocational work. Since a man is, after all, one man and not several, he will probably put the same sort of personality into what we call his vocational work as into the rest of his doings, if only we knew how to look for it there. And yet it is certain that the sole justification, or the chief justification, of science and art is not to be found in their immediate effect on moral character, and the direct aim of art and science is never moralistic. Both deteriorate at once, as soon as they are made consciously subservient to a purely moral purpose. Art and science both do us good, but the good they do is not, in the first instance, to improve our discharge of our duties to our families, our customers, or our clients. Art does us good directly by teaching us to detect and revel in beauty, science by teaching us to care for truth.

Just so it is with religion. Like science and art, and more markedly, it has its repercussions on our daily moral practice, but, like them, it is primarily something quite different from a moral rule of life. As art has its source in the intuition of the beautiful, and science its source in the vision of the true, so religion arises directly from, and is the creature's response to, the dim and vague, but intensely vivid, perception of the presence of the uncreated and adorable. The characteristic attitude of the religious soul is that of worship, and worship springs from assurance that the uncreated and complete good is no mere *Sollen*, but is given as intimately present here and now, as the overpowering reality. Now this sense of the actual presence of the divine, though, when accepted as such, it can infuse a new quality of life into all our practice, is in itself something transcending the merely moral. The furthest that moral practice, and philosophical theory based on reflection upon practice, will take us is to the inferential conclusion which Kant reaches, that *if* moral obligation is more than a mere generous illusion or *bellum somnium*, the uncreated good must be a reality too. But to draw this conclusion as a philosophical inference is not the same thing as to live in the conscious presence of the divine as *given*. Morality, at its best, and the "practice of the presence of God" are two and not one; it is because they are two, not one, that the Kantian moral autonomy, obedience to a self-imposed law of conduct, is not the same thing as what our fathers called "Gospel liberty", but only a second-best. So long as we are living only at the level of Kantian autonomy, we have not really anchored our life on the "Rock of Ages", and it is a consequence of this that the note of joy, so characteristic of religion, is so entirely absent from Kant's philosophy of life. Once more, we must say that the direct vision which gives a great religion its supreme and unique value is not an affair of commands and precepts, a vision of what we *ought* to do, but a vision of what that from which we come, and to which we return, actually *is*, and what *it* is doing and will do, in and for us. The regenerating moral effect of our religion on our conduct is most genuine and profound when the direct object of our attention is not the self and its tasks, but God; and, for this reason, the supremely important thing in any religion is its "revelation" of God. Either we must deny that religion has any relation but one of accidental conjunction with moral practice, or, if the facts of life and history are too strong for us, we must, as it seems to me, frankly admit, for all the great religions which have really elevated humanity, the presence of a genuine element of direct self-disclosure of the divine, and so of "revelation", immediately given knowledge of God.

If so much is conceded, we may attempt an answer to the argument which maintains that there can be no finality about revelation because its content must be conditioned by the antecedents of the recipients; that there can be no "truth for all time", just because every truth, to be true at all, must be a truth for its own particular time. In a sense, I grant, the fact is so, and has to be frankly admitted. It is true that, as the schoolman's phrase ran, *quidquid recipitur, recipitur ad modum recipientis*, or, in more familiar words, "not all can receive this saying, but those to whom it is given". And this is a principle with an applicability not confined to the domain of religion and theology. Art, science, philosophy, to be significant at all, must speak the language of a particular community and a particular age. There is no work of art which is neither a work of Greek art, nor of Flemish, nor of Japanese, nor of Italian, nor of any other age or place, but just a work of art *überhaupt*. A great tragedy, like *Agamemnon*, or *Othello*, is not simply *a* tragedy; it is a tragedy instinct with the spirit of a definite people, the Attic or the English, and a definite age, the age of Cimon, or the age of Elizabeth and James, and we do not properly understand the tragedy until we can recreate in ourselves something of the spirit of the place and the time to which it belongs. *Othello*, a characteristic product of the London of the reign of James I., is necessarily more or less of a sealed book to any man who can only feel and think like a man, perhaps not even like a Londoner, of our day. Even a great philosophy is always, in some sense, the product of its place and age, and is never fully understood, if it has to be studied in isolation from the whole concrete life of the society to which it belongs. If one has spent years in trying to understand a great thinker, such as Plato, and to help others to understand him, one knows well from one's own experience how dependent one is for success on the double process of purgation and enrichment of one's own mind. One has constantly to be resolute to forget so much that one knows, or supposes one's self to know, about the world, because it was unthought of in the Athens of Socrates and Plato; on the other side, one must constantly be awake to the possibility that ignorance of apparently irrelevant facts about the life of their age may have the gravest consequences for one's work of interpretation.[1] And the double process is one which can never be brought to completion. After years of purgation by the resolute effort to think historically, one can never be certain that one's interpretations are not still vitiated by undetected elements of the unhistorical; again, our documentation is so imperfect that, when every extant scrap of historical and antiquarian evidence has been utilised, our knowledge of a long-vanished age is bound to be schematic, abstract, and full of ugly gaps, and we can never be confident that the filling up of the gaps, the clothing of the skeleton with flesh, might not gravely affect our understanding of the thought of the age.

It is true everywhere that the determinable is never found actually existing, except as modified by specific determinants. Truth, to be spoken to any age, must be spoken in the age's own dialect, and the dialect of different ages is never quite the same. Nor could we escape the problem by reducing it to one of mere verbal expression, as is done by those who have said, for example, that the "language of the Christian creeds is Greek, but their meaning universal". Meaning and its expression are not related as my body and my clothes,

[1] How often, for example, it is forgotten that Socrates was a man of the Periclean age, that Plato came of a family in which "democratic" politics were traditional, that Aristotle had no personal experience of the life of the "citizen", and that we are bound to misunderstand all three if we neglect these facts. Even Descartes is often misrepresented and unjustly accused of insincerities from mere disregard of the fact that he was a seventeenth-century French Roman Catholic, not a concealed "free-thinker".

but rather as my body and its skin. I may disguise myself in garments of a score of different fashions, retaining the same body unchanged; to be fitted to a different skin, I should need to have a differently built body. So the transference of knowledge or thought from one society to another is no mere affair of adaptation to a new vocabulary; it is a matter of adaptation to a different set of habits of mind.

If all this has to be admitted, as it surely must be, it should be plain that it applies just as much to thought which may have originated in a specific disclosure of the divine as to any other thought. We have this treasure in earthen vessels, and the excellence of the wine makes no difference to the fact that the vessels are earthen, and that many of them may be earth of very common quality, not superfine porcelain clay. Yet, when the fullest allowance has been made for such considerations, the question still remains with us whether, because every truth communicable to man must be a truth for its own time, every truth must also be one *only* for its own time. The conclusion is congenial to a certain type of philosophy, not unfashionable in some quarters, the philosophy of pure becoming or sheer impermanence. It is fashionable to-day in these quarters to say that "nothing is, everything becomes", just as it was fashionable to say the same kind of thing in the Athens of Socrates. The favourite modern way of saying it is, as we should expect, epistemological rather than ontological. Truth, we are told, is itself a mental fashion, and fashions are proverbially changeful. A philosophy, a theology, a scientific doctrine, must perish, and rightly so, by mere lapse of time, not because the answers it gives to its problems have been found to be false, but because, with the change in intellectual fashions, the problems themselves have lost their significance. No truth can be the "truth of God", valid for all time and all places, for the same reason that no costume can be the wear for all mankind, always and everywhere. This way of thinking has more than one name, and shows itself in more than one quarter. It may appear now as "pragmatism", now as "humanism", now, perhaps, as the *filosofia dello spirito*, but all these would seem to be variations on one theme, the doctrine that permanence is an illusion. Without us, there is no law in nature; within, there are no fixed principles of truth; without or within, there is nothing but "motions", the more slowly or more rapidly passing whims of *la mode*. In the language of the Heraclitean aphorism so often quoted by Nietzsche, "Time is a child playing draughts; the kingdom is a child's".[1]

When we try to meet and counter theories of universal impermanence with special reference to what concerns us most for our present purpose, their epistemological side, our most natural first thought is to look for some definite isolated body of truths which may plausibly be said to be truths for all time, because they are manifestly not clothed in a linguistic garb peculiar to any one time, and consequently do permit of transcription from any one idiom into any other without loss or increment of significance. Then we inevitably tend to think, with Plato, Descartes, and Spinoza, of the system of the propositions of pure mathematics as the great outstanding example establishing the existence of truth which is permanent, just because it is truth at the extreme limit of depersonalisation. We to-day, were we arguing for mere persuasive effect, might make an impressive point by simply exhibiting the three massive volumes of a work like the *Principia Mathematica* of Whitehead and Russell, where the

[1] Heraclitus, Fr. 79 (Bywater), *αἰὼν παῖς ἐστι παίζων πεσσεύων· παιδὸς ἡ βασιληίη.*

"timeless validity" of the body of pure mathematical propositions seems to have been demonstrated in act by the rendering of them all into a stereotyped language which has never been, and never will be, the living idiom of anyone anywhere, but, in compensation, can be equally apprehended by individuals of the most various idioms. The mere fact that the propositions of mathematics have been so successfully translated into a language which, being still-born, cannot grow or change might seem to have met the epistemologists of impermanence as Diogenes is fabled to have met the deniers of motion. But such a defence would be inadequate to our purpose, for a double reason.

For one thing, even in *Principia Mathematica*, the stereotyping of thought is not, and could not have been, complete. There are intrinsic limits to the capabilities of a "universal symbolism". Its not innumerous symbols for primary "indefinables" have to be accurately apprehended before their combinations can be understood, and thus presuppose preliminary explanation in an idiom which is not dead and impersonal, but personal and living. Here is, at the outset, an opening for what may prove to be serious misunderstandings. And again, in every such symbolic system, there must be some supreme principle or principles, governing all its inferences, and these obviously cannot be expressed in the symbolism itself. Thus, every symbolically expressed demonstration in *Principia Mathematica* depends on the principle that "what is implied by true premisses" is itself true", but neither this proposition nor the meaning of the terms "implication" and "truth" can be expressed in the symbolism of the authors, or any other.[1] Explanations on such

[1] Cf. L. Couturat, *Les Principes des mathématiques*, p. 11: "il est remarquable que ce principe ne peut pas s'exprimer symboliquement. Comme le remarque

points have to be given in ordinary language, and this makes it possible that the explanations may, from the first, have been confused or ambiguous, and again that they may cease to convey the sense intended, as the words employed shift their meaning "in use". Thus, the most rigorous system of symbolically expressed mathematical truths would not wholly escape the criticism of a resolute denier of permanence.

It is a more important consideration, for our purposes, that even if it were possible to put the *whole* body of pure mathematics, including the primitive indefinables and primary principles of inference, into a stereotyped symbolism, as a guarantee against change of significance, all we should have achieved by this would be the construction of a purely abstract and formal pattern, inadequate to the description of the simplest piece of concrete fact. The "world" with which the physicist professionally concerns himself is a sufficiently poverty-stricken abstract from the world of individual events and purposes in which we all, including the physicist, have to live as men and women, but even the physicist's "world" itself defies all attempts to build it up out of mathematical formulae. Even in physics, the formulae function as describing the structure of an elusive something which slips through their meshes; a fact, however empty of content we try to make it, is not to be manufactured out of formulae, there is an *haecceitas* about it which is proof against our analyses. It is *this* fact, and there can be no "symbol" for *this*.

If, then, we are looking for examples of permanent truths, with an interest for life which persists through

M. Russell [cf. *Principles of Mathematics*, i. p. 34], ce principe marque la limite du symbolisme. Il n'y a rien d'étonnant, d'ailleurs, à ce que le symbolisme ne réussisse pas à traduire tous les principes, car il faut évidemment définir verbalement les premiers symboles et les premières formules."

all the ages, it is not to pure mathematics, with its formulae from which the vitality has been carefully drained, that we should turn. We may perhaps derive a more helpful suggestion from consideration of the analogous case of the works of art and imagination which are found to retain abundant life and significance for generation after generation. We could all name some of the great outstanding works, in literature and the arts, which most successfully defy all vicissitudes of time, all differences in customs, manners, morals, institutions, to make them antiquated. Now a curious thing about these works which are never "out of date" is that the fact of their universal appeal to the human mind, in all times and places, seems to be connected with the other fact that they are so deeply rooted in the life of the society from which they spring. They seem to be "for all time", not *though,* but *because,* they are so very definitely of their own time. The creations of genius which remain perfect after the lapse of centuries, and the rise and fall of commonwealths, are not works which reflect the life and thought of no particular age or place, and might, so far as can be seen, have been equally well produced almost anywhere, or at any time, but those which are so full of a rich and complex life that they could only have come to birth in the soil from which they did, in fact, spring.

The play of *Hamlet* may serve as an example. In a way, *Hamlet* is a specimen of a kind of composition which has made its appearance at more than one period in the history of European imaginative literature, the tragedy of revenge.[1] Tragedies of revenge may be, and I suppose have been, composed in most societies which have any drama at all. But what makes

[1] We can trace the "family tree", so to say, of the play *Hamlet* back through Kyd and the *Spanish Tragedy* to Seneca and his *Thyestes*, and through Seneca back to the older Greek tragedies which dealt with the same and similar themes.

Hamlet unlike most other works of the type, a perennial delight, what gives it its interest for men whose intellectual and moral convictions may be very different indeed from those of the English of the year A.D. 1600, is precisely its saturation with the qualities which stamp it as the product of the whole social life of a particular community, acting as a stimulus to an individual man of genius. A tragedy of revenge, of some sort, might be composed by almost anyone in Europe at any time. *Hamlet* could only have been the work of an Elizabethan Englishman, and only of just the one Elizabethan Englishman who did, in fact, write *Hamlet*. (If any of you doubt this last statement, I recommend a careful perusal of the other contemporary dramas of the same type.) The paradox is that it is just this which gives the play what is called, in the hackneyed journalistic phrase, its "universal human appeal" to a world in which only a few students have ever heard of the *Spanish Tragedy*, *The Duchess of Malfi*, *Titus Andronicus*, *The Revenger's Tragedy*, or *Women beware Women*. And we must note that this does not mean that *Hamlet*, or any other work of the same immortality, has, for mankind at large, an interest which is primarily historical or antiquarian. *Hamlet* is saturated with the spirit of Elizabethan England, but the reason why it retains its hold on us is not that it gratifies our natural historical curiosity to observe the obsolete and unfamiliar outlook of Englishmen of a remarkable age, now some ten generations behind us, on the world and life. This *is* very largely why the minority of students find some of the other contemporary tragedies of revenge which we have just mentioned interesting. But *Hamlet* "grips" us of to-day, and not only those of us who are English by birth or education, because it is full of an attitude towards life and its problems which we still feel to be *our* attitude. The often-lauded universality of Shakespeare does not mean that in his vision of life he misses out what is characteristic of his own people and his own time; it means that his vision penetrates to the depths.

What is true of the great poet's vision is, I should say, equally true of the thought of the great philosopher contemplating life concretely. I meet in my reading the repeated allegation that the great constructive philosophies of antiquity, or of the Middle Ages, have lost their value for us, not by being refuted and shown to be false, but by a change in the temper and spirit of the age, which has made the problems of the past and the solutions given them equally unmeaning. I doubt whether even the able writers who say this kind of thing most glibly really feel altogether as they profess to feel, at least when they are actually opening their minds to the influence of the great teachers of the past. If they do, how comes it that they can still be aware of the greatness of that which, according to their professions, no longer means anything to them? For my own part, when I try to enter, for example, into the thought of Plato, I know well enough that there are *nuances* which must be lost on me, because I am unavoidably ignorant of so much of the mental life of the Athens of the fourth century before Christ. But I do not find that I am in an intellectual fog where I have lost my bearings, as I might be if I could listen to the conversation of a group of "Martians". The great problems man's life suggests to Plato seem to be recognisably the same with which our own society still has to reckon; the precise form in which they are stated may often not be that which would occur most readily to ourselves, but, after all, we can translate the Platonic problem significantly into terms of our own intellectual currency. If at times we feel that the rendering cannot be made a perfect equivalent, that is no more than the common difficulty which besets us whenever we try to turn a page of French, or German, or Italian into English. It does not mean that the understanding of Plato's thought is in any way analogous with the attempt to decipher an inscription in a tongue which has vanished and left no traces behind it. There is no ancient philosophy which is undecipherable in the same sense as the picture-writing of Easter Island.

It should be clear, then, that the mere fact that any truth less abstract and superficial than the propositions of pure mathematics must be the truth of a specific age need not mean that such a truth must be the nonsense or falsehood of other ages. Those who think thus seem to forget that, after all, our precursors, ourselves, and our distant successors—if we leave any—in the course of history are alike in being *men*: we all have the same ground-pattern, are all variations on one theme. A philosophy which ignores the reality of "universal human nature" as at least an *universale* IN *re* is a philosophy which does not look "under the skin". If these considerations apply to all human thought, they apply, of course, independently of any question of the historical origination of the thought. Thus, the fact that whatever is "received" is received only "after the measure of the recipient" is not in itself a valid objection against the reality of revelations made through specific channels and at specific times. Unless it is nonsense to speak of any utterance of man to man as having abiding significance, there is no reason why utterances prompted by such self-disclosures should not possess that abiding significance and, in that sense, be final.

But we shall also do well to remember certain things which advocates of the claims of a particular historical "revelation" to finality are sometimes inclined to forget. We have to remember that the conditioning of the disclosures received by the limitations of the recipient must be twofold. If we may judge by the historical records about those who have claimed to be recipients of such illuminations, the thing revealed is nearly always descried dimly and with much confusion; it can never be expressed in speech in a way which is wholly adequate. This is no peculiarity of the revelations of the world-religions; it is true of all that any man feels to be at once supremely significant and eminently personal to himself. Our deepest thoughts, as Shelley said to Trelawny, are "unintelligible even to ourselves"; they are what a greater than Shelley has called "thoughts beyond the reaches of our souls". Even in Christianity, which asserts a relation of unique intimacy between the human mind of its Founder and the mind of God—"the Son knoweth whatsoever the Father doeth"—this problem is not absent, as may be seen by the way in which Christian theologians have been exercised by the question of the human knowledge of Christ and its limitations.[1] Curiously enough, the philosophical theologian who has gone nearest towards denying the existence of this problem in the case of Christ is one who stood all his life outside the Christian community. "To Moses", says Spinoza, "God spoke face to face, but to Christ He spoke mind to mind."[2] That

[1] A problem forced on the most conservative mind by the express statement of the Gospel that Ἰησοῦς προέκοπτεν σοφίᾳ καὶ ἡλικίᾳ καὶ χάριτι παρὰ θεῷ καὶ ἀνθρώποις (*Luke* ii. 52).

[2] *Tractatus Theologico-Politicus*, i. 23-4. "non credo ullum alium ad tantam perfectionem supra alios pervenisse praeter Christum, cui Dei placita, quae homines ad salutem ducunt, sine verbis aut visionibus, sed immediate revelata sunt; adeo ut Deus per mentem Christi sese apostolis manifestaverit, ut olim Mosi mediante voce aerea . . . si Moses cum Deo de facie ad faciem . . . loquebatur, Christus quidem de mente ad mentem communicavit."

may be so, but it is surely equally clear that, even to Christ, God did not speak by the communication of the only thing which deserves the name of adequate knowledge on Spinoza's principles, an exactly articulated system of propositions about the relations of "clear and distinct ideas". No one, orthodox or unorthodox, I conceive, will maintain that Our Lord was either speculative metaphysician or speculative theologian. His revelation of the Father was not a speculative system, it was the whole of his own concrete personality and life; and such propositions as are ascribed to him are expressions, wholly unsystematic, and mostly, as von Hügel has somewhere said, "exoteric", of an immediate perception.

And, apart from this, a revelation on which a religion is to be built is not a perception to be kept to the immediate recipient; it has to be imparted to the community. Even if it has been received by the immediate recipient, "mind to mind", as Spinoza phrases it, it has to be conveyed to others in the language they understand, and thus adapted to their limitations, and this creates a second problem. If the conservative Christian theologian, for example, is unwilling to admit that Our Lord himself had, in his conception of past history, his expectations for the future, his outlook on the world of nature, in many respects the mind of a Galilean of his century, the only alternative is to assume that, in communicating his teaching to his disciples, whose limitations no one denies, the Lord must have translated what, as conceived in his own mind, was simple *Wahrheit* into a *Wahrheit* sufficiently leavened with *Dichtung* to be appreciated by them and fruitful in them. If he did not himself expect to reappear in the immediate future in the clouds before the eyes of his enemies, at least he must have used language which the first generation of his followers could only understand in that sense, or the New Testament would not be permeated, as it is, by the conviction of the imminent nearness of the Lord's return and the "end of history". The reality of a revelation, however assured, cannot dispense from the duty of repeated scrutiny and careful distinction between that in it which is the permanent substance and that which belongs not to the substance, but to its adaptation to the measure of the recipients; and this should make the theologian more scrupulous than he has frequently been to avoid the assumption that the separation has already been accomplished, and that what he has now on his hands is pure and unmixed "substance of faith".

Yet, on the other side, it is unjustified dogmatism to assume that because we cannot be certain that what we have left after our winnowing is pure and unmixed substance, there is really no substance at all. This is that "emptying out of the child with the bath" of which the proverb warns us. What *is* substance, I take it, we only learn in what might fairly be called an empirical way. *A priori* we are hardly entitled to say more than this. A religion is true religion just in so far as it achieves the purpose, on which we dwelt so long in our former series, of thoroughly remoulding the self, so as to make God, the supernatural good, and eternity the very centre of a man's thought and will. Whatever, in the life and practice of an actual religious community, is an obstacle to this inward renewing of life is plainly incompatible with true religion, and whatever, in the alleged revelation possessed by the community, encourages and perpetuates the obstacle cannot be of the substance of revelation. But also, what cannot be dismissed without impoverishing spiritual life, and hindering the remaking of the self into eternity at its source, clearly is of the substance. If we would judge how the test is to be applied, I do not see that we have any sure course but to study the types of life and character actually promoted by given affirmations and denials. If we find that a high level of the right kind of spirituality and other-worldliness is regularly attained in dependence on certain convictions which have their origin in acceptance of a given "revelation", but regularly missed when these convictions are ignored or denied, we shall, if we are prudent, be very slow to treat these particular affirmations as temporary and unessential; we shall feel fairly persuaded that they at least *contain* something which is sterling substance, and that they must not be met by bare denials. It may be that the affirmation is not thus proved to be all substance without alloy; the future may yet show that there may be qualifications of the affirmation which can coexist with, or even be favourable to, the richest spirituality. But the test, if it has been fairly applied, may, for all this, entirely dispose of an unqualified denial.

We may consider a simple illustration of this point. We probably all remember Kant's violent opposition to prayer, an opposition directly due to his determination to see nothing *sui generis* in the religious, as distinguished from the moral, life. A man, being autonomous, ought, Kant holds, to do his duty in his own strength by the unaided exercise of the morally good will; to pray for "grace" to live aright is therefore no better than unethical superstition,[1] if the prayer is more than the expression of a hope that we may persevere in our virtuous resolution. We know, too, how widely even anti-materialistic philosophers in the second half of the nineteenth century were infected by the coarse

[1] Kant, *Werke* (Hartenstein[2]), vi. 294 ff.

deterministic prejudice that prayer, if it means anything more than meditation, is an absurdity, because to pray implies the belief that the "laws of the physical world" can be modified or suspended by the will of God. One might debate the Pelagianism of Kant's argument, or discuss the ambiguity and arbitrariness of the "determinist" scheme to the end of time and "find no end, in wand'ring mazes lost", so far as any decisive theoretical result is concerned. In practice the question whether prayerless life is not also wholly worldly life admits of a much readier solution. It is not to dialectic we need to turn to discover that a prayerless good will, reliant on its own strength, does not remain permanently at any high level of inward goodness, or that, even in respect of the "external good things" of life, a man's *moral* always suffers, if his theories forbid him to ask for the provision for his needs, and to give thanks when he receives it. There are many methods of prayer, not all equally compatible with a true spirituality, but it should be plain from experience of "fruits" that, whatever elements of superstition may disfigure the practice of some forms of prayer, a philosophy of religion which has no place at all for "prayer and supplication" is a false philosophy.

Some suspicion of this may be detected in the language of philosophers who, after proscribing prayer proper, concede that "meditation", at any rate, may be a real need of the religious life. The pity of it is that those who speak thus too often abstain from specifying the *object* of the meditation they are willing to permit. Whether meditation is to do us good or harm must surely depend on the nature of that on which we meditate. It will not be all one to our characters whether the object of our habitual meditation is a Father who knows how to give good things to those that ask him, or a Stoic εἱμαρμένη, or a purely non-moral "law of necessity". Spinoza, to be sure, fancied that by meditation on the "absolute necessity" of all events we might be led to the *summa mentis acquiescentia* of the saint.[1] In actual life, if the meditator has not, like Spinoza, a predisposition to saintliness, such "morose contemplation" is more likely, I take it, to lead to the defiant vapourings of Mr. Russell's "free man",[2] or W. E. Henley's brags against the "bludgeonings of Fate," and oftener still to something even worse than vapouring or bluster, that listless apathy which the Middle Ages reckoned a deadly sin, and called by the name of *acedia*. Even meditation on my own autonomy as giver of the moral law to myself is more likely to end in a Stoic self-idolatry than in anything noble, and meditation on the Absolute of the more optimistically coloured nature-pantheisms in spiritual voluptuousness. The meditation which can be counted on as a source of strength and sweetness of spirit is meditation on a God to whom one can and must *spontaneously* pray. Clough,

[1] *Ethica* v. 5-8, 11, 26, 27.

[2] "When, without the bitterness of impotent rebellion, we have learnt both to resign ourselves to the outward rule of Fate and to recognise that the non-human world is unworthy of our worship, it becomes possible at last (? why) so to transform and refashion the unconscious universe, so to transmute it in the crucible of imagination, that a new image of shining gold replaces the old idol of clay" (B. Russell, *Philosophical Essays*, p. 66). (Exactly: the "free man" of Mr. Russell, like Nebuchadnezzar, only "worships" an image of gold, the "work of his own hands". Spinoza knew better than this.) "Brief and powerless is man's life; on him and all his race, the slow, sure doom falls pitiless and dark. Blind to good and evil, reckless of destruction, omnipotent matter rolls on its relentless way; for Man . . . it remains only to cherish, ere yet the blow falls, the lofty thoughts that ennoble his little day; disdaining the coward terrors of the slave of Fate, to worship at the shrine that his own hands have built", etc., etc. (*ib.* p. 70). But *what* does the "free man" worship at this "shrine"? On Mr. Russell's own showing, something which is a pure product of his own imagination, and known by himself to be nothing more. And what is the quality of the "worship"? Is not the plain prose of the situation—Mr. Russell, as the rhythms of his sentences show, is "dropping into poetry", of a kind—that the "free man" is sheltering himself in "make-believe" from a merely disgusting reality? Might it not be more advisable to ask the question whether Mr. Russell's bugbear, "omnipotent matter", is anything but an *alias* for "old Noboddady"?

for example, in a well-known stanza, seems to be explicitly surrendering prayer; yet the attitude of his "prayerless heart" to the object of its meditations can be described in such words as these:

> Man's inmost soul, before Thee inly brought,
> Thy presence owns, ineffable, divine;
> Chastised each rebel self-encentred thought,
> My will adoreth Thine.[1]

That is a meditation on the living God which is itself already a prayer.

We have still to consider the allegation that revelation, the direct disclosure of the divine, is in principle either impossible, or at least superfluous, since a revelation, even if possible, must coincide in its content with what we can independently discover about God by the "natural light". The allegation of *impossibility* may be very lightly dismissed, as the mere prejudice of a mind which has not learned to think historically. An unhistorical age is usually sceptical, at once and for the same reason, of revelation and of genius in its various manifestations. For like revelation, genius, whether it be that of the poet, the dramatist, the musician, the painter, the mathematician, the mechanician, is always a *disturbing* factor in things for the type of mind which finds its satisfaction in clarity, definition and the conscious orderly arrangement of thoughts, rather than in their depth and "grip" on reality. For it is notorious that the genius, like the poets examined by Socrates, cannot, as a rule, tell anyone whence his "inspirations" come, nor analyse their content, or reduce it to a neat and transparent structural pattern. His insights come to him, as perceptions come, direct, with the appearance of being unsought disclosures of a reality given to him, not constructed by himself; they *impose* them-

[1] *Qui laborat, orat.*

selves, violently and intrusively, as "impressions of sense" do, and again, as with "impressions of sense" there is a wealth of confused concreteness about them which resists analysis. This rich, but confused and intrusive content is offensive to all the intellectual habits of an age of "enlightenment" and "good sense", which, accordingly, tends to deny the fact of genius, just as it tends to deny the fact of revelation. As such an age is prone to reduce the claimant to revelation to the status of a conscious moral and social reformer, who conceals his purpose under a cloud of mystifications and pretences, with a view to impressing the imagination of the "vulgar", so it reduces the great poet to the status of a craftsman deftly insinuating moral and political "lessons" by artificial "fiction" and allegory. As it sees in the prophet only the reformer, so it sees in the poet only the teacher.[1] Both are supposed to make, in their own minds, a clear distinction between the matter they are presenting and the adventitious and artificial form in which they clothe it, and the form is regarded as a mere instrument, deliberately adopted for the conveyance of the matter. It is not, I think, a mere accident that it is also characteristic of the philosophy of such ages of "good sense" to lay great stress on the "subjectivity" of sensible qualities, to treat the inexhaustible wealth of colour, tone, fragrance, and the like, as merely superposed by "the mind" on a reality consisting only of fully analysed and articulated interconnections between monotonously simple elements, and then, finally, to suspect these very elements, just because they have been so denuded of everything obviously intrusive and qualitatively given, of being

[1] The eighteenth-century critic of Shakespeare tended, for example, to ask about every play what was its "moral", and even to make the value of a work like *Macbeth* dependent primarily on its supposed usefulness in teaching us that it is commonly "bad business" to murder a king and usurp his crown.

themselves "mental fictions". In the process of being divested of its mystery and refractoriness, reality is, in fact, evaporated.

Now, as regards both the sensible world and the world of art, this whole mental attitude may, I trust, be considered hopelessly discredited. I do not think we are likely to hear much more from the really competent of the mere illusoriness and "subjectivity" of the amazing wealth disclosed to us by the senses. As Mr. Meyerson somewhere puts it, the working physicist is at heart an obstinate realist, convinced that he is confronted in his work with a world which he does not *make* out of nothing by some process of mental synthesis, but *finds* given to him. If he could ever succeed in analysing the course of events without remainder into an elaborate logical construction, transparent to the intellect, he would instinctively feel that its reality had slipped through his fingers; the real, to him, *is* that which defies such complete analysis. (This explains why a coherent thinker like Dr. Whitehead will hear nothing of the "subjectivity" of the sensible. "Qualities" were pronounced to be "subjective", precisely because they are ultimates for analysis: that is, because they have just the character which should be proof of their reality.)

Again, with all its crudities, the age of romanticism has at least taught us that the genius of poet and artist is something wholly different from deft artifice; it is something which controls the artist, and is not controlled by him.[1] Homer, Dante, Shakespeare, are something very much more intriguing than men coolly devising a "fable" as a convenient vehicle for the conveyance of instruction. All of them, presumably, do

[1] On the philosophical significance of the "romantic" reaction against "good sense" see *inter alia* Whitehead, *Science and the Modern World*, v. pp. 109 ff.

this kind of thing incidentally, as we all do, but it is not the doing of it that stamps them as supreme poets. The *Iliad*, the *Divine Comedy*, *King Lear*, full as they may be of conscious artifice, are in *kind* very different from the frigid allegories of an Addison. Each has its source in a direct and eminently intrusive vision of a life which is overpoweringly real and inexhaustibly complex, and full of surprises—something disclosed to the poet, not fashioned by him, nor completely understood by him.[1] The form of his work is not simply selected as a well-chosen device for expounding a matter alien to itself, which might, but for assignable reasons, have been conveyed by a different vehicle; the matter itself dictates the form. The hard and fast distinction between end and means, effect and instrument, a distinction in fact borrowed from the realm of industry, if taken over-seriously, is as pernicious in the theory of art as it is in the theory of morals.

All this, to be sure, is commonplace by now, but I have a motive for reminding you of the *locus communis*. It is not in the region of religion only that we meet with the startling and apparently unaccountable, sudden self-disclosure to particular persons and at special times on the part of a reality which does not equally obtrude itself on the notice of all men every-

[1] I do not forget the famous *Letter to Can Grande* in which Dante himself apparently treats his *Commedia* as though it were a mere contrivance for the preaching of an elaborate "lesson". But I think it safe to say that the whole four-fold lesson described in that letter might have been perfectly set forth in a work which would have had no *poetical* value whatsoever, and further that the account is itself an obvious "rationalisation" of the real facts, based on the assumption, traditional in Dante's time, that a great poem has to be justified by showing it to be didactic. It is not a transcript of the poet's real personal experience. In fact, the letter only shows that the greatest of modern poets would have been unable to stand examination by Socrates on the question "what he meant by his poem". One can be sure that Shakespeare's sense of humour would have forbidden him to "explain" *Lear* as intended to prove that professions of affection do not always mean all they say, or that it is not always wise to anticipate one's death by a *donatio inter vivos*.

where and always; we meet it wherever we have to recognise the presence of that which has been called genius. Genius is not, as it has been called, infinite capacity for taking pains; that would rather be a definition of superb and conscious craftsmanship. But we might say, perhaps, that genius is capacity for being arrested by and sensitively responsive to characters of reality which elude the average man's notice; that it is rare and unique *receptiveness*. We might then add that, apart from supernatural revelation, which has God for its object, there is *natural* revelation, and that the men of genius are its depositaries. Indeed, I should like to go further, and say that, below the level of disclosure we call genius, *sense* itself is a kind of natural revelation. Even the man who, without any title to be considered a genius, has an exceptionally fine sensibility to delicate variations of tint and tone which the rest of us allow to pass unnoticed, might be said to be the recipient of a revelation of real riches,[1] which only reaches us through him, so far as we learn, under his tuition and by starting from an act of faith in his utterances, to see with his eyes and hear with his ears. It is a familiar fact that this can be done; we can actually learn from the work of a great painter, interpreted by a true critic, to see the visible world itself with new eyes. But the lesson is never learned without a meek docility. The work of painter and artist will be thrown away on

[1] Cf. what a poet of our own day has written of "the body":

"Thy senses close
With the world's pleas. The random odours reach
Their sweetness in the place of thy repose,
Upon thy tongue the peach,
And in thy nostrils breathes the breathing rose. . . .

"Music, all dumb, hath trod
Into thine ear her one effectual way;
And fire and cold approach to gain thy nod,
Where thou call'st up the day,
Where thou awaitest the appeal of God."

us, if we persist in the prejudice that what we cannot see for ourselves, "with our own pair of eyes", is not there to be seen, and so must be an illusion superadded to the given and real. What is real, in the realm of colour *is* what is given, but it is not given to all in the same measure and with the same immediacy.

We may say the same thing of the vision of human life which inspires the great poet. He does not embroider the reality of life with trappings of pure illusion, or, if he does so, he is falling below the level of his own genius. What he sees is there to be seen, though the rest of us must go to school to him, if we are to learn to see it; this is why poetry could be called a "criticism of life".

If then, the very world of nature and everyday human life would largely be closed to us, but for our readiness to trust disclosures which come, in the first instance, to the exceptional few, it is unreasonable to deny the probability that the same thing may hold true of God, the transcendent reality. We should rather expect that the analogy would hold good here also; that there would be exceptional persons to whom this reality, too, is immediately disclosed in a special manner, and that here, as elsewhere, the best of what is to be discerned will be lost on us, if we refuse to learn to see through their eyes. So much, indeed, is actually admitted when it is proposed, as it often is proposed, to recognise the reality of what is called "religious genius". Unfortunately, there is a widely diffused notion that we somehow get rid of the recognition of *revelation*, actual self-disclosure on the part of a real divine, by using this phraseology. It is fancied that the "religious genius" somehow *creates* the content of what he himself regards as the "revelation"; it is magnificent, but we must not suppose that it has "objective validity", or is strictly entitled to be called *truth*. As against all such loose ways of thinking and speaking, we need to be clear that to speak of "religious genius" is not to *explain* a fact, but merely to give the fact a new label. To explain revelation by calling it genius is merely to explain one mystery by another. And if we have been right in maintaining that genius, in its various forms, is special *receptiveness*, and its so-called "intuitions", as the very name implies, apprehensions of a reality actually there and given, we have not done even so much as to replace one mystery by another by introducing "genius" into the argument. We have only admitted the fact that there are special apprehensions of a self-disclosing God, which are not bestowed equally on all of us. We have admitted not only the possibility, but the actuality of revelation, however we may please to boggle at that old-fashioned name for the fact.

These same considerations should dispose of the contention that, at any rate, revelation, if actual, can only disclose, a little sooner in point of time, what might be made out sufficiently without it by patient unaided "natural reason", and is therefore superfluous, though convenient. One might as well say, in the same fashion, that by my own account of genius, the great painter or poet only sees in nature or human life what is there to be seen, and that the rest of us, in time, learn to see from him. After all, then, the painter or poet only sees what, in a sense, the rest of us may come to see for ourselves, "with our own eyes". Is the painter, or the poet, then, not also a superfluity?

We all know well enough the answer to such a suggestion. What we come to see with our own eyes, by learning the lesson of poet or painter, we only come to see because we have first, as we say, learned from him to look through *his* eyes. If he had not seen first, and seen distinctly, we should not have learned to see at all. And, besides this, if the artist who teaches us is a sufficiently great artist, the time never comes when we say: "I have now learned to read nature, or life, from him so thoroughly that he has no more to teach me about them. Henceforth, I can dispense with his hitherto valuable, indeed indispensable, help, and look at the object unaided." When does any of us reach the stage at which he has learned *all* that Dante, or Shakespeare, can tell him about human nature, or all that is to be learned from the great painters about the natural world as a kingdom of colour? It comes—never. It is not merely that while we are beginning to know human nature, Shakespeare's vision of it may guide us, and his knowledge furnish us with "opinions" which will be a temporary surrogate for first-hand knowledge of our own. To the end, for any man who is not a second and greater Shakespeare, there will be truths about human nature which he has not verified by his own personal vision, and knows, if he knows them at all, by trusting to Shakespeare's vision where his own fails him.

"He is most natural", says Sir W. Raleigh of Shakespeare, "when he upsets all rational forecasts. We are accustomed to anticipate how others will behave in the matters that most nearly concern us; we seem to know what we shall say to them, and to be able to forecast what they will say in answer. We are accustomed, too, to find that our anticipation is wrong; what really happened gives the lie to the little stilted drama that we imagined, and we recognise at once how poor and false our fancy was, how much truer and more surprising the thing that happens is than the thing we invented. So it is with Shakespeare. His surprises have the same convincing quality. . . . We are watching the events of real life; from our hidden vantage-ground we see into the mystery of things, as if we were God's spies."[1] This is finely said, and as truly as finely. But in principle it applies as much to revelation of the divine as to the revelation of human nature, and may supply a justification to the theologian for his belief in the possibility of "truths of revelation" about God, transcending the range of "natural reason".

God, as all who believe in Him acknowledge, must have a being infinitely richer than our own. If there is so much about human nature which would be dark to us but for the intuitions of Shakespeare and his fellows, there must be much more that is true of God which would be completely hidden but for the flashes of intense and direct insight which are granted to a privileged few. Here, too, when the recipient of the disclosure has conveyed it to us, we may recognise its "convincing quality", may discover "how poor and false our fancy was, how much *truer*[2] and more surprising" the reality than "the thing we had invented". The relation between a knowledge of God through a genuine revelation and "natural" knowledge of God, such as we may reach by analysis of the presuppositions of the moral or physical order, has an analogical counterpart in the relation between truth about human nature disclosed to us by the "intuitions" of a Shakespeare and truth about human nature reached by our own reflections on our everyday experience. If we found that Shakespeare's "surprises" were in contradiction with what we know for ourselves about human motive and purpose, we should not pronounce them "convincing", or turn to Shakespeare for

[1] *Shakespeare* (E.M.L.), 143-4.

[2] Italics, of course, mine, not the author's.

insight. This is exactly what we do find about the "surprises" of too many dramatists,[1] and we reject their claims to be "true to nature" in consequence. So if we find that God, as pourtrayed in what claims to be a revelation, has a character flatly contradicting that which "natural reason" is forced to ascribe to the author of physical and moral order, we may safely pronounce that we are dealing with a product of misguided imagination, not with the self-disclosure of the transcendent reality. It is because we find Shakespeare's "surprises" at once so surprising, and yet so true to the human nature of which we independently know something, that we accept them, even when they surprise us most utterly, as divinations into a reality, not as fanciful distortions of it. In the same way, if there is a doctrine of God, claiming to rest upon genuine revelation, which provides us with surprises, but surprises recognisable *après coup*, though not antecedently, as inevitable, as of one piece with, though not discoverable from, that which a strictly natural theology can tell us of the divine character, there should be no rational objection against the acceptance of such a doctrine as a further and fuller disclosure of the divine nature, and the recognition of divine self-manifestation as its source.

In historical fact, apologists for the several revelational religions have made an unnecessary complication for themselves, and weakened the defence of revelation as a source of knowledge about God, by yielding too much to the polemical desire of representing their own religion as the only one possessing such knowledge, and its rivals as mere pretenders to a wholly unreal revela-

[1] And about some of the surprises in Shakespeare's own lighter and cruder work. Who "believes" in the sudden conversion of Sir Proteus or Duke Frederick, or the sudden reformation of Oliver de Boys?

tion. Thus the apologist for one particular historical religion provides the rejector of all with an argument, by using against his rivals weapons it is easy to turn upon himself. But it is not really necessary to defend the reality of revelation as a source of truth in one historical religion by refusing to admit its presence in every other. Since the historical religions do not simply contradict, but also, on many points, confirm one another, it is more natural, as well as more charitable, to recognise that they cannot be summarily dichotomised into one true religion and several false, but that truth, in different measures may be found in all of them. Since this is so, there is no sufficient reason to deny the presence, again in different degrees, of a genuine revelational element in them all. Thus, for example, since Christianity and Mohammedanism are in conflict on fundamental points, if one of them is the truth, the other cannot be. But this does not justify a Christian controversialist in simply dismissing Mohammed as the "false prophet", and his religion as an "imposture". That religion, like Christianity, testifies emphatically to the divine unity, and the reality of providence. I can see no sufficient ground for assuming that we have not here an element of Mohammedanism which came as a direct disclosure of the divine to the Arabian prophet, though, from the Christian point of view, it would be important to distinguish carefully between, for example, the truth of the divine unity and distortions of the conception of God in Islam by reckless and one-sided insistence on unity. The real antithesis is not between one religion which is true and a plurality of others which are simply false, but between a religion—if there is one—which is the whole truth, *ad modum recipientis*, about man's relations with God, and others which are partial and infected with error, because they do not, in the poet's phrase, look at the Lord "all at once".[1] From this point of view, while it would be possible to find an element of the revelational in all the great religions, it would remain an open question for speculation whether or not any of them is *the* true religion, the final self-disclosure of God to man. It would be conceivable that there are only more or less imperfect religions, but not a true and final religion; but it would be equally conceivable that there should be, or actually is, an historical religion which is also final, and can properly be called *the* true religion, because it integrates harmoniously, in one fuller and deeper vision of God, the different "broken lights" of the others, thus incorporating the truths of all, without the one-sidedness of any.

Whether any actual religion can advance this claim is not a question for this place. If it is made, it requires, or so it seems to me, to be substantiated by the successful application of a double test. No religion under which a genuine spiritual life has flourished can be *simply* false, and the religion which would establish its claim to be the one true faith must therefore stand the test of showing that it actually provides full recognition for all the elements of abiding truth in all the others, and does so by integrating their various insights into a real unity. It must also stand the test of being able to sustain the spiritual life of men as men, irrespective of circumscribing conditions of time, locality, race, or manners. A religion cannot be *the* true religion if, for example, it can become part and parcel of the life of the European and American West, but cannot truly naturalise itself elsewhere, and so remains something exotic for the Jew, the Hindu, the Chinese, or the Arab. The visible and

[1] R. Browning, *The Heretic's Tragedy*:

"The Lord we look to once for all
Is the Lord we should look at all at once."

outward sign of the true religion would be its success as a universal *missionary* religion, not in the superficial sense of ability to make proselytes all over the world at the cost of denationalising them, and on the condition that they are dependent for their life as a community on control, supervision, and stimulation from outside, but in the sense of power to make itself, in its entirety without mutilation, deformation, or contamination, part and parcel of a life which is not a borrowed one. Such a test of the claims of Mohammedanism would be, for example, its ability to produce British or French Moslems who remained British or French to the core; of the claims of Christianity, its power to produce Indian or Chinese Christians who should be not, as too many "converts" have been, inferior imitations of Europeans, but at once Christians, and Indians or Chinese, as the case may be, "in their bones".

These last remarks are by the way, and merely "illustrative". But they may conceivably serve to suggest the right way of dealing with a real difficulty. How can the mind hold together two lines of thought apparently antithetic and yet both necessary to any genuine belief in revelation? A revelation with God as its source clearly must be, in some quite real sense, "final", and yet theology, the systematised intellectual elaboration of the content of revelation, never is final, but always *in fieri*. If we feel any doubt of the fact, we may readily allay the doubt by studying the history of the theology with which we are ourselves most familiar, *Christliche Dogmengeschichte*. Every considerable Christian society has sincerely professed to regard its Christianity as something in a real sense given once and for all, a "deposit" to be transmitted unchanged down the generations. The controversy between the most unyielding of the conservative-orthodox and the most venturesome of modernists has never really been as to the existence of an unchanging "substance of the faith", but always as to its content. The modernist, admitting that there is such a "deposit", merely adds that his conservative opponent confuses that priceless deposit with accretions which have grown up round it and disfigure it. And yet, it may fairly be urged, does not history seem to show that *every* affirmation which has been regarded as part of the "deposit" has repeatedly changed its meaning? Is it so certain, for example, that the same Trinitarian formula really bears the *same* meaning in Boethius and in St. Thomas? The doctrine of "original sin" is regarded as indispensable to Christianity by St. Augustine, St. Thomas, and Kant; but do not these three eminent men mean three different things by the formula which all of them employ? It might be said, with a considerable show of justification, that the more resolutely a religious society tries to live up to the motto *semper eadem*, the more impossible it finds the task, unless it is prepared to translate the Latin audaciously into a living vernacular as *eppur si muove*. The "Liberal Protestant" of 1927 would, no doubt, have been disowned as a mere "deist" by the "Liberal Protestants" of 1727, as our friends in the Roman fold like to remind us; but may we not equally suspect that an "orthodox" Roman of our own time, a Leo XIII., for example, would have found it hard to talk theology with the Angelic Doctor, without discovering that, for good or bad, the man of the thirteenth and the man of the nineteenth century meant different things by the same phraseology?

There is a way of meeting the difficulty which is popular and tempting, but to my own mind profoundly unsatisfactory, by the drawing of a hard-and-fast distinction between the "faith" which abides, and its intellectual expression in doctrine and dogma which is merely mutable and subject to the law of indefinite modifiability. I do not myself understand how so many philosophers have been content to acquiesce in this depreciation of "dogma" which is part of the current superior journalism of our times. The only consistent logical position for the rigid separatist of "faith" from all intellectual formulation, I take it, is the extreme position which simply identifies religion with some kind of emotion, and the mere identification of *any* fundamental activity of the human spirit with emotion, cut loose from a *specific* object, is the degradation and, in the end, the paralysis of the emotion itself. Emotions of all kinds so manifestly derive their value for human life from the character of the object on which they are directed. Emotion inappropriate or disproportionate to the objective situation by which it is evoked is the bane of life. We can all see this clearly enough in moral theory when the question is raised of the worth of this or that emotion as a "motive" to action. It is, or should be, the stalest of ethical commonplaces that emotions cannot be classified into the morally good and the morally evil, and that if "motive" is taken to mean what Mill took it to mean, the "feeling" which "makes a man act" by breaking down a kind of mental and moral inertia, the view that the worth either of our acts or of our character is a function of our "motives" would be the ruin of coherent thinking about conduct.

There would, for example, be no sense in saying that pity is a good motive, but resentment a bad one. The worth of either depends on the question who it is that is pitied, what it is that is resented. Pity for the wrong persons, or even ill-regulated pity for the right persons, has repeatedly led to the most dreadfully wrong moral action; anger, if it is righteous anger against oppression or meddling, is one of the most precious ingredients in the character of the moral "hero". The moral worth of wonder or curiosity, again, depends wholly on its object. To wonder about the right things, as Plato knew, is to be on the way to become a master in knowledge; to "wonder with a foolish face of praise" at the wrong things is to be for life a *curioso impertinente*.

Nor would the edge of this criticism be turned by appealing to the now familiar distinction between belief in a statement and belief, or faith, in a person. That distinction is real, and we may have to revert to it, but it will not serve this turn. Faith in a person will not be a quickening and regenerative influence, if it is faith in the *wrong* person; nothing will wreck the moral life more utterly than an unquestioning faith in an unworthy person. The important thing is that our faith should be reposed in a person who is really adequate to sustain it, and thus it makes all the difference in the world to the spiritual fruits of such faith what we take the person we believe in to be, and whether he really is what we take him for. This surely disposes once and for all of the proposal to find the real value of religious faith in mere intense emotion, divorced altogether from any element of intellectual conviction. We may, no doubt, acquiesce intellectually in any number of propositions about a person without being moved by the acquiescence to any practical surrender of the direction of our will and conduct by our "convictions", as the devil has been imagined to accept the whole of Christian theology without being even faintly stirred to conformity of will to God. But such assent remains a merely "dead" faith, if we are to call it faith at all. It would be mere unreason to infer that since "living" faith is *more* than such intellectual assent to a number of propositions, it involves no such assent. To "believe in" a man is, indeed, always more than to believe certain statements *about* him, but it is no less true that I cannot "believe in" a man without believing something "about" him, even if that something is no more than that "this is the best and wisest man I have hitherto met", and what one believes thus is always capable of being stated in an intelligible, though commonly very incomplete, form.

A faith which was *mere* emotion—if there really can be, as I gravely doubt whether there can be, any such thing as a *mere* emotion—would be a faith devoid of anything deserving to be called conviction. Genuine faith, because it reposes on conviction, cannot be other than a *fides quaerens intellectum*. For that reason, I should say, we owe a real debt of gratitude to the much decried "dogmatists", whose concern has always been to make explicit the implicit convictions which justify faith in a person. Being, like the rest of us, human, and incident to the common intellectual and moral weaknesses of humanity, the dogmatists may execute this task very imperfectly, but it is a task which rational beings cannot decline. Thus I suspect that the secret reason why so many of us to-day incline to resent all attempts to put our convictions about God into clear doctrinal form is an uneasy suspicion that, if we were quite honest with ourselves, we should find that we have no real convictions to support our emotionalism, and are naturally unwilling to be driven into making this discovery. I should suspect the same thing of a man who professed unqualified faith in his teacher, or his country, if he resented all questions about the precise achievements of either which elicit and demand his faith.

Thus Fr. G. Tyrrell's epigrammatic declaration, "I share the faith of Simon Peter, not his dogmatic theology", seems to me to come perilously near converting a needful distinction into a dangerous false antithesis. I do not see how we can have a faith in common with Simon Peter, unless there are also *some* intellectual convictions which we share with him. It may be impossible to isolate just that element of common intellectual conviction completely from other elements which are not common, as it is, I presume, impossible in practice to isolate one chemical element absolutely from all others, and yet, in both cases, it may be a proper, even a necessary, exercise to make our approximate analysis as thorough as we can.

The problem is, of course, one which meets us in every sphere of human intellectual activity. Thus the "external world" of the ordinary practical man and that of the physicist "physicising", especially if he is a physicist of the latest type, may seem to have as little in common as the simple unspeculative faith of Simon Peter, the fisherman of Bethsaida, and the systematic theology of the *Summa* of Thomas, or the *Institutes* of Calvin. Yet the attempt sometimes made by the physicist to set the two "worlds" of common experience and physical theory in absolute antithesis to one another leads nowhere, and cannot, I should say, represent the real belief of the philosophical physicist himself. It is not many months since I had the privilege of listening to a brilliant statement of the antithesis from the lips of Professor Eddington.[1] If we took the professor at his word, there seemed to be so complete a severance between the common man's world and the physicist's world that the mere reference of an object to the one would be enough to exclude it from the other. The table upon which Professor Eddington, as a man speaking to men and women, rested his manu-

[1] *Nature of the Physical World*, c. I.

script or his crayon, and the table which, as a physicist, he regarded as an object for investigation and description, were made to seem so wholly disparate that any statement which must be made about one of them would be simply false if asserted of the other. There was not even justification left for so much as calling the "physicist's table" a ghost or shadow of the "real table". And yet I am sure that the speaker never meant seriously to suggest that the physicist is only amusing himself with capricious inventions of his own unregulated fancy, or that "verification" by reference to the common man's "sensible objects" and their behaviour is not the standing test of the physicist's hypotheses. He did not really believe himself as a professor of astronomy to be concerned with an "intelligible sun" and "intelligible stars" to which the eccentricities of the sun and stars we can see have no sort of relevance. For he proceeded in subsequent lectures[1] to draw all sorts of conclusions about the probable past and future history of the sun and stars, and, of course, the sun which has had a history in the past and will have a history in the future is the sun which we all see and whose warmth we all feel. There was no serious question of forgetting that all the problems of the physicist are set for him by the sense-experience which he shares with the rest of us, and that the supreme test of his success in solving them must be found in his ability to anticipate other experiences of the same kind, or that the only kind of scientific hypothesis which can be dismissed once and for all as "illegitimate" is an hypothesis which, from its nature, is capable of possible disproof by confrontation with "facts in the sensible world". Whatever Professor Eddington might permit himself to say for the purpose

[1] *Op. cit.* c. 4.

of impressing his audience with the abstract and schematic character of physical science, it was clear that he knew—no one better—that the physicist means all the time to be talking of the world which "is the home of all of us", and that his genial attempts to "make our flesh creep" by telling us, for example, that the human body consists almost entirely of "empty space",[1] would have had no point if this were not so. For if the physicist really means when he talks of *my* body to be speaking only of something which has even less connection with what I, as an ordinary man, mean by my body than my shadow has, why should I feel perturbed, or even mildly interested, by anything the physicist may please to say about it?[2]

Now, a physicist like Professor Eddington really stands to you and me, in his utterances about human bodies, tables, suns, stars, precisely as the scientific theologian stands to the simple believer, Simon the fisherman, or another. The physicist is the systematic theologian of the natural world, that θεὸς εὐδαίμων of Plato's *Timaeus*. The *viri Galilaei* and their lived religion set the Christian theologian his problems, as the sense-experiences of the common man normally equipped with eyes, ears, nostrils, tongue, skin, set the physicist his. There is no legitimate physical speculation which has not its point of departure in common pre-scientific sense-experience, and there is similarly, I take it, no legitimate theological problem which has

[1] *Op. cit.* pp. 1-2.

[2] Cf. Professor Eddington's own observations in another volume: "Science is not the describing a world invented to save trouble; it is following up a problem which took definite shape the first time two human beings compared notes of their experiences; and it follows it up according to the original rules. . . . I simply do not contemplate the awful contingency that the external world of physics, after all our care in arriving at it, might be disqualified by failing to 'exist'. . . . It is sufficient that it is the world which confronts our common experience and that therefore we are interested in knowing all we can about it." ("The Domain of Physical Science" in *Science, Religion, and Reality*, pp. 196-7.)

not its point of departure in the actual life of contact with God. In this sense, the whole of legitimate theology is implicit and given once for all in the life of the man practising his religion, as the whole of physical science is implicit and, in a way, given once for all, in the actuality of the sensible.

Now, to say thus that the "dogmas" of a true physics are, in a real sense, given once for all in our everyday apprehension of the sensible means, to be sure, that there must be an element of intellectual conviction common to the physicist with the ordinary man. Their respective certainties are not, after all, of wholly disparate orders. The physicist does not live in one world with his intellect, as a physicist, and in a "wholly other" world, that of human life, with his emotions and reactions to stimulus. He takes the "world" of common life with him into his laboratory, when the disclosures of the senses set him a problem for investigation, and he recurs to that "world" when he tests his solution by comparing his theoretical results with the record of another set of immediate disclosures of sense. Thus there are convictions, as well as emotions and motor responses, in common to him with the plain man, though it is true that he could not set out these common convictions in exact and abstract logical form completely and unambiguously. For he must speak either the language of common life itself, or the technical "jargon" of his special science. The one is always pregnant with masses of unanalysed and imprecise suggestion, which make it hopelessly ambiguous;[1] the other has been devised specifically to deal with the physicist's abstractions *as such*, and the more adequate

[1] Cf. Plato, *Ep.* vii. 342 E πρὸς γὰρ τούτοις ταῦτα οὐχ ἧττον ἐπιχειρεῖ τὸ ποῖόν τι περὶ ἕκαστον δηλοῦν ἢ τὸ ὂν ἑκάστου διὰ τὸ τῶν λόγων ἀσθενές· ὧν ἕνεκα νοῦν ἔχων οὐδεὶς τολμήσει ποτὲ εἰς αὐτὸ τιθέναι τὰ νενοημένα ὑπ' ἀύτοῦ, καὶ ταῦτα εἰς ἀμετακίνητον.

it proves for this purpose, the less is it fitted to express convictions which are not peculiar to the physicist as such, but shared by him with the rest of mankind. Yet these convictions are none the less present and all-persuasive, that we have no idiom in which to give them well-defined expression.

In the same way, I suggest, we should conceive of the all-pervasive presence in theology of intellectual convictions which are common to the theologian and the simple unspeculative believer, but defy precise formulation, whether in the rich but systematically ambiguous language of direct and vivid faith, or in the highly specialised and artificial technical vocabulary of theology itself. We may reasonably expect that the difficulty of formulation will be even more formidable for the theologian than for the physicist, since all our apprehension of God, the supreme reality of realities, is necessarily so much dimmer and more inadequate than our apprehension of everyday sensible body. And theology may surely learn a much-needed lesson from the procedure of the physicist. The once-for-allness and finality of the sense-experience through which the bodily world is given makes itself felt in physics in the recognition that a theory which demands consequences to which our senses definitely give the lie is thereby discredited. This, I take it, is the only finality known to physics. May we not say that there is only one way in which a theological doctrine is finally discredited? It is discredited if its truth would require that the religious growth of the soul should be fostered by conditions which, in fact, impede it, or hindered by conditions which, in fact, promote it. A refutation of this kind may be hard to obtain, but sometimes it is obtained, and then it is indeed final. Where it cannot be obtained, it seems premature and dangerous to convert our best attempts to find formulae for the intellectual expression of the convictions by which we live into "articles of a standing or a falling Church".

But the rival attempt to dispense altogether with intellectual formulation is itself equally dangerous to real spiritual life in a different way. Faith may die, often has died, of internal ossification, when it is not allowed to stir except under the weight of a cast-iron panoply of ready-made doctrinal formulae; it may die, no less surely, by a sort of liquefaction, when suffered to evaporate in vague emotionalism. And of the rival dangers, there cannot be much doubt that the second is the more imminent for the average member of the "educated" society of our own country at the present day. Most of *us* are in no very great danger, as we might have been in some former ages, of spoiling our religion, our morality, our politics, or our art, by excess of rigid intellectual conviction. Our danger is rather that living, as we do, at the end of a "romantic" age which ran riot in the glorification of emotion for its own sake, we may try to make out, in religion, morals and politics, art alike, with a superficial scepticism, feebly coloured with thin sentimentality. In an age in which scepticism—a languid scepticism—about the "certainties" of science, not so long ago apparently the most assured of all "certainties", has become the favourite intellectual attitude of the "educated public", our most crying intellectual need, perhaps, is the need of men who will, by their robust assertions, arouse us, not from our "dogmatic", but from our lazily anti-dogmatic, "slumbers". There was something heroic about the temper of the "Mid-Victorian" time, with its cry of

> It fortifies my soul to know
> That though I perish, truth is so.

There is nothing heroic about "keeping the mind open" on all questions, simply because we are too indolent to give ourselves the trouble of shutting a door. Nor is it well to leave all doors indiscriminately open, for, though the open door often provides an avenue for the entrance of much that is welcome, it also, as we too often forget, affords an exit through which what we can least afford to lose may disappear. The important thing is to judge rightly which doors should be left open and which should be shut.

III

RELIGION AND THE HISTORICAL

Ist es der *Sinn*, der alles wirkt und schafft?
Es sollte stehn: Im Anfang war die *Kraft*!
Doch auch in dem ich dieses niederschreibe,
Schon warnt mich was, dass ich dabei nicht bleibe.
Mir hilft der Geist! Auf einmal seh' ich Rat
Und schreibe getrost: Im Anfang war die *Tat*.

GOETHE.

THE object of our last lecture has been to urge that there is nothing inherently unreasonable in the recognition of specific "revelation" as a source of knowledge of God and the eternal. But it would be possible to concede all for which we have so far pleaded, and yet to object that we have not so much as touched the real problem created by the claims of the great positive revelational religions of the world. At most, we have only vindicated the reasonableness of recognising the possibility that significant truth about God may be made known to, or through, particular persons at a particular place and time. We have left it an open possibility that the truths thus historically disclosed—if such a disclosure has indeed taken place—might be one and all of a supra-temporal order, concerned entirely with the eternal and timeless, like, for example, the Christian doctrine of the triune nature of God, or the great Jewish doctrine of the divine Unity. Even if we adopt the view that the proposition "the Lord our God is One" is at once vital to religion and incapable of rational proof, so that it can only be received, where it is received, on the strength of faith in an immediate historical revelation—to Moses or to another—still, the doctrine itself, however we have come by it, is not a statement about the historical course of events; it is a statement about the supra-historical reality, God. But when we examine the *credenda* propounded for acceptance by any of the great positive religions, we find that in every case there are included among them some propositions which are themselves statements about events of the historical order, allegations that certain transactions have taken place in the past, or will take place in the future. The creed of each of these religions is found to contain specific assertions about the course of history in the past, and specific anticipations or prophecies of the course which events are to follow in the future. In the creed of orthodox Christianity we see this presence of an historical element in its most pronounced form. Side by side with propositions concerning the eternal divine nature, it contains a number of distinct statements of fact about the life of Jesus Christ, and one definite prophecy of an historical event to occur in the future, a "coming" of Christ to bring the temporal history of humanity to a close.

Now here, it may be said, and not in the mere concept of revelation, lies the real *crux* for a philosophy of religion. The revelational religions regularly treat the whole of their *credenda* as alike "saving truth", no portion of which can be denied without the "loss of the soul". But how is it possible for the philosophic mind to attach this kind of value to any statement of historical fact? As for serious error about the divine nature, since such error means acceptance of an unreal and unworthy object for the soul's unqualified worship, we can understand that it must lead to impairment of the soul's life. For we inevitably grow ourselves into the likeness of that which we contemplate with adoration and self-surrender. There is thus, in principle, no mystery about the dependence of our attainment of eternal life upon the worthiness and truth of our real convictions about God. But how can there be any such connection between spiritual vitality and a man's convictions about the events of the past? How, to take an extreme example, can a man be the better or worse according as he believes or doubts that the Roman procurator who gave the order for our Lord's death was named Pontius Pilate?[1] How would the truth of the Christian religion as a revelation of God be affected, even if it should be discovered that the Gospel tradition had made a mistake of a few years, and ascribed to Pilate an act which really belonged to his precursor's or his successor's tenure of office?[2] Must it not be false in principle to assert that our beliefs about such historical points have any bearing upon the spiritual life? And is it not also a sin against intelligence to demand of any man that he shall affirm propositions of this kind on any ground but that of the goodness of the historical testimony for them? Must we not say that in dealing with assertions about historical events there can be no appeal from the standards of historical evidence, as in dealing with assertions about the physical there can be no appeal from accurately recorded and registered scientific observation? The philosopher, indeed, might conceivably be justified in accepting as true all the statements about

[1] The example is actually given by Abelard—whom I name at second-hand from Wicksteed, *Reactions between Dogma and Philosophy*, p. 115—as proof that the text of Holy Scripture alone does not contain all things necessary to be believed. (Either Abelard's memory must have played him false, or he used a bad text of the Vulgate, since the *nomen* Pontius occurs at least thrice in the New Testament, *Luke* iii. 1, *Acts* iv. 27, 1 *Timothy* vi. 13.)

[2] And *a fortiori*, how could our religion be affected by the discovery that the *nomen* of the procurator is inaccurately given in the two passages just cited, and consequently in the Creeds? (The Gospel narrative uniformly uses only the *cognomen*, Pilate.)

historical events contained in the "creed" of a given religion, but he would only be justified if he had independently convinced himself that these statements satisfy the ordinary tests applicable to all allegations about facts in the past, and assent of this kind is something quite different from religious faith, and may, in fact, exist without being accompanied by such faith. It would be easy, for instance, to name writers who have combined rejection of the Christian *faith* with assent to the mere historical truth of such articles of the Christian creed as "born of the Virgin Mary", "the third day he rose from the dead", and such assent is not what any orthodox Christian has ever meant by the faith which saves.

One might go on to support the main position thus outlined in more detail by appealing to the indisputable fact that the great historical religions have, one and all, been convicted of putting forward among their *credenda* assertions about historical fact which have undergone definite disproof, and, in the end, been abandoned, not without grave sacrifice of dignity. We have only to think of the widespread and complete surrender of "orthodox" Christianity, within the last half-century, to "critical" research in the matter of Old Testament history.[1] There is the further problem created by the fact that so many of the events included among the *credenda* of the historical religions are of a kind unparalleled in the "ordinary course" of nature. All these religions have their "miracles", and a "miracle" creates a very real difficulty for a mind in earnest with the conviction on which all philosophy is based, the conviction

[1] It may be objected to me that the Roman Church, at any rate, seems not to have made the surrender. It is not for an outsider to pretend knowledge of the official attitude of any Church, but *if* the Roman Church really has committed itself to some sort of "Fundamentalism" on this issue, I can only remark that, in my own opinion, that is so much the worse for the Roman Church.

that the world is an intelligible unity. Here, then, is a special problem of which the significance cannot well be exaggerated. How "actual" it is we can see for ourselves by studying, for example, the recent series of works by Dr. Gore, who may fairly be taken as representative of the position of the educated "conservative" in these matters of history, at its best. Dr. Gore is resolute in his insistence that there are certain statements of matter of historical fact which are so vital to the Christian religion that no compromise about them, no permission to take the words of the "articles" which affirm them in anything but their "plain, literal" sense, can be allowed to anyone who claims to adhere fully to the faith of the Church. Yet it is manifest that all along the line Dr. Gore is standing on the defensive in a fashion very different from the buoyant, occasionally truculent, aggressiveness of the apologists of two or three generations ago. Again, one is struck by the fact that Dr. Gore reduces his list of positions which must be defended at all costs to a minimum. What is really instructive is that a High Anglican Bishop and former Principal of Pusey House should be satisfied to draw his line round two or three propositions expressly enunciated in the so-called *Apostolicum*, where Dr. Pusey would have stood out, and did stand out, for the whole body of Scripture narrative. Even within the four corners of the *Apostolicum* Dr. Gore finds himself driven to make a distinction. There is to be no "latitude of interpretation" of the clause *natus ex Maria virgine*, but a generous latitude enough when we come to *ascendit ad caelos*, *inde venturus est*. In fact, the policy of "no surrender" is apparently not to be insisted on in its full rigour for more than perhaps two clauses of three or four words apiece, and this looks much as though Dr. Gore himself were conscious of being the conductor of a "forlorn hope".[1] One is naturally tempted to ask whether the foreseeable end must not be the general abandonment of all insistence on the religious value of assertions about the historical. May not Tyrrell have been a true prophet when he wrote that all that will survive permanently of Christianity is "mysticism and charity", with the possible addition of the Eucharist, reduced to its simplest form, as an impressive symbol in act of the spirit of mysticism and charity? And may not the method of "allegorical interpretation", so dear to the earliest Fathers, come once more to be adopted as the only "way out" for a great religion which has entangled itself in a web of dubious assertions about history?

We all know men of deeply religious spirit and fine intelligence who have already reached a position like Tyrrell's, or are certainly on the direct road thither, and we should all be able to understand both the strength of the temptation to secure one's religion once for all from the historical critic at a stroke, and the cruelty of the practical problem created for such men by the conflict between their conviction that one cannot cut one's self loose from the life of communal worship without grievous impoverishment of spiritual personality and the demand, still formally made by the Churches, that the participant in the common worship shall profess a belief which includes a great deal in the way of statements about history. There is, at the very least, ample excuse for those who hold that the future of the Churches depends on their willingness to rise to the opportunity of ridding their teaching about

[1] For a defence of the position in question, of which I wish to speak with the deep respect due to all the pronouncements of the author, and with which I find it hard not to feel real sympathy, I would refer to Dr. Gore's summary of his doctrine in the volume *Can We Then Believe?* (1926). I sincerely hope that I have succeeded in describing the general attitude taken up throughout the volume without unconscious misrepresentation.

God of what has been the source of so many burnings of heart and so much disloyalty to truth. Others than "ultramontanes" might well be pardoned for feeling that they would heartily thank God to be "done with history."[1]

Still, the real question is not whether this attitude of mind is intelligible and pardonable, as it assuredly is, but whether it is justifiable. To myself the unqualified Modernist solution of this particular difficulty, like most simple solutions of serious problems, seems too simple to be trusted. It would be at least a singular paradox that one and the same age should find it necessary to save its physics, after the fashion urged by Dr. Whitehead—by reconstructing traditional doctrines in the light of biology, as a remedy for the incurably unhistorical character of the "classical" mechanics—and also to save its theology by the elimination of all historical reference. If "misplaced concreteness" has really been the curse of nineteenth-century physics, it should presumably be an equally objectionable thing in divinity. And what it would really mean to "have done with history" we may perhaps gather, if we will make a simple *Denkexperiment.* Let us suppose the elimination of the historical to have been successfully "carried to the limit". To make the illustration the more telling, we will suppose this to have happened with the religion in which we have been ourselves brought up, and whose influence is written large in the life of our own society at its best. We will suppose, then,

[1] Cf. Inge, *Philosophy of Plotinus*,[1] ii. 227: "Neo-Platonism differs from popular Christianity in that it offers us a religion the truth of which is not contingent on any particular events, whether past or future. It is dependent on no miracles, on no unique revelation through any historical person, on no narratives about the beginning of the world, on no prophecies of its end. There is a Christian philosophy of which the same might be said. . . . Christianity . . . can only exert its true influence in the world . . . when it stands on its own foundations, without those extraneous supports which begin by strengthening a religion and end by strangling it."

that the theory which denies the very existence of the founder and central figure of Christianity as a historical person should cease to be the private fad of a few amateurs of little judgement who have wandered into history from other fields, and become the accepted and unchallenged teaching of historians at large, and thus pass as a standing assumption into the "general mind". That is, we will suppose that all but the entirely uneducated, devout and undevout alike, have acquired a habit of mind to which it is as unquestioned a "truth" that the life of Christ is pure fable or allegory as it is now an "unquestioned truth" that existing animal species have "evolved" within a measurable period of time. We will imagine a society which will regard the dwindling minority among those who have passed through its schools who still cling to the belief that Jesus Christ was a real man much as our own society regards minorities who deny that "the earth is round", or that the dog and the jackal are descendants of a common ancestor. If it were true that the spiritual value of a religion is *wholly* independent of beliefs about matters of historical fact, it should follow that the Christian life would flourish just as well in these supposed conditions as in any others, and possibly better. It should be as easy in principle for the Christian religion and worship to make terms with the resolution of Christ into an astronomical or moral symbol as it has been for it to adjust itself to the view that the story of Adam, Eve, and the serpent has only symbolic value. The only difference should be that the unreasoned sentimental prejudice against reducing the Cross to the status of a mere symbol might be expected to be deeper rooted, and to require a longer time for its evaporation than a similar prejudice in favour of the botanical reality of the tree of the knowledge of good and evil. The spiritual power of the "word of the Cross" for the regeneration of human life should remain unaffected. But I venture to think that we have only to envisage the suggested situation clearly to be convinced that this is preposterously false. The whole "power of the Gospel" to remake human personality is intimately bound up with the conviction that the story of the passion and exaltation of Christ is neither symbol nor allegory, but a story of what *has been done* for man by a real man, who was also something more than a real man, a story of a real *transaction* at once divine and human. You cannot cut the motivation conveyed by such words as "*if* God so loved us, we ought . . ." out of the practical Christian life without destroying *that* specific kind of life at its root.

Similarly, if the triumph of a human "Lord of life" over death is no more than an allegorical way of conveying some philosopheme about the "conservation of values", the story surely loses all its power to inspire us with the hope which

creates
From its own wreck the thing it contemplates.

The *whole* point of the Christian story is that it claims to be a story of an *opus operatum*, an act which has, in fact and not in fiction, been achieved by God through man and for man. The point is that love and goodness have, in perfectly plain and downright fact, "power as they have manifest authority", and that in the face of all the apparently overwhelming testimony of history to the superior *power* of evil, and the apparent complete failure of nature to disclose an "All-great" who is also an "All-loving". If the story is not fact, and has no permanent value but that of a symbol, it loses all its depth, for it is a symbol of what may be dreadfully *un*-fact. If we ask ourselves seriously what it is in Christianity which is the element of supreme value to Christians, that is to men who are actually trying to live the Christian life, what it is *they* find in Christianity and nowhere else, I do not think there can be any doubt about the answer; it is, as Soloviev has said,[1] the person of Christ himself, taken as the completest revelation of God. But a religion without any historical *credenda* would be a religion without the *person* of Christ, and thus, even if it retained a host of *theologumena* expressed in Christian terminology and a mass of traditional Christian devotional practices, it would no longer be Christianity. It would be—to adopt Huxley's mordant definition of the Comtist "religion of humanity" —Catholicism (or Protestantism, as the case might be) "*minus* Christianity".

Now I can understand and respect a man who says that, whether we like it or not, this is all that loyalty to truth can leave standing in the way of a religion for mankind in the future. Perhaps we all of us sometimes feel a misgiving that it may be so. What I cannot understand is that any thoughtful man should maintain either that this is the substance of Christianity, and that the evaporation of the historical would still leave the Christian religion potent to produce the types of character we see in the Christian saints and heroes, an Augustine, a Xavier, a George Herbert, a Bunyan, or that, though it may be true that the world must never expect to see that type of man again, the world, and religion itself too, will be none the worse for the loss. And unless one is prepared to say one or the other of these things, one must admit that Christianity, at any rate, could not be simply relieved of its historical

[1] See the brilliant and suggestive dialogue "The End of History", in *War, Progress, and the End of History* (E. tr., p. 213).

credenda without being transformed into something of radically different character.[1]

It might, no doubt, be suggested that this is an accident of one particular historical religion, and I can conceive that this might actually be made a ground for depreciating Christianity by comparison with some of its rivals for world-wide allegiance. The person of Christ, so I can imagine some non-Christian but devout student to reason, is certainly central in the religion of Christians, and the obscure and perplexing "doctrine of the person of Christ" consequently central in their theology; so much the worse for it and them. By deifying their Founder (for I may fairly assume that the imagined critic will regard the Christian worship of Christ as simply a striking instance of the *post-mortem* deification of a great man by the love and admiration of his followers), Christians fatally committed themselves from the outset to a hopeless conflict with history, which knows nothing of *praesentes divi* and has the duty to reduce their figures to the proportions of flesh and blood; naturally, such a religion must not hope to survive the exposure of its initial mistake. But other historical religions have not committed the error of what the Mohammedan doctors call "association" (*shirk*), the giving of a partner to their Deity. They have kept their founders and prophets on the strictly human level, and there is thus not the same reason why the fate of their traditions of their great men should affect their value as "religious knowledge". Judaism and Islam are faiths whose message to mankind has, as its content, simply a doctrine about God ; the worst

[1] Here rather than in the "Copernican revolution", to which Dr. Inge attaches so much significance, I should find the secret of the now acute *crise du christianisme*. The supposed theological consequences of the deposition of our planet from its unique status appear to be in process of dissipation by the return of astronomers themselves to the old belief that the status of the Earth is unique, or at least, most exceptional. Cf. Eddington, *Nature of the Physical World*, pp. 169 ff.

that destructive criticism of their historical traditions could do would only be to disprove the supposed fact that this doctrine was integrally proclaimed at a given place by Moses the Levite, or Mohammed, son of Abdallah, a fact which obviously has no relevance to the truth and importance of the doctrine itself. It is wholly illegitimate to mistake for a universal character of revelational religion what is, in truth, an incidental weakness of one special religion.

The contention at least sounds plausible, and we should be careful not to underestimate its force. Yet, when all is said, I feel the greatest misgivings about it. Is it so obvious, after all, that Mohammedanism or Judaism is in substance nothing more than a "philosophical" Theism, or Deism, with the relatively unimportant characteristic of having been, according to tradition, first promulgated by a particular person on a particular occasion? Does common experience show that the Jew or Moslem who jettisons his historical *credenda* fares so much better than the Christian who is in the same case? Take the case of the Jew who eliminates what is, after all, the central *motif* of Old Testament religion, and a *motif* of distinctively historical kind, the "covenant" once made by the one God with the Israelite Fathers. Does he usually find that what is left him of his Judaism still serves equally well to sustain a life of active faith in eternal realities, or does he not more commonly tend to lapse into a mere agnostic worldliness? And what happens to the "young Turk" who has simply thrown overboard the great historical *credendum* of his inherited beliefs, the Day of Judgement, and everything in the traditions of his fathers which stands or falls with the Day of Judgement? These are questions which we cannot well avoid raising, and serious consideration of them may possibly suggest that it is by no accident that our own religion is as closely bound up with convictions about the significance of an historical personality as we find it to be. It may rather be that Christianity shows itself to be the most true to type of all the great universal religions, precisely by exhibiting in that intensest form a character which is present in all, though in the others its presence is less obtrusive and more easy to overlook.[1]

This, in fact, is no more than one might expect, if we have been right in holding that the great function of religion in human life is the transformation of personality by the substitution of the abiding and eternal for the merely temporary and transient, as the centre of man's interests. We should expect that in proportion as a religion succeeds in effecting this transformation, it will show a quickened and keener sense of the reality of both terms of the opposition. Unless our whole conception of the relation between "nature" and "grace", "this" world and the "other", as we tried to develop it in our former series, was false in its principle, it might have been foreseen that the religion which grapples most successfully with the practical task of reorganising life with an eternal good as its centre will be the religion which brings its God down most intimately into contact with the temporal historical process, not one of those which simply set Him outside and beyond it, and consequently that it will find its historical connecting link between God and man in a personality standing in a much closer relation to God than that of the prophet, the mere bearer of a "message from the other side" which might equally well have been put

[1] St. Paul's attitude, as we gather it from his epistles, seems to me very instructive. The covenant under Moses appears to have lost its main significance for him, and to be reduced to the status of a decidedly secondary episode. But his depreciation of the Law only throws into stronger relief his unwavering faith in the earlier covenant with "Abraham and his seed" as a central fact in the history of mankind.

into the mouth of another. We should naturally expect in such a religion what we actually find in Christianity, that its historical revelation of God consists primarily neither in a body of propositions about God, nor in a code of precepts from God, but in the whole of a concrete divine personality and life; that, in fact, the "revealer" would be the content of his own revelation. And for the same reason we might, as I think, anticipate *a priori* that the intellectual elaboration of such a self-disclosure of the divine through the detail of a concrete human life, its abstentions and silences, no less than its acts and utterances, would inevitably involve, as the theology of a religion which still leaves its God more or less remote need not involve, a doctrine of the person of an historical "Christ". To a religion which leaves God more or less aloof in the beyond, to be known only by the instructions and commands which come to us from Him, the teaching or the commandment is the primary thing, and the only importance which the bearer of them need have for us is that he is the conduit through which the communication has reached us. So long as we accept the message he transmits, it is really irrelevant what we believe or do not believe about his personality. But if a religion actually brings God down into the heart of temporality, as working through it, not from outside it only, then it will be the person and life in which the complete interpenetration of the eternal and the temporal has been actualised which is itself the revelation, and to believe will be primarily not to assent to the utterances of a messenger, but to recognise the person in whom the interpenetration of the two "worlds" has been achieved for what he is. In a religion which still leaves God and man, the eternal and the temporal, in their relative aloofness, the intermediary between them will be honoured for the message which he brings; when the aloofness has been abolished "by unity of person", the sayings and precepts of the intermediary will be honoured because they are *his*.[1]

If what we have tried to say in earlier lectures about the relation between eternity and temporality is at bottom sound, we can thus see that the prominence of *credenda* of an historical character in our own religion, all of them connected with the conviction that the complete interpenetration of Creator and creature has been realised in fact in an individual life, is evidence of strength rather than of weakness. It could not be otherwise with a religion which is to do justice to the given reality of human life, as the region where the eternal and the temporal are bound up with one another as the antithetic poles of a single tension. So, and only so, is eternal life, in fact, brought down within the reach of mortal men. The ultimate justification of the refusal to make religion wholly "philosophical" by the reduction of the whole element of historical *credenda* to mere edifying allegory or symbolism is to be found, then, in the character of specifically human life itself, as a life which can be, and ought to be, one of "participated eternity", one in which successiveness is increasingly penetrated by permanence and abidingness, but where, because we are and must remain men, not gods, the successiveness which marks us as "creatures" never wholly vanishes. Its complete disappearance would mean that each of us had himself become an independent *ens realissimum*, self-contained and self-supporting. If that were *our* nature and *our* destiny, it would

[1] Cf. Soloviev, *op. cit.*, p. 173: "Until you show me the goodness of your lord in his own deeds and not in verbal precepts to his employees, I shall stick to my opinion that your distant lord, demanding good from others but doing no good himself, imposing duties but showing no love, never appearing before your eyes but living *incognito* somewhere abroad, is no one else but *the god of this age*."

be as true as it is, in fact, revoltingly false to say of that finest of all creaturely virtues, which Christians have called the one virtue which is wholly supernatural, what Spinoza unhappily said of it, *humilitas virtus non est, ex ratione non oritur.*[1] It would follow, in the same way, that the ultimate aim of the religious life is to supersede itself, to conduct us to a heaven where, if it could ever be reached, each of the beatified would have ceased to have anything to worship, being simply "shut up in measureless content" with himself. And I conceive we might draw the further corollary that even now, while we are still *in statu viatoris* towards such a consummation, prayer of all kinds would be a hindrance, not a help to the life of the spirit, since the very point of prayer is that it is the expression of a sense of utter dependence. These are, I think, all inevitable consequences of permitting ourselves to forget that we are, and must always remain, historical beings, just because we are dependent beings, creatures and not our own creators.

"The historical", says an eminent philosopher recently taken from us, "is what we *understand* least and what concerns us most. How far below us, how far above, the historical extends, we cannot tell. But above it there can be only God, as the living unity of all, and below it, no longer things, but only the connecting, conserving acts of the one supreme."[2] By way of comment I would subjoin two reflections. Below the historical, I should say, and I think I should be in accord with the trend of the contemporary philosophy of the physical sciences in saying so, there could be nothing actual, but only the *materia prima* or *informis* of the Aristotelians, that ghost of just nothing at all which Dr.

[1] *Ethica*, iv. 53.
[2] Ward, *Naturalism and Agnosticism*[1], ii. 280 (after Lotze).

Whitehead is wrestling so hard to lay. And when God is said to be above the historical, this does not mean, and I take it that the philosopher I have quoted did not suppose it to mean, that God, being eternal, cannot intimately inform and work through the temporal and historical. Time, indeed, cannot be made, by stretching at both ends, so to say, to envelop eternity, but eternity can and does envelop time, and penetrate it through and through at its every point. This, as we thought we saw long ago, is the open secret of the moral and spiritual life of man, depending, as it does, all through on the delicate balancing of right attachment to and noble detachment from temporal good, and sustained, as well as initiated, by an outgoing spontaneous movement from the eternal, God, to the temporal, humanity. Carried to its extreme limit, such a self-disclosure of the eternal in and through its own creation, the temporal, would be an actual individual temporal life, subject in each of its details to the contingency inseparable from creatureliness, and so the life of a creature with its own *apparently* accidental place in the "kingdom of nature", as just the historical creature it is, when and where it is, and yet also, in every detail, the complete and adequate vehicle of the eternal. Such a life, plainly, would not be that of a creature which had somehow *achieved* beatitude, like a Buddhist *arahat*, by victory over its own initial vices and defects, nor yet the life of a creature which, though uniquely faultless, was still a *mere* creature. So long as we have the strictly eternal on the one side, and the merely creaturely, however faultless, or the other, the actual interpenetration and enfolding of the temporal by the eternal remains incomplete. If the full resolution of the ultimate dissonance is to be achieved, what is necessary is a life which is at once everywhere creaturely and yet also everywhere more than creaturely, because its limitations, circumscriptions, and infirmities, whatever they may be, interpose no obstacle to the divine and eternal purpose which controls and shines through it, but are themselves vehicles of that purpose. That there has been one human life of which this is a true description, and that the life of the Founder of Christianity, is the undemonstrated and indemonstrable conviction which gives the Christian religion its specific character.

It would be inconsistent with my duty, as defined by Lord Gifford, to assert or deny the truth of this conviction. Here it is in place only to make two observations: that the conviction, if true, though lying outside the limits of a strictly "natural" or "philosophic" theology, is in full harmony with such conceptions of the divine nature and the divine way with men as a sound philosophy leads us to entertain; and, again, that the surrender to such a conviction is definitely an act of walking by "faith", and not by "sight". That the Word has been "made flesh", and made flesh in just the specific person whom a Christian calls Lord, is a proposition which admits of no establishment by the empirical appeal to certified fact.

Some apologists for the Christian faith need, I think, to recognise this more unreservedly than they are apt to do. It is, I submit, a mistake to suppose that the unique cosmical significance Christianity ascribes to its Founder and Master can be sustained by a simple induction from the recorded events of his earthly life. In the first place, the Gospel narratives, like all records of human doings, permit of very different interpretations. Even the moral perfection of our Lord's character cannot be established beyond all possible question by the appeal to the record. Even of him, Kant's observation holds true, that, since we cannot read the secrets of men's hearts, we can never be sure as a matter of ascertained fact of the moral purity of the motives behind any act of any man.[1] The current anti-Christian attacks on various recorded acts of Jesus as indicating moral imperfections are, for the most part, malignant and stupid enough, and reflect grave discredit on those who can stoop to them; yet there really is no means of *proving* beyond cavil that all such unfavourable interpretations are false. The actual record, as it stands, *might* without logical absurdity be read as the story of a well-meaning and gracious, but self-deluded, sentimental "idealist" gradually embittered by contact with disagreeable realities; or again, even as that of an ambitious, or patriotic, "nationalist" insurgent against the political supremacy of Rome. Even apart from such crudely hostile interpretations, we have only to contrast the "liberal Protestant" reading of the story with that of the apocalyptists who find the key to Christ's conduct and teaching not in the *Sermon on the Mount*, but in eschatology, to appreciate the extreme difficulty of constructing an unambiguous and convincing portrait of "the historical Jesus".

Again, we must remember that on the most favourable estimate of our biographical material, it is painfully scanty. Even if the record permitted no alternative interpretations, it remains the fact that apart from the narrative of the week between the entry into Jerusalem and the return of the frightened women from the empty tomb, it consists only of a few anecdotes and a handful of discourses. Of the Lord's life as a whole we know hardly anything, and this of itself seems to vitiate all attempts to justify the Christian conception

[1] *Werke* (Hartenstein[2]), iv. 256.

of the significance of that life by appealing to the testimony of plain fact. And finally, we are bound to take into account the results of careful and unbiassed scrutiny into the sources of our narratives and the stages through which they have passed, as seriously affecting our right to regard them as trustworthy in their details. We are bound in honesty, I think, even from the standpoint of the most judiciously conservative criticism, to admit that we really know much less about the Master's life than might be supposed at first sight, or than we could wish. It is not too much to say that there never has been, and never will be, a trustworthy *Life of Jesus Christ*; we have no materials for such a work outside the Gospels, and the purpose of the Evangelists was not that of a biographer.

Similarly, if the chief emphasis is laid not so much on the Gospel narrative as upon the asserted incontestable perfection of the Gospel rule of life, it might be objected that it is not evident that the Gospels contain anything which can properly be called a *rule* of life; that what they do contain is rather a number of particular decisions on special moral issues; that it has always been a disputed question among Christians themselves what body of consistent moral principles, if any, can be extracted from these incidental decisions; and that they afford no unambiguous guidance in many of the most important moral problems of societies living in conditions very different from those of the Galilee or Judaea of the first Christian century. All this, so far as I can see, has to be conceded, and it would seem to follow that the utmost we can expect to do by appeal to the records is no more than to show that it is possible and permissible to interpret the recorded acts and teaching of Our Lord in a way which does not conflict with the claims Christian theology makes for his person.

Hostile criticism can be shown not to have made out its case; it seems doubtful whether empirical methods can show more than this. The specifically Christian "faith" in the person of Christ can be defended against attacks based on unfriendly interpretation of the records of his life and teaching, but not adequately substantiated by examination of those records.

It is clear, in fact, that the first believers were led to their belief neither by inference from the observed moral perfection of their Master, nor by reflection on the excellence of his moral precepts. What weighed with them, as we see clearly enough from the synoptic story and the *Acts of the Apostles*, was, first and foremost, the direct and immediate impression made by his whole personality of the presence in him of something "numinous", not to be understood in terms of the categories of ordinary human life, and next, the confirmation of this impression by the transcendent events of the resurrection on the third day and the wonderful manifestations of the day of Pentecost. And it seems that when the message of the Gospel was to be conveyed to a world at large which had known nothing of the Master before his death, the only facts of his career to which importance was attached were just the facts that he had been crucified "for our sins", "declared to be the Son of God by the resurrection from the dead", and was now actively "sending the Spirit" on believers. Thus it is notorious, though the fact is an awkward one for some "liberal" reconstructions of early Christianity, that St. Paul records only one incident of the life of Christ antecedent to the passion on Calvary,[1] and that an eminently "numinous" and

[1] 1 Cor. xi. 23. St. Paul's insistence on the point that he had "received" the narrative seems to me to demand the interpretation that it had been *officially* communicated to him by St. Peter and other eye-witnesses of the scene, and thus to be evidence for the Christianity of the date of his own conversion.

"other-world" act, the declaration that the bread and wine of the Last Supper are "my body on your behalf" and "the new covenant in my blood".

One might, I believe, go a step further and say truly that the first Christians primarily read even these facts wholly in the light of the Pentecostal "outpouring of the Spirit". If they were persuaded that their Master's death was something more than, what the world has seen so often, the murder of a wise and good man by the blinded and wicked, and his reappearance on the third day more than a signal vindication of the truth that the righteous man is not finally abandoned by his Maker, that, as they said, "Christ died *for our sins* and rose *for our justification*", they were so persuaded because they were first convinced that they had in themselves the actual experience of a new kind of life with God as its centre, and that this life had begun with the Pentecostal "giving of the Spirit".[1] They did not infer the transcendent significance of Christ from an antecedent belief in the moral perfection of his character, or the ethical elevation of his recorded sayings: rather they inferred these—though it is singular how little appeal any of the New Testament writings outside the Synoptic Gospels make to ethical precepts of Jesus—from their antecedent belief in the transcendent significance of Christ as the "glorified" sender of the Spirit. And one may fairly doubt whether, in later days, any man has ever really been converted to the Christian faith simply by the impression made on him either by the story of Christ's life or by the reports of his moral teaching. It is perhaps noteworthy that Christianity has never developed any counterpart to the enormous Mohammedan collections of Aḥādīth,

[1] Cf. the valuable chapter on "The Christ of History" in E. G. Selwyn's *Approach to Christianity* (1925).

traditions of the sayings of the Prophet, genuine or apocryphal, relative to the discharge of duty in all the conceivable situations in which the good Moslem may find himself. Something of this kind is indispensable in a religion whose Prophet has no significance for life beyond that of being a preacher and a moral exemplar, but Christianity has never felt the need of such a literature. Apocryphal Gospels were at one time freely invented, either to recommend specific *theologumena* like the *Gospel of Peter*, or to satisfy a craving for the marvellous, like the *Protevangelium of James* and the *Gospel of the Infancy*, but not to meet a demand for sayings of the Lord regulating in detail the moral duties of the Christian life. That need was met not by falling back on parables and precepts of Jesus, but by reliance on the guidance of the present and living Spirit.

This is not to say that there is not an appeal to history by the success or failure of which Christianity, or any other faith, may fairly be judged. But that appeal has very little to do with what are known as the "historical evidences" of a religion; it is the application to religion of the Gospel maxim "by their fruits ye shall know them". The vital question is not how much or little of the chronicled detail of the Founder's life can be authenticated in a way which will satisfy the exacting historical critic, or how far his certainly genuine utterances can be made into a code of "categorical imperatives"; it is whether he has brought, and continues to bring, a new quality of spiritual life into humanity, or not. This *is* an issue which can only be tried, so far as it can be tried at all, at the bar of history. But the historian who is to sit as judge must, of course, himself have the gift of genuine spiritual vision, if he is to discern the fact, just as he must have the dower of imaginative vision before he can pronounce on the question whether a given poet has or has not enriched our reading of nature with a new quality. (No one who understands the issues would, for example, accept the superficialities of Macaulay as the verdict of history on Loyola, or Bunyan, or George Fox; of St. Teresa, Macaulay fortunately had no occasion to say much.)

No doubt, this means that there must always be an element of the "subjective" and personal about such verdicts. Erudition, critical acumen, and honesty will not of themselves ensure the justice of any man's answer to the question whether Christ has brought us a new and true revelation of God, any more than the same gifts, by themselves, will ensure the justice of his answer to the question whether Wordsworth has brought us a new and authentic revelation of nature, or Beethoven dowered us with new thoughts and a new language. Yet true as this is, it does not leave us at the mercy of merely "subjective" impressions dictated by the prepossessions of the individual historian. The same problem arises, in a less accentuated form, whenever history is conceived as more than the construction of a register of births, accessions, and deaths, battles, treaties, and Acts of Parliament. Erudition and acumen alone will not suffice to answer the modest questions whether a statesman has, or has not, breathed the breath of life into the programme of his party, or a statute or tariff moulded the destiny of a society. Yet these questions are precisely those we ask our historians to answer for us, and the study of history would not long retain its high place as a chief instrument in liberal education if we seriously thought the historian could present us with nothing more satisfactory as an answer than a series of brilliant but wilful and contradictory "personal impressions". This may be magnificent journalism, but it is not history, and I think it would not be hard to name more than one eminent *littérateur* among us whose reputation has been already shattered by the discovery that the work by which he dazzled our fathers was, in spirit, brilliant journalism and nothing more.

For a time, no doubt, it may seem as though the historian of the religious life and thought of mankind had nothing more than his "personal impressions" to offer us. The strictly "orthodox" historian of a religion will tend always to assume as beyond question that the faith he professes does for its followers something wholly different in kind from that which any other faith can do for its own adherents; the historian of a religion in which he does not himself personally believe will equally tend to assume, again as known and certain, that it does nothing of the sort. Among ourselves, even at the present day, we have still the type of "historian" who can see nothing in the still living non-Christian faiths which even prepares the way for the light of the Gospel, and the other type who obstinately persists in seeing nothing in the provision made by Christianity for man's spiritual needs but what was equally provided by the host of more or less obscure "mystery cults" of late antiquity. It should be possible for the opposing subjectivities of the two types to cancel out against one another. The questions whether there is something unique and imperishable in the spiritual life which has its historical origin in Christ and his little band of followers, and what that something is, however complex, ought not to be in principle insoluble.

Indeed, I think it may fairly be said that so far as the presence of something entirely unique in the spiritual life historically traceable to that actual historical personality is concerned the verdict of sober history is already clear. The attempt to retain the secret of the specifically Christian life, when the figure of Christ and the events of the Gospel narrative have been resolved into symbolism, is not, after all, an experiment of recent years. We call this tendency to dispense with the historical element in religion "Modernism", but there is really nothing peculiarly modern about it, or, as we might prefer to put it, our own age is not the first which has felt itself "modern" by contrast with those which have gone before it. George Tyrrell and his friends called themselves modern, mainly with the great scholastics of the thirteenth century in their minds as the "ancients" from whose domination they were determined to free themselves. But these very ancients, who fashioned the Christianised Aristotelianism which Tyrrell and the rest wished to replace by a philosophy of the "pragmatist" or "activist" type, spoke of themselves, as St. Thomas does, as *moderni*, by way of opposition to *their* antiquity, the Platonic-Augustinian tradition. Nor is the particular kind of modernism which resolves historical *credenda* into symbol a new thing in the history of the Christian Church. It is as old as the beginnings of speculative theology itself. The very first "heresy" with which the Church was confronted, even before the later of the New Testament writings, such as the *First Epistle of John*, had been composed, was Docetism,[1] the doctrine which resolved the human personality and recorded life of Christ on earth into a long-continued symbolic illusion. It is to

[1] See the useful article "Docetism", by Adrian Fortescue, in *E.R.E.* iv. 532 ff. And with what follows in the next paragraph cf. E. Bevan, *Hellenism and Christianity*, p. 100 ff. "What strikes one in this Gnostic account of the descent and reascension of the Redeemer is that it is just a *reduplication of the Hellenistic story of the soul.* But in these fragments which we have of Hellenistic theology, unmodified by the influence of Christian faith in a human Person, there is no Redeemer. . . . Salvation by such *gnosis* and salvation by Christ present the appearance of two alternative schemes which have been imperfectly joined together."

combat this doctrine, as we know, that the Johannine epistle insists on the denial that "Jesus Christ has come in the flesh" as the distinguishing mark of an "antichrist", and it is apparently for the same reason that the Johannine Gospel gives a curious prominence to points of detail which illustrate the reality of the Lord's physical life, his weariness as he sat by the well in Samaria, his tears at the grave of Lazarus, his sufferings from thirst on the Cross, the water and blood which flowed from his side. Docetism, in that early age of the Church, seems to have spread like wild-fire among the educated, and to have been as hard to extinguish. It was the common basis of the whole bewildering growth of half-Christian speculations known as Gnosticism, in which a symbolic theosophic figure is substituted for the historical human "Son of the Carpenter". In the end the Church succeeded in casting out Gnosticism, but the success was only won by a hard struggle, to which the presence of statements of historical fact, or what was meant to be taken as such, in the traditional baptismal Confession of Faith still bears witness.

In some respects, we are sometimes inclined to think, the Church suffered in the conflict, as a man commonly suffers from wounds or maiming in a life-and-death struggle with a formidable opponent. But the known facts of the development of Gnosticism seem to have convinced serious historians that the Church did well in setting its face stubbornly against it, even at the cost of arresting philosophical speculation and losing for long enough a firm grip on the distinction between what is and what is not sufficiently attested fact. For the alternative was that Gnosticism, with its substitution of a symbolic figure for a real historical person, would kill the spiritual life of the community, and the essential thing was to preserve that life, even if it could only be preserved as a wounded life. The choice was between religion and faith, things tremendously alive, and theosophy, a lifeless thing which stands to living faith as the "bloodless ballet of impalpable categories" of Hegel's *Logic* to the breathing life and the movement of the world of sense. One cannot have a religion without something or someone whom one can trust, and to whom one can pray; but no one can trust in a category, or address heart-prayer to a symbol. Worship of a category (or a law, or a tendency) would be the most tragic of all forms of the "fallacy of misplaced concreteness".

It seems to me, then, that the actual history of Gnosticism is a sufficient warning against repetitions of the attempt to divorce the spiritual life, which we know in fact only as mediated by religions with roots in historical facts and happenings, wholly from its historical attachments. At bottom it is an attempt to manufacture God, the most tremendous of all realities, out of universals, and if there is any result that can be taken as final in philosophy, we may say that it has been finally established, beyond possibility of dispute, that the real, though pervaded everywhere by universals, cannot be constructed out of them. The metaphysician trying to make a fact out of categories is only repeating the task of twisting ropes out of sand imposed by Michael Scot on his fiends. However cunningly you complicate category with category, the process always leaves you with something which *may* be, or *should* be, or *ought* to be, and, as Baron von Hügel was fond of saying, "No amount of Ought-ness can be made to take the place of one Is-ness". As we have been trying to urge all through our argument, the great and unbridgeable gulf between a morality which remains morality and any religion which is religion is that morality remains an affair of the *ought*, religion is concerned with something which overpoweringly *is*.

If we once let the mere *ought* usurp the place of the *is*, however unconsciously, we may indeed try to retain, as some of the Roman Catholic ultra-modernists of twenty years ago tried to retain, all the wealth of devotional life which has been called into being by the felt need of feeding the soul's life on contact with a supreme "Is-ness", but whether we know it or not, we shall really have reduced religion to the status of a mere instrumental adjunct to an independent morality, and history is there to bear witness that this reduction of religion to a position of mere subservience to morals regularly has two effects. The religion so treated soon ceases to be genuine worship, and it is not long before it also ceases to be an effective stimulus to earnest moral action. In the hands of the Gnostics, worship became theosophy, and a morality with no better sanction than theosophy then ceased to be a vigorous and elevated morality. We see the same thing illustrated by the subsequent history of some of the "modernists" censured by the Roman *curia*. One cannot but feel deep sympathy with men who, as I suppose most of us think, were so largely right in their opposition to traditional intellectual idleness and stagnation, and were met by angry and largely stupid official violence on the part of authorities who should have mingled encouragement with admonition and caution. Probably it is just those among us who feel most respect for the great Church of the West who are most vehemently stirred to indignation when we see her authorities engaged in "putting back the clock". Yet the fact does remain that too many of the Continental leaders of the movement, after their breach with the representatives of official tradition, rapidly sank into contented secularism.[1] Unintelligent as the authorities at the Vatican showed themselves in their attitude alike to critical scholarship and to genuinely personal philosophical thinking, we must do them the justice to add that they do not seem to have been wrong in their conviction that the detachment of extreme "modernism" from all vestiges of historical tradition is as incompatible with the deepest spiritual inwardness as it is with the practical necessity that a religion which is to be available for all must be one and the same for the subtle and the simple, the critical and the uncritical.

I feel sure, then, that it is not from any defect or temporary accident that there is, in all the great world-religions, more or less of insistence on an element of historical fact which cannot simply be dismissed or denied without striking a formidable blow at the substance of the religion itself. But it does not follow that it is ever possible to say with finality just how much of what has been handed down as historical fact in the tradition of the community really has this character, or that the last word can ever be said for all time by men of one age upon any single historical *credendum*. At most, we can only safely formulate very general principles; the application of them to particular cases is always a matter of infinite difficulty. One can, no doubt, see that in the case of any actual positive religion there are some *credenda* of an historical kind which cannot be denied without challenging the value of that religion as a genuine disclosure of the divine character and purpose, and that there are others which at least have not the same manifest spiritual value. Thus, merely for

[1] For evidence on this point I may be content to refer to the volume of *Selected Letters* of von Hügel (1927) and the accompanying *Memoir* by Mr. Bernard Holland.

purposes of ready illustration, we may consider the assertions about the historical facts of our Lord's life which figure in the great Christian confessions of belief. As I have said, Docetism, which cuts away all these assertions by denying the reality of the Lord's actual historical existence *in toto*, would clearly destroy the specific character of Christianity itself. Again, a denial, for example, of the article *tertia die resurrexit a mortuis*, if taken to mean that our Lord's personal existence ceased when he breathed his last on the Cross, and that the band of followers who believed him to be still living and directing and inspiring their activities, and shaping the whole course of history, were simply deluded, would be almost as directly fatal to Christianity as Docetism itself. Whatever religion might survive general acceptance of the thesis that from the first until now Christians have been worshipping a dead man and mistaking their reminiscences of him for experiences of direct contact with God, it would not be a religion with any right to the name of Christianity.

We can only blind ourselves to this manifest truth by committing the common confusion between the theological formulae in which men give an account of what they suppose themselves to believe and the faith by which they, mainly subconsciously or unconsciously, shape their lives. A man, in fact, often really believes so much more than he is himself aware that he believes. He says and thinks, perhaps, that he believes Christ to be no more than a good man who has been wholly non-existent for nineteen centuries. But in his life he acts on a very different assumption. He professes to think that Christ belongs to the dead past; he acts as though Christ belonged to and dominated the living present. But to be convinced that Christ is an abiding living personality, and that our own destinies are in his hands, is not exactly the same thing as to regard the New Testament narratives of his "resurrection appearances" as one and all beyond historical criticism, or to have any particular theory about the nature of those appearances. One may intelligibly hold that the belief in the real continued personal activity and the supremacy of Christ, and in the reality of the contacts between the still living Christ and his disciples, out of which Christianity arose is what is essential in the historical *credendum*, and everything else matter for criticism and speculation, not affecting the true substance of the Christian faith.

For, we may say, that Christian conception of the relation of Christ to God and to man which would be ruined by the view that Christ has been non-existent for nineteen hundred years is no more affected by an uncertainty whether he did or did not eat honey-comb or fish with his friends after his Passion than by a difference of opinion on the point whether St. Paul, on his day of Damascus, actually *saw* a vision of the features of Christ, or only *heard* the memorable words which St. Luke records in the *Acts*; or again by the possibly unmeaning question whether this hearing itself should be called an "external" or an "interior" audition. From the most completely traditionalist point of view possible to a rational man it has to be admitted that the events in question are, *ex hypothesi*, so remote from the familiar order that they can hardly be described in language devised to serve familiar daily purposes without obscurity; and again, that the descriptions we possess, like all *bona fide* independent narratives of real and striking events, are not completely consistent: and even these elementary admissions have far-reaching implications. Consensus as to the historical character of the central incidents in such narratives should be recognised to be compatible with wide divergences in estimation of details.

So much seems to be conceded, even by the conservatives of Christian theology, at least so far as concerns some of the *credenda* of an historical kind specified in the classical Christian confessions. Dr. Gore,[1] for example, with all his anxiety to fence round some of these *credenda*, frankly puts a symbolic sense on the phrase *ascendit ad coelos*, with the qualification that the symbol must be understood as representing a real transaction of an order indescribable in ordinary language, and he is here, no doubt, speaking the sense of the majority of strictly "orthodox" educated Christians of the present day. None of them, if confronted with the question, would be likely to assert that by "ascension into heaven" they mean physical displacement in a direction perpendicular to the horizon of Jerusalem. (And in respect of this particular article it is, of course, easy to claim, as Dr. Gore does, the authority of learned Fathers such as Gregory Nyssen and Jerome for the "symbolical" interpretation.) What I myself find it a little difficult to understand in a position like Dr. Gore's—which I desire to treat with all the respect rightly due to its author—is the hard and fast line which is drawn between *credenda* thus admitted to contain symbolic elements and others which are taken to be bare records of happenings with no such intermixture.

It is not that I deny all validity to this distinction, so long as it is regarded as one of degree; of course, I am aware that, when we use words in a popular fashion, we can say that the statement that Christ "ascended" or that he "sits on the right hand of the Father" is

[1] *Can We Then Believe?* p. 206 ff. Cf. J. H. Bernard, art. "Assumption and Ascension", in *E.R.E.* ii.

symbolic in a way in which the statements that he was crucified and buried are not. What I dispute is the right of any man, or body of men, to claim once and for all to limit the right to recognise the presence of the symbolic element to the case of certain specified articles and to exclude from active participation in the devotional life of the Christian community those who do not make the same precise restriction. I do not understand on what *principle* the line of delimitation between the two classes of historical *credenda* is to be drawn, and—a still more fundamental difficulty—I think it actually impossible to describe *any* real event in language wholly non-symbolic.[1] No language, if I may be pardoned the merely apparent "bull", is even approximately free from the symbolic, except the artificial language of "symbolic" logic,[2] and that idiom is impotent to describe the simplest and most familiar event. I gather that Dr. Gore's own view is that the principle of distinction is itself an historical one—certain *credenda* have long been understood (but by whom?) to be expressed in symbolic language, others not so, and the line must continue to be drawn always just where it was drawn in the past (in the fourth century?). I own that I feel some doubt about the fact. I cannot help thinking that one would only have to go sufficiently far back in the history of the Church to find a time when a Council of Dr. Gore's episcopal

[1] Let me illustrate by an example. Dr. Gore notoriously would include the article *natus ex Maria virgine* among those which must be understood "literally". But how much is to be meant by this? We know the interpretation put on this *credendum* by St. Thomas and in the *Catechism* of Trent. Ought we, then, to insist on the whole of it, or only on some part, and if not on the whole, how shall we justify ourselves against the criticism, which might be brought against us from the Tridentine point of view, of not really accepting the article without diminution? Must we regard it as *de fide* to hold that Christ, as a physical fact, *ex mulieris alvo sine ullo maternae virginitatis detrimento editus est*? If not, are we not permitting a latitude we professedly reject in the interpretation of the word *natus*?

[2] And even this exception seems apparent rather than real.

predecessors would either have condemned his "symbolic" Ascension, or have left it uncondemned only because a distinction so clear to his mind would have been unintelligible to theirs.

The real difficulty, however, arises chiefly in connection with traditional historical *credenda* which appear to stand in no discoverable connection with the great central *credendum* of any religion, its doctrine of God and of God's ways with men. Such propositions, it is often said, have no "spiritual value"; a man's personal walk with God is in no way affected by his opinion about them: they are mere assertions about incidents of past history irrelevant to the spiritual life, and therefore *religiously* insignificant. These at least, then, should be expunged, should they not, from a confession of faith, before a rational man can be asked to accept it? But here again there are several considerations which ought to be carefully pondered.

In the first place, it is not always apparent on inspection what allegations of historical matter of fact have, and what have not, a spiritual value such that the rejection of them would seriously impair the personal religious life of the rejector. There may be such a connection in cases where it is not so patent as in those which I began by alleging. And it should be remembered that the very presence of a statement in a great communal profession of faith at least affords some presumption that it was originally placed there to rule out some opposing position which had been found practically mischievous to the religious life of the community, and may be mischievous again, if it is suffered to revive. It may, of course, not be so; the *credendum* in question may owe its place to the contentious ingenuity of theologians dogmatising for dogmatism's sake (though this motive does not appear historically to have been very prominent in the great creed-making age of the Christian Church). But the initial presumption, at least, is the other way, and modesty suggests that before we declare an "article" to have "no spiritual value", we should go to history to learn why and how it obtained its place. We may find that there has been an excellent reason for this, as in the case of certain biographical statements about Our Lord in the Christian confessions. At first sight the inclusion in these confessions of the chronological detail that the Crucifixion took place in the procuratorship of Pilate might seem to be pure irrelevance. But the clause acquires a different significance when we learn from history that the purpose of insisting on such details was to make it clear, once and for all, that the Saviour confessed by Christians is a real man of flesh and blood, not a phantom or a theosophical symbol. Docetism—as we may see from the fantastical revival of it by the faddists who deny the "historicity of Jesus" in our own day—is an ever possible perversion of a religion of incarnational type which is fatal to its spirit, and a philosopher cannot quarrel with Christians for their determination to keep Docetism out of their religion.[1]

Of course, it may be said that, even after the appeal to history has been made, the case is not equally clear with all *credenda* of this kind. Even when we have been at pains to discover why they were originally adopted, we may be left unable to see, in the case of some of them, that they are denials of anything which would injure religion by impairing a soul's intercourse with its God; or such mischief as might have been done in

[1] It seems to me important, in view of current controversies which I need not specify, to remember that the original purpose of all the statements made in the Creeds about the earthly life of Jesus was to insist on the reality of his *humanity*. They are directed against Docetism, not against "humanitarianism", which was not a theory of the creed-making ages.

this way in a past age may be dependent on modes of thought and feeling peculiar to that age, and no longer formidable. Hence it is a real possibility that there may be no close or clear agreement between thoughtful and sincerely religious men about the presence of a real spiritual significance in such *credenda*, and it might plausibly be argued that what cannot be seen to be thus directly connected with a true belief in God, being at best superfluous, must be actually injurious to personal religion; that whatever is more than the *unum necessarium* is, for that very reason, harmful. Here, again, I suppose we may say that private judgement needs to be tempered with humility. Even if I cannot myself see any connection between acceptance of a certain *credendum* and the quality of a man's belief in God, yet, if it also appears to be widely true that persons and societies which cherish that *credendum* enjoy a rich and vigorous spiritual life, while those who reject it do not, it is wise to suspect that there really is a connection between the belief in question and "growth in grace" which a more penetrating scrutiny would make manifest, though possibly it would also reveal hitherto unsuspected points of distinction between the substance of the *credendum* and temporary accidents of the form in which it has traditionally been held. It is not the part of the true wisdom, which is always humble, to pronounce too confidently that there is "nothing in" any conviction which has fed the spirituality of generations.

It may, no doubt, be urged by way of objection to this appeal to the *consensus* of the great multitude of the spiritually minded that, as Dr. Bevan has said,[1] fine spirituality and sound historical insight are not *in pari materia*. It is reasonable to defer to the judgement of the spiritually minded against my own when the

[1] *Hellenism and Christianity*, p. 245 ff.

question is one of the tendency of some practice to promote or check spirituality of mind, but what reason is there to suppose that the exceptionally spiritually minded man is an exceptionally trustworthy authority about historical fact? It is, after all, only in his own "art" that the "artist" may fairly claim to be listened to. I own that the argument would be final but for one consideration. When such an appeal is made, the point on which one is appealing to the judgement of the spiritually minded man is *not* a point of naked fact. We do not ask him whether or not there is good documentary evidence to establish the asserted fact; what we are really asking him is whether denial of it would involve deterioration in our conception of God and God's dealings with ourselves. The question itself is, in the end, one of "spiritual value", and therefore the verdict of the "spiritually minded", if it is clear and accordant, as it seems to me, does count, exactly as an accordant verdict of musicians on the question of historical fact, "Did Mozart, or Beethoven, write this piece of music?" or the accordant verdict of great men of letters on the question, "Had Shakespeare a hand in *The Two Noble Kinsmen*?" really counts, even though none of those who accord in giving it should have been specially trained in the critical investigation of documentary evidence. It seems to me, therefore, not unreasonable to allow real weight to the intuition of the spiritually minded, where they are clearly in agreement, even on the question whether acceptance of certain statements as to matters of historical fact is of the substance of religion.

But I would also add that the very ground I have just urged in favour of genuine deference to this kind of intuition is also equally a ground for recognising that the rights of such intuition are rather closely circumscribed. The whole argument rests on two broad general presuppositions: (1) that, as is implied in the assertion of the existence of God, the disjunction between "value" and "fact" is not absolute, the supreme "value", God, being also the ultimate source of the whole course of historical "fact"; (2) that the religion to which it is essential that a certain assertion about historical fact should substantially be true is a religion which conceives God rightly, so that the conviction "here is something which is significant *fact*" is equivalent to the conviction "if this is not fact, then God, the source of all facts, is something less than God". In the application of the principle to a specific case it is also presupposed that what leads the spiritually minded man to insist on the "historicity" of a certain event really is a perception that denial of the fact would involve surrendering a more for a less adequate conception of God.

If the true motive for the insistence is different, if it is no more than intellectual inertia, *a fortiori* if it is only the reluctance of officials with a prestige to maintain to admit their own liability to error—and none of us are so spiritual that these motives can be wholly excluded—the apparent consensus may lose much, or all, of its significance. In fact, I think we may say we know that a good deal of conservative traditionalism in "matters of religion" has often been inspired by little more than the intellectual apathy of good men, or the fear on the part of official men that their prestige is in danger. Even when motives of this order are not dominant, there is always the possibility to be reckoned with that they are present, and that, under their influence, a great deal which has really a very different origin may masquerade as the genuine intuition of spiritual minds. Even when we can be sure that we are dealing with real spiritual intuition, we still have to remember that the affirmations based on such intuition have regularly been elicited by specific denials; their legitimate object has been to safeguard something felt to be vital to the spiritual life which has been challenged by these specific denials, not, in the interests of "pure thought", to settle once for all the question exactly how much in the received assertions of historical fact constitutes the significant "substance". The formulation of a *credendum* cannot reasonably be regarded as intended to solve in advance problems which have never been present to the minds of the promoters. The highest regard for the intuitions of the spiritually minded need not blind us to the patent fact that such intuitions, like the immediate judgements of men of high conscience and moral insight on practical problems of conduct, are regularly evoked by concrete situations and as responses to these situations; intuition does not function *in vacuo*.

If these considerations were only borne in mind as they should be, we might anticipate not only greater humility on the part of the individual "historical critic", when he finds himself confronted by a genuine deliverance of the body of the spiritually minded, but an answering greater humility on the part of those who claim officially to speak in the name of religion. The individual critic of the traditional would have to admit that a living religion, because its God is a God of an historical world, does imply *credenda* of an historical kind among its foundations. He would have to abandon the claim, sometimes advanced by the negative critic of tradition in our own day, to be doing high service to the spirit of a religion by merely destroying its body. I would add that he would be less prone than he sometimes is to confuse the very different assertions, "This cannot be shown to be matter of fact by testimony which will satisfy the religiously indifferent, or the anti-religious", and "There is nothing in this but illusion". But equally the guardians of a religious tradition would have to admit that, in the last resort, their own claim to be "guided by the Spirit" can only be justified in so far as they really embody neither the mental indolence of the unthinking, nor the lust of officialdom for prestige and power, but the genuine insight of "holy and humble men of heart"; and, again, that however decisive the pronouncements of intuition upon the concrete situation which has elicited them, they cannot by anticipation foreclose issues which have never been presented *in concreto*.

If these limitations are remembered, it is not necessary that there should be any irreconcilable conflict between the demand of a living religion for an indispensable basis in genuine historical fact and the right of critical historical investigation to deal with all "evidences" freely and fearlessly, by its own methods and without interference. Most of our acutest trouble in this kind seems to be due to the proneness of theologians and historical critics alike to an unconscious assumption of their own infallibility in metaphysics. The theologian tends to assume too hastily that religion demands not merely that God should have disclosed Himself through the past, but that we should already know in all detail what the pattern of the past through which God has disclosed Himself is. The historical critic too often assumes, with equal rashness, that we know that certain patterns never were, and never will be, exhibited by any fact. Each is trying in his own way, with equal unreason, to canalise the same living current, which the one might call the "march of events", the other the "great river of the grace of God".

IV

THE SUPERNATURAL AND THE MIRACULOUS

τὴν θατέρου φύσιν δύσμεικτον οὖσαν εἰς ταὐτὸν συναρμόττων βίᾳ.—PLATO.

I CAN conceive that it may be felt that the considerations we have so far advanced, even when all possible weight has been allowed to them, do not remove the main difficulty presented to a philosophical mind by the historical religions. It may be conceded that if there is a God who discloses Himself to man, it is only reasonable to expect that the disclosure will have a wealth of character harmonising with, but going far beyond, anything we could discover by mere general analysis of the implications of the bare reality of a natural or a moral order, and that this is enough to justify the great positive religions in attaching importance to some *credenda* of an historical kind. The trouble, it will be said, is that, in point of fact, they are found to insist upon historical *credenda* of a very special and questionable sort. They propound for our belief assertions about alleged facts which are avowedly *miraculous*, events which are surprising, and all the more surprising to us the more fully we become acquainted with the general pattern of experienced fact. A miracle is, *ex vi termini*, a break in the order of "customary experience", even if it is not, as it is sometimes called, a violation of a "uniform law of nature", or an event without a "natural" cause; such an event is perhaps intrinsically impossible, and it is, at any rate, a kind of event which we learn to think steadily more improbable, as we learn more and more from science and history of the actual course of nature and human behaviour, and of the psychological conditions which explain the rise of ungrounded beliefs in such events. But the positive religions are so bound up with this belief in miracles that it cannot be eliminated from them without fundamentally altering their character. A God who does not reveal Himself by miracles is not the God of any of these religions. There is therefore an element of falsehood in them all, against which philosophy is bound in honour to take up an attitude of permanent protest. A religion for the truth-loving man must be a religion without miracles, and it is only by disingenuous sophistry that any of the great historical religions can be identified with non-miraculous religion. The philosopher must, therefore, in loyalty to truth, reject them all on principle.

This familiar objection to what is loosely called the miraculous element in the positive religions may take any one of three distinct forms. (1) There is the old "high *priori*" contention, now for the most part relegated to the polemics of the uneducated or half-educated, that a miracle is intrinsically impossible because its occurrence would be a violation of the principle on which all distinction between truth and falsehood rests, the principle that the world is intelligible. (2) There is the contention, familiar to the readers of Matthew Arnold and Huxley, that though the question of the *possibility* of miracles is merely idle, increasing acquaintance with the facts of natural science has shown, as Arnold puts it, that miracles *do* not happen, or, as Huxley suggests, that the testimony to any miracle in which the followers of a religion have believed proves, on examination, to be insufficient as testimony.[1] (3) Finally, there is what is probably felt by our contemporaries to be the gravest objection of all, that which Dr. Bevan has called the *anthropological* objection.[2] This has been pithily condensed into a single sentence by Sir R. Burton, who remarks that Hume disbelieved in miracles because he had never come across one, but if he had lived in the East, he would have come across so many that he would have been even more incredulous.[3] Or, to adopt the less epigrammatic but more careful statement of Dr. Bevan, the anthropologist finds himself constantly dealing in his work with miraculous stories which have a marked *prima facie* resemblance to those found in the traditions of the great positive religions. He sets them all aside, because his particular studies have made it so plain to him that they arise from an ignorance and an illusion characteristic of mankind all over the globe at a certain level of intellectual development. Why should an exception be made for the particular stories which have been attached to the names of the great figures of the world-religions? If the Christian dismisses a thousand stories of a virginal birth, why should he deal differently with the thousand and first because it is told of Christ, or the Jew discriminate between two such similar stories as that of the disappearance of Romulus in the thunderstorm and that of the translation of Elijah in the tempest?

This, as I should agree with Burton and Dr. Bevan, is the one and the very formidable line of argument which impresses us all at the present day. Whatever our agreements or disagreements with Kant, there is one lesson which we have all learned from the *Critique*

[1] *Hume* (E.M.L.), c. 7. [2] *Hellenism and Christianity*, p. 233 ff.

[3] The remark is taken from Burton's version of the *Thousand and One Nights* (Night 236).

of Pure Reason, that logic, functioning *in vacuo*, can tell us nothing of the course of events. No assertion about the actual course of events can be shown to be unreasonable, apart from an appeal to specific experiences, unless it is found on analysis to be internally self-contradictory, and then only, if we accept the Law of Contradiction, as a real Irrationalist in metaphysics would not, as an ontological truth. Even the more moderate-sounding assertions of Arnold and Huxley are of a kind which produces no confident conviction. It is not quite clear what Arnold meant by his dictum that miracles "do not happen". If he meant only that they do not commonly happen, the remark is true, indeed truistic, but irrelevant; we should not call an event of a kind we see occurring every day a "miracle". If he meant that they *never happen in our own age*, this is a statement of fact which would be traversed by a greater number of intelligent persons than is often supposed, and ought not to be made without some attempt at justification. If he meant, as he may have done, that our knowledge of physical science, though not our knowledge of metaphysics, enables us to exclude certain types of event confidently and finally from the pattern of the real world, the argument has already lost its force as we have become increasingly alive to the abstractive and artificial character of all physical hypotheses.[1] But if he only meant that European societies in the sixties and seventies of the last century were generally incredulous of the miraculous, he was actually alleging the mere prevalence of a habit of mind as its own justification. Probably the most charit-

[1] Cf. E. W. Hobson, *Survey of the Domain of Natural Science*, p. 490, and the whole of the essay by Prof. Eddington in *Science, Religion, and Reality*, pp. 189-218 (references which I owe to Dr. Gore, *Can We Then Believe?* p. 52). See also the singularly able essay by H. D. Roelofs on "The Experimental Method and Religious Beliefs" in MIND, N.S. 150.

able interpretation would be that he really intended to be stating the anthropological objection in untechnical language. Similarly, when Huxley[1] insinuates that though on good and sufficient testimony we ought to be ready to believe the most astounding statements about the course of events, there never has actually been good and sufficient testimony to any of the events which the theologians of the various faiths have claimed as miracles, he seems to fall into a manifest confusion of thought. If credibility is wholly a matter of external testimony, as it should be if the rest of Huxley's theory is sound, there is better testimony for some "miracles" than there is for many non-miraculous events which are commonly accepted as historical. There is, *e.g.*, better testimony for the appearance of Our Lord alive after his crucifixion than there is for the death of St. Paul at Rome, better evidence for the stigmatisation of St. Francis than for the murder of the "princes in the Tower". It should seem that what Huxley intends to suggest is precisely what he professes not to be suggesting, that the testimony which would be sufficient for more customary events is insufficient to establish the particular *sort* of event meant by the word "miracle". Hence I should suppose that he also has the anthropological objection at the back of his mind.

If I had either the right or the desire to make my remarks on this problem into an *apologia* for the miracles of a particular religion—as, speaking in this place, I am not likely to do—I think I could offer some grounds for holding that the analogies alleged by the sceptical anthropologist between the unusual incidents in the stories of the heroes of savage folk-lore and those which figure among the *credenda* of great positive religions professed by communities of civilised men are

[1] *Hume* (E.M.L.), pp. 133-9.

not altogether as impressive as they are sometimes made to appear. There are similarities, it is true, but there are also dissimilarities which are equally significant. (The Nativity narratives in the Gospels, for example, do not strike me as being particularly like any of the folk-lore stories of virginal births I have read in the works of anthropologists, though they do remind me of Old Testament stories of a very different kind, like those of the births of Samson and Samuel, in which a virgin plays no part.) My actual purpose, however, is not, and ought not to be, that which is the legitimate business of the Christian apologist. The issue with which I am concerned is the more general one, what kind of view of the relation of the world to God is implied in the conception of the "miraculous" as a constituent of real becoming, and is there any incompatibility between acceptance of such a conception and loyalty to philosophical principle. I am not asking whether a truly philosophic mind ought to believe in this or that particular miracle, or indeed in any specific miracle in which men have ever been called on to believe, but with what antecedent convictions the problem should be approached. Is it our duty as lovers of truth to come to it with minds made up against the admission of the miraculous, in any intelligible sense of the word, into our scheme of things? Since our choice between participation in the devotional life of the actual religious societies around us and individualistic detachment cannot well fail to be influenced, and may, for some of us, be decided, by our answer to this question, the issue is a live one enough, and one which, if philosophy indeed has any function in the direction of life, the philosopher has no right to evade.

If we are to think with any approach to clarity, we must begin the discussion of the problem by drawing a distinction of the first importance which is too often obscured by loose and careless language—the distinction between the supernatural and the miraculous. Nothing but disaster can come, for our thinking about religion, from the common confusion of the two, illustrated, for example, in the last century by the title of a too-famous anonymous work on *Supernatural Religion* which was nothing more than a polemic against "miracles". We need to understand clearly that the *supernatural* is the generic term, the *miraculous* only a subordinate species of the genus, and even more clearly that the vital and primary interest of religion is in the supernatural; for religion, the miraculous is, at best, secondary and derivative. Religion is only concerned with the miraculous if, and so far as, the miraculous can be taken as an indication of the reality of the supernatural. Religion exists whenever, and only when, there is the conscious domination of life by aspiration towards an absolute and abiding good which is recognised as being also the supreme reality upon which the aspirant is utterly dependent. Where we have as the fundamental motive of life "love towards an infinite and eternal thing", there we have living religion; where we have not this motive, at least implicitly, we have not religion. Religion itself is thus consciousness of the strictly supernatural, the transcendent something which is above all mutability, passage, and history, or it is nothing. When a man really loses, if anyone ever loses, all belief in the reality of that which is ultra-temporal, and therefore strictly supernatural, at a level *above* that of the "complex event we call nature", he *ipso facto* loses religion; where, if anywhere, men have not yet attained to at least a virtual recognition of the entirely abiding as the supremely real and the true centre of interest in life, there may be cults propitiatory of non-human powers, hostile or friendly, but there is nothing we can class with Christianity or Judaism; if we are to call such cults religious, we can only do so "equivocally".

This seems to me the sure and certain kernel of Otto's now famous conception of the *numinous*, however much there may be to criticise or correct in Otto's own elaboration of his thought. But it should be clear that though religion, in our sense of the word, *is* the active recognition of the supernatural, and nothing else, this recognition of the supernatural *need* not carry with it any recognition of the miraculous, in the sense of abnormalities and singularities in the historic sequence of events, as specially revelatory of the supernatural. There is no more entirely irreligious conception of the world than that of Epicurean philosophy, the ancient theory which, more than any other, by its doctrine of the incalculable *clinamen principiorum*, insisted on the reality of the singular and abnormal. On the other hand, there is no room for the miraculous in a philosophy like that of the Stoics, or their modern counterpart, Spinoza, nor again in that of Plotinus; but a man would have to be very blind not to see the genuine spirit of religion in the hymn of Cleanthes, in many a discourse of Epictetus, or "moral epistle" of Seneca, in almost any essay of the *Enneads*, in the "fifth part" of Spinoza's *Ethics*. A Christian may, and will, hold that there are more adequate expressions of spiritual religion than any of these, but he cannot deny that in their measure they do express it, and sometimes with great beauty and nobility. That there is religion genuine and undeniable in the Stoics, in Plotinus, in Spinoza, is of itself complete proof that though there can be no religion without the supernatural, there can be religion, and profound religion, without miracle.

Prima facie, then, it might be suggested that the complication of religion with miracle which meets us in the great positive religions is purely accidental, a mere consequence of the fact that these religions had their beginnings in ages of widespread ignorance of the facts of the natural order, and that by a wholly beneficent process of development they may be expected to get clear of their miraculous accretions, as of so many unhappy encumbrances, though still retaining to the full their assured conviction of the reality of the supernatural. They will end by ceasing to look to any special events as evidence of the supernatural, because they have learned to see its presence everywhere.

> God is law, say the wise: O soul, and let us rejoice,
> For if He thunder by law, the thunder is yet His voice.

This is, as we cannot deny, an attractive and plausible, as well as a very widely held position; to many of you I may seem to be wilfully surrendering to unreason in suggesting that it is possibly not the last word on the matter, as it appeared to be to the generation for whom Tennyson wrote the verses I have quoted, and that "natural law in the spiritual world" may not prove to be the great secret of God's way with mankind. The question, to my mind, is whether the position is not *too* plausible on the surface to be quite above suspicion.

With theories, as with men, one does well not to trust the exceedingly plausible without very careful consideration. And there is at least one reflection which seems to have some pertinency at this point. The savage and the primitive man are often said by the more popular of our anthropologists to be simple-minded creatures who have not yet learned to distinguish between fancy and fact; they are held to be in the habit of treating the visions of dreams, delirium, and artificially induced hallucination as all on the same level with the perceptions of waking life, to have no conception of causality, or of the existence of a regular routine in the sequences of nature. With them, we are told, casual association is the one sufficient ground of belief, "primitive credulity" is unbounded, and here we have the simple and sufficient explanation of the origin of belief in the "miraculous". Now even if this is an accurate account of the workings of the savage mind—and I have a suspicion, encouraged by much that I have read of the work of recent and careful anthropological students such as Malinowski, that it errs seriously by over-simplification[1]—it is at least pertinent to remember that the great positive religions have all had their beginnings in historical times and among "civilised peoples"; none of them is really a simple unbroken development from the days in which the ancestors of Jews, Christians, Moslems may have been "savages" with the habits of life and thought of Australian aboriginals.[2]

As it happens, the only cases in which we have contemporary evidence about the mental life of the persons with whom a great positive religion originated are those of Christianity and, perhaps we should add, Islam,[3] the two youngest members of the group. And however different the mental habits of the first Christian disciples may have been from those of a modern European Bachelor of Science, it is at least certain that the apostles and their converts were not "primitive savages" who could not distinguish between waking

[1] *E.g.* "savages" appear from the evidence, in many cases, to see no causal connection between the commerce of the sexes and the birth of children. But this does not mean that they do not assign a cause of some kind for conception. They have their own rival theory of the cause, which they can defend with some ingenuity, as readers of Malinowski, or Spencer and Gillen, are aware.

[2] This becomes all the more evident if those critics are right who regard Judaism as originating in "post-exilic" times.

[3] See for a strong statement of the paucity of the evidence in this case Professor Margoliouth's article "MUHAMMAD", in *E.R.E.* viii.

life and dreams, or had never bethought themselves that a resurrection from the dead is a startling departure from the "familiar routine". It was precisely because men like St. Peter and St. Paul were as familiar as we are with the distinction between "customary experience" and "miracle" that they saw the hand of God so conspicuous in the miracle which they put in the forefront of their message to the world. If St. Paul, under bondage to "primitive credulity", had thought it just as likely that the "next best" man would rise from his tomb on the third day as that he would not, plainly he could not have found in the resurrection of Christ any proof that Christ had been declared to be the Son of God "with power". No doubt, the routine of "customary experience" as conceived by St. Paul and his contemporaries included sequences which it does not embrace for us, but this should not blind us to the more important fact that they were as much alive as ourselves to the existence of such a routine. If they appealed to a miracle as evidence of the presence of God behind the routine, this was not because they had never learned to discriminate between the familiar and the marvellous, or miraculous, but precisely because they did habitually make the discrimination.

It is a true remark of some nineteenth-century writer—I believe of F. W. H. Myers[1]—that though we should be led into misconceptions if we thought of the apostles, as eighteenth-century apologists sometimes seem to do, as men with the minds of average British jurymen, we should be led much more seriously astray if we thought of them as men with the minds of hypo-

[1] I have now found the precise reference: "They (the apostles) were more like a British jury than like a parcel of hysterical monomaniacs" (Myers, *Essays Classical and Modern*, p. 448).

thetical "primitive savages", or even of actual Hottentots or Central Australians. After all, they were members, though most of them humble members, of a society which had possessed a high civilisation for centuries, and the mental traditions shaped by the superior intellects of a high civilisation work down to and stamp themselves on every section of the community, and must do so in virtue of their incorporation in its very vocabulary. It is nonsense to assert that the society which saw the rise of Christianity acquiesced in the marvellous elements of the Christian story simply because it was its habit to believe any marvel related of any one and by any one without discrimination. What is really illustrated by the comparative ease with which the miracles of the New Testament won credence and have retained it to this day, except in the relatively small circle of scientific and historical critics and those who have come under their influence, is not inability to distinguish between what is customary in experience and what is not, but the persistent tendency of the human mind, *after* it has learned to draw this distinction, to expect that the abnormal and exceptional will attend the doings of the men through whom God makes a special disclosure of Himself, that the "prophet" will be accredited by a "sign".

The same tendency is interestingly illustrated by the rise of Islam. Mohammed, as is well known, expressly, and prudently, disclaimed all appeal to miracle in support of his own revelation. His "sign" was to be, apparently, the inimitable intrinsic divinity of the verses, or sentences, of his Koran, and inquirers were to expect no other. This did not prevent his followers from developing a tradition of evidential "miracles", some of them on a cosmic scale. Now, of course, all that is proved by the history of these two faiths is the vitality of the tendency of the human mind to connect the performance of wonderful works with the possession of a special message from God and about God; the mere existence of the tendency is not its own sufficient justification. As Arnold said too flippantly, it would be no proof that my statements in my writings are true that I could turn my pen into a pen-wiper, though, if I could do so, men in general would be ready to believe anything I might assert. Still the very persistency of the tendency here acknowledged might tempt a cautious thinker who shares Aristotle's conviction that a view held strongly and quasi-instinctively by the "many" is not usually a pure delusion to wonder whether the popular association of the true prophet with "signs and portents" is quite so irrational a prejudice as it is made to appear by Arnold's caricature. Possibly even in the Jew's "seeking after a sign", as well as in the Greek's demand for metaphysical "wisdom", there may be exaggeration of a thought which is not in itself unreasonable.

To myself it seems that this really is so. If we grant the reality of the distinction, necessary to any religious view of life, between the temporal order of natural succession and a transcendent unseen order which pervades and dominates the sensible and natural, we still have, as it seems to me, a choice between two ways of conceiving this pervasion of the sensible by the supra-sensible, neither, on the face of it, irrational. We might think of the dominance of the supra-sensible as always strictly pervasive, but never obtrusive. The divine purpose might underlie and control the course of the familiar sensible order without anywhere disturbing it, as the conscious intelligent purpose of an artisan who is a master of his craft controls the running of adequate machinery employed on a material thoroughly pliable to the ends of the craftsman, with a mastery which is all-present, but presents no shocks or surprises.[1]

This is the way of thinking most congenial to the temper of my own generation, with its historically explicable prejudice in favour of finding gradual growth and slow and continuous "evolution" everywhere. Even the most strictly orthodox divines of that generation habitually think of the establishment of the kingdom of God itself by preference in terms of the parables of the unseen growth of the grain of mustard-seed and the slow working of the leaven hidden in the mass of dough; they allow the comparison of the revelation of the Son of Man with the sudden flash of lightning which lays the heavens bare[2] to fall into the background.

But if we believe in the reality of the transcendent, it is equally possible to think of the sensible order, with its system of "customary experiences" articulated in the process of adapting ourselves to our immediate bodily environment, as being always something of a "misfit" for a reality so much richer than this extract which has been shaped from it under the pressure of urgent physical need. If we think along these lines, we may be led to expect that there will be occasions when the "misfit" will make itself specially manifest. There will be something catastrophic, violently irruptive, at moments of critical importance in the relation between the transcendent reality and its sensible temporal disguise, and at such times anticipations based on "customary experiences" will be liable to be suddenly

[1] This is, in fact, the way of conceiving the divine control of the course of nature which is adopted in Plato's reply to the deniers of providence and the moral government of the world in *Laws* x., and explains why the Platonist makes the recognisable order and "uniformity" of the celestial revolutions a principal argument for Theism.

[2] *Luke* xvii. 24.

and startlingly shattered. I cannot myself see that antecedently either of these ways of conceiving the relation of the two orders is more rational than the other. Such analogies as we can employ, and they are necessarily very imperfect analogies, are not wholly on either side. The nearest of such analogies, that based on the relations between purpose and routine in the life of an eminently wise and good man, for example, cuts both ways. Intellectual and moral dominance of one's environment and the material from which one has to fashion one's life is not the same thing as wild and unaccountable eccentricity. Neither the saint nor the genius is an "eccentric", and the man whose behaviour is one succession of astounding "adventures" does not rank high in the scale of either greatness or goodness. Most of the good man's life exhibits a routine of its own; he is, as we say, a man of "regular" habits, one on whom we can "count". And so also with the great man; in the main, his greatness is not shown by attempting things it would never have come into the head of another to imagine, but by doing the obvious things, the things another could not well avoid attempting in his place, but doing them in a perfect way. He does what a score of his inferiors may be trying to do; the difference between him and them is that they, not being masters of their opportunities, try and fail; he, being the master of his situation, does the thing he attempts, and does it lastingly. It is this, so largely sound, thought that is exaggerated into falsehood when genius is said to be "capacity for taking pains".

And yet the thought is not wholly sound. In a sense, indeed, the eminently good man does not "surprise" us; in a sense, we always can "count" on him. But this is only true in the sense that we can always count on him to act like a good man. It is not true that there is never anything surprising to us in his behaviour when he has to make a critical choice, or that we can always tell beforehand what he would do in a given emergency. We may be startled by the act, when it comes; it may be a reversal of all the expectations we had based on knowledge of the agent's "habits". It is *après coup*, when the choice has been made, that we discover its rightness and reasonableness. And, as I have long ago urged in another connection, the same is true of the man of genius. If, after study of some of Beethoven's symphonies or Napoleon's battles, we went on to make a study of a fresh symphony or battle, and found that it presented us with nothing we could not have anticipated on the basis of our previous study, I think this very absence of "surprises" would itself be felt in a rather painful surprise. It would be said that the master was "repeating himself", and there would be conjectures that, for some reason, he was "not quite himself" when he composed the music or fought the engagement. (In fact, Wellington, as quoted by the historians, seems to have been surprised that Napoleon had no surprises to spring at Waterloo. "Napoleon", he wrote, "did not manœuvre at all: He just moved forward in the old style, in columns, and was driven off in the old style." [1]) It is neither the absence of surprises, nor the perpetual recurrence of surprises of every conceivable sort, that reveals intelligence behind a career or a work of art; it is the presence of the right kind of surprise at the right place. There is a real element of the "irruptive" and incalculable about the relation of human purpose and intelligence to the "routine" of events, and by analogy, we might expect the divine purpose behind history, if it really exists, to display the same quality. If the course of events is indeed subdued to a supreme

[1] Quoted from York Powell and Tout, *History of England* (1900), p. 866.

divine purpose, it should neither be chaotic, nor yet a mere routine; it too, as a whole, should present shocks and surprises of the right kind, and in the right places.

It might further be urged, with some force, in favour of the view which is prepared to meet with the abrupt and irruptive invasion of the familiar order by the transcendent, that the expulsion of the element of surprise, marvel, and the wholly incalculable from nature and human life cannot be consistently carried out, except at a price which intellectual honesty itself forbids us to pay. However we may try to disguise the fact, the presence of something uncomfortably like "miracle" obstinately confronts us whenever we try to look at any section of the concrete becoming of things steadily, and this is no more than we may expect if we are careful to remember how much richer is the concrete reality than any of the systems of categories by which we try to stabilise it. This is the plain lesson of the now patent failure of the many and patient attempts to reduce physics to mere kinematics, biology to mere physics, psychology to mere biology, history to psychology. "Rationalisation" of this Cartesian kind is a stubborn attempt to get rid of the abrupt, startling, discontinuous, and an attempt which is being perpetually renewed, and always fails. To an intellect determined to work with the apparently transparent and self-justificatory concepts of pure kinematics, physical and chemical quality presents an intractable mystery: to one which confines itself to the concepts of physics and chemistry there is the same appearance of abruptness and sheer miracle about the entrance of organic life on the scene of becoming: the reality of consciousness is equally a pure "irrationality" to the mind resolved on explaining everything in terms of biological processes, and the reality of intelligent plan and purpose to one which will see in conduct nothing but the elaboration of highly complex patterns of sense-reflexes. The mind may, for a time, disguise the difficulty, after the fashion of the fabled ostrich, by simply pretending that what will not fit into its own picture of the world is not really there. Then one gets such doctrines as those of the "subjectivity" of sensible qualities, the purely "mechanical" character of vital processes, the epiphenomenalist version of the relation between body and mind. All these theories may now be said to have been fairly "tried out" over their respective fields and found incoherent, as, in fact, all are condemned in principle by the consideration that no feature of the historical world is really got rid of by the verbal trick of calling it an "illusion". When you have made all possible play with that disparaging "name", it still remains that what is there *is* there.

The recently prevalent fashion of talking freely about "emergent" evolution, as though the adjective could take the place of an explanatory theory, is a glaring illustration in point. The epithet is tantamount to an open confession that there is something really present in historical processes which ought not to be there if the substantive really means what it says. Something has "come out of" an alleged set of antecedent conditions which was never in the conditions, and therefore is not rationally accounted for by specifying them, though we are still to pretend, by the use of an adjective, that it has been accounted for.[1] In all such cases we have, in fact, been trying to exhaust the whole content of the individual and historical by analysing

[1] I need hardly say that I am not attacking the phrase "emergent evolution" as a useful *description* of certain historical processes; my comments only apply when the words are treated as conveying an *explanation*.

it without remainder into a combination of a few "universals", and so to reduce the unique and surprising to routine, and in all we have failed for the simple reason that the individual is not to be built up out of universals; being individual, it always contains the possibility of surprise for the abstractive understanding.

One might add that there appears to be a point at which the most resolute enemies of the "miraculous" are ready to abandon the undertaking of eliminating it. Even those who scruple most at admitting the occurrence of a physical "nature-miracle", an appearance of the wholly unforseeable and genuinely individual, in the course of strictly physical process, usually make no difficulty of the same kind about what we may call the human "nature-miracle" of genius, or the "miracle of grace". Yet when all is said, familiar routine is not more intrusively broken by the surprising events recorded, for example, in the Gospels than by the abrupt appearance of high poetical genius in the youthful Shelley with his antecedent record of commonplace ancestry and particularly worthless adolescent verses, or the youthful Keats, or, again, by the extraordinary reversals of character and habit, often instantaneous and singularly complete, illustrated by some of the "conversions" known to history. These are facts which the serious student of human life cannot deny or deprive of their individual and incalculable strangeness. And I would ask you to note that we cannot, without doing violence to historical testimony, confine these abrupt manifestations of an individuality not to be reduced to formula within a closed system of the psychical. For example, if there is any fact about the historical career of Christ which may be said to be thoroughly guaranteed by testimony beyond possibility of suspicion, it is the fact that he attracted attention on a large scale primarily as a worker of extraordinary acts of healing, and that his teaching was listened to on this ground. This is so manifest that hardly anyone who has seriously occupied himself with the records thinks of a simple denial of the fact, though there are numerous students who are willing to accept the record in so far as it concerns only such acts of healing as they personally think not *too* startling, and no further. We then disguise our real breach with the principle that the abrupt and intrusive is not to be reckoned with as fact by loose talk about the influence of the mind on bodily condition, conveniently forgetting that this very influence itself, as the history of psycho-physical hypotheses sufficiently shows, is just one of the outstanding "mysteries" which defy reduction to routine.

Partly, I suppose, this tendency to restrict the abrupt and really novel to the domain of mind is a mere survival of the obsolete prejudice that only the bodily is strictly real and historical, the mental being a superimposed "illusion"; partly, perhaps, it springs from the opposite equally unjustifiable prejudice that only the mental has any true individuality, whereas the physical may be treated as a mere complex of universals. But it should surely be plain that both prejudices are alike unreasonable. It is strictly absurd to treat the mental as "illusion", for the obvious Cartesian reason that illusion is only possible on the condition that there really are minds to be imposed upon; it is equally absurd to deny the individuality of non-mental things such as the Koh-i-nūr, or the planet Mercury. There are not really two water-tight compartments of the historical process, a "physical" sphere and a "mental" sphere; there is the one concrete given process with its mental and physical elements interrelated and interacting. Thus the attempt to make a clean cut between one sphere of the historical, in which room may be found for the abruptness and surprises of individuality, and a second sphere, where there is to be nothing but routine, capable in principle of complete reduction to general formula, is thoroughly arbitrary and indefensible. This means, I take it, that it is quite unjustifiable to approach the study of the actual historical process with the antecedent assumption that, however the supernatural may make its presence recognisable, it *cannot* take the form of sudden and startling intrusiveness into the course of physical happening, reversal of the routine of "customary experience"; whether it does, in fact, take this form can only be known from acquaintance with the course of the historical in its historical concreteness. It is wrong in principle to assert that testimony to the occurrence of alleged fact may ever be dismissed on the plea that the facts alleged are miraculous, after the fashion suggested by Hume in his curiously incoherent onslaught.[1] The mere consideration that a proposed interpretation of God's dealings with the world involves the recognition of the surprises we call miracles does not stamp that interpretation as unphilosophical.

To admit this is not to say that reality is ultimately irrational, nor to blink the fact that, on any theory, the great majority of narratives of alleged miracles are thoroughly untrustworthy. When we say that the world of the historical is rational and that its rationality is a postulate of sane philosophy, all that we have a right to mean is that this world has a definite pattern which connects its parts in a thoroughgoing unity. We have no right to say, in advance of historically-minded examination of detail, what that pattern is, nor pre-

[1] *Enquiry Concerning Human Understanding*, section x. For an examination of Hume's reasoning I may perhaps refer to my own brochure, *David Hume and the Miraculous* (Cambridge, 1927).

cisely how it dominates its constituent sub-patterns, nor to assume that our understanding of any of these sub-patterns and the mode of "ingression" of the dominant pattern into them is, or ever will be, complete and final. The proposition that the historical, that is, the actual, is rational, or intelligible, is, rightly conceived, an *imperative* of the *practical* reason. It is a command to ourselves never to stop short in the business of looking for a higher and more dominant pattern in the course of the historical than any we have yet found, not an assertion that the task has been achieved.[1] The world

[1] The perfect typical example of the process is the evaluation of a "surd" numerical value defined by a series. However far we go in the evaluation, we have never expressed the *exact* value of our "surd" (π or e or what not). But we can, in this ideal case, assign limits within which the error of our estimate falls, and by carrying the evaluation far enough we can make the interval between these limits as small as we please. In this case, of course, we do, in a way, know precisely what the "dominant pattern of the whole" is. Our "sub-patterns" are the successive approximations to the "value" of our "surd"; the dominant pattern is the, precisely-known, form of the series by which the "surd" which is its "limit" is defined; this is "ingredient in" the sub-patterns, because each departs from it by an excess or defect which the known form of the series enables us to restrict within a determined "standard". The formulae which we employ as our "laws" of physical process do not, of course, represent anything like so complete a "rationalisation" of the concrete observed facts.

For suppose, to take a very simple example, we wish to determine the fraction of its own length by which an iron rod expands when heated as a function of the increase of temperature. Our formula has, in the first instance, to be determined by measurements made when the rod has been heated to certain definitely known points, but it must also hold good when the increase of temperature is intermediate between two of those from which we start, or is less than the least or more than the greatest of them. Hence a formula which fits any series of observed results may be shown by further experimentation to demand modification if it is to fit "intermediate values" of our "independent variable", or values lying beyond either of the originally examined extremes. This is the problem of "interpolation" and "extrapolation". And, again, the general character of the formula itself is conditioned from the first by the consideration that the "law" to be discovered must be a series of a type which we can readily submit to mathematical operations (must be readily integrable); and, again, for practical reasons, must be such that a consideration of two or three initial terms of the infinite series will give a sufficiently close approximation to the "limit" of its sum. Thus, in the case just supposed, practical considerations lead us to *assume* that if x represent the fraction of its own length through which the rod expands when it receives the increment of temperature θ, the law connecting the two will be of the form $x = a\theta + b\theta^2 + c\theta^3 + \ldots$ where $a, b, c \ldots$ are arbitrary coefficients, which must now be chosen in such a way that, for all practical purposes, $a\theta + b\theta^2 + c\theta^3$ may be taken as a sufficiently exact equivalent for the value of the "sum to infinity" of the whole series. This explains why such laws are always open to revision as our knowledge of facts grows in a is there as a problem; we have to "rationalise" it, but in fact, we never succeed fully in carrying out the work and, for that reason, no science which is not avowedly one of pure abstractions can dispense with a sane empiricism in its methods.

To put the point in a terminology made familiar to us by Hume, our duty as thinkers is never to be satisfied with bare "conjunctions" between events, to insist on looking behind the conjunctions for necessary *connections*. When Hume declared that the *connections* are simply "feigned", that is to say invented, by the scientific man who is looking for them, and unconsciously imported into the objective world without any real warrant, he was—as he himself very well knew—denying the very possibility of science. If that is what is meant by one who says that "the understanding makes nature", that statement is simply false. But Hume would have been absolutely right if he had been content to say that, however far we carry our process of search, we never actually reach a stage at which we have converted conjunction into connection without remainder. There always are, and always will be, loose ends, "bare" conjunctions not understood, in all our actual natural knowledge, just because it all starts from and refers to the historical and individual, which analysis cannot exhaust. To say the same thing again in different language, it is never a *conclusive* argument against the reality of a *fact* to say that it cannot be harmonised with a known "law of nature", since the law, if asserted as having objective reference, only embodies our partial divination of a pattern which we never grasp in its concrete entirety. Though our formu-

---

way in which purely mathematical "approximations" to limiting values are not. (Throughout the whole of the present paragraph my indebtedness to the brilliant work of É. Meyerson, *L'Explication dans les sciences*, will be obvious.)

lated "laws" are never merely "subjective", yet, as the history of natural science proves only too abundantly, they always contain a subjective constituent which affects them to a not precisely definable extent. Hence the fact we find so stubbornly recalcitrant *may* provide the very suggestion we need for introducing an illuminating correction into our "law".

Again, and this has a special bearing on the anthropological argument of which we have been speaking, the reality of "miracles" as a feature of the historical process is not in any way disproved by the true contention that the vast majority of narratives of alleged miraculous events are untrustworthy. The same thing is equally true of the so-called "miracles of genius". The reality of genius is not disproved by the true observation that most of what, in any age, is acclaimed as the expression of genius is a very sorry imitation. To recur to our old illustration of the "surprises" of Shakespeare, it is no disparagement of their inevitableness and truth to life to say that what are intended by the inferior dramatist to be "strong" situations, or subtly divined characterisations, are mostly hollow, theatrical, and fantastic. The "Machiavellian" villain of the ordinary Elizabethan stage, a Barabas, a Bosola, a De Flores, may be unreal and mechanical enough; it does not follow that Iago is a mere puppet of the theatre. So, I think, we may say it is with the drama of the historical process. The play as we re-shape it in our own imagination may be as unlike the work of the divine artist as *The Spanish Tragedy*, or *The Unnatural Father*, is unlike *Hamlet*; it does not follow that the divine artist's play is without its astonishing incidents, and, if we may reverently call them so, its sensational situations.

It seems to me, then, that there is nothing inherently irrational or unworthy in the conception tha the relation between nature and supernature may b compatible with, or even require, that element of specia abrupt and intrusive surprise which we mean to in dicate when we speak of "miracles". To expect such surprises in the course of events is no proof of inferior to deny them no proof of superior, intelligence. It i therefore, so far as I can discern, no sufficient philo sophic objection to a positive religion that it involves the belief that such surprises have actually occurred or do still actually occur. The objection would only become valid if the *kind* of surprise asserted to occu were one which, if genuine, would involve a false con-ception of the divine nature itself. Indeed, for my own part, though I give this, of course, as a purely persona confession, I find a scheme which allows for the occur-rence of what is popularly called "miracle" apparently *more* reasonable than one which excludes it altogether. For since we cannot deny the presence in the historical world-process of the intrusive, abrupt, and discontinu-ous, in the form of what we call a "miracle" of genius, or a "moral" miracle, or a "miracle of grace", to con-fine it to these spheres seems to me to amount to one of those "bifurcations" which are in principle forbidden by the supreme postulate of a sound philosophy.

I venture, then, to make the following suggestions, in the hope of doing a little to diminish the mass of am-biguities and confusions which seem to beset current thinking on this issue of "miracles". (Beyond this initial work of clarifying the issues, I doubt whether philo-sophy, as such, can legitimately concern itself with the problem; I am sure it is idle to look to metaphysics either for proof that "miracles" occur, or for proof that they cannot.)

(*a*) In the first place, since the whole issue in dispute

is concerned with "nature-miracles", it is necessary to note that, when a natural event[1] is called a "miracle", two distinct assertions are being made about it. It is part of the understood meaning of the word that the event itself is in a high degree startling and unusual; it is a sequence of a kind not familiar in "customary experience", a breach of the normal routine. The miracle is a τέρας or *prodigium*, a *wonderful* event. If it were an event of a kind which we know to be common and frequent, it might still, like so many everyday events, baffle our powers of explanation, or even seem to be incompatible with recognised physical theories, but we should not on that account call it a miracle; we should only say that it presented a difficulty in the present condition of our scientific knowledge of nature. The most resolute enemy of the miraculous, if he is not a singularly ill-informed man, is aware that in all departments of science there are such stubborn facts, in apparent conflict with duly established "laws", but it never occurs to him to urge that we should extricate ourselves from the difficulties they present by a bold "denial of the fact". But, secondly, a miracle is also something more than a mere astonishing "freak" or "oddity", however extreme, in the course of events. It is also, in New Testament phrase, a σημεῖον or *sign*, an event which, in an exceptional way, reveals something of a transcendent purpose, assumed to underlie the whole course of history, but not usually transparently present.[2]

[1] By "natural" event I mean here, of course, simply an event belonging to the sensible order, whether it conforms to, or departs from, "customary routine".

[2] Cf. St. Thomas, *S.T.* ii.ª ii.ªᵉ q. 178, art. 1 ad tert. "in miraculis duo possunt attendi: unum quidem est id quod fit, quod quidem est aliquid excedens facultatem naturae, et secundum hoc miracula dicuntur *virtutes*. Aliud est id propter quod miracula fiunt, scilicet ad manifestandum aliquid supernaturale: et secundum hoc communiter dicuntur *signa*." As here given, the definition of *virtus* is obviously open to the criticism that we cannot say in advance of *any* event that it

To put the point in very simple language, a miracle is, in the first place, as I once heard an Anglican divine remark, "something which makes me say *Oh*!" To be sure, when one reflects, no event ever is completely explicable; there is always about every sequence of effect or cause something which we cannot reduce to "connection", but have to accept as bare given "conjunction". At bottom, then, there is something wonderful in all events; *omnia abeunt in mysterium*. But usually we are not alive to this; it is only the unfamiliar and exceptionally surprising which "makes us say *Oh*!" We may add that, in the customary use of the word, it seems further to be implied that a surprise which is called a miracle, except when the name is employed by a conscious *catachresis*, is always an event of the *sensible* order, something which gives a shock to our senses, a reversal of the "customary routine of our *perceptions*". There are many true propositions in the pure mathematics, and, again, in the accounts physicists give us of their imperceptibles, which cause an intellectual surprise when we first make their acquaintance, but we commonly do not speak of "miracle" in connection with them. Thus the Epicurean *clinamen* of the atom, or the sudden jump ascribed in Bohr's recently famous, but as I am given to understand, now antiquated theory, by an electron from one orbit and velocity to another, are as surprising as any ecclesiastical marvel, but they are not called miraculous, because, being imperceptible, they could administer no shock to our senses. Similarly, as I am informed—I can speak only at

excedit facultatem naturae, since we do not know what the *facultates naturae* may prove to be. In this same *quaestio* Thomas says that the frogs and serpents produced by the magicians of Pharaoh (*Exod*. vii. 12, viii. 7) were real frogs and serpents, but their production was not a true miracle, since it was due to "natural causes". One wonders how Pharaoh was expected to know that this was not the case with Aaron's serpent, or Moses' frogs.

second-hand—it has been questioned whether the transubstantiation of the sacramental elements in the Eucharist taught by the Roman Church can properly be called miraculous or not; those who deny that it can basing their denial on the fact that the "sensible accidents", shape, colour, taste, and the rest, undergo no change. And though we speak of miracles of intellect, or moral miracles, we are always conscious that, however permissibly, we are here extending the primary significance of a word, by metaphor, or analogy.

(*b*) But it is not every startling event of the sensible order that we call miraculous. The sudden occurrence of a gigantic earthquake would probably startle most of us much more than the quiet rising of a palsied man from his couch at the word of an apostle; yet we should certainly be at least disposed to regard the curing of the disease by a word as miraculous, and the earthquake, however startling, as a purely "natural occurrence". The miracle not merely makes us "say *Oh!*" it makes us aware of the immediate presence and operation of God. Hence the frequent appearance in theological definitions of the *differentia* that a miracle is an event in which the supreme cause acts directly, and not, as commonly, through second, or intermediate causes.[1]

(*c*) The two characteristics may consequently be disjoined. There are startling events which are not "signs", and, I take it, there are events which are "signs", but

[1] *E.g.* St. Thomas, *S.C.G.* iii. 101 "hoc sonat nomen miraculi, ut scilicet sit de se admiratione plenum, non quoad hunc vel quoad illum tantum. Causa autem simpliciter occulta omni homini est Deus. . . Illa igitur simpliciter miracula dicenda sunt quae divinitus fiunt praeter ordinem communiter servatum in rebus." Cf. *De potentia*, q. 6, art. 2 "illa quae sola virtute divina fiunt in rebus illis in quibus est naturalis ordo ad contrarium effectum, vel ad contrarium modum faciendi, dicuntur proprie miracula." *S.T.* i.ª q. 105, art. 7 resp. "miraculum autem dicitur quasi admiratione plenum, quod scilicet habet causam simplicem et omnibus occultam. Haec autem est Deus. Unde illa quae a Deo fiunt praeter causas nobis notas miracula dicuntur."

are not unique and startling enough to be spoken of as miracles. Thus, to recur to our example, a great earthquake would presumably not be called a miracle by a divine, even though he saw in it a "sign" of the Creator's power. The "proximate causes" of earthquakes are, in part at least, ascertainable, and this would probably be held to remove earthquakes from the class of the miraculous. For the same reason, if our scientific knowledge of nature should ever lead to such practical control of events that we succeeded in our laboratories in converting water into wine, or even in restoring the indubitably dead to life,[1] no one, I conceive, would speak of such achievements, effected by laboratory methods, as miracles. If we could effect them for ourselves, they would, when so brought about, cease to be signs of the immediate special presence of the divine; they would, in the supposed conditions, only be signs of our human mastery over nature. The "miracle" in the strict sense of the word, must combine the two characteristics of being a superhuman "wonder" and being a "sign".

(*d*) But the special interest of religion in the miraculous event is due wholly to its interpretation as a "sign" of the direct operation of God. If it were not such a sign, however astonishingly wonderful it might appear, the event would not have the special religious significance the theologian attributes to it. Hence, provided that this character is indubitably present, the element of mere surprise and unfamiliarity, though it must not be absent, may be reduced to a minimum. So we find St. Thomas, for example, arranging *miracula* in three classes, one of which includes such cases as

[1] If we should ever discover how to effect such results in the laboratory, we might still continue to regard their analogues in the Gospel narratives as "miraculous", but the "miracle" would then be taken to be constituted by the absence, in these instances, of the "laboratory process".

recovery *virtute divina* from an ordinary malady which might have been successfully treated by a physician,[1] and Dante even giving the name miracle to the legendary opportune cackling of the Capitoline geese when the Gauls were making their nocturnal assault.[2]

(*e*) It follows from the combination of the two characteristics that in dealing with the credibility of narratives of alleged miracles it is always necessary to distinguish between two questions which are too often confounded—the *quaestio facti*, whether the events narrated actually occurred as narrated, and the *quaestio iuris*,[3] as we may call it, whether, if they occurred, they have the religious significance of "miracle", whether they are *signs*. The opponents of the miraculous, I think, are specially prone to forget this distinction. What they really want to discredit is commonly the value of the alleged miracle as "evidence" of the truth of a certain religion. They wish to argue that the event is not to be rightly taken for a sign accrediting a given doctrine as a revelation from God, or a given person as a messenger of God. But they frequently assume that it is further necessary to their case to prove that the alleged event was not even a "portent"; that it either did not happen, or, if it did, was a commonplace event of a familiar kind. Their antagonists, again, are only

[1] *S.C.G. loc.cit.*"Summum gradum inter miracula tenent ea in quibus aliquid fit a Deo quod natura nunquam facere potest . . . secundum autem gradum in miraculis tenent illa in quibus Deus aliquid facit quod natura facere potest, sed non per illum ordinem . . . tertius autem gradus miraculorum est cum Deus facit quod consuetum est fieri operatione naturae, tamen absque naturae principiis operantibus." The examples given of (1) are occupation of the same place by two bodies at once, the standing still or going back of the sun, the opening of the sea to provide a passage; of (2) the restoration of the dead to life, of the blind to sight, of the halt to the use of their feet; of (3) the healing of a naturally curable "fever", or the production of rain *virtute divina*. Cf. the shorter statement, *S.T.* i.ª q. 105, art. 8 resp.

[2] *Monarchia*, ii. 4.

[3] More accurately, we might borrow a distinction from the technical language of ancient rhetoric and distinguish between the question of the *quid* and that of the *quale*.

too prone to suppose that they need only establish the fact that the surprising event occurred to put its "evidential" character as a sign beyond all question. It is this standing confusion of two distinct issues which gives most of the literature of the controversy about miracles its unsatisfying and unedifying character. To me it seems clear that the fullest vindication of marvellous narratives as accounts of facts which have actually happened would leave the question whether the facts have the quality which makes them of moment for religion still undecided, in point of rigorous logic.

Thus, to take the most crucial example which presents itself, I can conceive it possible, though not probable, that it might be established beyond all reasonable possibility of doubt that Our Lord actually died, was actually buried, and actually seen alive again "on the third day". But to establish these facts, I should say, would not bring one any nearer proving the reality of what Christians mean by the "miracle" of the Resurrection. It would still be possible for men satisfied of the facts to dispute their significance. There would be no formal absurdity in the position—I do not say that it is one ever likely to be widely adopted—that it has been proved by a well-certified historical instance that, under conditions not yet accurately ascertained and perhaps not accurately ascertainable, the transition of a human organism from life to death is reversible, and yet to deny that this is anything more than a curious and puzzling scientific fact; to deny, that is, that its occurrence is any reason for believing that the person to whom it happened was one standing in any unique relation to God, or having any special significance for the history of humanity. Presumably this was the actual position of Seeley, who appears to have regarded the fact as historically certain, and also to have definitely rejected the Christian conception of the relation of man to God.[1]

For my own part, I do not see how anyone who had once taken up such a position could be driven from it by argumentation. You might, I take it, establish the historical character of the most unprecedented events, provided only that the testimony to them were sufficiently good. Hume's attempt[2] to draw a distinction between two different classes of events, both equally at variance with "customary experience", but of which one type may be accepted if there is sufficient testimony, while the other ought to be rejected without so much as a scrutiny of the testimony, appears to me, as I suspect it must have done to Hume himself, arbitrary and logically worthless. But when the fact has been established, when, if ever, for example, the resurrection of Christ has been made "as certain as the assassination of Julius Caesar", the question of our right to interpret the fact as Christianity interprets it still remains an open one, and cannot be closed by any appeal to "testimony". To compare the two questions is like comparing the question of the authorship of a given work with that of its scientific or literary worth. Thus, whenever some startling and arresting event is accepted not merely as a singular event, but as a miracle with a significance for religion, as disclosing the divine character or purpose, one is, I should say, in the presence of an act of "faith". This particular act of faith would cease to be possible if the believer were to be

[1] Cf. Bevan, *Hellenism and Christianity*, p. 234 (commenting on Seeley's words in *Ecce Homo*, c. 2, "the evidence by which these facts are supported cannot be tolerably accounted for by any hypothesis except that of their being true").

[2] *Enquiry Concerning Human Understanding*, x. pt. 2, pp. 127-8 (ed. Selby-Bigge).

convinced that the alleged fact had never occurred, but the completest *probatio facti* would not compel the further act of faith in its significance, as demonstration compels assent to its conclusions when you have assented to its premisses. The act of "faith" which converts mere belief in a *marvel* into belief in a *miracle* is, in its very nature, one of *free*, not constrained, assent.[1]

Thus belief in a miracle, like belief in God itself where it is genuinely religious belief, always involves free assent to something which cannot be proved; as the scholastic theologians rightly held, it involves a specific attitude of *will*,[2] and is thus a reaction not merely of the "intellect", but of a man's whole personality to influences from without. This is why the scholastics regard it as "meritorious", and why we are bound to recognise that a man's *faith*, what he *believes*, unlike his "opinions", makes a profound difference to his character. From a psychological point of view we may say of any act of assent of this kind that in the recognition of an event as a "sign" we have an immediate divination, comparable not so much with the drawing of an inference from premisses in which the conclusion is already fully implicit, as with our direct recognition of beauty, or aesthetic significance, in a product of nature or art, and our direct recognition of rightness, or moral significance, in a human act.

(*f*) These reflections suggest to me a further question which is not, so far as I know, often raised. Is there any meaning in speaking of an alleged event as simply, or

[1] Assent to a demonstrated conclusion is certainly a determination of the will, as Descartes, in adherence to the scholastic tradition, maintained in the fourth *Meditation*, but there is no freedom about it. Free assent is always assent to what has not been completely proved.

[2] *E.g.* St. Thomas, *S. T.* ii.ª ii.ªᵉ q. 4, art. 1 resp. "actus autem fidei et credere . . . qui actus est intellectus determinati ad unum ex imperio voluntatis. Sic ergo actus fidei habet ordinem et ad objectum voluntatis, quod est bonum et finis, et ad objectum intellectus, quod est verum."

absolutely, miraculous?[1] Is not "miraculous" a *relative* term, like "probable"? (It is only by a pardonable inaccuracy that we allow ourselves to talk of estimating *the* probability of a given event, as though the same event could only have one probability.) What we actually estimate is always probability *relative* to some set of data which constitute our assumed frame of reference.[2] ("The probability of x", like log x, is a many-valued function of x, though in both cases, for practical purposes, we may confine our attention to one specially important value; as for these purposes we take no notice of the infinitely numerous "complex values" of log x, so in dealing with the "probability of x" we take no account of its probability relative to "freak" sets of data.) I mean that if it is part of what we understand by a miraculous event that it is one which astounds and perplexes, it would seem that we cannot properly call any event miraculous without a reference to the mental habits and expectations of an experient of the event, as a frame of reference. Thus it might be quite reasonable to say that events rightly called miracles by one age may be rightly regarded as non-miraculous in another age which has grasped more of the general pattern of natural process, or that to an intelligence with a grasp of that pattern transcending the human, for example to an angel, as conceived in the scholastic philosophies, much that will always astound, and so be rightly called miraculous, *quoad nos homines*, might very possibly appear to be "just what might be expected", and therefore *not* miracu-

[1] In the passages already quoted from St. Thomas it will be seen that a genuine miracle is discriminated from events which are only *mira* to some men (*e.g.* to the unlearned, or the rustic); the *miraculum* must be *mirum* OMNI *homini*. But this leaves it still a question whether what is *mirum omni* HOMINI need be *mirum* to a higher "angelic" intelligence or not, as will be remarked below.

[2] Cf. J. M. Keynes, *Treatise on Probability*, pp. 6-7.

lous. In the same way, if we allow the existence of a whole hierarchy of intelligences, what would be miraculous to an angel of lower rank might be non-miraculous to one of higher, though it would still remain the case, seeing that complete knowledge of God *per essentiam suam* can only be possessed by God Himself, that there are works of God which are profoundly astounding, and therefore miraculous, for the highest of created intelligences. If this is so, we might still agree with men of an age and society less familiar than our own with the regular natural order that certain events which they called miraculous really happened, and really were "signs" of the power, the justice, or the mercy of God, as they had rightly discerned; but to us these events have become "natural" signs, part of the *cursus ordinarius*.

It is true that such a view would be inconsistent with the traditional hard-and-fast distinction between events traceable to God as working through the instrumentality of "second causes", and events for which there is no second cause, *res immediate a Deo productae*; but it seems in any case impossible to attach much real value to this traditional distinction. It could never be safely used as a *criterion*, for the simple reason that we could never "constate" the absence of a second cause in a given case.[1] At the most we could only say that the "second" cause, or causes, of the event cannot be discovered in the present state of our general knowledge.

[1] Thus on a previous page we have seen St. Thomas pronouncing that the restoration of sight to the blind is entirely beyond the power of the system of "second causes" we call nature. It is most improbable that St. Thomas would be confident on the point if he were living in our own day. According to Leibniz there is a mechanism of "second causes" everywhere; the miracles of the faith have their "second causes" which go back to the creation, when the system of nature was constructed expressly to produce these unique events at just the moments when they were called for by the divine purpose. Whatever we may think of this view, I do not see that it in any way hazards the interests of religious faith. (*Théodicée*, pt. i. § 54).

The thought presumably at the bottom of the distinction seems to me to be obscured by the scholastic expression of it. What is really meant, I suppose, is that the ultimate reason why the event which is said to have God for its immediate cause happens is that just it, and nothing else, is demanded at just this juncture by the purpose of God in His dealings with His creature, man. If anything else happened at this juncture, the "counsel of God" would be brought to nothing. God, so to say, has no alternative course of action open to Him, if His end is not to be frustrated. Consequently, so long as we leave this necessity for the realisation of a divine purpose out of account, it is useless to try to discover antecedent conditions for the event which would permit us to say "whenever these conditions are fulfilled, this kind of event must follow." For the one supremely relevant consideration, the necessitation of the event in view of a divine purpose, belongs to the order of finality, and can never figure among constateable "antecedent conditions". (Just so when the poet

> takes his pen and writes
> The inevitable word.

What makes the word inevitable is its unique aesthetic fitness for its present context; this is seen by the "amazed" poet in a moment of inspiration. It would be idle to find the explanation of the inevitableness anywhere else, *e.g.* in the "laws of the association of ideas".[1]) The thought, as I say, seems to me a perfectly sound one, but the expression given to it is unfortunate, since it suggests the possibility of deciding whether an event is a "divine miracle" by *first* ascertaining that it has no "natural cause".

To put the whole matter once more in yet another

[1] Cf. Stout, *Analytic Psychology*, bk. ii. c. 6, § 4.

way, a miracle, if there is such a thing, is an event which is recognised as having what Otto has taught us to call a *numinous* character. No amount of criticism however justified in other respects, will really seriously shake Otto's central position that it is this immediate recognition of the numinous, the wholly other and transcendent, in persons, things, events, which is at the root of worship, and so of religion. It does not follow that there is no such thing as misrecognition of the numinous. It may be wrongly taken to be where it is not, exactly as beauty, moral goodness, or professed truth have been, and often are, supposed to be where they are not. It is *conceivable* that the majority of the objects men suppose to be beautiful are not beautiful; that most of the acts human societies have thought morally noble have only been thought so because our current moral notions are perverted by false sentimentalism, that most of the statements which have been acclaimed as profound truths are only plausible errors; it is *certain* that spurious beauty, sham virtue, flashy half-truths do often impose on mankind. But just as the fact that bad pictures and bad music are often admired, and spurious heroism often belauded, is no proof that there is no true beauty or moral heroism, so the aberrations of silly, lewd, or cruel worships are no proof that there are not events, things, persons, really endued with the numinous quality. If there are, then we may expect the task of distinguishing the true numinous from the counterfeit, or the more fully from the imperfectly numinous, to prove at least as difficult as that of discriminating true beauty from false. The education of mankind in recognition of the numinous should, by all analogy, be as slow and hard a business as their training in the discernment of beauty, and we might anticipate that, in both cases, the training would only advance *pari passu* with, and in close dependence on, the general mental development of man. The unity of human personality does not, indeed, guarantee that there shall be any precise correspondence between intellectual, moral, and aesthetic accomplishment. The age which is most sensitively responsive to beauty is not necessarily also that which is most eminent in the sciences, or most distinguished by lofty moral practice. But it is at least true that intellectual and moral childishness, or deep-rooted perversity, is commonly reflected also in the aesthetic life of a people, or an age. The art of a savage group may be in advance of its morality, or what we may, by courtesy, call its science, but, for all that, it remains the art of savages, childish, crude, or grotesque. And the same thing is true of the savages' worship and religion, and it is a part of Otto's own theory that this is so, though his more unfriendly critics seem to forget the point.

This is all that I have to say in principle on the philosophical issues raised by the miraculous. I do not pretend that the recognition of possibilities of the abrupt, invasive manifestation of the supernatural in special events of the natural order has no disturbing consequences. Any view of the relation between the eternal and the temporal which finds room for the miraculous must be disturbing to our *penchant* for what W. James used to call a neat and tidy universe. If there are such things as miraculous events, the actual historical order must be less visibly orderly, less regimented, I might say, than we like to suppose it. A world where such things happen, however rarely, must be one which is "uncanny", a place where we are not, and cannot be, quite at home. And we all tend to resent the uneasy suspicion that we are not wholly at home with our surroundings, and so cannot implicitly count on them, for the same reason that we should dislike to be living where an earthquake may at any moment shake the solid foundations of our houses. Also, of course, on such a view of the world, the ascertainment of historical truth becomes harder, the very unfamiliar cannot simply be brushed aside, with the ease permitted by a philosophy which refuses to have anything to do with real "breaches in the customary routine of experience". If there are miracles, the task of distinguishing the true from the false is likely to be hard. Hence one can readily understand why the philosopher, more than most men, should have a special bias against miracle, because he feels more acutely than others the need for a coherent representation of the world.

Yet, as has been already said, it is at least certain that whatever the central purpose which makes the historical into a unity may be, it is not the purpose of gratifying our natural indolence by making thinking easy. Even apart from miracles, the historical world as we know it is disconcerting, untidy, and, on a surface view, wildly disorderly, and the advance of science has, in fact, only increased the appearance of disorder. How much more disorderly and untidy, on a first view, is our present astronomical scheme than the system of Eudoxus with its twenty-five or twenty-six concentric rotations and their absolutely uniform velocities; or, again, our present perplexed attempts to construct an intelligible account of the behaviour of the electron than the truly childish simplicity of the Epicurean scheme of atoms falling—apart from the rare moments of παρέγκλισις—steadily in a single direction with a single constant velocity. And the world of human life and human relations, again! Does a week pass without something to remind us that its safe and settled ways and regular habits, even in the societies where these things count for most, are very much on the surface? In dealing with one's fellows, one never knows when the ground may not fail under one's feet and reveal the crude, violent, and bloody reality of elemental human passions. We who have seen the thing happen to the human race at large during the past fifteen years must surely be aware that it may happen to our little personal "world" any day. Real life is eminently disorderly and dangerous, with a disorder which is not sensibly increased by the admission of an occasional "miracle" into the pattern, and it would not be surprising if the old-fashioned "rationalist's" vision of the physical order as one where "miracles do not happen" is as wide of the mark as the "Sunday-school-book" vision of the moral world as a realm in which there are no worse crimes than an occasional over-indulgence in liquor, or a stray act of poaching. If rationality really meant, as it is sometimes mistakenly supposed to mean, monotony, it would be true to say that every step taken towards fuller comprehension of the historical structure of the world is a step away from rationality. Thus the mere consideration that to let the miraculous into the course of events makes their pattern less easy to pack into a formula affords no ground for regarding the miraculous as irrational in any sense in which the irrational must be disavowed by a sane philosophy.

Indeed, the very notion of miracle should be possible only to a conscious or unconscious rationalist. If there were really no connection, no unity of plan, in the march of events, it would be meaningless to distinguish between what is miraculous and what is not. In a world where all that happens happens without plan and purpose, any event would be just as much or as little miraculous as any other; there would be no basis for the distinction between what may reasonably be expected and what may not. Were the world what Hume professed to think it when he said that events are "conjoined but never connected", we could, of course, note the fact that some sequences occur frequently, others rarely, and, if we only allowed ourselves to forget that the observer's mind is assumed to be part of the world to which this dictum applies, we could go on, with Hume, to offer a psychological *explanation* of the fact that men expect the course of events to run on familiar lines and are incredulous of the wholly unfamiliar. But we could do nothing to *justify* this habit of expecting the familiar, give no reason for thinking that it yields more "intelligent" anticipations of the course of events than expectation of the most fantastic occurrences. This seems to be the explanation of the apparently perverse conclusion of Hume's famous essay on *Miracles*,[1] where a page devoted to the suggestion that Christianity requires us to accept stories which are on a par in improbability with the fairy tales of the nursery is followed by the declaration that there is nothing in what has been said to disturb the orthodox theologian; it is true that he believes what is irrational; but why should he not, seeing that he is conscious of a standing miracle in himself? His assent to the unfamiliar is itself as much a miracle as any of the events narrated in the scriptures to which he assents; thus he actually has in his own personal experience the certainty that miracles do occur.

If we leave out of account the touch of satire in this language, we see at once that the conclusion drawn is no more than must necessarily follow from the principles Hume adopts as the basis of his own professed theory of the world. If it is true, as Hume maintains, that there is no intrinsic reason why any one event may

[1] *Enquiry Concerning Human Understanding*, sect. x.

not be followed by another, it is also true that there is no reason why our expectation that an event of given kind will be followed by the kind of event with which it has been "customarily" conjoined in the past should not be disappointed at any moment. Our psychologically explicable prejudice in favour of the customary is no guide to the real pattern of the historical process. Hence the fact that a single miracle has been believed in by anyone *proves* that "customary experience", though a common source, is not the only source of conviction, and proves nothing further as to the wisdom or unwisdom of holding convictions due to some different causes. There are persons, as is proved by the mere existence of Hume's more orthodox friends and antagonists, who in fact hold, and hold with strong conviction, some beliefs which are not due to customary experience. That they actually hold these beliefs is that consciousness of a miracle within themselves of which Hume speaks. On the question of the truth or falsehood, reasonableness or unreasonableness, of these beliefs the argument has no bearing; that question cannot even be asked without absurdity by an irrationalist who regards belief itself as nothing more than an unaccountable "propensity" to view things in a certain light.[1] The ordinary divine and the ordinary "free-thinker" can only discuss the question and disagree in their answer to it, because both, whether they know it or not, mean to be rationalists in their metaphysics. Both hold, or should hold, that there is a real, objective, coherent pattern in the historical course of events; their dis-

[1] Strictly speaking, the only conclusion to which Hume is entitled by the argumentation of part i. of his essay, where "customary experience is treated as the *only* cause of belief, would be that no one ever *has* believed in a miracle, since there has been *no* "custom" to cause the belief. But this conclusion is so glaringly false that, to avoid it, he has to correct his original assumption into the form that customary experience is only the most usual cause of belief.

agreement is only about the precise character of the pattern.

It is even more clear that the specifically religious question about startling events, whether they are "signs", is only in place if we accept a rationalist metaphysic. On genuinely irrationalist principles, as I said, we could distinguish between rare and frequent sequences, and take note that some suggested sequences are not known ever to have occurred, though we should have no right to say that a rare, or even an unprecedented, sequence is less likely to occur at any moment than any other. But if the unprecedented sequence presented itself, we could not ask whether it might not be a "sign", a significant clue to the ultimate pattern underlying all events, since the whole point of metaphysical irrationalism is that there *is* no such pattern. Events awaken various mental expectations in us, and what expectations they will awaken depends on our personal history, but no event is a "sign" of anything, for the reason that all events are merely loose and separate; "all our distinct perceptions are distinct existences", and "the mind never perceives any real connection among distinct existences".[1]

(*g*) It is further in this double character of the miracles of the great religions that we may perhaps find the possibility of an answer to the "anthropological" difficulty. The kind of "miracle" which is only too common in the folk-lore studied by the anthropologist is one which is merely a portent without being a sign, a surprise, but an insignificant surprise. There is a real and relevant difference between such mere surprises and surprises which, if they are real, are significant disclosures of a self-coherent supernatural source of the temporal process. There is accordingly rational justifi-

[1] Hume, *Treatise of Human Nature*, Appendix (Selby-Bigge, p. 636).

cation for the refusal to treat surprises of such different kinds as though they stood on the same level of rationality. If eminent anthropologists of the type of Sir James Frazer are curiously blind, as I think they sometimes are, to the relevance of the distinction, the reason of their blindness is presumably that they start with the uncriticised assumption of a sheer metaphysical irrationalism. They are at heart persuaded that history has *no* meaning. Discussion of the miraculous, or of any other subsidiary issue, is mere waste of time, unless the parties to it are antecedently agreed on this most fundamental of all metaphysical issues, the question whether "becoming", the course of history as a whole, has a meaning or has none, or, in plainer words, whether God exists or does not exist.

However we answer that question we shall, of course, have to admit that, in view of the limitations consequent on our situation, that of beings who only become very gradually aware of a small part of the indefinitely extended historical process of becoming, we must expect violent surprises, events which upset all calculations built on *our* customary experience, to present themselves from time to time. But acceptance or rejection of belief in God, and, for the matter of that, acceptance or rejection of the specific conception of God conveyed by a great positive religion, will necessarily affect our view as to the character of the surprises which may reasonably be expected, and their distribution through space and time. As I have put the point elsewhere, "in an atheistic or neutral metaphysical scheme there would be no reason to expect the surprises to wear any special character, or to be distributed in any special way over space and time. We should expect them to make their appearance as simple *freaks*. If our philosophical world-scheme is definitely theistic, the case is altered completely. For we shall then conceive of the pattern of events not merely as providing a connection between them, but as providing a connection which is intelligible, in the sense that, like the structure of a symphony, or a well-lived life, it exhibits the realisation of an end of absolute value. We should thus antecedently look for the 'irregularities' in nature and history to exhibit a special kind of concentration, exactly as the surprises in the construction of a great piece of music, or the conduct of a life of wise originality, exhibit the same concentration. . . . Thus the difference in ultimate metaphysical outlook between a theist and a non-theistic philosopher would make a difference between the two sets of initial premisses relatively to which each estimates the probability of certain events. It is not unreasonable in a convinced theist to be satisfied with evidence for the resurrection of Jesus Christ which would not satisfy him of the resurrection of a next-door neighbour, since he may well ascribe to the resurrection of Christ a unique spiritual value . . . which he could not ascribe to the resurrection of his neighbour."[1]

It may be said, I fear, that there is, in the words just quoted, a confusion of two distinct problems which have no bearing on one another—the problem of fact and the problem of value—that the "spiritual value" attaching to an alleged event, supposing it actually to have occurred, has nothing to do with the reasonableness of judging it to have occurred; *that* is dependent solely on the amount and quality of the available "testimony". But I would rejoin that, so far as I can see, though the probiems are distinguishable, they are not discon-

[1] *David Hume and the Miraculous*, pp. 46-8. Of course I am assuming that the theist spoken of does not base his theism itself upon belief in the fact of Our Lord's resurrection, since his reasoning would then be circular.

nected; the question of value has a real bearing on the question of fact. We all recognise this in practice, when, for example, we take into account what we call "evidence to character". We do regard evidence of facts which would be treated as altogether insufficient to convict one man of a charge—*e.g.* of "loitering with intent"—as ample in the case of another. If I am a "suspicious character", I am reasonably regarded as not having cleared myself of an allegation by evidence which would be more than enough to clear the man who is "above suspicion". Of course, though the principle is sound, there is always a good deal of danger in the application of it, and in human society, which, being human, is never quite free from snobbery, it often works out cruelly or absurdly, but I do not see that this affects its soundness as a principle. As such it is just a form of the refusal which, as I hold, sound metaphysics must make, to divorce reality from value. In the last resort, I should say, the *raison d'être* of any fact must be a "value".

However that may be, I would at least end this discussion by repeating once more that the credibility of miracles, in the theological sense of the term, can never be regarded as independent of the central issue of all religion, the reality of God. For the frame of reference by which an intelligent man estimates credibilities will itself be different according as he believes in God or disbelieves. For that very reason it seems to me impossible to appeal, as some of the old-fashioned apologists for Christianity used to do, but as philosophers of the calibre of St. Thomas were careful not to do, to the assumed actuality of miracles as a ground for the belief in God itself. Except as interpreted in the light of antecedent belief in God, no marvel, however stupendous, however well authenticated, and however marked its results on the life of mankind, would be more than a rare and curious fact. As Francis Bacon said long ago, no miracle was ever wrought to convince an atheist.[1] If a man does not see God in the *cursus ordinarius* of nature and human life, "neither will he believe, though one rose from the dead". Or at least, we should perhaps say, he may in fact be converted by the rising of one from the dead, but he will owe the fact of that conversion to the weakness of his logic; his conversion will prove that, whatever his good points, he is no *esprit juste*.

[1] *Advancement of Learning*, bk. ii. (E. and S. iii. 345): "There was never miracle wrought by God to convert an atheist, because the light of nature might have led him to confess a God: but miracles have been wrought to convert idolaters and the superstitious, because no light of nature extendeth to declare the will and true worship of God".

V

THE MEANING AND PLACE OF AUTHORITY

> A prophet? Prophet wherefore he
> Of all in Israel('s ?) tribes?
> *He teacheth with authority,*
> *And not as do the Scribes.*—CLOUGH.

> Nulli ergo dubium est gemino pondere nos impelli ad discendum, auctoritatis atque rationis. Mihi autem certum est nusquam prorsus a Christi auctoritate discedere: non enim reperio valentiorem.—AUGUSTINE.

I CAN readily believe that an auditor of our foregoing discussions might be willing to allow the force of all we have said, and yet might contend, with a great show of reason, that we have carefully avoided facing the real problem. In the last resort, he might argue, there is an inevitable and ineradicable opposition between the very spirit of rational philosophy and the spirit common to all positive and revelational religions: philosophy is committed to the principle of "private judgement"; it is a state and habit of mind rather than a set of dogmas; it has no value unless it is the fruit of a free personal effort to understand, and it is even more important for the philosopher that his convictions should have been reached by such strenuous personal effort than that they should be true. But all the positive religions, avowedly or implicitly, are no less deeply committed to the recognition of an absolute authority before which private judgement may properly be bidden to submit itself without reserve. In a word, philosophy is, in its very nature, "Protestant", positive religion "Catholic";

the one would have us hold our convictions because we are personally persuaded of their truth, the other because of the *auctoritas*, or dignity, of the source from which we have learned them, and no man can loyally adopt both these attitudes at once. I have heard an amusing anecdote, true or false, which puts this point very neatly. It relates that a Roman Catholic theologian was in conversation with an outsider, who remarked that there seemed to be no real difference between the position of Rome and that of a well-known and widely respected "Anglo-Catholic". "Pardon me", replied the theologian, "we are at the opposite pole from *X*. He holds every doctrine that we hold, but holds them all for the entirely irrelevant reason that he thinks them true." You see at once the point of this epigrammatic criticism. By the critic's own admission, what *X* holds in theology is the truth, and the whole truth, so far as the whole truth is accessible to man; the trouble is that *X* takes it to be the truth for a wrong reason. He should take it for truth because it comes to him on the authority of the Church, but in fact only takes it as true because it commends itself to his personal judgement, and is thus, formally, though not materially, a "Protestant heretic". If a particular dogma happened not to recommend itself to his personal judgement, he would not assent to it, whereas he ought, in fact, to believe the dogma without so much as raising the question whether it approves itself to his judgement or not, on the sole ground that God, speaking through the officials of the Church, has declared it; when God speaks, we believe, not because what God says can be seen or shown to be correct, but because the speaker is God.

Though the Roman Church has given this conception of authority as the one real and sufficient basis of faith in "revealed truth" its most elaborate expression, the position is not, of course, peculiar to that Church; indeed, it may fairly be argued that it is common in principle to all the positive religions. One may reject the authority of the Church in favour of that of an infallible written Scripture, as the original Reformers did, or one may reject the authority of the body of Scripture as a whole, as some of the successors of the Reformers do, in favour of that of those utterances which, as it is held, can safely be taken to have come from the actual lips of the supreme revealer of God, the authenticated sayings of Christ, relieved of everything which can plausibly be regarded as later exegesis or amplification. But differences of this kind are only secondary disagreements about the precise channel through which infallible authority speaks; they do not affect the principle that there is somewhere an authority which is that of God Himself, and that when this authority has spoken, the question whether its deliverances recommend themselves to a man's personal judgement becomes irrelevant. If God has never spoken in this way, is there not an end of all the claims of any positive religion on the universal allegiance of mankind? If He has so spoken, *causa finita est*. The *foi du charbonnier* would thus appear to be an indispensable constituent in every positive religion.

But, it may be said, the one thing which a rational philosophy cannot tolerate on any terms is just this *foi du charbonnier*. For, as Ferrier has maintained,[1] it is even more important that a philosophy should be reasoned than that it should be true. That a man, in that resolute effort to think things out which is philosophy, should come to erroneous conclusions is a com-

[1] *Institutes of Metaphysics*, p. 2: "Philosophy, therefore, in its ideal perfection, is a body of reasoned truth . . . it is more proper that philosophy should be reasoned than that it should be true; because, while truth may perhaps be unattainable by man, to reason is certainly his province, and within his power".

paratively trivial matter. If his conclusions are erroneous, the patient following of the method of "thinking things out" will of itself, in time, lead to their correction; patient thinking can always be trusted, in the end, to repair its own mistakes. But if we once allow an assent which is more than consciously tentative and provisional to be given to that which has not been thought out by a personal effort, but taken on trust without question or criticism—and this is the kind of assent a positive religion necessarily demands when its God has spoken—the central conviction which lies at the heart of all rational philosophy—the conviction that reality has a structure which is intelligible—has been surrendered. We may call such dutiful submission to authority asserted to be divine assent to the declaration of the supreme source of truth, but it is, in plain fact, no more than a "strong propension" to view things in a certain light, dignified by a name to which it has no right.

The point, it may be said, is made abundantly clear by the history of apologetics. The philosophically minded apologist may start, like Anselm, with unbounded belief in the possibility of justifying his faith at the bar of intellect by showing that when you "think things out" you are always led to the very convictions you had begun by taking on trust. But even Anselm, when he speaks of *fides quaerens intellectum*, does not mean, as the modern Agnostic does when he takes as his motto "*we seek for truth*", that the search is begun in the dark. It never occurs to him to doubt the indispensability of beginning with absolute and unqualified assent to the whole received content of *fides*, or to suspect that the thinking out of things might possibly lead to substantive modification of the "deposit" of faith. It is *itself*, not the "manifold of science", or the "great mystery" that his *fides* is seeking to understand. If he had found himself completely unable to urge anything in answer to Gaunilo's apology for the "fool" who says in his heart that there is no God, his faith in the Christian creed would no more have wavered than Gaunilo's own wavered when he constructed his pamphlet. At bottom Anselm's conviction that he is already in possession of a truth which merely needs to be cast into a logically articulated form to become evident amounts to an assumption that metaphysics is, to parody a *mot* of Bradley, "the finding of *good* reasons for what we believe on instinct".[1] But, we may ask, is not that which we "believe on instinct" usually any set of ideas, true or false, which has the advantage of being deeply interwoven with the whole social fabric of our particular place and time? *Fides quaerens intellectum* will be led to a Western Christianity in the atmosphere of eleventh-century Paris or Canterbury, to Islam at the court of Bagdad or Cordova.

Nor is the case visibly mended much by drawing a distinction between natural theology, that part of the contents of a positive creed for which we can succeed in finding good and sufficient probative grounds, and the revealed truths for which the most close and patient thought can do no more than to show that the reasons urged against them are inconclusive, and where, therefore, the last word must be with authority. St. Thomas' words, indeed, read well: "To argue from authority is supremely proper to this study, because the principles of the study are had from revelation, and it is therefore right that there should be belief in the authority of those to whom the revelation has been made. Nor does

[1] The word "instinct", indeed, is perhaps not the best that could be chosen to convey Anselm's thought. But neither does it really convey Bradley's meaning.

this derogate from the dignity of this study; for though the appeal to authority founded upon human reason is exceeding weak, the appeal to authority founded upon divine revelation is exceeding efficacious."[1] This may be true enough, but you have first to identify your divine revelation before you make your appeal to its authoritativeness, and thus there would seem to be only two alternatives, either to take as the accredited divine revelation whatever happens to enjoy the prestige of a revelation in your own community, or else to judge of the credentials of professed revelations by the exercise of your own intelligence, though when once the credentials have been found satisfactory, you propose for the future to ascribe your assent to reverence for divine authority.

In either case, it might be said, the whole of your faith really rests in the end on the *locus ab auctoritate quae fundatur super humana ratione*, which is *infirmissimus*. If it is a poor reason for accepting a revelation as truly divine that it seems to be so "to the best of my personal knowledge and belief", it is a worse reason still that *on dit* "this is a divine revelation". "And so", to borrow the words of Hobbes, "we are reduced to the Independency of the Primitive Christians, to follow Paul, or Cephas, or Apollos, every man as he liketh best . . . because it is unreasonable in them who teach that there is such danger in every little Errour, to require of a man endued with Reason of his own, to follow the Reason of any other man, or of the most voices of many other men; which is little better

[1] *S.T.* i.ª q. 1, art 8 ad sec. "argumentum ex auctoritate est maxime proprium huius doctrinae, eo quod principia huius doctrinae per revelationem habentur. Et sic oportet quod credatur auctoritati eorum quibus revelatio facta est. Nec hoc derogat dignitati huius doctrinae: nam licet locus ab auctoritate quae fundatur super ratione humana sit infirmissimus, locus tamen ab auctoritate quae fundatur super revelatione divina est efficacissimus."

than to venture his Salvation at crosse and pile."[1] The only divine authority left with a right to demand absolute submission thus proves, after all, to be the authority of the "God within", the reason and conscience of the individual. But the cause of a positive religion seems to be inseparably bound up with the recognition of a supra-individual supreme authority, that of a "God without", by which the aberrations of individual judgement may be magisterially corrected and controlled. If we are in earnest with the demand that each man shall be left to follow "Paul, or Cephas, or Apollos, as he thinketh best", we cannot in consistency draw the line there; a man must also be left free, "if he thinketh best", to follow none of the three, but to strike out his own line, to be of a school in which there is "no man doctor" and no man disciple, except himself, and however we may seek to disguise the fact, there will thus really be as many religions as there are individuals—a state of things far removed from the "independency" of the primitive *Christians.*

To Hobbes this does not very much matter, but the reason why it does not matter is that he really cares nothing about religion and wholly disbelieves in its worth as a knowledge and worship of God. Knowledge of God, according to his philosophy, is impossible, because God is "ingenerable", and knowledge is all of motions, generations, and their effects;[2] conformity to the established worship has nothing to do with convictions; it is "not philosophy, but law",[3] merely an indication that, as good citizens, we do not propose

[1] *Leviathan*, c. 47.

[2] *De Corpore*, c. i. 8 "excludit a se Philosophia Theologiam, doctrinam dico de natura et attributis Dei, aeterni, ingenerabilis, incomprehensibilis, et in qua nulla compositio, nulla divisio institui, nulla generatio intelligi potest."

[3] *Seven Philosophical Problems*, Epistle Dedicatory (English Works, ed. Molesworth, vii. 5): "But what had I to do to meddle with matters of that nature, seeing religion is not philosophy, but law?"

to disturb the King's peace for any metaphysical quillets of our own. From the individualistic premisses of the sectary we thus reach the conclusions of pure indifferentism.

This seems, at first sight, a paradox, but reflection may possibly show that it is no paradox, but an inevitable consequence of consistency in individualism. For the thoroughgoing individualist begins by making a double assumption, both parts of that assumption being equally necessary to him. My religion is strictly a purely personal affair, a concern between myself and my God to which there is no third party; it is primarily a matter of the salvation of my own soul, and nothing else. ("Nothing", says a hymn I have heard sung in my boyhood, "is worth a thought beneath, But how *I* may escape the death That never, never dies".) It is because the whole transaction is so strictly individual that it appears so reasonable to hold that the only authoritative guide for me in the transaction is the interior voice of God, recognised as such by my own judgement and conscience. One only succeeds in combining such a view, as it has historically been combined, with the further conviction that there is a religion which is true and obligatory for mankind by the further tacit assumption, regularly made by enthusiasts for all creeds, that every other man's personal judgement and conscience will agree in its deliverances with my own, if only he shows good faith in consulting them. This proposition of fact is just what the cool-headed student of men and manners, with no strong personal enthusiasms, finds it impossible to grant. "No honest man", said Johnson, "could be a deist, for no man could be so after a fair examination of the proofs of Christianity."[1] At the present day—*experto credite*—an edu-

[1] Johnson to Boswell, February 1766.

cated layman who ventures to write in the most modest way on the side of Christian, or even theistic, belief may expect to receive communications from "infidels" who are entire strangers to him, informing him in unambiguous language that he must be a dishonest person, because no one who has considered the refutations of Christianity (or of Theism) with attention can possibly retain any belief. To a dispassionate mind it is meanwhile patent that there are very honest Papists and equally honest Protestants, sincere Christians and Jews, and also sincere atheists, at all levels of general education and intelligence. The reason and judgement of all the individuals cannot be trusted even to lead in the same general direction, on the single condition that it shall be loyally followed. If there is no other authority, it seems natural to draw one of two conclusions: either there is no truth to be reached in matters about which equally intelligent and sincere persons draw such divergent conclusions from the same data, or if there should be any truth which will ultimately emerge from the endless welter of inquiry and controversy, truth so hard to find cannot be of much moment for the practical conduct of life and the attainment of the "good for man". And this is Indifferentism.

But a positive religion can flourish only when it is recognised that the direction of life by its light is the supreme and very practical concern of mankind; no such religion can tolerate reduction to the status of an interesting speculation which may prove to be not entirely unfounded, but has no pressing importance for the ordering of conduct and life. We can thus readily understand why it is that, in actual fact, even those religious bodies which theoretically push the rejection of "external authority" to an extreme almost always, in practice, prove to retain some authority to which they expect private judgement, in the last resort, to submit itself; and, again, why every movement which effects much for the quickening and deepening of the personal spiritual life seems regularly to be accompanied by a revival of insistence on the authoritativeness of something which is not "private judgement", whether the something is the organised Church, the letter of a Scripture, a particular interpretation of a Scripture, or some new revelation, attested by physical or moral wonders.

Thus, to illustrate the point by the history of a particular religious community, it is manifest fact that the gravely enfeebled spirituality of the English Church of two hundred years ago has been wakened into new vitality chiefly by three great movements—the Methodist, the Evangelical, the "Anglo-Catholic". The broad fact remains certain, however badly any man may think of some of the incidental characteristics of some or all of these movements. (I can understand that to some minds the ardent Methodist, the eager Evangelical, and the earnest Anglo-Catholic may all be distressing, but I should not understand the denial of the proposition that all three are alive, if sometimes disconcertingly alive, while the decorous Latitudinarians of George I.'s time were dead, or moribund.) Each of the three movements was, in its own way, a somewhat violent revolt against the domination of individual judgement and "good sense" in matters of religion, towards some form of "non-rational" authoritarianism. Wesley, Toplady, Newman are, in various ways, unlike enough, but they all agree in seeing the enemy in what Newman called "Liberalism"; all, like the priest in Blake's poem,[1] or, for the matter of that, Blake himself, regard it as the supreme blasphemy to

[1] "A Little Boy Lost", in *Songs of Experience*.

Set up reason for the judge
Of our most holy mystery.

We see the same thing, in a highly grotesque form, in the curious contemporary American movement which calls itself Fundamentalism. That the Fundamentalists, being for the most part extremely ill-educated, should be violently obscurantist in their attitude to natural and historical science is only what might be expected, though I doubt whether their *caeca fides* is really more obscurantist at heart than the equally blind confidence of the aggressive "rationalist" in the competence of scientific methods, of which he most commonly knows next to nothing, to answer all questions "in the earth, or out of it". But it is, I should say, a mere mistake to see nothing in the Fundamentalist movement but its hostility to Darwin and Huxley and the "higher critics" of Biblical documents. What is really at the back of the movement, and supplies it with its driving force, is the conviction that any attempt to eliminate absolute supernatural "authority" from Christianity, or any other great positive religion, is destructive of its character as religion. Such attempts convert "the faith" into a philosophy, and by consequence, since there can be no such thing as an authoritarian philosophy, into a mere body of tentative "personal opinions", a collection of *Privatmeinungen*. And a man for whom his religion has become an affair of *Privatmeinungen* has ceased to have a religion.

The real issue is not whether the opening chapters of *Genesis* are "fundamental", but whether there is anywhere a genuine *fundamentum*, a "sure corner-stone", on which positive religion can build. It is felt that such a corner-stone cannot be found in any purely rational theology or metaphysic, since the God of such a system is a God whom we have succeeded in understanding, a God who is not a *deus absconditus*, and does not "move in a mysterious way". We accept His disclosure of Himself through theology or metaphysic because, so far as one can see, it contains no mistakes, not because *haec dicit Dominus Deus*. But such a God divested of mystery, a God whom we understand, as we understand the properties of integers or triangles, would be a God who "has no more in Him", or, indeed, "has less in Him", than the mind which can thus understand and dispose of Him, a mere *dieu des savans et des philosophes*, and therefore not a being whom we can adore, and so not a true God at all, in the sense in which "heart-religion" demands a God. Worship, indeed, is not mere abjection and abasement before something which baffles our intelligence, but without the element of the baffling there is no worship. If, then, such a God has ever declared Himself to mankind, the communication cannot owe the claim of its content to acceptance to the transparent intrinsic reasonableness and good sense which pervades it; there must be something in it which has to be accepted, not because, with the expenditure of sufficient industry and acumen, we can see it to be "what could not be otherwise", but because God has spoken it, and it rests on *His* word for it.

State contenti, umana gente, al *quia*;
chè se possuto aveste veder tutto,
mestier non era parturir Maria.[1]

Now, I own that it is just this recognition of the principle of absolute authority, in one form or another, which is, in the end, the *scandalum* offered by all positive and historical religions to the philosophical mind, honestly bent on the understanding of things. The mysterious always presents a problem to intelligence,

[1] Dante, *Purgatorio*, iii. 37.

and the intellect would be playing the traitor to itself if it merely sat down idly in the presence of the problem without any serious effort to grapple with it. Yet, on the other side, it seems impossible to remove the scandal by denying that there is any ultimate mystery at the heart of things. When we consider how utterly the attempt to locate absolute authority in a definitely circumscribed seat, and to codify its deliverances, has always broken down, we may, indeed, be strongly tempted to cut the knot in this fashion. To consider only the solutions of the problem of the seat of authority which have been propounded within the limits of Christianity itself, it seems impossible, without great feats of sophistry, to place it in the official declarations of Popes or Councils, or of both together, for some of them seem to contradict others openly, and some to be in disagreement with independently ascertained truth. The same and similar difficulties attend the appeal to the written text of the Bible; the text appealed to is sometimes corrupt, sometimes speaks with an ambiguous voice, sometimes asserts what we know to be historical or scientific error. Moreover, before we can so much as know what Bible it is to which we are appealing, since the Bible itself never enumerates its own component parts, we have to go to an extra-biblical authority to learn what "books" are part of the infallible Bible, and what are not. (So far the "Fundamentalists" apparently have shirked the question what is the authority which fixes the canon of Scripture, but it is a question which they must be prepared to face—with curious consequences for Fundamentalism.)

If we fall back from the Biblical writings as a whole on the recorded personal utterances of Our Lord, there is the desperate problem of ascertaining how far these utterances have been accurately transferred from the idiom in which they were primarily spoken to another, and then transmitted to us without mutilation, addition, or deformation.[1] (If careful and unbiassed criticism is steadily delivering us, as it seems to be, from the more extravagant speculations which once threatened to dissolve the whole Gospel story into a tissue of "tendencious" misrepresentations of fact in the interests of early quarrelsome theological controversialists, it is no less steadily making it plain how very little we know of the actual words and deeds of the Lord with anything like certainty.) And the various ingenious devices by which the theories of the infallibility of Popes, of Councils, of Scripture as a whole, of the reports of the sayings of Christ, is kept intact under difficulties, what a lame affair they all are! The Pope infallible? Yes, of course; but somehow one can always make out a case for holding that *this* Pope, making *this* pronouncement, has omitted to comply with some condition necessary to make his utterance one of the infallible ones. General Councils liable to err? Why, no; but it may always be possible to discover that *this* Council had some defect which made it not really oecumenical, or that its Acts are interpolated, or have been misunderstood. The words of Scripture are inerrant, but we may disagree about the canon, or allow for unlimited corruption in transcription, or may take strange liberties of interpretation. The actual words of

1 The problem has its very practical bearings. *E.g. if* we are to take the *ipsissima verba* of Christ as they fell from His lips as our absolute authority and our only absolute authority, how is a Christian Church to deal with the problems of divorce? Everything will turn on the questions—(1) Did Christ actually utter the words "apart from a case of fornication", which appear in *Matt.* v. but not in *Mk.* x.? (2) What is the precise signification of the word "fornication" in this clause? (3) In view of the actual institutions of Galilee in the first century does the presence or absence of the clause make any difference? It seems impossible to hold that all three questions can be answered with certainty. I am not asking, be it understood, whether divorce in case of fornication is Christian or unchristian, but whether anything could be determined either way by simple appeal to the *litera scripta*.

the Lord are beyond question, but He may be credited with a double meaning, or a recorded utterance may be shown to have suffered from imperfect rendering out of Aramaic into Greek, or to have been misunderstood from unfamiliarity with Galilean tradition, or to have undergone "development", whenever it suits our convenience. All transparent subterfuges by which our absolute authority is nominally respected, while in fact we trim its deliverances to suit our changing fancy. It is an old story over which the world has made merry until it is ashamed of its own jest.

And yet when all has been said, it is as hard to conceive of an adequate religion without mystery, and consequently without the note of authority, as it is easy to smile at the shifts to which the theorist is driven when he attempts to provide authority with its clearly defined seat and to compile a register of its declarations. It remains true that "God comprehended" would be no God, but a mere artificial construction of our own minds. *Christianity not Mysterious* is no proper title for a work on the Christian religion by a writer who seriously believes that religion to be something more than an invention of ingenious moralists and statesmen. Butler's famous *Analogy*, it has been said, cuts both ways, for it seems to make "revealed religion" superfluous by demonstrating that it leaves the course of the world as mysterious as it finds it.[1] But the criticism is surely much more smart than sound. It is true, after all, though it is an unwelcome truth, that in the Aristotelian phrase so often repeated by the great schoolmen,[2]

[1] Leslie Stephen, *English Thought in the Eighteenth Century*, c. 5.

[2] *Met.* α 993 b 9 ὥσπερ γὰρ τὰ τῶν νυκτερίδων ὄμματα πρὸς τὸ φέγγος ἔχει τὸ μεθ' ἡμέραν, οὕτω καὶ τῆς ἡμετέρας ψυχῆς ὁ νοῦς πρὸς τὰ τῇ φύσει φανερώτατα. In the *versio vetus Latina*, the νυκτερίς is replaced by the *noctua*. Is there some chance reproduction of the original image in Blake's words,

"The Bat that flits at close of Eve
Has left the Brain that won't believe"?

the eye of man's mind for truth is like the eye of the owl for daylight. A theology which finds mystery it cannot explain away at the centre of things may not be true, but it is certain that a theology which professes to have cleared away all the mystery out of the world must be false. In any true account of the concrete and individual reality one must somewhere come upon something of which it can only be said, "Why this thing should be so, or even just what it is, is more than I can tell, but at all costs it must be recognised that here the thing is". If this is all we mean by "irrationality", we may safely say that historical individuality is the great supreme irrational from which thought can never succeed in getting free. If by the "rational" we mean that which is wholly transparent, that which *va de soi* for the logical mind, the one ubiquitous irrationality is the very fact that there should be anything more than the "bloodless ballet of impalpable categories", the fact that something exists. For the something that exists is always individual, and this means, in the first place, that it is not constructed by, but *given* to, our thinking, and in the second, that it is inexhaustible by analysis, an implicit and dimly apprehended "infinite". The actual function of thought is neither to create its own data, nor yet to fit data otherwise given in a number of clear-cut simple apprehensions into an alien pattern, or relational scheme, of "universals", independently given by a second kind of simple apprehension, but to analyse and articulate the present experience, which is our one, always confused, real datum; to transmute apprehension, if I may so express myself, into recognition.[1] It is of the essence of the situation that this transmutation is never complete; there is

[1] This, I should say, is the real meaning and the permanent truth of the Platonic doctrine that all knowledge is ἀνάμνησις.

always in the confused, concrete, given fact a remainder of the perplexing, the not yet recognised, which intrigues us, and yet cannot be ignored without killing the experienced fact. A mere "laboratory" fact, from which this element has been artificially subtracted, is no longer the living fact.

So far as I can see, the function of authority is just to insist upon the reality and omnipresence in religion, as in all our contact with the objectively real, of this element of refractoriness to complete intellectual analysis which is the stamp of objectivity, this never wholly removable misfit between the real and the categories in which we try to confine it. "A God comprehended is no God"; also, a "nature" completely comprehended would not be the real natural world. But the misfit is so much more patent when it is God who is the object of our thinking, because of the incomparable wealth of intrinsic reality in the object. In dealing with a God who does not simply stand aloof "on the other side", but has entered into the historical and become truly immanent in it, though never merely immanent, authority provides us with the way of escape from the agnosticism which is the despair of the intellect. For *ignorabimus* it substitutes the happier watchward, *console-toi, tu ne me chercherais pas, si tu ne m'avais trouvé.*[1] The possession is in the puzzling form of dim and vague contact, but it is a genuine fact, which guarantees us that the *au delà*, where we can detect no clear and definite outlines, is not, after all, a mere *terra incognita* which may prove, like the unexplored regions in mediaeval maps, to be filled by fantastic man-destroying monsters. Or, to put it rather differently, what I would suggest is that authority and experience do not stand over against one another in sharp and irreconcilable

[1] Pascal, *Pensées*, 553 (Brunschvig) (*Mystère de Jésus*).

opposition; authority is the self-assertion of the reality of an experience which contains more than any individual experient has succeeded in analysing out and extricating for himself. It is indispensable for us as finite historical beings who need a safeguard against our inveterate tendency to supplement the statement "this is what I can make of this situation" by the perilous addition, "and this is all there is in it".

It is instructive, I think, to consider the analogy of what we often call the "authority" of sense-perception, and the part it plays in our knowledge of the natural world. As has been remarked before, we may safely say, following in the steps of Mr. Meyerson, that it is just the impossibility of resolving the course of physical becoming without remainder into a complex of universal connections, in accord with exactly formulable laws, that forbids us to regard the whole of physical nature as no more than a coherent dream of the physicist. If the physicist could ever succeed in getting rid altogether of the element of intrusive and perturbing brute fact which will not square wholly with his scheme of formulae, he would probably feel, as I think Mr. Meyerson has said, that the real world had evaporated before his eyes into a mere collection of logical or mathematical symbols. Now, of course, the brute facts which thus save the natural world from being sublimated away into a system of differential equations are, in the end, facts about our *sensations*, and what they disclose. The natural world is obstinately real because, however far we have carried the reduction of its processes to "law", we have always still to take account of experiences in the way of sensation for which we can give no justification beyond the fact that they are there. Sense furnishes a standard of appeal which seems to be external to thinking, and by which the results of thinking have to be corrected. In the end, if there are undeniable facts recorded on the testimony of sense which refuse to square with the apparently best assured analyses and deductions of the intellect, it is the intellect, with its deductions and analyses, which has to submit.[1] This is as annoying to the typical "thinker" as the theologian's demand that "reason" should give way before "authority"; the same repugnance to admit the control of thought by anything beyond itself which gives rise, in one sphere, to the contemptuous rejection of all "authority" produces, in another, the types of philosophy which, in various ways, attempt to deny that sense as sense makes any contribution to the fabric of natural knowledge. In the one case, as in the other, theories which try to deny or conceal the fact that in all our thinking, whether about physical becoming or about God, the eternal Being, thought is working on an object which it has neither created nor "postulated", but finds there, given in a contact which is not mere thinking, seem doomed to failure, as all unqualified *a-priorism* must be, by the consideration that the thinker is himself an historical being, and that nothing has significance for him except in so far as it affects him by historical contacts.

In the case of the sensible experiences[2] which give us

[1] This explains what Democritus meant when he made the senses say to the intellect τάλαινα φρήν, παρ' ἡμέων λαβοῦσα τὰς πίστεις ἡμέας καταβάλλεις; πτῶμά τοι τὸ κατάβλημα (fr. 125 Diels). Cf. the observations of É. Gilson with reference to the ultra-rationalism of Descartes: "à un phénomène réel qu'il ne pourrait pas s'expliquer s'il le connaissait Descartes préfère de beaucoup un phénomène qui n'existe peut-être pas mais qu'il peut expliquer pour le cas où ce phénomène existerait. Tels ces escadrons de fantômes qui combattent en l'air. . . . Les scolastiques croient au phénomène et renoncent à l'expliquer. [They ascribe it to the agency of God, or of good, or bad, angels.] Descartes n'y croit guère, mais il indique cependant les causes qui lui semblent capables de le produire" (*Études de philosophie médiévale*, p. 285).

[2] If I am asked exactly what I mean by *sensible*, I do not know that I can do better than quote the definition of Augustine: "iam video sic esse definiendum, ut sensus sit passio corporis *per se ipsum* non latens animam" (*de quant. animae*,

our historical contacts with nature there are several points which call for remark. In the first place, it is obvious that there is no possible *proof* that all present sensation may not be mere illusion, as some of the ancient philosophies seem to have taught that it is. Descartes may make his immediate inference to an objective reality, the *sum*, from a single *cogito*, the fact, for example, that he is aware of colour or warmth, but that he *is* aware, that he *cogitat*, is not even an immediate illation.[1] If it is denied, the denial cannot be met by the production of grounds, but must be swept aside by a mere reiteration of the original assertion. In the second place, though the whole edifice of philosophy and science is built, in the end, on a basis of direct simple apprehension, of which no further account can be given, this does not mean that one could ever isolate the simply apprehended content from the context of interpretation and "construction" with which it is complicated. Sense and thought, direct apprehension and the interpretation of what is given to it, may both be involved in any articulate perception, but we can never sort them out, so as to be in a position to say "*this*, and no more, is the element in my present perception which is *given*, simply apprehended as present; *that* is the result of recognition, analysis, comparison, and so is not given, but *made*".

Kant, indeed, seems to undertake such a separation in his doctrine of the forms of intuition, but Kant, as I imagine we should all agree now, did not probe deep enough. Apparently, he would be content to assign to

23, 41). See the exposition of É. Gilson (*Introduction à l'étude de saint Augustin*, 72), from whom I borrow the reference.

[1] We must be careful to avoid the mistake of Huxley in his essay on Descartes, who argues that the premiss of the inference should be stated in the hypothetical form, *si quis cogitat, est*. The absence of existential import in such a premiss would make it incapable of yielding the existential conclusion Descartes needs. *His* premiss is really *ille homo qui est Renatus Descartes hic et nunc aliquid cogitat*.

the side of construction everything in the perception recorded in a simple perceptive judgement which has to do with the spatial or temporal shape, size, position of what is perceived; but supposes that when you get down to the purely qualitative, when, for example, your perception constates no more than could be adequately conveyed by the monosyllable "green", or "sour", you have reached the merely given. In that case, the element of construction would only come in with that which the exclamation "green!" may imply, but does not convey—the implication "just here and just now". Yet it seems plain on reflection that merely to say "green" with significance is to perform an act of comparison and recognition; interpretation has already begun, before we proceed to the implication "here, not there; now, not then". If there ever was a time, as we may fairly doubt, in our own past history when we were purely receptive, the time must have passed before we could so much as name things, and to recapture the condition must be beyond the power of "articulate-speaking men".[1]

The analytic psychologist may produce reasons, and possibly good reasons, to show that there must be such a thing as "pure" sensation, but it is abundantly clear that no such thing as a sensation pure of all elements of interpretation can enter as such into the fabric of our perception of the natural world, or be produced for the inspection of the psychologist who is reflecting on the problem of perception. In any bit of what we call our sense-experience, however elementary, which can be detached for examination, we find the given,

[1] Plato shows more insight, when he subjoins to an account of the intellectual activity implied in the grasping of a geometrical truth the words *ταὐτὸν δὴ περί τε εὐθέος ἅμα καὶ περιφεροῦς σχήματος καὶ χρόας, περί τε ἀγαθοῦ καὶ καλοῦ καὶ δικαίου, καὶ περὶ σώματος ἅπαντος σκευαστοῦ τε καὶ κατὰ φύσιν γεγονότος, πυρὸς ὕδατός τε καὶ τῶν τοιούτων πάντων, καὶ ζῴου σύμπαντος πέρι καὶ ἐν ψυχαῖς ἤθους, καὶ περὶ ποιήματα καὶ παθήματα σύμπαντα* (*Ep.* vii. 342 D).

or received, and the interpretative work of mind on this datum already inextricably complicated, a fact too readily ignored by the many promising young philosophers who treat the theory of knowledge simply as an affair of theorising about "sensa" and the relations between them.

In the third place, there is an important consequence which follows from this impossibility of making a quasi-chemical separation between a definite, exactly describable *given*, in respect of which we are simply receptive, and an equally definite and describable construction performed upon it, in respect of which we are active, and, it may be, wrongly active. The so-called authoritativeness, or infallibility, of sense is based wholly on the presence in it of the given and simply received. It will not cover anything which must be assigned to interpretation of the given, or construction on the basis of the given. And since we can never, as a fact, make an unambiguous separation, by reflective analysis, between one element in an experience which is all givenness, and a second which is all construction, the so-called "infallibility" of sense in respect of its proper sensible is never a sufficient guarantee that a specific experience involving sense is simply veridical. We *may* be mistaken when we appeal to any particular "sense-experience", for none of the experiences we call by the name is pure unalloyed receptivity of a *given*. In part, all are manufactured, and we can never say certainly and exactly *what* part has been manufactured.

It is true, as Locke used to say, that there is a difference between real life and a dream, between actually burning my hand and only dreaming that it is burned. But there is no certain criterion by which, in *a given* case, we can distinguish waking from dreaming, actual perception from imagination. A careful psychoogist may accumulate a number of distinctions which commonly stand us in good stead, for example, the superior vividness of actual waking perception, its steadiness, its coherency. Yet, in a given case, we know that any, or all, may fail us. In general, "images" may have less vividness than the corresponding percepts; they may be incoherent, or may flicker in a way in which the percepts do not. Yet there is always a real difficulty in discriminating a distant and faintly heard noise, or a colour seen by a dim and flickering light, from a sound or colour which we have only imagined; again, it seems undeniable that a "pure hallucination" *sometimes* has all the intensity, the fullness of detail, the steadiness and persistency which are, as a rule, marks of a true perception of the physically real. It is always hazardous to tell a man that he has not really observed, but only imagined, what he claims to have observed, because his observation, if genuine, would upset an important and apparently well-accredited theory. If we allow awkward observations to be disposed of in this fashion, we are plainly taking a dangerous step towards the arrest of all progress in natural knowledge. Yet there are cases where the procedure would be justified, and we can lay down no rule for their detection. There is a meaning, and an important meaning, in the assertion that sensation is authoritative, and even, if you prefer the more emphatic word, in a way infallible, and yet it is also true that no "observation" can be guaranteed as beyond criticism and correction.

I do not mean only that an observation may prove to have been made with defective instruments, or in neglect of some condition which might conceivably have been relevant to the result observed. I mean, further, that when all possible precautions have been taken to exclude error arising from such causes, error, that is, due to definitely identifiable special misinterpretatio there is still a more insidious source of error. We tal of "reading off" a record made by our "instruments o precision", but in actual fact all "reading off" is itse inextricably mingled with interpretation because th very construction of the "instrument" itself involve and embodies interpretative theory; we never can b sure that we have successfully made ourselves th purely passive and recipient registers of "external fact' The use of a measuring-rod presupposes the previou selection of a whole system of geometrical postulate the appeal to a chronometer involves a theory of th "flow of time". "Omnes perceptiones, *tam sensus quan mentis*, sunt ex analogia hominis, non ex analogi universi. Estque intellectus humanus instar specul inaequalis ad radios rerum, qui suam naturam natura rei immiscet."[1] Thus, though there could be no rea knowledge of physical nature if we had not in sense with its core of receptive passivity, an authoritativ "control" of active speculation, we can never treat th particular "observation" as though it were all pure re-ceptivity, and therefore absolutely infallible. It is no our *thinking* only that *recipit infusionem a voluntat et affectibus*.[2]

We may reasonably expect to meet with similar diffi-culties when we turn to examine our human knowledg of God, just because the *subiectum* which owns both kinds of knowledge is the historical human individual. Here also, if knowledge is to be more than persona

[1] *Novum Organum*, i. 40.

[2] *Ib.* i. 49. One might almost say that the "theory of Relativity" is no more than an illuminating comment on these two aphorisms. As an illustration of the source of difficulty I have here in mind, the reader may ask himself, carefully comparing Einstein, *Theory of Relativity* (E. tr.), pp. 53-4, with Eddington, *Nature of the Physical World*, p. 11, whether or not the "FitzGerald contraction" is a fact, and just what he means by his answer to that question. And cf. the whole of Eddington's essay "The Domain of Physical Science", in *Science, Religion, and Reality*, particularly pp. 209-18.

opinion (δόξα), there must be control of our personal intellectual constructions by something which is not constructed but *received*. Not only must we begin as little children, if we would *enter* either the *regnum hominis super naturam* or the kingdom of God, but we must retain the submissiveness and docility of the childlike mind all through our subsequent progress. A true humility of soul in the presence of the given is as much a condition of advance in natural knowledge as it is of "growth in grace". The problem in both cases is how to combine rightly two characters, both of which are distinctive of gracious and unspoiled childhood, humility and the spirit of fresh and fearless adventure, τὸ πρᾷον and τὸ θυμοειδές, to speak with Plato; we should, like the best and most attractive kind of boy, be at once receptive and eager—receptive without servility and eager without presumption and waywardness. The combination will only be effected if we remember always that there is, in the case of our knowledge of God also, that which is simply received, not invented by ourselves, and is therefore, in its nature, simply authoritative, a genuine control on the wilfulness of our individualism. It is not by "searching" that we find out God. And it is clear what this control must be. It must be the experience of rich, but confused, contact with the supernatural which plays, in our knowledge of God, the same part that immediate contact through sense with a confused "other" does in our knowledge of nature. The difference between the two cases is partly that the contacts with the supernatural are at once dimmer and richer than our contacts through sense with the natural, partly that whereas contact with the natural, being a necessity of physical existence, is common to us all, and exhibits only moderate variations, except when there is definite bodily disease or malformation, *impressive* and frequent contacts with the supernatural are given to the few, and there is a much wider range of variation in sensibility to them. It is not hard to find the human individual of "good normal" acuteness of sense-perception, and the divergences between the reports of such "normal" individuals on the same situation can be made negligible, or nearly so. In respect of natural eyesight, most men in health and the prime of vigour are beings with fairly "normal" delicacy of vision; the myopic or markedly astigmatic are a minority, sufferers from serious ophthalmic disease a smaller, and the downright blind a still smaller, minority. But in the matter of spiritual vision not a few of us are perhaps the born blind, the vast majority are myopic; the clear-sighted are the very few. Clear-eyed spiritual vision seems to be at least as rare as penetrating mathematical insight or exquisite musical sensibility.

Hence, while we rightly take as the authority to which we must, in the end, defer in questions of natural fact the perceptions of the "normal" man, exercised under carefully prearranged conditions of observation, in questions about facts of the supernatural order we cannot similarly make our authority the "common", or "average" man. It is as though the great majority of a certain population were markedly short-sighted, or colour-blind, and were therefore forced to take as authoritative the visual perceptions of the few who stood out as exceptionally free from those defects—a case which would presumably actually occur if there were a group of human beings who had become, by past "adaptation" to a special environment, generally colour-blind, or myopic.[1] In such a kingdom of the

[1] Cf. the famous parable of the cave-dwellers at the opening of the 7th book of Plato's *Republic*, 514 A ff.

blind, the one-eyed would actually be king. And, in fact, we do act on this principle in the closely analogous case of aesthetic perception. We do begin by trusting the authority of the few of exceptionally keen perceptivity, *e.g.* in music, on the question whether a composition has beauties to be found in it, and what those beauties are, and it is only by our initial submissiveness to their authority that we come, if we do come, to acquire ability to perceive for ourselves. Even so, none but the few among us ever come to perceive for ourselves independently more than a part—in my own case, alas, how small a part!—of what the more favoured few perceive, though we are content to believe that much which we shall never learn to discern is really there, because the few agree in assuring us that it is so. We have found that we perceive the more clearly for having believed them, and therefore we continue to believe their assurances, even where we never expect to be able to see directly for ourselves. In the same way, it is reasonable to recognise that if a great religious tradition has ennobled and purified human life, over a wide range of space and time and circumstance, by bringing the supernatural down into it, and is actually, so far as we have been able to assimilate its content, doing the same thing for our own lives, what has been intensely perceived and lived by the chosen spirits who have shaped the tradition, even where we have not been personally able to assimilate it and build it into the substance of our own lives, is no mere "subjective" illusion, but embodies real apprehension of a real supernatural.

But the point on which I am personally most concerned to insist is a different one. It is that in immediate apprehension of the supernatural, as in immediate apprehension of the natural, we are dealing with concrete, individual, historical, experiences which resist complete intellectual analysis, at the same time that they demand it. In both cases, no man can communicate what he sees in its totality and individuality. Any attempt at communication involves rationalisation and analysis, at least in an unconscious form, and communication, in consequence, brings with it loss and gain together. In the effort to say what one sees there is always an intellectual concentration which makes it clearer to the beholder himself what certain central features of the *chose vue* are. This is why a prudent man distrusts "impressions" of which he cannot "give clear account" to another; and, again, why it is a good rule never to be satisfied with one's own proof of a proposition unless one can "set it down in black and white on paper". But the central features of the *chose vue* are always in fact given in a setting of *penumbra* or marginal vision, and this setting falls more or less completely outside the range of that which can be imparted by communication. No one can answer the simple question, "What do you see at this moment?" in a way which will convey "the truth, the whole truth, and nothing but the truth". The thing simply cannot be done, even if the statement is being made to a second person with vision as perfect as the speaker's;[1] much less, if the second person is lamentably colour-blind. It follows that it is with perception of the supernatural as it is with perception of the natural; it is impossible to make an unambiguous presentation of the actually given and the reflective interpretation of the given in separation from one another. In every attempt to communicate the content of the experience there is inevitably an accompaniment of interpretation, and therefore of construction, even if the construction amounts to no more than the negative

[1] At least the answer would have to be "much what you see yourself", and this is an evasion of the difficulty.

mission of the "marginal", and it is never possible to ay with precision *how much* is construction. (Even if he construction is no more than a leaving out of the 'marginal", you cannot say just what and how much ou have left out; if this could be done, the "marginal" vould have ceased to be marginal.) And, as in the case f sensation, so in the case of contact with the super- atural, the reality and authoritativeness of the given s given does not guarantee the infallibility of the in- lividual declarations based upon immediate contact.

It seems to me, then, that the rightful demand of the ntellect for individual freedom to think sincerely and earlessly, and the equally rightful demand of religion or objectivity and protection against the vagaries of ure subjectivity, can only be harmonised in one way, hrough the cultivation, by all parties who are con- erned that human life shall be the prey neither of vorldliness nor of superstition, of the two comple- nentary qualities of docility and adventurousness. In he past untold mischief has been wrought by their eparation. The *ecclesia docens*, the official body of eachers in the religious community, has often shown high degree of adventurousness in its bold formula- ions of articles of faith, or other propositions claiming o embody the content of what is authoritative; from he rest of the community it has demanded unqualified ubmissiveness. Or, in the reaction against this demand, ndividual thinkers have denied the right of authority, eposed in any external body, to exercise any control ver, or receive any deference from, the solitary mental dventurer. Indeed, not so long ago, there seemed to e, at least in Western Europe, a still more complete nversion of the parts played for so many centuries y the *ecclesia docens* and the individual. We have vitnessed something hardly to be distinguished from a claim on the part of self-constituted representatives of the secular sciences to be the sovereign authority which dictates but does not obey, while official theologians have, in large numbers, been almost comically anxious to show their docility by accepting almost any speculation put before the British Association by a Professor or a Fellow of the Royal Society, or communicated to the newspapers by a medical man of any notoriety as the latest deliverance of an infallible authority, to which religion must at once conform itself, at its peril. Neither the ends of pure religion, nor the purposes of sound science are well served by these attempts to make authoritarian dictation the duty, or privilege, of one set of men and teachable humility that of another. No man will be either a true saint or a man of the right scientific temper who does not know how to be at once docile and adventurous in his own personal thinking.

This fairly obvious truth has very important bearings on the duties of those whose office it is to be, for their time, the representatives of authority in the religious community. It is inevitable that, for the necessary purpose of avoiding pure anarchy in thought and consequent anarchy in practice, there should be somewhere in the community a body thus charged with the duty of safeguarding the foundations of its life. The whole *raison d'être* of the religious community as such depends upon its possession of a genuine disclosure of the supernatural, too precious for human life to be surrendered at any man's bidding. But where there is not a true and deep docility of spirit in these official custodians of the "deposit", there is certain to be, along with rightful jealousy for the real spiritual treasure of the community, a great deal of unreasonable jealousy of surrendering, or even modifying, much in the existing tradition which is mere temporary incrustation upon the true jewel. The motives for this conservatism in authorities need not always be, and most often, perhaps, are not chiefly the more discreditable ones of lust of dominion, or professional *esprit de corps*, though a "man in authority" does well to be vigilantly on his guard against the unsuspected presence of both in himself. But the excellence of the motives in no case removes the mischievousness of their effects. If one age, from the worthiest motives, persists in defending the indefensible, the next is likely to see a panic surrender of the indispensable.

Now the danger to the spirit of religion itself from an improper exercise of authority is not sufficiently guarded against by merely drawing such distinctions and marking such limitations as have already been recognised by even rigidly authoritarian religious communities. It is true that even when the claims of an infallible authority—Pope, Councils, Bible—have been most insisted upon, it has been customary, in theory at least, to admit a whole mass of such limitations. Thus there has always been some sort of recognised distinction made between the primary and indefeasible authority of the official person, or persons, as custodians of the truth and a second and temporary authority of a purely executive or administrative kind to determine what, in view of existing conditions, may be taught or practised with the consent of the community, and I suppose it would be pretty generally conceded that actual repositaries of authority have not infrequently misused their position by confusing the two different kinds of authority. If, for example, in the too famous case of Galileo, it had simply been decided that, at the existing juncture, the Church must not be distracted by the teaching of Copernicanism as a definitely established truth, there would, I take it, have been no serious reason to complain of the decision; the scandal arose from the presumptuous declaration of the Cardinals Inquisitors that Copernicanism is *false*.[1] So, again, it has generally been held by the supporters of an infallible authority that the range of its infallibility is circumscribed; authority is only infallible in matters of "faith and morals". And, once more, even within this domain itself, a distinction has been taken between the express words of an authoritative deliverance itself and the explanations given of them, or the inferences drawn from them, by individual theologians, which are said to be authoritative only in the sense that they deserve a respect based on the eminence of the expositor in his own speciality. Unfortunately, in practice Popes and Councils determine for themselves what questions are questions of faith and morals. Where the authority recognised is the text of a written Scripture, either the determination of this point is left with some group of divines who happen to be prominent and influential, or, as in societies of "Fundamentalist" views, the text of Scripture is taken indiscriminately as equally authoritative in all spheres whatsoever. What is really needed, if there is to be no faltering of specifically religious life and thought, as well as no dictation by theologians, acting in the supposed interests of religion, to natural and historical inquiries, is, I suggest, the making of a distinction between authority and inerrancy, and the recognition on all sides that the claim to rightful authority is not a claim to inerrancy.[2]

[1] Of course there was a further issue, viz. how far any decisions of the Inquisition are binding outside the Pope's dominions. Were the Universities of France in any way bound to respect such a decision? But this is a wholly secondary matter.

[2] Cf. the distinction always felt by the Romans, from whom we have borrowed the very word *authority*, between the *imperium* of the consul, or praetor, and the *auctoritas* of the senate. As W. G. de Burgh says (*Legacy of the Ancient World*, p. 191 n. 1), "*auctoritas* means 'moral influence'; the English word 'authority' in the sense of executive power would be expressed in Latin by *imperium*

The justification of this distinction has already been provided by what we have said of the impossibility of making any intelligible statement, whether about the natural or the supernatural, which shall have as its content the simply objective and given, with no element whatever of the subjective and constructed. It is worth while to reflect that even the unique authority ascribed by orthodox Christianity to Our Lord, as the man in whom humanity and deity, nature and supernature, the temporal and the eternal, are in perfect interpenetration, does not seem to affect the application of this distinction to the authoritatively enunciated doctrines of the Christian religion. From the Christian conception of the person of Christ it follows, no doubt, that the spiritual vision of the one man Jesus Christ, unlike that of any other of our race, must be thought of as adequate, never obscured by wilfulness, self-centredness, consciousness of alienation from the divine. But we have also to remember that equally, according to the conception of orthodox Christianity, Christ is no *Mischwesen*, not something more than human but less than divine, like the daemons and heroes of Hellenic fancy, but at once truly divine, and no less truly and utterly human. Both the soul and body of Christ are held to be, in the fullest sense of the word, "creatures"; the historical, human experience of Christ is thus a creaturely experience, though an absolutely unique creaturely experience, of the divine; hence the strictest traditional orthodoxy has found itself confronted with the problem of the limitation of the human knowledge of the incarnate Christ, a problem raised from the first by the simple statement of an Evangelist that, as he advanced from childhood to manhood, he "grew in wisdom and

or *potestas*". What some of us find amiss in the attitude of "authoritarian" divines is precisely that they seem to us to confuse *auctoritas* with *imperium*.

grace with God and man",[1] by the record of his frank admission of ignorance of the day and hour of the final triumph of the divine purpose,[2] and still more impressively by the narrative of his devastating experience of sheer dereliction at the crisis of his history, the prayer of passionate prostration in the garden, and the dying quotation from the most heart-broken of the Psalms. It is only the creaturely that can pray, and when a Christian speaks of the adequacy of the Lord's human experience of the supernatural, he must not, I take it, forget that the adequacy meant is still relative to the conditions of creatureliness inseparable from genuine humanity. The human experience even of a humanity "personally united with the Word", being human, is still temporal experience of the supra-temporal, and of it, too, it must hold true that *quidquid recipitur, recipitur ad modum recipientis*. If it were not so, Christian theology would have had no obstinate Christological problem to wrestle with.

It is hardly necessary to recur again in this connection to the point already dealt with earlier, that in dealing with the recorded utterances of the historical Christ, even if we could be sure of their actual words, we have to allow for qualification of the received by the very real limitations of the recipients to whom the utterances were addressed, and of those for whose immediate benefit they repeated them. But we must add, finally, that before a doctrine, however derived, becomes a defined *dogma*, a formula approved by the community or its representatives, there is still a further stage of more conscious reflection, regularly attended by prolonged, and often prejudiced and inflamed, discussion and debate; there are also always, or nearly always, the dissentients who, at most, silently acquiesce in the formula finally

[1] *Luke* ii. 52.

[2] *Matthew* xxiv. 36; *Mark* xiii. 32.

adopted for the sake of peace because adoption is the alternative which "divides least", and even among those whose acceptance means more than this acquiescence to avoid strife, verbal agreement often covers a wide divergence of interpretation. On all these grounds it seems a dangerous confusion to treat a rightful claim to authority as if it could ensure the formal infallibility of a dogmatic formula. The permanence of truth, I hold, is perfectly compatible with the transience of the precise formulae in which we try to give truth its expression.

We are all, I hope, alive to the reality of this distinction in the realm of natural knowledge. There we rightly revere the authority of the great names: we regard the Galileos and Newtons as having really made imperishable additions to our stock of apprehended objective truth, additions which will never have to be simply removed or dismissed as subjective fancies, but we do not dream of declaring that the formulae in which they gave expression to their truth are lifted once and for all above all possibility of modification. There seems to be no sufficient reason why the same distinction between authority and inerrancy should not be quite frankly recognised in connection with the theologian's attempts to formulate human knowledge about God. If it were recognised, we might look for a double advantage. We might fairly expect the candid lovers of science to lose their natural, but unfortunate, prejudice against theology, as they came to realise that the kind of authority claimed for himself by the theologian is, in principle, the same sort of authority with which they are familiar, and to which they properly attach weight, in their own sphere. With the clear distinction between authority and inerrancy once before them, it would become increasingly apparent that what the theologian is really asserting as the foundation of his claims is simply the reality and autonomy of experiences of contact with God as a genuine feature of human life, and the legitimacy of co-ordinating the contents of such experiences into a coherent system by trusting the testimony of those in whom it is richest and most pronounced. There are many signs in the present attitude of outstanding leaders in natural knowledge to the great religions that a claim of this kind would be understood and respected, if it were not supposed to carry with it the further claim of some specific man, or body of men, to decree the truth of anything they please, without condescending to any account of the why and wherefore. If the official custodians of religion would but cultivate the virtue of wise docility, the gain would not be only to their own characters and reputation. Theology itself, I believe, would once more win a more general recognition as a true science, and we should be delivered, to our great spiritual and moral profit, from the ruinous compromise which makes over the whole field of real knowledge to the various branches of secular study, and reduces religion to a mere affair of elegant but meaningless emotionalism, our latest method of honouring God with our lips while our hearts are far from Him. Unfeigned docility in the representatives of theological authority would have as one consequence a salutary advance, on the part of philosophers and men of science, from religiosity to religion.

And, moreover, such an advance would carry with it also an increased inward respect, from the scientific side, for the positive doctrines and even the dogmatic formulae of the great religions. When the claim to authority had been put on its true basis, appeal to a spiritual insight and experience which have proved their power to sustain a definite and unique type of life of supreme value, it would no longer be possible to regard the agelong systematic reflection on the principles underlying and regulating that life embodied in the dogmas of great theologies, and the expositions of them by great theologians, as mere intellectual curiosities which stand in no vital connection with the realities of spiritual experience, and may, without loss to our personality, be relegated to a museum of obsolete fashions. It would be increasingly understood that where there is a genuine *given* for the intellect to work on, the fruits of generations of continuous elaboration of the *given* by those whose aptitudes make them specially at home in the field are never to be lightly set aside as having exhausted their significance.

We know how, a century ago, this sort of treatment was meted out to the great constructive philosophies of the past; the thought of Plato, of Aristotle, of Descartes, was treated as a curious, but mainly wrong-headed, divagation of the human intellect with no significance for the direction of the modern mind, which would, in fact, best prepare itself for its own conquering advance by freeing itself once and for all of all this antiquated lumber. We all know, also, how within less than a century, the quickening of interest in the great philosophical systems has not only made the history of philosophy and science a living subject, but has also helped to provide some of the most modern and "progressive" of our scientific and philosophical thinkers with significant "direction-cosines" for their own work and their own specific problems. Even in my own youthful days, most of my teachers would have said that at any rate the physical speculations of Plato, Aristotle, Descartes, were things simply dead, mere monuments of perverse and wasted mental ingenuity. To-day we see Professor Whitehead, in one work,[1]

[1] *The Concept of Nature.*

consciously and avowedly going back to the *Timaeus* and in another,[1] less consciously perhaps, but none the less really, to the *Physics* of Aristotle for the foundations of a singularly fresh and living and eminently "modern" doctrine of the principles of natural knowledge; and Mr. Meyerson[2] throwing a new and brilliant light on the tendency and the logic of the "theory of relativity" by exhibiting it as the unforeseen outcome of the conception laid down in its great outlines in Descartes' *Principia*, as, in fact, the fulfilment, in an unexpected form, of the Cartesian demand for the geometrising of physics. If, to our own grave intellectual detriment, we have so long missed the light we might have drawn from thought wrongly supposed to have lost its vitality, one cause which excuses, though it does not justify, our error has been, as we all know the way in which earlier generations had converted the authority attaching to the doctrines of great men into something like a formal inerrancy of their dicta. Now that, as we may hope, this reaction has fairly spent itself, it is not too much to say that the *authority* of great thinkers, like those I have named, has once more become real to us, just because we no longer confound it with this formal inerrancy. Because we do not treat their utterances, still less the official pronouncements of members of their "schools", or the explanations of their commentators, as verbally infallible, we do not need to understand their teaching in a forced and unnatural sense, or to explain it away into truisms, in order to safeguard their words against all modification. This sets us free to look for their real meaning with a reasonable conviction that even when their express statements can be seen to require most modification, they

[1] *Science and the Modern World.*
[2] In *La Déduction relativiste*, pp. 135 ff., 267 ff.

mean something which has real and permanent significance. We appreciate their authority better because we do not mistake it for a mechanical inerrancy. When there is no longer danger that the same mistake will be made about "authority" in the theological sphere, we may look to see the real significance and authority of the great theologies regain the same kind of general recognition.

It will, no doubt, be said that the suggested analogy between authority in the domain of theology and authority in philosophy or science is misleading, since the claim made by every theology of revelation is that it has behind it the *absolute* authority of God, whereas the authorities in other fields are avowedly no more than human. But I do not think that this historically famous distinction can really be maintained as ultimate. So far as it exists, it is a difference in degree rather than in kind. On the one side, we must remember what has been already said about the way in which both actual contact with the supernatural and the communication to others of the disclosures made in such contacts are conditioned by the inherent creatureliness of the recipients. On the other, when we speak of the purely "human" character of philosophical and scientific authority, we must not forget that, according to the authors of the very distinction we are discussing, supernature and nature have the same source. It is the same God who discloses Himself, at different levels, through the order of nature, through prophets charged with a special message, through a Son who is the "express image" of His person. In all three cases we have a contact with the supreme source of actuality and value, mediated by a contact with something or someone historical and temporal. The mediation may be more or less remote, and the type of life it sustains correspondingly poorer or richer, merely natural, simply human and ethical, or vividly supernatural. The content of the disclosures may be as loosely connected with the occasion by which it is afforded as a scientific law with the particular incidents which set its discoverer on the track of his discovery,[1] or as closely bound up with it as the doctrine of the great prophets with the special spiritual experience through which it has been won and without which it would lose the best part of its meaning. But in all cases alike, in different ways, the same fundamental type of situation recurs. There is an element of the wholly given and trans-subjective which is *absolutely* authoritative, has unquestionable right to control our thinking or acting, just because it is so utterly given to us, not made by us; also in any communicable expression of the experience, there is the other element of construction, always relative to the mental habits, or rather to the whole physical and mental condition, of the experient at the specific moment of experience, and so always, to an unknown extent, infected with "subjectivity". It is the presence, in however subordinate a form, of this second factor which seems to make it impossible to equate authority with inerrancy. Whenever, in nature or supernature, we are face to face with objectivity not to be explained away, God is speaking, but whether God speaks through the processes of nature, through a specific message brought by a specific messenger, or through a unique human life as a whole,[2] the communications, of very different worth and depth,

[1] Cf. the disputes on the question whether an incident of the year 1665 connected with an apple had or had not anything to do with the genesis of Newton's planetary theory.

[2] "The work of our redemption was an intire work, and all that Christ said, or did, or suffered, concurred to our salvation, as well his mothers swathing him in little clouts, as Josephs shrowding him in a funerall sheete; as well his cold lying in the Manger, as his cold dying upon the Crosse" (Donne, *Sermon for Christmas Day*, 1625). It would be relevant to meditate upon the implications of this.

coming to us in these different ways, all come through a channel which is creaturely, and none of them ever wholly loses all marks of the creaturehood of the channel.

Perhaps the reality and worth of an authority which, for all its reality, is not the same thing as a formal inerrancy, is most readily illustrated from the sphere of the moral life, a life which is more than merely natural and yet not fully and consciously supernatural. How impossible to maintain the inerrancy of a man's conscience, and yet how necessary to any serious morality to insist upon its authority, and even its absolute authority! Kant, it is true, if he is to be tied down to the letter of his teaching, appears to confound the authority of conscience with a formal inerrancy. In his anxiety not to weaken the sense of obligation in man he actually maintains that an honestly mistaken judgement on the morality of an act I am contemplating is impossible; "an erring conscience is a *Chimaera*"[1] an imaginary danger not to be met with in the real world. But Kant only takes himself in by this pronouncement because he has first made a false simplification of the typical situation in which we "consult conscience" about a course of action. The only "conscientious difficulty" he contemplates is that of the man who knows quite well that what he is proposing to do is a violation of positive moral law, but is looking for some plausible "colour" for the transgression. Had he considered the kind of decision which is really critical, choice between alternative lines of conduct where there is no traditional rule to afford any guidance, and the whole responsibility of deciding right or wrong thus actually falls on the individual conscience, the decision, for

[1] *Werke* (Hartenstein[2]), iv. 251, vii. 204 (where an erring conscience is expressly called an *Unding*, the word rendered in our text *Chimaera*).

example, to accept or refuse an offered post, to make or not to make a proposal of marriage, he must have seen the extravagance of maintaining either that in every such case we pronounce one alternative right and the other wrong, or that when we do with difficulty arrive at such a pronouncement, its honesty is sufficient guarantee of its correctness. Yet when the pronouncement has been arrived at, in any case, it is authoritative, and even absolutely authoritative, for the person who has reached it. I know that my conscience is not inerrant, but the knowledge does not excuse disobedience. When we are once clearly awake to the relative extreme infrequency in our actual moral life of uncertainties of the kind Kant selects for sole consideration, uncertainties whether we are morally at liberty to break a generally sound moral rule, we may perhaps be tempted to say that an erring conscience, so far from being an imaginary "bogey", is an ever-potent source of moral mistake. When we have to make up our minds to a really critical choice, is not our *maximum* of conviction represented by language like that of the Prince in R. L. Stevenson's story, when he throws the Rajah's diamond into the river, "God forgive me if I am doing wrong, but this is what I mean to do?"

Most moralists, after all, have admitted that an erring conscience is only too common in actual life, but have not held that the possibility that my conscience may be in error diminishes my obligation to follow it. St. Thomas, for example, is as convinced that an erroneous conscience absolutely obliges as he is that it does not relieve from responsibility.[1] Hutcheson is teaching the same doctrine of an authority which is absolute, though not formally inerrant, when he distinguishes between the *material* goodness of the act

[1] *S.T.* i.[a] ii.[ae] q. 19, art. 5, 6; cf. *ib.* q. 76, art. 3.

which is in fact demanded by the situation and the *formal* goodness of the act which the agent honestly believes to be demanded;[1] so is Henry Sidgwick,[2] in different language, when he says that conscientiousness, though not a sufficient, is always a necessary, condition of virtuous action. The *opinio melior* among moralists is unmistakably that conscience may, and sometimes does, err, but that this want of complete inerrancy does not affect its authority. The light it gives is not always that of the sun at noonday, and may at times be as fitful as that of a taper in a dark night, but it *is* light, and is all the light I have. I could wish always to have the sun, but if the brightest light I can get is that of the taper, I must guide myself by it. In other words, conscience, when it speaks, is authoritative and, if you like, absolutely authoritative, but its authority is not inerrancy. Even Butler, the great classical moralist of the doctrine of the unqualified authoritativeness of conscience, never, so far as I can remember, credits the "principle of reflex approbation" with simple inerrancy.[3]

Next observe that the drawing of this formal distinction between the *authority* of conscience and inerrancy does not imply that all consciences are equally liable to err in all matters. How far my conscience can in practice be treated as secure against the danger of error will depend on many things: on the questions, for example, whether I am a callow youth, with all the inability of the young to see the full bearings of a confused and complex moral situation and to fix on those

[1] Though, to be strictly accurate, Hutcheson expresses himself rather differently about formal goodness; an act is formally good "when it flows from good affection in a just proportion" (*System of Moral Philosophy*, i. 252).

[2] *Methods of Ethics*, bk. iii. c. 1.

[3] Though he does regard its possible "aberrations" as confined within a narrow range (*Sermon* ii. par. 2, iii. pars. 5, 6).

which are most truly relevant, or a man made clear-sighted by experience of life; whether I have made it my practice to reflect on moral issues and to wait for the determination of conscience before committing myself, or have habitually allowed myself to act on headlong first impressions; whether the issue on which I have now to pronounce is, in its general character, of a type which experience of the situations presented by life has made familiar to me, or is, to me, unprecedented; whether I am facing a choice to be made by myself, or trying to give sound advice to another, and the like. Yet our moral experience may fairly be said to show that the surest way to get a more clearly illuminated conscience is to be steadily loyal to the light one already has, partly within one's self, partly in the practice and the counsel of those whom one discerns, by the light one possesses, to be better and wiser than one's self. A caterpillar, says James Ward,[1] eats to fill its skin, but in doing so it gets a better skin to fill. Even so, by loyalty to the conscience one has—if we carefully remember that amenability to the admonition of those whom that conscience reveals as one's betters is a point of this very loyalty—one gets a better conscience to be loyal to. The one *certain* way to miss getting a better conscience is to treat the conscience one has as less than absolutely authoritative, by living at random, or by handing over the direction of one's conduct blindly to another. The more loyally one thus follows conscience, the more assured and delicate do one's own personal discriminations between right and wrong become, and the more surely does one also learn who are the "others" who really stand out, in virtue of their moral insight, as guides whose help may be most safely relied on. There is thus nothing very paradoxical in a remark, made somewhere by Bosan-

[1] *Psychological Principles*, p. 268.

quet, that a man of habitual loyalty to conscience may, with sufficient experience of the situations of life, reach something not very different from infallibility of moral judgement, *for himself and his own personal choices*.

If, further, we find that, throughout a great historical civilisation in which our own life forms an integral part, and which has the prospect of indefinite further extension from age to age, and race to race, the deliverances of conscience, as interpreted by those who are most delicately sensitive to them and listen most loyally for them, steadily tend to integrate themselves into a coherent system, covering the whole sphere of human action and pervaded by definite principles, we may fairly say that in such a moral tradition we have, not indeed as yet fully given, but as in process of being given, a truly objective morality which is not only of obligation and authoritative for man as man, but guaranteed in all its essentials against error, a morality which is an adequate basis for an ethical *science* at least as assured and certain as the most indubitably scientific of physical sciences. I do not myself see why we might not entertain the same hopes for the future of theology as a genuine, assured, and yet progressive *science* of God, if once the claim for authority could be disassociated from the very different claim of formal inerrancy for the precise words of statements made in the past, or to be made in the future, under certain strictly defined "standard" conditions. "Dead" authority and "living" experience are sometimes talked of as if they formed a natural and irresoluble antithesis, but the two are only antithetic when the authority is conceived of as dead and sterotyped.

"I should not believe in the Gospel", says Augustine, *nisi me catholicae ecclesiae commoveret auctoritas*, "were

I not constrained by the authority of the Church universal".[1] Had Augustine meant by the *auctoritas ecclesiae catholicae*, as has sometimes been meant by the words, a formal order issued by ecclesiastical officials, it might be said that he is committing the circle of crediting the inerrancy of officials on the strength of passages in the very Gospel which he professes to receive only because it is vouched for by the inerrant officials. But the thought permits of a very different interpretation. The *auctoritas* of the Church universal is not dead and canalised, but intensely alive. It is the weight attaching to the undeniable reality of a new and vivid experience which transforms life. In the life actually lived by the members of the Christian community there is a unique dominant quality, and it is historical fact that the source of this new life is, by the consenting utterances of all generations of the community in which it is manifested, a new relation to the supernatural, mediated through the human personality of which the Gospel narrative is the record. Understood so, the "catholic" appeal to the authority of the Church as a ground for belief is not opposed to the familiar "evangelical" appeal to the personal experiences of the individual. Both are forms of the appeal to a direct and personal experience, but when the experiences thus appealed to are those of the whole community throughout its existence, the impressiveness of the argument is immeasurably increased. The testimony of one man to the source of his own changed life, if it stood alone, might easily be discredited. He may be thought to have wrongly found the genuine

[1] *Contra Epist. Manichaei*, v. 6. The context is to this effect. How is the claim of Mani to be an apostle of Jesus Christ to be defended against one who denies it? It is suggested that the Manichaeans may appeal to passages in the text of the Gospels. Augustine replies, "I only accept the Gospel because it comes to me with the *auctoritas* of the Church behind it. But it is the same Church which denies the apostolic mission of Mani. Its *auctoritas* is valid to substantiate both positions or neither."

source of the change in someone or something only incidentally connected with it. Or that which has really been mediated to him through one channel may be equally capable of being mediated with the same success to a second man through another, just as some other work than Chapman's Homer may do for another youth of poetic genius what Chapman's book did for Keats. The concurrent testimony of generations of a community with members from every "people and nation and kindred and tongue" is a different matter. It is not in the nature of things that the whole of such a community should be under a standing collective hallucination, either as to the reality of the special quality of its life, or as to its source.

You cannot explain away the entrance of a new spiritual life into the world through Christ as a consequence of "Jewish apocalyptic" ferment in the Palestine of the first century, for the *ecclesia catholica* embraces Greek and Scythian as well as Jew, and its history covers many generations; yet you find it bringing the same specific new quality into men's lives, whereever and whenever it comes into contact with them. So, again, you cannot account for "conversion" to the life of the *ecclesia catholica* as a psychological accompaniment of the attainment of puberty, a by-product of sexual development, for the "converted" are not all adolescents: some are children, some men and women in the prime of life, some in advanced age, and it is the *same* new quality which the "conversion" brings into the lives of them all. The "catholicity" of the community is precisely that which gives the driving force to the appeal to its authority, for what it means is that since the community does not belong to one sex, or one period of life, or one special age, or place, or national or social tradition, there can be no explaining away of its experience as illusory, unless one is prepared to believe in the recurrence of the same identical illusion, with the same identical *dominus Christus* as its centre, in all places, at all times, and in spite of all variations in individual and social endowment and tradition. The wider one spreads one's net the more "universal" the *ecclesia* which exhibits the common experience, the more incredible that it should be under an illusion about the genuineness of this experience, or the source of it. A scepticism which sees "collective illusion" here cannot well see anything else in any conviction of humanity, and if all our convictions may be an illusion, the very meaning of the distinction between truth and illusion is lost. That, I take it, is what is really meant by the *auctoritas* of the Church universal, and there could be no better illustration of an authority wholly independent of the claim of any set of officials to a formal inerrancy. And this is precisely why, with all respect for the "great church" of the West, I cannot but think that the attempt to locate the "seat of authority" in a specific official, or group of officials, is on a level with the attempts of some political theorists to localise "sovereignty" in the same fashion within the body politic and of some psycho-physicists to localise "the mind" in some delimited region of the nervous system.

VI

INSTITUTIONALISM

πάντα δὲ εὐσχημόνως καὶ κατὰ τάξιν γινέσθω.—1 Cor. xiv. 40.

To the type of man who is bent, before all things, on doing his thinking for himself, the great stumbling-block in the historical religions is, no doubt, that authoritarianism of which we have been speaking. Such a man, as Newman says of himself, can no more think to order than he can see with another's eyes, or breathe with another's lungs. But most men probably do not seriously resent authority in matters of belief as such; they are only too ready to have their thinking done for them in advance by others. If they reject the dictates of one "authority", it is usually only to surrender themselves to another. The mentally indolent—and we are all mentally indolent in many things—must have a pillow for their heads; if they throw away St. Paul or Calvin, it is only to repose on Karl Marx or Bernard Shaw. Less deep, but more widely diffused, is the resentment aroused by the tendency, shown by all the great historical religions, to evolve an elaborate system of ritual and ceremonial words and acts, and more particularly to develop *mysteries*, or *sacraments*, in which material objects and external acts terminating on them are treated as channels through which a specially rich and direct contact is made with a supernatural spiritual reality. The history of any great positive religion abundantly illustrates both the universality and depth of this tendency to ceremonialism and the persistency of the opposition it evokes.

Thus it would be hard to imagine anything much simpler, more spontaneous, less formal than the worship of the early Christian congregations, as known to us from the New Testament, the Apostolic Fathers, and the first apologists, or more complex, conventionalised, and artificial than the systems which have grown out of those beginnings and still regulate the practice of the great majority of Christians. In the former the element of freedom and spontaneity of approach to the divine is at a *maximum*, that of artifice at a *minimum*; within a framework of the simplest, all detail is left to free improvisation. In the latter there is a fixed rule for almost everything—the words to be said, the tones in which they are to be uttered, the gestures to be made, the postures and garments of the officiants, the precise fashion of all sorts of accessories. Simplicity seems to have given place everywhere to rather cumbrous complexity, nature to artifice, spontaneity to rigid traditional formula. And the curious thing is that, after every reaction towards simplification, the same development seems regularly to begin again. The "reform" which started as a "return to nature" commonly ends in the adoption of a new conventional ceremonial, often less complex and usually less aesthetically rich than the old, but equally rigid and as little spontaneous. Thus, among ourselves, I suppose, we should expect to find spontaneity and freedom from fixed ceremonial form in the Salvation Army, if it is to be found anywhere. Yet I well remember being present years ago at a great "rally" of that body and receiving a very strong impression that in the "knee-drill", "volley-firing", and handkerchief-waving executed to order, I was witnessing the initial stages in the growth of a new ritual, cruder and noisier than those with a longer history, but no less truly artificial and conventional. (Whether the growth has resulted in further development to-day, I regret that I cannot state.)

It is a mistake to confuse this tendency of the historical religions to conventional ceremonial and ritual with a mere movement towards display, pomp, or materialistic splendour. Ritual, as such, is neither beautiful, nor pompous, nor glowing; it may be bald, ugly, drab, without ceasing to be ritual. There is nothing glowing or pompous about the Gregorian "modes"; the bands and Geneva gown of a Presbyterian minister, the garb of a Captain in the Salvation Army, are just as much ritualistic or ceremonial vestments, in the proper sense of the word, as alb or chasuble, since all are alike the conventional "uniform" appropriated to persons set apart to discharge specific functions. Ritualism, reduced to its simplest elements, is just the tendency to confine the expression of a specific human activity to one artificial form prescribed by convention; the antithesis to it is not simplicity, or baldness, but free spontaneity, permission granted to the activity of the moment to find its expression for itself unhampered by precedent, convention, or custom.

Both the tendency to ceremonial, or ritual, and the revolt against it are universal features of human life, present in many spheres besides that of worship. The difficulty, indeed, would be to find any human activity in connection with which both tendencies do not make themselves felt. Every human social activity inevitably tends to develop its own conventions, and so to create a ritual for itself. There is a recognised ritual of the breakfast-table, the dinner-table, the drawing-room, embodied in the rules which we speak of sometimes as those of etiquette, sometimes as those of civilised manners. Whenever we have intercourse of any kind with our fellows, there are always ways in which things are done and other ways in which they are not done, rules of mannerly behaviour to be adhered to, whether we are personally disposed to follow them or not. We all know that careless infraction of the rules, disregard of all the "conventions", is commonly the beginning of that neglect of the "decencies of civilised life" which, surrendered to, means relapse into "barbarism", loss, in great measure, of the rational man's command over himself and his moods. We can understand well enough what Mr. Belloc means when, in one of his stories,[1] he speaks of a man assailed by mortal illness as preserved from the complete collapse of his manhood by "habit, or ritual, the mistress of men sane". Nor do we hesitate to condemn, as at least an early symptom of what may grow by neglect to be a serious moral disorder, needless or wilful departure, when there is no adequate reason, from the conventionally fixed way of conducting ourselves, even though we may be able to give no further ground for conformity than that the established way is established.

That the members of a family, for example, should ask after one another's health, or greet one another with a kiss when they reassemble daily in the breakfast-room is, in itself, only a piece of conventionalism, a bit of ritual. But we know that disregard of the convention only too readily leads to a real preoccupation with self and a dulling of one's concern for the other members of the family group. The habit of answering letters when possible, within twenty-four hours of their arrival, is a ritual which it is often a little "costing" to practice, and of no great moment to neglect, but—I speak with shame as an offender in this matter—refusal

[1] *Emmanuel Burden*, c. 12.

to have some rule of the kind, and to keep to it always, means that our "unconventionality" will, sooner or later, cause serious detriment to our own, or our correspondents', interests. A rule of conversation, like that which forbids a well-bred man to gesticulate, or raise his voice, in the drawing-room when he feels justifiably excited or aggrieved, is never more necessary than at the moments when observance of it is hardest. We need an artificial barrier as a protection against the very real moral danger of "letting ourselves go", and the impulsive man whose natural tendency is always to the unrestrained expression of all his moods in bawling, strong language, sharp contradiction, table-banging, needs the safeguard of the convention more than any of us.

Mr. Chesterton,[1] indeed, has glorified freedom from all these conventional restraints as the essence of true masculine *camaraderie*, but I should suppose that even he would find the respect of some conventions necessary in one whom he could regard as *bon camarade*; he would not like to be hugged and slobbered over, or even perpetually thumped on the back, or prodded in the ribs, by his "comrade", and still less to have the comrade performing all necessary natural functions in his presence. Without some foundation of respect for my whole personality, body as well as soul, a man, or even a dog, cannot be a "comrade" to me, and what lies at the bottom of ritual and convention is just this respect, which involves recognition of barriers which must not be broken down. The two most intimate associations of human life are, I take it, the "dear love of comrades" and the *consortium totius vitae* which is marriage;

[1] *What's Wrong with the World*, p. 96. Mr. Chesterton was ill-advised when he took the social behaviour of Johnson as his classic example of "unconventionality". The "Club" was something different from a boozing-ken, and the records of Johnson's actual conversation are marked by a degree of regard for "conventions" which strikes us to-day as exaggerated.

neither can exist without respect and the sense of inviolable privacies, and where these are there must always be some element of convention which finds its embodiment in ritual.

Of course, like all things which are of good use in life, convention and ritual have their obvious abuses. In all relations of life there must be certain barriers and self-repressions, and it is natural that mankind, once alive to the fact, should go to excess in setting up barriers and multiplying forms beyond what is needed; convention, the sustainer of wholesome human relations, then passes into a conventionalism which withers them. The proper respect for the bodily presence of another which is modesty, a thing no less salutary than beautiful, whatever Blake and his idolaters may have said falsely to the contrary, passes into the false modesty, or prudery, which affects to ignore the very fact of the body and its functions. The respect for parents which is the foundation of human relations between the young and the old is no less easily converted into an affected self-abasement which makes mutual confidence, true affection, and right guidance of the young by the old impossible. The different, but equally necessary, courtesy of equal towards equal, without which there could be no honourable friendship, is as readily overlaid by the forms of a ceremonialism which makes real friendship impossible. And thus, while convention is indispensable to sustain all the relations which give civilised life its superiority over savagery, the sense of the value of convention needs always to be kept in due restraint by wholesome impatience of the multiplication of superfluous rules of ceremony, etiquette, ritual. We can take our pattern of civilised life neither from a *Roi soleil* or a Castilian *grande*, nor from a *sansculotte* zealot for "fraternity", or an Elijah Pogram. Civilised existence is "art", not undressed "nature"; but art must not be allowed to ossify into artificiality. Here, as in all the problems of life, our business is to find a "right mean", and the finding of the "mean" is never easy. We only find it at all on the condition that the two antithetic tendencies, to fixed form and to free spontaneity, compensate one another.

I have dwelt so long on what may appear obvious for a simple reason. If we are to appreciate the true strength and weakness, in the religious sphere or any other, of both the antithetic tendencies which we may conveniently call the ritualistic and the anti-ritualistic, it is important not to confuse the essence of either with some of its accidents; a confusion which is made only too often, especially in connection with the manifestation of the ritualistic tendency in the institutionalising and conventionalising of a community's religious practice. In popular controversy among ourselves, it is common to hear ceremonial, or ritual, spoken of by those who sympathise with it as "imposing", or "magnificent", and equally common to find it confused by those who dislike it with such things as a taste for millinery and fancy-dress. In much the same spirit William James has somewhere, a little complacently, contrasted the European demand that rulers should exhibit themselves, on public occasions, in uniform with the gratification which, as he avers, the "democratic" sentiment of Americans derives from seeing a President discharge his public duties in a badly fitting morning coat.

Talk of this kind seems to me to betray complete misapprehension of the source of the opposing tendencies. What is really at the bottom of the demand for ceremonial is not the desire to be "splendid", or "imposing", but to be *formal*. The object of a fixed ritual is not to *impose*, but to *impress* in a certain specific way, and the impression may be, and often is, produced even more effectively by unusual austerity and artificial simplicity than by gorgeous show. There is, for example, a great deal of pomp and splendour about the ceremonial of a *Missa Pontificalis*, with its brilliant and varied vestments, its wealth of music, lights, and incense. A "plain celebration", correctly conducted, dispenses with nearly all this show, and is sensibly austere and bare; the traditional worship of Good Friday, with its open and empty "sanctuary", stripped altar, unkindled lights, and sombre black vestments, is artificially simplified to the extreme of austerity. But attention to the correctness of the worship is equally "ritualistic" in all three cases, and, to some temperaments at least, the austerest ceremony is much the most impressive.

Similarly it would be pure misunderstanding to suppose that the leaders in what is often called the "ritualistic" movement within the Anglican Church in the last century took any very profound interest in millinery and perfumes as such; indeed, the gentle satire of humorists like Thackeray, who saw the beginnings of the movement, is as often directed against its austerity in some respects as against its magnificence in others. The "Tractarian" of Thackeray's satire makes it one part of his pose to affect an unusual simplicity in the cut of his surplice and the hang of his stole; like the early Methodist preachers, he crops his hair close and brushes it straight; in general, he makes a point of sacrificing the personal adornments of the older type of fashionable clergyman and even of cultivating an artificial monotony of delivery in his sermons, by way of protest against the meretriciousness of rhetoric and elocution.[1] If he also wanted vestments and ceremonies,

[1] See the amusing account in *The Newcomes* of the effects of "Puseyism" on the Rev. Charles Honeyman.

he wanted them not because they were rich, or artistic, but because they were traditional, charged with a certain conventional significance as symbols. To be sure, there were persons who attached themselves to the "movement" for different reasons; because, for example, their slightly barbaric aesthetic cravings found satisfaction in a riot of colour, light, and fragrance. It is conceivable even that there may have been a few foolish young curates here and there who did really at heart simply want to dazzle milkmaids and servant-girls by a showy costume. But it would be childish calumny to confuse such weaklings with the men who bore the brunt of the prosecutions and imprisonments for "ritual offences".

On the other side, also, I can hardly believe that the typical American of whom James speaks is really much concerned that the coat worn by his President on public occasions shall be a misfit. His feeling, I take it, is one of protest against the principle of "uniform",[1] not a preference for ill-made and badly sitting clothes. The real issue is directly between convention and spontaneity. What the supporter of "forms" and "ceremonies" feels, often unconsciously, is that without regulation by convention there is no guarantee that expression, in word or act, will be adequate and appropriate to the thing to be expressed. The spirit which should dominate an occasion will not do so, as it should, if it gets a wrong embodiment, and without guidance by regulations carefully conformed to, it will constantly be getting an embodiment which is, more or less, a

[1] A "uniform", I take it, displeases him because he regards it as a kind of livery, a badge of the "menial", who is not a really "free" citizen. His livery is the outward and visible sign that he is not *dominus sui*, his own master. The zeal of Puritan reformers against vestments had a different source. The traditional vestments were objected to not because they were uniform, and uniform is *in se* objectionable, but because they were the *Pope's* uniform, "rags of Rome", as the urbane phrase went. James's American possibly also has a touch of more special animosity against a "militaristic" uniform.

wrong one. What the enemy of "set forms" feels no less strongly is that the conventionalised embodiment of a spiritual activity is always in danger of becoming a *dead* body. If he sometimes talks as though he were positively attracted by slovenliness, crudity, and disorder, he only does so because he thinks, rightly or wrongly, that those things are inseparable from life; life itself is an untidy, disorderly, crude affair.

The whole controversy is, in the end, only one form of the wider disagreement between the votary of significant form and the enthusiast for a rude vitality which cannot be confined within any bounds of form, precisely because it never knows fully what it would be at. We find a precisely similar clash in letters between the worshippers of "style" and the worshippers of rough force, and in philosophy between the "intellectualist" and the partisan of the *élan vital*. To ignore this is to be unjust to both parties. And if we are to be discriminatingly just, we must be careful, in discussing the issue thus raised, to take it at a sufficiently universal level. We are not principally concerned with the worth of a certain kind or amount of ceremony, as against more or less ceremony, or the relative worth of the various "uses" of different communities; these are not questions for philosophy. Whenever it is maintained that certain activities, to flourish at all, must get special expression at special times and places, and in special ways, what is being asserted is the necessity of ritual, in the wide sense, for life. Complete denial of the principle, involving the position that set times, places, forms, are matters of indifference, or are even dangerous to the spiritual life, means unqualified adoption of a strictly individualistic "quietism".[1]

[1] I use the word, perhaps not quite conventionally, to mean any kind of "waiting for the spirit to move" one, and letting the expression take care of itself.

Now we have, I think, only to conceive of "quietism" as systematically applied to the whole range of human activities to see that its results would pretty certainly be the very reverse of those at which the advocates of unfettered spontaneity aim. Consider, for example, what would be the probable effect of the unqualified suppression of form and conventional ritual on the most intimate of our personal affections. What would happen if the ritual of family life were entirely abolished? It would follow, in the first place, that we should recognise no special occasions on which family affections manifest themselves in some way consecrated by tradition. The keeping of birthdays within the family, with its traditional accompaniment of special salutations, letters, dinners, presents, the manifestation of the sense of loss after bereavements by the observance of a season of mourning, and the wearing of the garb of mourning, would have to be discontinued; though marriages, in view of their legal consequences, would still require to be celebrated with some sort of official formality, the formality would be reduced to the indispensable minimum; one must suppose that a wedding would cease to be a scene of festivity, and that the married would cease to mark the annual return of the wedding-day by any of the little customary observances.

Nor would this be all. Strict carrying out of the principle would even forbid the use within a family circle of such formal conventional gestures as the kiss of welcome and good will at morning and evening, at return from and departure on a journey. These are all pieces of customary ritual, and against all it may be argued that those who are most careful in observing the conventional form are by no means always the persons who feel most deeply and steadily the affection the form is meant to symbolise; and, again, that the truly loving father or brother does not really feel more love on the anniversary of a birthday than on other days of the year, or that those who display their grief in bereavement by the punctilious donning of mourning garb often seem to lay the memory of their lost friends and kinsmen aside with their sables. All this is true enough; one can easily understand the feeling which has often prompted sincere and warm-hearted persons to make a point of defying the conventions by disregard of these rituals. We can appreciate, even if we do not unreservedly approve, the contention that when a man's heart is full of sorrow, or of family affection, he has no need to put on mourning or to celebrate birthdays.

Yet it is no less certain that, since men are very forgetful creatures, if they do not assist nature with art by providing themselves with occasions for contemplating the object of their affection and giving outward expression to the emotions aroused by the contemplation, remembrance and emotion must tend to fade. "Out of sight" really is "out of mind". And if there is one point which has fairly been established in the psychology of the emotions, it is the falsity of the popular notion that emotion is deepened by inhibition, when the inhibition is more than temporary. James was at least right in saying that our real object in training children to suppress facile displays of emotion is not to make them feel more, but to make them *think* more and feel *less*.[1] One may safely say, justified by one's personal experience of life and the known practice of universal humanity, that if a man means to keep his own deepest personal affections alive, there is only a choice for him between two alternatives. Either he must fall back on the opportunities for recollection, and the expression of emotion in act, provided

[1] *Principles of Psychology*, ii. 466.

by social convention, or if he finds the provision for any reason unsuitable, he must devise a fresh ritual for himself, as a surrogate for that in general practice. If one will do neither, the "world", the βιωτικαὶ μέριμναι, always "too much with us", will infallibly choke the fountains of the inner life. For, without such an outlet,

> Each day brings its little dust
> Our petty souls to fill;
> And we forget because we must,
> And not because we will.

Further, even the most private ritual of occasions and opportunities never becomes completely individual. The little family circle, narrow as it is, is, after all, a circle, a community; it is indispensable to the wholesomeness of life that its affections shall be communal, and that the special occasions and opportunities which sustain them shall be opportunities and occasions for the whole group. For example, the keeping of a child's birthday is such a special opportunity not merely to remember and display the father's, and again the mother's, affection for the child, but also for the parents to remember and display their affection for one another, and their *common* participation in affection for the child, and also for brothers and sisters to remember and display *their* love, not only for the child whose birthday is being kept, but for each other and for their parents. A true birthday celebration, like an annual reunion of the household, is a feast of the family and of family affection. It comprises a whole complex of finely discriminated and graded affections, and demands a ritual which gives comely and appropriate expression to them all. It may fail of its purpose if it strikes too loudly, or not loudly enough, any one of the notes which it ought to sound. And this means that, to be utilised to the full, it must contain features which are less spontaneously prompted by the special mood of some of its celebrants than by those of others. The parents would not spontaneously exhibit their parental affection for their child in precisely the behaviour which is most appropriate and spontaneous in his small brothers and sisters; yet the birthday feast must not fall apart into two concurrent but distinct festivals, a festival of parental, and another of fraternal, love; that would be destructive of its whole significance as a manifestation of the spirit of the family. This, of itself, implies that the observance will necessarily embrace features which some of the parties concerned will feel to be definitely conventional and artificial so far as they in particular are concerned, features which the general spirit of the occasion would not have dictated to *them*, if they had stood alone, or even features they might definitely wish to be away, if they were the only parties to be considered. Even within the close family group, the individualist temper which refuses to take its part in any detail of the conventional observances not directly fraught with meaning to itself would shatter the unity of the group, if it were allowed unfettered free play. Even here in practice life requires a certain amount of give-and-take, such as is called for on a larger scale by all institutionalism.

Nor have we, even now, exhausted the significance of art and convention for the life of the family circle. So far we have spoken chiefly of the value of comparatively rare special occasions for contemplation and the exercise of the emotions which attend it. In point of fact convention has a subtler part to play in the daily routine. We need recollection daily, not only once or twice in the year. If we are to meet the demands made on us by personal intimacies adequately, we shall have to show ourselves loving and sympathetic, to give appropriate expression to what we have at heart, not only on special occasions but daily, and we cannot trust to the moment always to provide the best response to situations. Some of us are by nature reticent and awkward; we do not find it easy to meet a situation properly, if it calls for the expression of what is deepest in us; our habitual tendency is to very inadequate expression. We shall seem careless and cold when we are not really so, unless we are at some pains to make ourselves speak and act as the situation demands. Others are naturally prone to the expression of surface moods, and so are constantly making a wrong impression. We seem, for instance, to be irritated when we are really not so. And all of us are careless, thoughtless, and preoccupied. From some or all of these causes we may only too easily spoil the most precious intimacies of life, and there is no better way to guard ourselves against this ever-present danger than to protect ourselves by the habit of little observances which are "conventional" in the sense that we should often not practise them if we left ourselves to the suggestion of the moment, and that it costs some effort to keep them in being.

The point to be made, then, is that a certain element of art, even of artifice, is indispensable everywhere in life, if the activities which give it its highest value are to be permanently sustained at an adequate level. Nowhere can we afford to be wholly "free-and-easy". Least of all is it possible to be simply free-and-easy in the expression of activities aroused by the objects of our highest reverence, or even respect. If reverent devotion is to be kept at the level necessary for its rightful place in human life, there must be set occasions and opportunities for its special manifestation, and the forms in which it is manifested must not be left to improvisation, or they will inevitably be largely incongruous and jarring. We see this in connection with the maintenance of a national patriotism, a profound and ennobling sense of the worth of our national ideals and history and our gratitude to our national past. It would be impossible to keep a true patriotism alive without particular occasions for commemoration of the great achievements and deliverances of the past, and worthy celebration of the memory of those whom, under God, we have to thank for them. We should not be better Frenchmen, Englishmen, or Scots, nor even better Europeans, but worse, if we refused to honour the recurrent anniversaries of our deliverance from oppression or danger, if we forgot the memory of St. Joan of Arc, or Nelson, or Wallace. We cannot be always dwelling on these things in the routine of daily life, and it is well that we should not do so too often, or too obtrusively; but if daily life is to be unconsciously leavened through by the right kind of love of country, it is needful that there should be regular provided occasions when we may dwell very specially with the recollections which specially evoke the feeling of patriotic devotion.

Again, because the very function of such commemorations is to raise us, for the time, out of the atmosphere of every day, it is specially important that the forms taken by our "patriotic exercises" should be, in a high degree, conventional and, in no bad sense, artificial. If a whole community is to be lifted above its common level into a mood of worthy patriotic thought and emotion, we cannot trust for that effect to the inspirations of a haphazard spontaneity. Even a minor inadequacy in expression will, for example, pervert what might have been a stimulus to the finest type of national public spirit into a degrading exhibition of vulgar complacent or truculent "flag-flapping". In any really appropriate public expression of true patriotism, the form taken by the expression will be consciously "conventional", or "ceremonial"; it will be felt, to some degree, as an imposed restraint, just because it is so difficult to keep any mood, at its best, clean of the degradation which attends any lapse from the highest standard.

What Kant says of reverence for the moral law is true, in some measure, of all respect for an object of the mind's contemplation. The attitude is hard to keep up; it is one of conscious constraint, and so "painfully tinged", as Kant puts it, because of the inhibition of the commonplace and less worthy which it involves.[1] It is the function of proper ceremony, or ritual, to maintain this inhibition at the same time that it gives expression to the exalted mood. We ought, therefore, to understand that there is real justification for the common feeling of mankind that the solemn public acts of national functionaries should be marked as having a public significance by an external dignity and decorum which stamps them as having a character out of the ordinary. There is something reasonable in making the inauguration of magistrates, the holding of courts of justice, the assembling of the legislature, notable by an etiquette of costume, gesture, utterance, which impresses the imagination, inhibits commonplace associations, and makes the spectator or auditor aware that he is being taken, for the time, out of the sphere of the merely domestic and private. There ought, for instance, to be a suggestion of the extraordinary and "otherworldly" about such a transaction as the administration of criminal justice. It would not be well that we should not be reminded by the surroundings that judge, jury, prisoner are engaged in a business which is not their private and personal affair; the "tonality" appro-

[1] *Werke* (Hartenstein[2]), v. 82.

priate to the office or the market would be out of place *here*. If we are among the audience when a convicted murderer receives sentence of death, we need to have it brought home to us that the speaker who pronounces the sentence is not Jones or Smith signifying his personal pleasure; he "bears *our* person" and announces a purpose to which *we* are consenting parties; the responsibility for the doom pronounced rests on each of us. The real judge in the cause is "Everyman", and this is why the execution of the murderer is not simply a second and premeditated murder. This is what the often thoughtlessly decried ceremonial of the courts of justice is meant to keep us from forgetting.[1]

Similarly there is just one department of life in connection with which even the type of American described sympathetically by William James seems to feel as the rest of us do. So far as I know, even he does not carry his hostility to ritual and ceremonial to the point of objecting to uniform in the Army and Navy. I do not believe that the explanation of this inconsistency is completely given by the utilitarian consideration that the very distinctive dress of combatants is a convenience to the combatants themselves and a protection both to them and to non-combatants. True as this is, it will not explain the universality of regulations requiring the wearing of uniform on public occasions in times of peace, or the strength of the sentiment that is outraged by the use of "colourable" imitations of the national uniform for purposes of advertisement, and by the exhibition of it in ludicrous circumstances on the comic stage. The truth, I believe, is that the national uniform is felt to be the symbol of a life dedicated to

[1] Something of the same effect is produced in our own country even by the use of the old Norman-French formula in signifying the royal assent to an Act of Parliament. There is a feeling which is satisfied by the formula *Le roy le veult*; it would be dissatisfied by "very well", and outraged by "Yep".

specially arduous devotion to the public service. We expect the sight of it to sustain noble public feeling at a high level. It marks out the soldier of the country to the rest of us for recognition and honour, and it should keep him from forgetting that he is under a special obligation of honour not to fall in his daily conduct below the standards demanded by his position as a dedicated man. I cannot help wondering, therefore, whether the anti-ritualism regarded by James as so typically American may not be connected with a certain failure in the population of the United States at large to take statesmanship and the administration of justice quite seriously. (There can be no harm in alluding to this failure, since American writers themselves have been among the first to proclaim and deplore it.) If the mass of any people are contented to see in political life, or in the administration of justice, only a set of artifices by which professional rogues compass their personal ends, it is quite intelligible that they should feel no need to invest the acts of the legislator and the judge with any special impressiveness. When the conviction has really come home to them that these acts are public and representative, and that the society as a whole, and its several members in particular, have a genuine responsibility in connection with them, I should think it most likely that the sentiment in question may be profoundly modified.

We may now apply what we have said to the special problem of the right place of the element of institution, ceremony, ritual, in the communal religious life. In principle, indeed, there seems nothing left to be said beyond what has been said already. But I think we can see why the conflict between the tendency to fixed forms and institutions and the complementary tendency to unregulated spontaneity should be exceptionally acute in this particular field. On the one side, it is in the acts which give expression to the religious life of the community that its members are lifted most completely into an atmosphere remote from that of all their everyday this-world transactions. In their communal worship they are conscious of being brought, as they are brought nowhere else, into direct relation with the wholly transcendent, supernatural, and "other". Here, more than anywhere else, the sense of being in the presence of something entitled to absolute and unqualified reverence will be paramount, and it will carry with it the completest inhibition of all incongruous lower activities. The state of soul in which a man is wholly taken out of himself and filled with an adoring sense of the immediate presence of God is therefore exceptionally hard to maintain. At best it can be maintained by most of us in its intensity and purity for only a short time; the concentration and withdrawal demanded are eminently hard and exhausting, and we feel the need that they should be supported and encouraged by all the suggestions of an environment differentiated in subtle ways from that of our more everyday and worldly hours.

Again, as all experience proves, the very depth and intensity of the emotional mood of worship is itself a source of grave dangers. The danger—it is one which besets all deep and intense moments of feeling—is that other and incongruous emotions, which in the ordinary affairs of life only figure on a reduced scale, may intrude themselves. If one merely shuts out, for the time, the commonplace outer world and its surface interests, and does nothing more, there is the risk that the house of the soul, which has been swept and garnished for the coming of the supreme guest, may be occupied by "unclean" spirits. The "tumults" of the soul may usurp upon its "depths"; excitement, and that of a very evil kind, may take the place of intense interior stillness and the "waiting" spirit. I need not particularise to make it obvious why importance should be attached to the fostering of the true temper of worship by devices which aim at shutting out both the commonplace and the unworthy, and so erecting an environment which makes it easier to maintain in the worshipping assembly the right, not a wrong, mood of unworldliness. No doubt, if we could make the soul entirely independent of "environment", we should have no need of these devices, but if we could do that we should have ceased to be what, in fact, we are, and must remain, "creatures". It is part of the humility of the "creature" to recognise that there is for it no absolute escape from "environment". This, as it seems to me, explains and largely justifies the tendency of all worships to take on a traditionally conventionalised form.

On the other side, there is no attitude in life which is so intensely *personal* as the attitude of the worshipper in the felt presence of his God. Unless adoration has occupied the inmost citadel of my personality, I am not really worshipping; I am merely complying with an external form. Religion is not, as the quietist holds it to be, merely a personal affair between myself and my Maker, but it is at least that, however much more it may be; when the intimate personal relation is absent, nothing can replace it. This is why we rightly feel that the *cultus* of a Greek city-state of the classical times is something quite different from what we mean by religion; it is *cultus* and it is nothing more. The philosophy of a man like Plato *is* profoundly saturated with religion, and for that very reason it treats the *cultus* with irony, or open hostility. Now there is always sure to be much in the conventional *cultus* of my group which does not stand in any felt relation to my own personality, much which to me individually is a matter of mere form imposed from outside, and perhaps felt to be more or less repugnant.[1] We can understand, therefore, why in this department of life, more than in any other, the institutional and conventional should provoke the individual's resentment. I want that in my worship of my God, so far as possible, there should be an utter breaking down of every barrier between my personality and His; that the two should come into a contact "closer than breathing"; that He should flow in upon me without let or hindrance. And the whole apparatus of conventional forms may readily appear to me no better than an artificial multiplication of hindrances and barriers, the banishing of God to an inaccessible distance. Hence it is often the most deeply religious men who feel the keenest resentment against the whole of the institutional and ceremonial element in the religion of their own communities. The very depth and sincerity of a man's devotion to his God will make him impatient of the suggestion that there is not a way of access to God which stands open to the human soul at all times, in all places, and independently of all prescribed formal avenues of approach. It is in this spirit that we find Plotinus refusing to take any part in the revived Hellenic worship which carried some of his friends off their feet. He refused to visit the temples on the ground that "it is for the gods to come to me, not for me to go to them".[2] That is, the true temple of God is a soul made fit for His habitation. When a man has done all that is in him to make his own mind fit for the heavenly visitation, it must be left for Deity to

[1] Is there any deeply religious Christian of any Christian church, I wonder, who does not find *some* features in the worship sanctioned by his church decidedly repellent?

[2] Porphyry, *Vit. Plot.* 10, ἐκείνους δεῖ πρὸς ἐμὲ ἔρχεσθαι, οὐκ ἐμὲ πρὸς ἐκείνους.

choose when and how He will come to His temple; it is not for us to control His movements. It is the same spirit which inspires the vehement protests of the greatest Old Testament prophets against the ceremonialism of a people who draw near to their God through sacrifice and ritual, while there is no real contact of their personality with His: "Their hearts are far from Him".

(In modern times these protests have often been exaggerated to the pitch of maintaining an absolute antithesis between two incompatible types of religion, a "priestly", which is *ex hypothesi* false in principle, and a "prophetic", which is true; but this is something of a caricature of the facts. It has not unreasonably been retorted that the two prophets who did most for the creation of the Jewish Church out of which Christianity has directly arisen, Jeremiah and Ezekiel, were themselves priests,[1] and that "prophetic" religion is so far from being the same thing as *true* religion that the majority of prophets appear to have been *false* prophets. Indeed, it might perhaps be said that what Jeremiah, the greatest of all the prophets, foresees in the famous anticipation which has meant so much to the Christian Church is not the disappearance of institutionalism, but the supersession of the special function of the prophet: "In that day a man shall not *teach* his neighbour . . . for they shall all know me".[2] And according to the same prophet, in the Messianic days, "Neither shall the priests the Levites want a man before me to offer burnt offerings, and to burn oblations, and to do sacrifice continually".[3] But it is true to say that

[1] The force of the retort would not be affected even if the recent theory that *Ezekiel* is a pseudonymous work of the Greek period should come to be generally accepted. In any case it is a "priestly" work.

[2] *Jer.* xxxi. 34.

[3] *Ib.* xxxiii. 18.

in the great Israelite prophets we see the tension between institutionalism and spontaneity at its acutest.)

The actual attacks upon institutionalism characteristic of certain quarters in our own times seem to me, indeed, to be very largely on a lower level. To some extent, to be sure, they are prompted by the impatience of an intense spirituality with things which are felt as hindrances in the way of free access of the individual human spirit to God. But largely, also, they appear, at least, to be inspired by different and inferior motives. Thus there is a widespread tendency to decry everything in the nature of institution, not so much on the ground that it is found to interfere with personal spirituality of temper, as on the ground that it is "childish" or "unreasonable". Why, it is said, should I trouble, for example, to go to a church on set days and at set hours, to find God, when I am just as near Him every moment at home or in the fields? Why should I even have any special times of the day for private prayer, when God can be addressed by the human spirit at any moment? It would not, I believe, be unfair to say that most of the anti-institutionalists who urge these considerations are not persons of exceptionally high and ardent spirituality; more often, probably, they are worldly and indifferent. When a man declines to pray with the "congregation", he does not most commonly decline with a view to making his prayer more intense and heart-felt; it is rather that he does not really feel any great need or desire to pray.[1]

There is also a position intermediate between that of the indifferentist and the passionately religious man of markedly individualist type. The one real function of

[1] That God is as truly present in the fields as in the church is an argument not unknown on the lips of the sort of man who really means that he prefers "joy-riding" to worship.

eligion, it is often said, is to promote the leading of morally good life. The whole institutional side of a eligion is valuable so far as it conduces to this end, but no further. And there is no close intrinsic connection between any part of it and the leading of a good life. Such connection as does actually exist is extrinsic and accidental, and it is chiefly those whose intelligence and reason are least developed who are "helped" in living a good life by institutional religion. It, with its apparatus of set times and places, prescribed forms and rites, may be temporarily allowed as a concession to the weak, but the aim of a rational piety should be to make men strong enough to live as they ought without such supports; a true and robust spirituality should be independent of them.

In large part this alleged irrationality and unspirituality of the specifically institutional in the historical religions may fairly be regarded as disposed of by the general considerations on which we have been dwelling. But some further points suggested by the particular anti-institutional arguments just rehearsed seem to call for separate brief examination. In particular there are two widespread and mischievous mistakes which are between them responsible for a great deal of the present fashionable depreciation of what used to be called "religious observances"; though both these mistakes spring from misconception of the specific character of religion, they may seriously impair the inner life of naturally deeply religious souls.

(1) It is a complete mistake to find the sole value of religion for life in its instrumental services to morality. The reality of these services, and the extreme difficulty of attaining a high level of social or personal moral practice except under the influence of the "religious sanction"—by which I do *not* mean expectation of mere

personal rewards and punishments—are facts paten and undeniable. But though religion, like art, may have and when it is good religion will have, a morally en-nobling effect, the effect is something different from it cause. To be religious is not the same thing as to try t be morally good, any more than to enjoy, or practise art is to try to be morally good, though a man's re-ligion is not worth very much if it does not lead him to try earnestly to be virtuous. And it is a familiar fact of life that the persons who try most consciously to be morally good are by no means always those who respond most readily to "religious impressions", while, on the other side, very real sensitiveness to the super-natural, like sensibility to beauty, is often found co-existing with grave moral weakness. It is still largely true that publicans and harlots — I do not mean *ex*-publicans and *ex*-harlots—can be much nearer to the kingdom of God than morally earnest Pharisees. The secret source of what is definitely religious in life is the vivid sense of creatureliness and the felt attitude of the creature towards its Creator, the experience of worship or devotion; and to adore is not the same thing as to cultivate moral betterment. To repeat what we have said so often already, morality which remains morality and nothing more is an attitude to that which *ought* to be; adoration and religion are attitudes to that which overpoweringly and tremendously *is*. To degrade wor-ship into a mere instrument of moral improvement would be to make the same sort of mistake as that made when art is degraded into a mere vehicle of instruction.

By consequence, much as art would be deprived of most of its power to influence character if the artist, in producing his work of art, consciously aimed at being didactic, or the contemplator of the work at learning a "moral lesson", so a religion would lose its best actual moral effects on life if its worship were consciously directed on moral reformation. A great religion produces noble moral fruit only because it is aiming, first and foremost, at something else. It aims at making a vision of God a real and dominant presence in life; moral ennoblement follows spontaneously on the vision. It is not myself and my "moral being", but God and God's being which occupy the centre of my attention in proportion as I have a really religious experience of reality.

(2) It follows, further, that a man's religion, to be worth anything, must be something more than a purely personal and private transaction between himself and his God. Religion is degraded from its rightful place in life not only when it is conceived as a mere support of moral endeavour, but also when it is thought of, as it so often is, as primarily concerned with the personal "salvation", however conceived, of the individual's soul. God, not the self and its private destiny, is the true centre of genuine religious interest, and the supreme religious motive to action is the "glory of God", not the safeguarding of a man's personal interests. For this very reason that my private selfhood is not the true centre of religious interest, religion, though an intensely personal thing, is emphatically not a *private* concern. The saint's interest in God, and worship of a God felt to be present, are no more the private affair of the saint than the scientific man's interest in truth and its discovery is his private affair, or the artist's interest in the making and contemplation of things of beauty his. In all these cases there is an experience of vision, or contemplation, and the experient, who is one term in the experience, has, of course, his own private, and in its concreteness incommunicable, personality. But the other term in the experience, the object

contemplated, Truth, Beauty, the God of the spirits of all flesh, is above these privacies, and it is the object which gives the experience its significance. The experience, in all these cases, is one with a core of direct cognitive apprehension, and *therefore* an experience of being possessed, "informed by", "assimilated to" the apprehended object, an *adaequatio cognoscentis cum re*, which takes the experient out of his private solitude without impairing his individuality. Worship, like the pursuit of truth, or the fashioning and enjoyment of beautiful things, is essentially a community-function, not because the individual person is something less real than the community, but for a different and deeper reason, because of the *supereminence* of the "form" to which the experient is "assimilated". An adequate human worship of God cannot be the attitude of one single human soul, for the same reason that the whole of truth cannot be the knowledge of one mind, nor the whole of beauty the intuition of one artist. From these theoretical considerations there follow two consequences of a practical character.

(1) It may be true, indeed I would admit that it is very largely true, that many of the forms of an institutional religion have no direct connection, nor even such an indirect connection as could be detected by analysis, with any particular moral improvement. But, however true this may be, it affords no reason to pronounce observation of the occasions and opportunities provided by institutional religion irrational, nor even for denying that neglect of them is likely to be attended by specifically moral loss, since, as we said, the characteristic function of religion is not moral improvement, and its real, though indirect, influence on character is exerted, like that of the pursuit of truth or beauty, in infinitely subtle and obscure ways. It is similarly true

that I shall, unless I am a very abnormal creature, be morally the better because I feed my mind on the greatest art, but in this case also it would be futile to undertake to show the precise moral benefit I derive from this and the other work of art. I cannot say precisely what particular moral profit I get from the contemplation of *Othello* or the *Third Symphony*; yet there is no denying that morally, as well as in other ways, I am the better for the contact of my mind with Shakespeare's or Beethoven's. True, a man may be morally excellent and yet unable to appreciate great art, and, as we know only too well, a man may be at once a true artist and a vicious man. But the question is whether the second man, in most cases, without his sensibility to art would not have been more vicious than he is with it. Some other man may be more virtuous than, for example, the art-loving man of strongly carnal appetites, and yet be without his sensitivity to art. But the comparison which is really relevant is not that of the sensual and art-loving man with the man who is neither sensual nor responsive to art; it is the comparison of the art-loving sensualist with *himself* as *he* would be without his love of art.

(2) Again, if worship itself is more than a merely private activity, it is not reasonable, but eminently unreasonable, to expect that the community's institutional provision for it shall contain nothing which I do not find clearly beneficial to myself in particular. That which means little to me, or is even repugnant to me, may to another be a very real occasion for the lifting up of the heart. To forget this is as unreasonable as it would be to wish to banish from the world's store of poems and pictures all works which leave me personally cold, or possibly actually annoy me. I have, in such a case, to remember two things. One is that I myself, like every-

one else, have my personal limitations of defective sympathy. There is true and genuine beauty, it may be of a high quality, to which I do not personally yield a quick and spontaneous response; a second man, who does respond to it, may have his difficulties in appreciating some of the particular beauties which speak most directly to me. It is good for both of us that each should have the opportunity of learning to correct his own defects and limitations by going humbly to school to the other. Each may learn from the other in a way which really enriches his own capacity for personal appreciation. Even when this is not the case, we have to remember that all members of the community are not on the same level of appreciativeness. The poem or the picture which really is only a poor or mediocre achievement, and is correctly seen by me to be so, may also, if it has any beauty at all, be a real avenue to appreciation of beauty for my neighbour, whose perceptions have been less cultivated. There is thus a double reason why a society anxious, for example, to provide its members with opportunities for the appreciative enjoyment of pictorial art would be acting unwisely and irrationally if it admitted to its public galleries no paintings except those which satisfied the tastes of a small body of experts and *connoisseurs*. The smaller the group of these experts, the more serious the probability that some works really of the highest value would be excluded; there would also always be the still graver danger that a collection exactly to the taste of even a considerable body of experts would be "over the heads" of the great bulk of the public for whose benefit it is designed.

These considerations apply with undiminished force to the provision of opportunities for the cultivation of the spirit of religious adoration. There, too, we have to uard against the ever-present danger of the spiritual in of priggishness. Religion, like art, is for everyone; ve cannot afford to leave any part of the community, whatever its crudity or hebetude of perception, unouched by either. Genuine religion and genuine art are both profoundly "catholic" in the sense that neither can tolerate appropriation by a small intelligentsia of superior persons, and in both there is a very real necessity, in particular for those of us who are occupied with some department of the "academic life", to protect ourselves against the danger of degenerating into 'superior persons". The grace of a true humility is just the grace we need more than any other, and we cannot afford to disregard the opportunities for growth in it. We ought to be alive to the truth that in literature and art we lose much, if we do not take pains to keep alive in ourselves the capacity for appreciating the simple and perhaps second-rate, or third-rate, poetry and painting which makes its direct appeal to the "common people". The superfine person who cannot, in his reading, condescend to be interested in anything less subtle and unobvious than the verse of Donne or the prose of Henry James is not the sort of person we ought to wish to be. Similarly, if we would keep the spirit of worship alive in us, we cannot afford to neglect the opportunities for contact, it may be at the cost of overcoming some personal repugnances, with the forms of *cultus* which are most potent in evoking worship and the sense of being in the presence of God in the mass of simple folk.

The same thing is true of the cultivation of the sense of national loyalty and love of country. The appeal of such things as the national anthem, or the flag, to the "common people" may be a crude one; it may cost us the overcoming of an intelligible repugnance to sympathise with these things, knowing as we do how often

they are traded on to provoke ignorant and pre
judiced explosions of feeling on wrong occasions. If w
know something of the detailed facts of history, we may
and often do, feel the same kind of annoyance with th
"patriotic" rhetoric which converts very faulty "nationa
heroes" of the past into figures without spot or reproach
No one can fairly expect me, for example, to see no
thing in Oliver Cromwell but sheer devotion to th
good of "God's people", or in Bruce nothing bu
Scottish patriotism, to imagine that the actual issue o
the fight at Naseby or Bannockburn was just nationa
freedom on the one side or "chains and slavery" on the
other. Yet it is also certain that a man does not really
promote intelligent love of his country by punctiliously
refusing to honour its flag, or national anthem, or to
join in the commemoration of its national achievements
and its national heroes. A good Englishman or good
Scot will not lie about facts for the greater glory of
Nelson or Bruce, but he will take his share, along with
his neighbours, in commemorating thankfully the deliverance of Trafalgar or Bannockburn, and will be
all the better for doing so, even while he may be
amused, or possibly annoyed, by some of the *naïvetés*
of the commemoration. He feeds on what is wholesome
in these things, and what is less wholesome does him
no more harm than the inevitable "impurities" of the
articles on which physical life is nourished. Neither for
the soul nor for the body does a wise man expect to find
a diet which can be assimilated wholly without remainder; he knows that if he refuses everything which
contains the least trace of an "impurity" he will merely
die of inanition. And so, I take it, philosophers have
had other motives besides that of self-protection for their
traditional recommendation that a man should worship
God νόμῳ πόλεως.

It ought to be added that in practice the great insti-
utional religions, in proportion to their inwardness, actu-
lly allow more scope for spontaneity in worship than
night appear from much that is said in the popular
ontroversies on the topic. In some of them, indeed,
ve seem to find a complete, or all but complete, con-
entionalising of the forms of public corporate worship.
But every great religion recognises and insists upon
he reality of a personal and intimate worship of its
God in the temple of the worshipper's own heart. There
re such things as private prayer and secret meditation
n the presence of Him who sees in secret, and no con-
iderable historical religion has forgotten to dwell on
hem as privileges and duties. None seeks to take the
pontaneity out of them. None, so far as I know, abso-
utely prescribes all words, postures, times for this private
vorship, though most, reasonably enough, as a matter
of guidance, recommend fixed times as a protection
against forgetfulness, or definite words and postures as
nost appropriate. Even when this recommendation is
nost emphatic and most systematised, it still leaves
oom for a very real spontaneity. When a religion has,
for example, enjoined the observance of set offices for
the "hours" of the day, it has never meant that the
access of the worshipper to God is confined to these
times and these prescribed forms. It is not meant that
there is to be no lifting up of the heart to God except
at the canonical hours, or that there are any prescribed
and conventionalised forms for this secret personal
devotion. Indeed, it is worthy of notice that among
Christians the very Church which has gone furthest
in developing a minutely systematised public worship,
n which every utterance, gesture, and posture is sub-
ected to precise regulation, has also the richest litera-
ure dealing with all the many ways in which the soul

of the individual Christian may directly approach God in personal prayer, and lays most stress on the importance of the adaptation of the type of prayer to be employed to the special needs of the individual soul.

Nor is the same element really forgotten even under all the elaborate systematising of the visible acts and audible utterances of public communal worship. To take the most obvious instance, the principle of institutional ceremonial regulation could not well be carried further than it is carried in the rubrics of the *Missale Romanum* for the celebration of the Mass. Rules are laid down there for all the minute particulars of accessories, dress, posture, gesture, vocal inflection, on the part of the officiants. And yet one has to remember that with all this stereotyping of the visible and audible, there is another and inner side to the public act of worship which is not stereotyped. Behind all that can be seen, or heard, there is the "intention" with which the celebrant is "offering the sacrifice", a matter between him and his Maker. And, again, each of the silent worshippers is also "offering the sacrifice", and each again with an "intention" of his own. One may be seeking guidance in perplexity; a second, strength to overcome or avoid some special temptation; a third, patience under bereavement; and so forth. Each worshipper may thus have his particular "intention"; what it is depends on his individual situation, and is a secret between himself and God. Thus, under all the apparent outward conventionality and fixity of such an act of worship, there may be intense and spontaneous prayer *in secreto* on the part of each of hundreds of worshippers. Each, if he is following the instructions of his Church and making *his* sacrifice really "acceptable", is *solus cum solo* though he is also one in a crowd. When all is said, the prayer of each is a spontaneous utterance of his own need.

The same thing is apparently to be seen even in Mohammedanism, a religion generally held not to be very favourable to the cultivation of inwardness of spirit. There, too, the hours of prayer and the words, tones, and gestures of the worshipper are exactly prescribed. But it appears that the Moslem's prayer is actually invalid without the direction of it to a particular "intention", as is humorously illustrated by Mr. E. W. Lane's story of the man who was overheard in the mosque prefacing his recitation of the evening prayer with the declaration, "I purpose to steal this excellent pair of shoes". The doctrine of the direction of intention is, of course, liable to be abused, and it is commonly in connection with real or supposed abuses that it is referred to in our own literature. But in its main principle it merely enforces the true perception that the purpose of the institutional in religion is not to replace, but to sustain, the spontaneous movement of the personal spirit. That a worship may be spiritual, it must be intensely personal; it is not necessary, and the history of Montanism, or again of the Anabaptist ferment of the sixteenth century, fairly proves it undesirable, that it should be anarchical.

When all has been said, it no doubt remains true that a due balance, both in the public and the private practice of devotion, between prescribed and hallowed form and free initiative is a "costing" thing, not easy to reach or to maintain. And it seems to be the fact that no one balance is equally adapted to the needs of all souls. What will be the right adjustment, even in private prayer, between the broken, perhaps wordless, aspiration of the individual creature to its Creator and the rethinking and reuttering for one's self of time-honoured petitions, must be largely a matter of personal temperament and interior state. And so also in acts of public and communal worship, I cannot doubt that while, for practical purposes, we have to be content with such an adjustment as experience over a long period and a wide area shows to be beneficial to a great majority of average men, there will always be the difficulty that a degree of fixed form and ceremonial which positively helps some souls to realise the presence of God is a real hindrance to others; and, again, that the very absence of these things which is felt by some as setting the soul free to mount up to God on her own wings is to others what the exhaustion of the atmosphere would be to a bird. If it were my business here, as of course it is not, to make practical suggestions to those in authority over me, I would say, with great deference, that it seems to me desirable for this reason that any worshipping society should have the benefit of a plurality of alternative "uses", leaving different degrees of external freedom in these matters; and, again, that individual congregations should not be allowed to become slaves to any single "use". I conceive that congregations accustomed to a high degree of fixity in forms of prayer and an elaborate ritual of worship, and finding such a system on the whole most beneficial to them, would be the gainers if, at times at any rate, they varied their practice by reverting to something simpler and barer. A Church, for example, which has "high Masses", celebrated with abundance of ritual, cannot well be too simple and unadorned in its "low" or "plain" celebrations. Again, I should say that a Church accustomed to the use of fixed forms of prayer, couched in words of chosen beauty and solemnity, would also do well to make provision for homely public utterance of "extemporary" prayers somewhere in its devotions.

And I think, on the other side, that a Church whose public worship is for the most part devoid of ceremony and fluid in form, would be wise if it actually enjoined the occasional use of these things. It is desirable not to let even our most serviceable habits get too complete mastery over us. The best of them, too seriously followed, will impoverish our experiences. But to follow up this line of thought would be quite alien to my purpose in these lectures; indeed, I should hardly have ventured to forget myself so far as to express the *Privatmeinungen* of the present paragraph at all had I been speaking in any place other than the familiar and beloved city of St. Andrews, and to any audience but one of old friends.

VII

SACRAMENTALISM

φαντάσματα θεῖα καὶ σκιαὶ τῶν ὄντων.—PLATO.

IT is not uncommon to find all that we have so far said about the institutional and ceremonial element in the historical religions of the world admitted by many who yet hold that these considerations do little or nothing to remove the real scandal these religions present to the rational philosopher. His trouble, it may be said, arises not from the bare fact that these religions are institutional, but from the peculiar character of the institutions which are fundamental in them. Full recognition of the value which ceremonial has for religion, as for other human activities, is no justification of *sacraments*, and sacraments, under one name or another, are prominent and central in positive religions all the world over. The sacraments of the various religions are alike, under all their differences, in possessing a character which distinguishes them sharply from mere ceremonial practices which are found effective as means of aiding the created spirit to realise the presence of the Creator, or as simple external symbols of devout states of mind. According to the claims regularly made for them, sacraments are physical acts, concerned with sensible objects, through which the Creator conveys a spiritual benefit, exercises a spiritual effect within the spiritual life of a rational creature.[1] Here we have the feature

[1] A few typical statements may be given here for reference. *Catechismus ex decreto Concilii Tridentini*, ii. 1: "definitio a divo Augustino tradita quam deinde

which distinguishes sacraments from rites in general. In a rite we may have nothing more than an action on the part of the human agents who take part in its performance; in a sacrament "God offers something to man". What makes a rite into a sacrament is that the ritual act is taken to be neither a device by which men induce a certain frame of mind in themselves, nor a mere symbolic declaration of their conviction that a certain state has been, or is being, induced in them by the action of God; the sacramental rite is itself an actual "channel" of grace, an "efficacious sign", or "instrumental cause" by the intermediation whereof the Creator affects the created spirit".[1]

I think that, in the light of all we know from the comparative study of religions, we must confess recognition of sacraments and sacramental acts, in this sense, to be so widely diffused a characteristic of actual religions that it must be regarded as typical; and, again, that it can hardly be eliminated from our own religion, by general admission at least the most adequate example of the type *historical religion*, without most gravely

---

omnes doctores scholastici secuti sunt. Sacramentum, inquit ille, est signum rei sacrae: vel, ut aliis verbis, in eandem tamen sententiam, dictum est: Sacramentum est invisibilis gratiae visibile signum ad nostram iustificationem institutum." (The passages meant seem to be Aug. *De civ. Dei*, x. 5: "sacrificium ergo visibile invisibilis sacrificii sacramentum, id est, sacrum signum est." Bernard, *In cena Domini*: "sacramentum dicitur sacrum signum sive sacrum secretum".) *Articles of Religion*, xxv.: "Sacraments ordained of Christ be not only badges or tokens of Christian men's profession, but rather they be certain sure witnesses, and effectual signs of grace, and God's goodwill towards us, by the which he doth work invisibly in us. . . ." *Anglican Catechism*: "*Q.* What meanest thou by this word *Sacrament*? *A.* I mean an outward and visible sign of an inward and spiritual grace given unto us, ordained by Christ himself, as a means whereby we receive the same, and a pledge to assure us thereof." *Shorter Catechism*, q. 91: "A sacrament is an holy ordinance instituted by Christ; wherein, by sensible signs, Christ and the benefits of the new covenant are represented, sealed, and applied to believers."

[1] These various expressions are, perhaps, not all exactly equivalent, but the distinctions between them, if there are any, are not easy to make out, and at least it is clear that the Roman, Anglican, and "Reformed" statements cited above are all in substance agreed in rejecting any reduction of sacraments to the level of declaratory symbolism.

modifying its character. A "non-sacramental Christianity" might, or might not, be an improvement on what has been known for nineteen centuries as Christianity; it ought to be impossible, in the face of a chain of witnesses from St. Paul's day to our own, to pretend that it is the same thing.

Now here, it may fairly be said, is the real *crux*. It is an affront to reason and intelligence to ask men to believe that an act resoluble by analysis into a contact, or series of contacts, between my own body and others can effect a change in my spiritual state. Such a belief has often been called, not merely in the heat of sectarian recrimination, a discreditable survival or artificial resuscitation of pre-civilised superstitions about the efficacy of "material magic", a throwback to the cult of the "fetish". Some of our contemporaries notoriously make the sacramentalism of historical Christianity a reason for pronouncing it no religion for a rational man; others find themselves driven to escape that conclusion only by the desperate expedient of declaring that a sacramentalism already found full-fledged in St. Paul's *Epistles to the Corinthians* and the Fourth Gospel is no part of "historic" Christianity. My own purpose, in this place, is neither to make an *apologia* for Christian sacramentalism, nor to discuss a problem of ecclesiastical history. What concerns me is the broad philosophical issue whether the conceptions on which all sacramentalism, Christian or non-Christian, rests are in their intrinsic character irrational superstitions or not, and, as a student of philosophy, I am interested in this issue because of its bearing on the still more general question, raised at the beginning of this course, of the relation between positive religion and a purely philosophical, or natural, religion. The question I have before me for treatment to-day is still the very general one whether what a positive religion professes to disclose of God, whenever it goes beyond what we are warranted in asserting by a metaphysic of nature and of morals, must be regarded as, at best, temporary illusion, or not. Hence the only issue with which I shall be concerned, in what I have to say of the sacraments of historical religions, is the broad one whether belief in physical objects and bodily acts connected with them as "means of grace", instruments through which a special contact of the created spirit with its Creator is effected, involves thinking of God and of the divine activity in a fashion incompatible with a sound and reasonable metaphysic. Any references I shall make to the sacraments of Christianity, or the sacramental doctrines of Christian Churches, in particular will be meant to be illustrative of general principles, and my illustrations will be taken from this quarter rather than another for the double reason that the Christian sacraments are those with which we are all most familiar, from our education in a Christian society, and that they have been made the object of the reflective study of theologians and philosophers in an exceptional degree, and throughout an extended period of time. Many other religions possess sacraments of some kind; none possesses the same kind of conscious sacramental theory.

When we look at sacramental practice and theory from this point of view, we can at least see without much trouble that controversial language about "materialistic magic", like most controversial rhetoric, merely confuses the issue. Whatever the sacraments of Christianity, or its precursor Judaism, may be, they are not a survival or recrudescence of "primitive" magic. In saying this I do not mean to imply that some practices of a sacramental kind found in the historic faiths of the world may not prove to be little more than the continuation of the nature-magic of savages into a more civilised age. That is a question for the anthropologist and the historian of "civilised origins". I may have doubts whether even they know very much about the matter, and I am quite sure that I do not. The ritual drinking of *soma* among the early Aryans, or of wine in some of the Hellenic mysteries, certainly has the character of a sacramental act as we have defined it, and at the same time *may* be continuous with, or a throwback to, practices which may fairly be called savage and magical, devices for the induction of an abnormal state of exaltation valued for itself merely as abnormal, independently of any thought of a special contact with deity. (As I say, I doubt whether anyone knows whether this statement is true, but I see no reason why it should not be true.) Circumcision, the great sacrament of the "older law", presumably had its origin in something very savage and superstitious, though the anthropologists seem at present as much in the dark as anyone else as to what that something may have been.[1] The same thing may be true of the ritual application of water to the body which has been adopted by Christianity from pre-existing practice as its sacrament of initiation. Nor do I wish to deny that investigation might reveal strange origins for a whole number of the secondary accessory details which, to this day, accompany the celebration of sacraments in the most spiritual and philosophical of the historical religions. The point I want to make is, that whatever may have been the far-away origin of specific ritual acts which in these religions are sacramental, the acts do not become sacramental in the sense in which our own religion, for example, possesses sacraments, until

[1] See art. "Circumcision" in *E.R.E.*

they have received a specification and sanction which take them wholly out of the class of the magical.

This ought to be suggested, in the first place, by a simple historical reflection which forces itself on us the moment we make a serious study of the facts about the sacraments of the "old" and the "new" law. Both Judaism and Christianity are religions which have been historically preceded by a conscious breach with the nature-cults we loosely call "primitive" because no one can say how they arose. Whenever and however the practices of circumcision and of ritual reception of bread and wine originated, the conviction of the believing member of the Jewish synagogue who circumcises his son, or the faithful Christian who approaches the Lord's Table, is that *for him* the act receives its significance and obligation from an historical divine institution, in virtue of which it procures him or his a definite divine gift. Many other nations might practise circumcision for known or unknown reasons; it *may* be that the Hebrew of the days of the monarchy himself practised it merely as a custom of which he could give no explanation. But the Jewish Church founded on "the Law" practised it (and it is irrelevant to my point whether the Jewish Church had an existence before the Exile or not) because it had been instituted by a divine command to Abraham, and made by that command the title-deed to a share in the divine promises to Abraham and his descendants. There might be, indeed, we know that there were, ritual meals in various cults of the first century A.D., but the Christian came to "the Lord's Supper" because the command to do so had been given on an historical occasion—"in the night when he was given up"—by his divine Master, and the Master had promised "eternal life" to those who fulfilled it.

For our purpose the important point is not so much

whether these beliefs were strictly accurate in point of fact, but that they were accepted as accurate, and that it was these beliefs which gave the acts their character as sacraments. There have been many divergent modern speculations about the origin of the widely diffused practice of circumcision. It has been pronounced to be a hygienic precaution of a purely utilitarian kind, or a prophylactic against imaginary dangers attending on entrance on the active exercise of sexual functions, or a symbolic consecration of the whole person to a deity, and these are only some of the conflicting hypotheses. But an orthodox and pious Jew, when he circumcises his child, may be presumed to be thinking neither of hygiene nor of protection against vaguely imagined dangers besetting the performance of sexual acts, but of the promise of God to Abraham, and it makes no difference in principle whether this promise to Abraham is an incident of authentic history or not. If it could be demonstrated that every detail of every act which is regarded as sacramental in a sacramental religion had pre-existed as a piece of so-called nature-magic for ages before the religion adopted it, this would not alter the fact, which is of primary importance for us, that the reason why the adherents of that religion practise these acts has nothing to do with the known or unknown reasons for its earlier performance. The reason why the act continues to be practised, and is regarded as sacramental, is that it is believed to be historically of divine institution, and to have specific effects attached to it in virtue of its character of being divinely appointed. This character would not be affected by the fullest proof that the same act had been performed by others without divine institution, and with no reference to consequences attached to it by an historical divine promise. The Biblical record of the covenant with Abraham, for example, does not pretend to be a narrative of the *origin* of the custom of circumcision; it is a narrative of its appointment to be a sacrament to Abraham and his descendants. We cannot really suppose intelligent Jews not to have known the notorious fact that the same rite was general with such a nation as the Egyptians, nor need we suppose them to have fancied that the Egyptians had borrowed the practice from themselves. But they did not regard the Egyptians as qualified by their circumcision to inherit the blessing. The rite was not, in their case, a sacrament.[1]

These reflections suggest at once the true *differentia* which distinguishes sacraments from "materialistic magic". A magical act, if we use the words with any precision, means an act which, provided it is correctly performed, produces its supposed consequences automatically. Magic, like early science, is a matter of technique. It may, and does, exist where there is little or no belief in the control of events by any kind of divine will or agency; in fact, in developed systems of magic, the performance of the prescribed acts, or the recitation of the prescribed spell, is thought of as actually compelling divinities, whether they will or not, to the execution of the magician's will.[2] At bottom, therefore, magic and religion, in the sense in which we have used that word throughout our discussion, are directly opposed in principle. The second draws all its signifi-

[1] It might be said that circumcision lacks the character of a sacrament, inasmuch as it is only a "token", or *declaratory*, not an *efficacious* sign. But such a view hardly does justice to the demand of *Gen.* xvii., that the "uncircumcised man-child" shall be "cut off" because "he hath broken my covenant". The implication here surely is that the Israelite enters personally into the "covenant" relation by being circumcised. If he neglects the rite, he has wilfully cut himself off from the covenant.

[2] Naturally, I cannot justify this view of the *essentia* of magic at length here. For a useful summary of the sort of evidence on which I am basing it, and a conspectus of the various anthropological theories, I may conveniently refer to the elaborate composite article "Magic" in *E.R.E.*

cance from the tension between this world of the temporal and the other world of the eternal, which so mysteriously encloses and interpenetrates this: the first is a purely this-world affair, as much so as sanitary engineering or electric lighting. In fact, it is not the priest, but the technician, who knows how to turn physical science to an utilitarian account, who is the real counterpart in our society of the wizards and sorcerers of darker ages. In the "temporal world" as conceived by Hume and his later disciples, that is to say, as conceived by the leading representatives of the *Naturphilosophie* of half a century ago, there is really no difference between the functions of science and the functions of magic. Science, on the Humian view, consists in discovering formulae which "sum up the routine of our sense-perception", and may therefore be used as practical receipts for the production of desired effects. Since, on the theory, all that the formulae record is conjunctions of events which stand in no sort of rational connection, the scientific laws which supply the modern inventor with his rules for procedure have exactly the same arbitrary character as the spells and incantations of magic. And the one justification admitted by a philosophy of this kind for its belief in its "laws of nature", the plea that, in some inexplicable way, they are found to "work" when applied to practice, is precisely the kind of justification a savage might allege for his belief in spells and charms. Without any desire to prejudge a case by rhetorical exaggeration, I must confess that I can see in principle no difference between physical science *as conceived by Mach or K. Pearson*, and the magic of an African medicine-man, except that the spells of the European man of science prove themselves in fact so much more trustworthy and potent; they are uncommonly "big" medicine.

The fact that *our* "customary experience" leads us to disbelieve in the particular conjunctions on which the magician of savage or semi-savage societies relies must not blind us to the much more important fact that it is purely "this-world" conjunctions which are the foundation of his procedure. It is true that "this world", as he conceives it, may contain constituents not recognised by the European secularist, ghosts of the dead, powerful spirits and demons, and the like, though those things are not indispensable to magic. Magic can flourish wherever there is belief in the potency within the sensible world of inexplicable and unintelligible "conjunction". And spirits and demons, as such, are just as much of the temporal and secular world as electrons or "wavicles"; it is only with the contrast of the eternal and the temporal that we reach the conception of the genuinely "other", and absolutely unsecular. When the superstitious revive the old magical practices in an age of high secular civilisation, it is true that they commonly attempt to give them a laughable dignity by calling them *occult* science. But, in principle, the conjunction in which the modern patrons of sorcery are interested are no more "occult" than any other conjunction which has to be accepted as a bare unexplained conjunction, that is, according to an empiricist metaphysic of nature, than any of the conjunctions summed up in our scientific laws.

For according to a consistently empiricist metaphysic, there is no real difference in respect of arbitrariness between the conjunction of administration of a dose of prussic acid and death and the conjunction between the same effect and the decapitation of the deceased's portrait by an enemy: the first is certainly the more familiar, but is every whit as unintelligible as the second. And if the proceedings of the medicine-man are occult in the different sense that the knowledge of the receipt for them is confined to a few experts, the same thing is equally true of the proceedings of the modern "wizard" of electrical science. Very few of us know how to make the "grand projection", or to "tie the knot"; very few also know how to construct a "wireless" set.

Thus, if we are to look for a modern equivalent for magical operations, we shall find it much more truly in the triumphs of applied science than in the sacraments of religion. In magic, as in "science," there is a complete absence of that which lies at the root of every sacrament, the free outward-moving activity of the divine. When "gods" are brought into connection with magic, they are degraded from their position as gods; their part in the magical act is not to be the sources of "grace", the bestowers of a gift, but to be passive instruments in the hands of the magician; the activity comes, in the end, from him. Hence the very fact that *ex hypothesi* a sacrament is a channel through which free and unconstrained divine activity expresses itself, an act in which "God gives something to man", as is indicated in religions like Christianity and Judaism by the stress laid on historical divine institution of the rite, definitely takes sacraments once and for all out of the domain of the magical.[1]

And as there is no "magic" in them, there is, for the same reason, no materialism. The sacramental act is, indeed, performed by contact with bodily objects, but it is never held that the bodies employed have any intrinsic efficacy to produce the effect of the sacrament. No theologian, to my knowledge, has ever held that

[1] The so-called *messe noire* of the "Satanists", if it really exists, on the other hand, is a deliberate attempt to convert a divine sacrament into a magical act, to "put a spell" on the Creator, to use His power for ends which are not His; hence its essentially blasphemous character.

wheaten flour and wine have in themselves any intrinsic efficacy in conferring on him who partakes of them "remission of sins and all other benefits of the Passion"; they are not analogous to the ambrosia and nectar of classical fables.[1] It has always been held that if their reception is instrumental to these effects, it is so simply by virtue of divine appointment, and that God might, had He pleased, have conjoined the same benefits with different instruments, or produced them without any physical instrument at all. *Ex post facto* theological reflection has discerned a symbolic appropriateness of the instruments appointed to the effects, but this is a very different thing from ascribing to them an intrinsic efficacy of their own. The whole of the instrumental efficacy actually ascribed to them is assumed to be freely conferred on them by the divine volition. References to "materialistic magic" thus misrepresent the true character of the objection they are intended to convey, and should be dismissed from serious self-respecting argument.[2]

The objection really intended gains in point and seriousness by being freed from these vulgar irrelevancies. The thought, at bottom, is that any action of the Creator on the created spirit should be direct and without physical instrumentality; it is conceiving unspiritually of God to imagine that the Spirit of all spirits needs, or employs, any bodily intermediary in His action on the spirits He has created. He is intimately present to them all; "to Him every heart is open and every volition speaks"; can we suppose that His re-

[1] Cf. the prayer in the Roman Office, "quod ore sumpsimus, Domine, pura mente capiamus: et de munere temporali fiat nobis remedium sempiternum" (said by the celebrant immediately after reception).

[2] Of course I do not mean to deny that popular superstitions connected with the Christian sacraments have sometimes degraded them into instruments of "magic", but such superstitions misrepresent the Christian conception.

sponse to our needs requires to be conveyed, or can be conveyed, through objects and acts in the physical world? This line of thought is further reinforced by the consideration that no religion of high ethical quality can conceive of graces of character as conferred on a man by the mere performance of a bodily act, independently of all internal state of soul. We need no witness beyond our common experience of men to see that the carnal, worldly, and proud do not derive spiritual life from mere bodily participation in the ordinances of any religion.

> Sumunt boni, sumunt mali,
> sorte tamen inaequali,
> vitae, vel interitus.

We can thus readily understand the wide diffusion of a strong prejudice against the belief that bodily acts and objects can be "instruments" and "efficacious signs" of spiritual benefits, even among those who would probably be shocked to discover that their prejudice, if carried to its logical consequences, would be fatal to rites and sacraments which they themselves prize and reverence. To take a trivial illustration, I have found a professedly Anglican writer denouncing, not merely as childish, but as actually blasphemous, the practice of blessing medals, crosses, and the like, on the ground that it is impious to ask the Holy Spirit to bless "purely *material* things". Yet I have little doubt that the writer makes no scruple about asking God, several times in the day, to "bless" his meat and drink, or that he is sincerely attached to the English *Communion Office*, with its formal and visible blessing of the bread and the cup, a prayer actually described in the rubric which accompanies it as one of "consecration". Clearly, if the principle is sound that God cannot without impiety be asked to bless anything which is material, we must be prepared to be consistent with it. If it forbids us to recognise sacraments as *means* of grace, it must equally prohibit the irrationality and impiety of praying that a leg of mutton or an apple-pie may be "blessed to our use". In neither case is the blessing on the physical object really disjoined from the blessing on the user. In the central sacrament of Christianity, for example, the oblation of bread and wine is blessed, or consecrated, "that it may become *to us*", *ut nobis fiat*, the Body and Blood of the Lord, or, as another rite says, "to the end that all who shall receive the same may be sanctified and preserved to eternal life", exactly as the meat on our tables is blessed that it may become to the partakers sustenance for the temporal life of soul and body. In both cases, improper reception is expected to effect disease, and not health; in neither is the beneficial effect conceived to follow in any purely mechanical way from the performance of an external act.

Thus the real question at issue is whether it is incompatible with a rational conception of God to hold that certain specific physical things and acts may be, not from an intrinsic necessity grounded in their character as these particular physical things and acts, but by free divine appointment, channels, or vehicles of a specific contact between the divine spirit and the created. It is important to remember that in Christianity, at any rate, it has never seriously been held that these specific contacts can only be effected by this specific mediation. It is a general position, accepted by the theologians of the most highly "sacramental" Christian societies, that "God has not *bound* His power by the sacraments", *i.e.* that though the things and acts in question have been appointed as the usual and regular channels for the reception of these specific gifts or graces, the effects can be and are produced directly, without the intervention of the physical things and acts when these are not to be had. This is what is meant, for example, by the well-known phrase of the *English Catechism* that the two great distinctive "sacraments of the new law" are "generally" necessary to salvation. The meaning is not that they are *universally* indispensable, as De Morgan asserts in a passage of his *Formal Logic*.[1] The framers of the sentence were too familiar with Aristotelian terminology to make a careless confusion between the καθόλου and the ὡς ἐπὶ τὸ πολύ, and too acute to miss the point that, if the meaning had been what De Morgan takes it to be, they would be asserting that the penitent thief was lost after all, in spite of the formal promise, "This day shalt thou be with me in Paradise".[2] The meaning of the proposition, a meaning admitted by the extremist sacramentalists, is that the sacramental acts are "as a rule", when they can be had, the vehicles of certain spiritual gifts; when they cannot be had, this impossibility is no bar to the bestowal of the gifts without them. This explains a whole series of positions, familiar in the literature of the sacraments, which would otherwise be unintelligible. It accounts, for example, for the *Crede et manducasti* of Augustine, an utterance not meant to excuse neglect of the sacraments, but to comfort the Christian who is physically cut off from them by no fault of his own with the assurance that he is not cut off from their Giver, or their benefits. It explains also the doctrine of the "baptism

[1] *Formal Logic*, p. 272.

[2] For, even if the penitent thief had been baptized, it is certain that he was not one of the company gathered a few hours before in the upper room. De Morgan also forgot that one Anglican rubric forbids the admission of children of tender years to the Communion, while a second pronounces that "baptized infants dying in infancy are certainly saved".

of desire" as replacing baptism with water, in the case of necessity,[1] and the still more famous doctrine that "desire" in its extreme form, that of martyrdom, "supplies the lack" of all sacraments.[2] Unless we are careful to bear in mind both the qualifications, that sacraments are held to owe their efficacy wholly to divine appointment and in no way to the intrinsic properties of their matter or their form, and also that "God has not bound His power by the sacraments," we shall be discussing a falsified issue.

It is, no doubt, true that one can find examples in various religions of *quasi*-sacramental rites which are thought of without these important qualifications, as producing their effects in virtue of a kind of natural necessity,[3] and therefore independently of any interior disposition on the part of the community[4] who receive

[1] St. Bernard (to Hugh of St. Victor, *Ep.* 77) "cum his (*sc.* Ambrose and Augustine), inquam, me aut errari aut sapere fateor, credens et ipse sola fide hominem posse salvari, cum desiderio percipiendi sacramentum, si tamen pio adimplendo desiderio mors anticipans seu alia quaecunque vis invincibilis obviarit. Vide etiam ne forte ob hoc Salvator cum diceret *qui crediderit et baptizatus fuerit, salvus erit*, caute et vigilanter non repetierit *qui vero baptizatus non fuerit*, sed tantum *qui vero*, inquit, *non crediderit, condemnabitur*." Cf. St. Thomas (*S.Th.* iii.[a] q. 66, art. 11 resp.), "eadem ratione aliquis per virtutem Spiritus Sancti consequitur effectum baptismi, non solum sine baptismo aquae, sed etiam sine baptismo sanguinis, in quantum scilicet alicuius cor per Spiritum Sanctum movetur ad credendum, et diligendum Deum, et poenitendum de peccatis." iii.[a] q. 68, art. 2, resp. "potest sacramentum baptismi alicui deesse, re, sed non voto . . . et talis sine baptismo actuali salutem consequi potest propter desiderium baptismi, quod procedit ex fide per dilectionem operante per quam Deus interius hominem sanctificat, cuius potentia sacramentis visibilibus non alligatur."

[2] *S.Th.* iii.[a] q. 68, art. 2 ad secund. "dicendum quod nullus pervenit ad vitam aeternam, nisi absolutus ab omni culpa et reatu poenae: quae quidem universalis absolutio fit in perceptione baptismi, et in martyrio: propter quod dicitur quod in martyrio omnia sacramenta baptismi complentur, scilicet quantum ad plenam liberationem a culpa et poena."

[3] The point is illustrated by the doctrine of Christian theologians on the necessity of an "intentio ministri" to make a sacrament valid. On this see, *e.g.*, St. Thomas (*S.Th.* iii[a] q. 64, arts. 8 and 10). His doctrine is that there must be an intention of the "minister" to administer a valid sacrament, or there is no celebration of the sacrament; an intention to celebrate a valid sacrament for an ulterior nefarious purpose (*e.g.* to consecrate a Host for purposes of sorcery) is a grave sin on the part of the ministrant, but does not annul the *veritas sacramenti*.

[4] A difficulty might be felt here in connection with the baptism of infants. It is raised by St. Thomas (*S.Th.* iii.[a] art. 68, q. 9, where it is objected against the

them; and, again, as, for the same reason, absolutely indispensable for the effect. But this only means that in such religions the notion of a sacramental has not yet been duly discriminated from that of a magical act. Our concern here is with the sacramental concept when it has been clearly formulated, and it is irrelevant to consider stages of thought and practice at which the important logical distinction between the sacramental and the magical has not yet been drawn.

Now that we have got our issue properly formulated, we should, I think, see at once that the prejudice against the sacramental in historical religions is only one of the many forms assumed by a more universal prejudice against the physical itself, the standing prejudice of that false spirituality which does so much mischief to the thinking and moral practice of many circles in our own society. There can be no sound logical foundation for *a priori* rejection of the possibility that certain specific spiritual benefits may normally be conveyed through special physical channels, apart from the allegation that it is, in general, irrational to hold that the physical can act upon the spiritual. If our physical state can, and does, in general make a specific difference to our spiritual state, there is no good philosophical reason for dismissing as "superstitious" the assertion that sacraments, in particular, are instrumental in specific ways to the spiritual life. And if we look at the world of experience as a whole, without preconceived bias, nothing seems more certain than that, speaking generally, the rule is that the physical is everywhere instrumental to the psychical. If we take the word *sacrament* in a wide sense to mean any physical occa-

practice that infants can have neither intention nor faith). St. Thomas's reply is in substance taken from St. Augustine: the faith and intention are there, on the part of the Church which is receiving the child into its fold.

sion which normally ministers as an instrument to the soul's life, we may clearly say that these are natural, as well as supernatural, sacraments, and that the physical world is everywhere pervaded by the sacramental principle.

It is the notorious fact, for instance, that the effect of the regular reception of proper food at the proper hours is instrumental to mental as well as to physical health; that we suffer in intellect and character, as well as in body, if we cannot get our proper sleep; that proper change of air and bodily occupation reinvigorate a man's moral being as well as his physique; on the other side, the explanation of bad intellectual and artistic work, and, again, of bad moral conduct, is often very largely to be found in unwholesome physical surroundings. You can seriously affect a man's thinking and his conduct for the better by seeing that he is fed as he ought to be, gets due sleep and exercise, and fresh and untainted air.

Here, again, it holds good that the connection between the instrument and the effect is found to hold *generally*, not universally, and that the benefit of the "natural sacraments", like that of the sacraments of religion, depends on co-operation in the recipient. A man may do work of the highest excellence, or lead a life of singular moral nobility, in spite of bad, or insufficient food, or air, or sleep; unfavourable surroundings may throw him back the more on his own inner resources, and impel him to make a specially vigorous assertion of his superiority to circumstance; bodily infirmity, as philosophers have noted, seems sometimes to provoke an exceptional activity of mind. But these qualifications do not destroy the truth of the general rule that vigorous and healthy intellectual and moral life needs the instrumental ministration of the physical;

the *mens sana* is not ensured by the possession of the *corpus sanum* and it may be found coexistent with a *corpus morbidum*, but it would be the height of presumption to count on retaining the *mens sana*, if I neglect to take the ordinary and available means of keeping my body in health. The possibility of a nature-miracle gives me no right to expect that the miracle will be forthcoming to counteract the consequences of my own negligence.

Further, over and above this general dependence of intellectual, artistic, and moral activity on physical environment, specific achievement in all these kinds is also, ὡς ἐπὶ τὸ πολύ, dependent on specific features of the physical environment. The "miracle of genius", it is true, occurs, from time to time, in the most unpromising surroundings. But, speaking generally, it is the rule that a man's specific intellectual, or moral, or artistic, accomplishment is conditioned by the way in which his interest has been awakened by his natural and social environment. A man is not likely, in spite of the dubious and exaggerated stories of the childhood of Pascal, to become a great mathematician if, in the most receptive period of life, he has never seen a mathematical book or diagram, nor to become a great painter, if he is brought up where there are neither paintings nor drawings to be seen, nor a great musician, if he has heard no music. He is not likely to develop a burning love of justice if he is born and brought up in the *zenana* of an Oriental Sultan, or of purity of thought, word, and act if his boyhood has been passed in a society permeated by the worship of the *lingam*.

We recognise this, when we speak, as we so often do, of the defects which may mar the whole work of even a rarely gifted artist for want of early opportunity to study good models, or the imperfections in the work of a scientific man caused by unavoidable ignorance of what has been done in his own subject before him. Opportunity to study the best models at the right time, to take the most obvious illustration, is, in the last resort, one provided by the physical order. It is a physical fact that a given northern artist had no access to any works of the great Italian masters, or a given poet to those of Sophocles or Shakespeare, until an advanced period of life, but it is a physical fact which may mar the artistic quality of his whole life-work. We may fairly say that, when all allowance has been made for the mystery of "genius", it is the normal thing that genius should get its inspiration and direction from specific occasions, furnished, in the end, by its natural surroundings. The same opportunities are not utilised in the same way without the genius, but without the right kind of opportunity the genius will be imperfectly developed, or developed on false lines. It may be a sentimental exaggeration to fancy that a common village churchyard holds a group of "mute, inglorious Miltons". A Milton is not likely to go through the world "mute", in any case. But it is at least true that if Milton had been condemned by circumstances to be all his life the thatcher or hedger of a country village, he would hardly have uttered himself in *Paradise Lost* or *Samson*.[1]

Indeed, one does not see how the rule could well be otherwise, in view of the elementary fact that a man is an embodied, not a discarnate, intelligence, and that the more we get to know of the whole life of man, the closer and more intimate we find the connection between the intelligence and the embodiment to be. The logical outcome of the tendency to deny or minimise the

[1] And if Blake had not been condemned by circumstances to lifelong semi-illiteracy, we may safely say that we should have had something from him very different from the fitfully splendid nightmares commonly called his "prophecies".

dependence of mental life on suggestions and opportunities presented by the physical would be the extravagant modern Docetism called, very improperly, "Christian Science", which, if I am rightly informed, declares that we really have no bodies, but dupe ourselves into fancying that we have them. This is a doctrine not merely intellectually fantastic, but morally dangerous, from its tendency to encourage unconscious hypocrisy in its professors. If one may judge them by their actions, many of them seem habitually to take exceptional care to surround themselves with a plentiful provision of theoretically non-existing comforts and luxuries for their theoretically non-existent bodies. They may persuade themselves in speculation that they have no bodies; in practice they seem commonly to behave as if they had, and as if the comfort of the body were a much greater good, and its discomfort or suffering a much worse evil, than most religions or philosophies admit. If we agree, not with their verbal profession, but with the operative beliefs revealed by their practice, we shall expect that the regular rule of life will prove to be that moral, intellectual, and aesthetic good is mediated to its human recipients through definite physical channels. "Spirituality" will mean to us not behaving as though we had no bodies, and were not set in a framework of bodily happening, but utilising the transactions between our own body and others to the full as opportunities for the discernment of truth, the practice of virtue, the creation or enjoyment of beauty. We need no proof of the falsity of the kind of "spirituality" which consists in pretending that the body is not there, beyond the moral havoc which it makes of the whole life of sex, marriage, and parenthood. Our true business with it is not to ignore it, but to keep it "in its proper place".

We should expect, then, in the light of analogies supplied by normal intellectual and moral life, that if there is a still further level of the life of the spirit concerned with conscious relation to the divine, at this level also the fact that such a life has to be lived by embodied creatures would be pertinent. We should no more expect the body, with the occasions and opportunities it provides, to play no part in ministering to such a "supernatural" life than we should expect the same thing in connection with life at other levels: thus we should anticipate as more probable than not that the highest gifts God has in store for us would, as a general rule, come to us in connection with, and dependence on, physical things and bodily acts as their channels, or instruments. In a world where nature is so full of sacraments, it would be strange that "grace" should not have its sacraments too. Nor would this anticipation mean that we look on divine agency as tied down to, and only able to exert itself through, these particular special channels, since their *raison d'être* lies not in the nature of God, but in the nature He has given *us* as *embodied* creatures. If there are wholly disembodied intelligences who are "separate" from "matter", like angels in the Thomistic philosophy,[1] we cannot well suppose that their intercourse with the Creator, however it may be conditioned, is mediated by the channel of "sacraments"; but we at least are not such angels, and nothing has ever come of

[1] But it is well not to be sure that there are. Even the most convinced Thomist will not deny that the higher "intelligences" communicate with, and have social relations with, one another. And he is forbidden by his own philosophy to credit any created intelligence with the power directly to read the thoughts of another: that, as Donne says, is held to be "beyond an angel's art". It would seem to follow that every such intelligence must have some such instrument and vehicle of communication with its fellows as is provided for us by our "weight of body and limb", though it may be well to avoid occasion for error by not calling that vehicle a "body". Only it would serve the same function as is now served by our familiar organism, that of being a standing instrument of intercommunication. But this is purely speculative, and by the way.

the attempts of men to forget that they are not angels except deadly evil; ignoring the body commonly ends in sinking below the level of the beasts that perish. Since, when all is said, at our highest we are and remain *men*, we should naturally expect our most direct contacts with the divine to be contacts under conditions which take account of our embodiment.

No doubt, it might be urged in reply to reasoning of this kind that there is a real difference between the part played by bodily channels and instruments in ministering to our moral and mental life generally and the part sacramental religions ascribe to their sacramental objects and acts. In the first case, the instrumentality is part of the *cursus ordinarius* of nature; in the second, it is, in a sense, arbitrary. This difference, however, ought not to create a difficulty for a philosopher who has already accepted the Theism without which there can be no rational religion. From the theistic point of view, the *cursus ordinarius* of nature itself ultimately depends on divine appointment; *la nature* is not a name for an independent agency, but for the instrumentality through which the Creator commonly acts; the one real difference between the two cases is that the instrumentality, for example, of food, sleep, and air in ministering to mental and moral health does not depend, as it is held that the efficacy of sacraments in ministering to the soul's "eternal welfare" does, upon specific divine institution at a definite time and place inside human history. And this difference itself does not seem to hold good for all the acts which can fairly be called sacraments of grace. It seems impossible to deny that we have in matrimony an institution which falls short of its full purpose, if its effect is merely to promote temporal happiness and prosperity; a marriage which deserves to be called a "marriage of true minds" is definitely productive of fine spiritual graces in the parties, and thus, as it seems to me, since the *dona matrimonii* transcend the secular, we do not think worthily of the institution unless we regard it as a sacrament of grace.[1]

Yet it is notorious that theologians have been hard put to it to answer the question precisely where and when the "sacrament" was instituted. Thus we are told in the supplement added to the *Summa Theologica* of St. Thomas[2] that "matrimony, in so far as it is ordained for the procreation of offspring", was instituted at the creation of Eve; "so far as it is a remedy against sin", it was instituted after the Fall, "in the time of the law of Nature"; so far as it involves restriction and specification of the persons, it was instituted "in the law of Moses"; so far as it represents "the mystery of the union of Christ and the Church", it was instituted "in the new law"; but so far as it promotes friendship and mutual *obsequium* between the parties to it, it is an institution of the civil—*i.e.* the Roman —laws. The first and last of these "institutions", however, do not concern marriage in its character as a sacrament.

In the light of our present historical knowledge, such an answer would amount to saying that the one definite historical occasion to which we can point as that of the institution of matrimony, "as far as it is a sacrament", is the occasion when Christ was asked a casuistical question about the legitimacy of divorce by opponents, who perhaps wished to involve him in trouble with

[1] The Anglican Church seems officially to "hedge" on this point. In the 25th Article Matrimony is said not to have "like nature of a Sacrament" with Baptism and the Lord's Supper, on the ground that it has no "visible sign or ceremony ordained of God". This might mean either that it is not a sacrament, or only that it is not on the same level as the two great "generally necessary" sacraments of the Gospel. The second interpretation *seems* most consonant with the language of the *Catechism* about sacraments, and with the assertion of the *Office* for Matrimony that "it is an honourable estate instituted of God".

[2] Q. 42, art. 2.

Herod Antipas. I confess that to me it seems fanciful to make a reply to such a question amount to a formal act of institution; I doubt, again, whether all theologians would be willing to make the status of Baptism as a principal "sacrament of the new law" stand or fall with the strict historicity of the words of the command, "make disciples of all nations, baptizing them", etc. It is interesting to read that the hard-and-fast limitation of sacraments conferring grace to the afterwards traditional seven did not, apparently, make its appearance until the twelfth century, and that in the thirteenth Bonaventura expressly ascribed the institution of two of the seven, Confirmation and Unction, to the *apostles*, while his master, Alexander of Hales, had actually traced the origin of Confirmation as a sacrament to a ninth-century Council. The effect on the Western Church of the hard-and-fast dogmatising of the divines of Trent, and the Reformers alike, about the number of the sacraments of grace and their immediate institution by Christ seems to me to have been wholly unfortunate.[1]

It would perhaps be a better taken point to attack on principle the validity of the analogy we have presupposed between the action of God as the source of the order of nature and His action as the source of "supernatural" grace. It might be said that we must look for no such analogy, since the bestowal of grace is *ex hypothesi* a strictly *supernatural* transaction between the Creator and the creature. Since the gift bestowed, then, does not belong to the order of nature, the divine action by which it is bestowed should itself be wholly independent of nature and of opportunities afforded by nature, as its channel. It should strike straight, without

[1] Cf. for the whole subject the articles "Sacraments" (Christian, Western), "Sacraments" (Christian, Lutheran), and "Sacraments" (Christian, Reformed) in *E.R.E.*

any "means" at all, from the depths of the Creator to the depths of the creature. Where there is a recognisable instrumentality, it might be said, its very presence is an indication that we are dealing with an effect which belongs to the natural order. This, I suppose, is the thought in the mind of an anti-sacramentalist critic when he says, as such critics have done, that he cannot see why any Christian should expect or receive any particular grace from participation in the sacrament of the Lord's Supper. (It is meant, in fact, that this rite, or "ordinance", is not really a sacrament, in the sense in which the word has been historically employed in the theology of the Christian religion.)

I confess that this line of argument seems to me not unplausible, though it appears to lead to consequences which are probably not before the minds of those who employ it. That the grace of God needs no physical channels is a favourite controversial argument in the mouths of those who give the supreme place in devotion and worship to the "ministry of the word", as against opponents who attach importance as great, or greater, to sacraments. Yet, after all, the "word" itself is ministered in dependence on physical occasions; its reception involves hearing or reading, and hearing and reading are as much physical acts as eating and drinking, or any others which are performed sacramentally in any religion. Again, the hearing or reading is just as liable as any other activity to become divorced from appropriate preparation and interior disposition, and to become merely external and mechanical. It is as easy to hear or read unspiritually as it is to receive a sacrament unspiritually.

It is quite impossible, with the best will in the world, to construct a worship for men which will be really independent of contacts with the physical. Thus the objection to sacraments on the ground of their physical character, carried to its logical conclusion, should issue in an extreme quietism hostile to all use of "means", though common sense really forbids the conclusion to be drawn. If it is not drawn, if marks apprehended through the eye, and sounds apprehended through the ear, are once recognised as a regular and ordinary "mean" by which the spirit of man may be awakened to consciousness of the presence of God, and may draw "grace to help" from that presence, there is no obvious reason why other physical experiences also should not be normal and appointed vehicles for the same contact with the divine.

But the truth, I take it, is that the whole question is one we cannot settle by appeal to *a priori* anticipations. It is irrational to attempt to decide on the strength of general metaphysical theory how God must act in bestowing good gifts on His creatures. The one question we can ask with sanity about such a matter is the *historical* question how in fact God is found to deal with us. Repugnance to give recognition to the sacramental element in historical religions as having abiding value seems to be, in the last resort, only one more form of the persistent reluctance shown by the numerous philosophers who, consciously or unconsciously, regard mathematics as the one type of what knowledge should be, to do justice to the reality of the historical. Far too many of our contemporaries—not all of them "idealists" —are still beset by the ambition to contemplate human life in all its detail under a supposed "form of eternity" which actually means the dismissal of time and history as illusions. Yet the whole poignancy of human life arises from the fact that it is an unsolved tension between the temporal and the eternal, in which the eternal, though steadily gaining on and subduing the temporal to its purposes, never absorbs it. To suppose that I can understand my own life without recognising the temporal everywhere in it is to repeat the old error of Lucifer, who mistook himself for God.

At the cost of some reiteration of the already said, I cannot escape recurring once more to what I regard as the true and important thought that it is just this presence of a never completely resolved strain of temporality in human life as we know it which makes the presence of uneliminated mystery and the stubbornly factual so characteristic of it. If we could compass a vision of life from which the last vestige of bare succession and contingency had vanished, all mystery would have disappeared with them. The work which God works from the beginning would stand revealed to us as something transparent and self-evident to the understanding; we should comprehend the ways of God finally and completely. But then also all opposition between the comprehender and the comprehended would have vanished; the world, thus completely comprehended, would present no single feature which stood over against the understanding as irreducibly foreign and given "from the outside"; it would be to each of us what a work of art might be to the artist who had constructed it with complete and conscious mastery, never for an instant uncertain as to his own meaning, never carried "out of himself" by an "inspiration" which mastered *him*, and never hampered by the intractability of a medium less than absolutely plastic to his purpose.

In fact no work of a human artist is ever of this kind. Every human artist is at times uncertain of the effect he means to produce, at times in the grip of an invasive inspiration which carries him to unforeseen effects, at times condemned to wrestle with difficulties due to the obstinate intractability of the medium in which he works.

And in our attempts as philosophical thinkers to understand a world which we have in no sense created, we are not even in the position of the human artist towards his product, but at best in that of the audience before whom a great drama or symphony is being rendered for the first time. We cannot say, before the curtain goes up on a scene, what the dramatist has in store for us. At the most we may hope so far to catch something of the spirit of the whole piece that the scene, when we have witnessed it, will be found to be in keeping with the none too clearly discerned purport of the whole. What that purport is we can only divine from the scenes which have already been enacted before us; we see the play only once, we have to leave the theatre before the performance is ended, and we are not allowed to bring a "book of the words" to the representation.

To complicate the situation still further, we are not merely an audience, we are also ourselves part of the cast for some of the scenes, and we are not furnished in advance with the text of our own part. The drama of history, as we sometimes call it, is like a play in which each actor is provided with some general knowledge of what has been said and done before he comes on the stage, and is perhaps aided by some whispered hints from an unseen prompter, but otherwise has to fashion and conduct his part for himself, as best he can. There is no going behind the scenes to secure a book of the play in advance, and the book of the play is what philosophers who set themselves to "geometrise" history falsely imagine themselves to possess. If they really had it, faith and proof would alike be swallowed up for them in vision.

It is wrong in principle, then, I should say, to attempt an *a priori* answer to the question whether belief in sacramental "means of grace" is rational or irrational, for the simple reason that the geometrising of the historical is wrong in principle. However strongly the philosopher may be convinced that history has the unity of a dominant pattern, he is bound to be equally assured that he can bring no knowledge of the pattern with him in advance to his study of history. Such light as he may gain on the character of the pattern will only come to him fitfully and tentatively, as the historical dance unfolds itself to his gaze. And the historical includes not only the interplay between man and man, but all the contacts there may be, in the depths of the soul itself, between man and his super-historical Maker. If He is beyond and above history, we are always immersed in it, and since *quidquid recipitur recipitur ad modum recipientis*, He can only reach us by an activity striking down into the temporal and historical. His dealings with us cannot be what they might be if we were non-temporal beings.

The real question we have to answer, then, is this. Granting that there is a quality or level of life which is specifically religious, not merely scientific, or aesthetic, or ethical, do we find, when the appeal is made to history, that life with this quality is normally and customarily exhibited at its rarest and best in connection with definite practice of sacramental acts, or in detachment from them? Is it, on the whole, true that religions lose or gain in the clearness and concentration with which they bring God and eternity as dominant realities into the lives of their followers, in proportion as the sacramental element is absent from them, or present in them? If the testimony of history is that such sacramental acts are normally most prominent in those religions, or in those periods of the history of a given religion, in which there is the most sensitive and abiding appreciation of the eternal values, this would be, not indeed mathematical demonstration, but historical proof that normally God does utilise the physical things and acts we call sacramental as genuine instruments for the conveyance of His best gifts. If the verdict of impartial history is found to be that the real appreciation of the eternal values and the control of life by that appreciation is equally well, or even better, sustained by the types of religion which rely least on sacraments, this would be fair historical proof that the sacramentarianism of some existing historical religions is a temporary accident, and possibly an unfortunate accident, which religion may be expected to outgrow as it reaches a clearer understanding of its own significance. This, as it seems to me, is the only form of the question whether sacramentalism is rational or irrational which admits of a determinate solution.

Naturally, it is no part of my business to answer the question for anyone else. But it may be in place to make some observations in defence of an over-hasty answer in either sense. The appeal, to be of real worth, must be made to history, not simply to the mere personal experience of a single individual. If we base our judgement only on our convictions about our personal experience, it is liable to be affected both by our own imperfect intellectual interpretation of our experience, and by mistaking our personal "temperamental" bias for something typically and universally human. The case is not sufficiently made out for sacramentalism by merely urging, however vehemently, that I believe my own spiritual life to have benefited from devotion to the sacraments of my Church. I may even be mistaken about the fact. I may take for personal growth in grace what is really something very different.[1] Or supposing

[1] *E.g.* advance in mere "refinement", or even that subsidence of carnal passion which is effected by growing physically older.

the fact to be indubitable, I may be committing the common fallacy of ascribing a real effect to a wrong cause. Finally, if I am right both about the fact and about its explanation, I may be wrong in arguing that a practice thus necessary and beneficial to me must have the same worth for everyone else, in spite of all individual variations of temperament. (This is actually recognised by ardent sacramentalists among Christians when they say, as they often do, that there can be no single rule equally valid for everyone, *e.g.* in the matter of frequency of Communions.)

On the other side, the anti-sacramentalist would not establish his case by merely asserting, however sincerely, that in himself a genuine spirituality exists in conjunction with abstention from sacramental observances. He, again, may be mistaken about the alleged fact; he may take for spirituality in himself what is only fastidiousness, as I believe is not uncommonly done.[1] If he is not mistaken about the fact, he may always be met by the suggestion that he would have received the gift of a still higher spirituality if he had not neglected "the means", or that he is possibly neglecting to allow for the special peculiarities of his own idiosyncracy, and forgetting that the whole question is not one of what is possible in exceptional cases, but of what is the general rule. To avoid all these sources of mistake it is necessary that the appeal be made to a super-individual experience, over a sufficiently wide range of space and time. And for the same reasons, I should say, it would be improper, in a thoroughly philosophical treatment of the question, to confine attention to the history of a single religion, with its specific hallowed traditions, since it

[1] As, *e.g.*, when the vegetarian plumes himself, as he sometimes does, on his superiority in spirituality to the flesh-eater. All that is true is that the vegetarian has the daintier palate, but there is no special connection between daintiness and spirituality.

does not seem possible to maintain the *simpliste* view that there are no genuine contacts with God outside the boundaries of some one historical religious community. In that sense, at any rate, *extra ecclesiam nulla salus* would be a palpable untruth.

It would thus not be dealing with the question on a sufficiently wide scale, for example, to study and compare the types of spiritual life provided, within the limits of the Christian religious tradition, by a highly sacramentarian community, like the Roman Catholic Church, and a non-sacramental body, like the Society of Friends. If one relied simply on that comparison, there would, I think, be serious risk of overestimating the spirituality compatible with rejection of the sacramental, for a reason which has been more than once dwelt on by von Hügel. One needs to remember that the Society of Friends sprang up and has continued to flourish in the midst of a wider Christian community which *is* sacramental in its practice, and that the type of religion which the Society seeks to cultivate was from the first conditioned and prescribed by the existing and powerful tradition, and has ever since been more or less fed by the great devotional literature, of this wider community. As von Hügel observes,[1] though George Fox turned his back on the sacramental system and believed himself to have received a new and special illumination directly from God, the actual content of the illumination is determined throughout by the Johannine Gospel, the high sacramentarian writing, *par excellence*, of the New Testament. And, of course, the Society at the present day, does not dream of trying to screen the life of its members from the influence of the great devotional literature of Christendom at large. Hence, though Fox and the Society he founded may not

[1] *Essays and Addresses on the Philosophy of Religion*, pp. 231, 293.

practise the Christian sacraments, his life and theirs could not be what they were and are but for the living influence of the sacramental tradition of the Church at large. When one is, so to say, within the "sphere of influence", even if one is outside the "occupied territory" of the organised historic Christian Church, one is never really far away from the operation of the Christian sacraments.[1]

For this reason an historical inquiry would not be complete if confined to a study of the types of spiritual life fostered by various Christian communities. One should further attempt a comparison between the spiritual fruits of a religion like Christianity, which, in its most significant historical forms, is intensely sacramental, and a religion like Islam, which is overwhelmingly non-sacramental. Of course, in such a survey, it would be indispensable to avoid the besetting unfairness of the controversialist. One would be scrupulously careful not to make the comparison one between Christianity, as it shows itself in the lives of its saints, and Mohammedanism, as shown in the lives of its average men. In fact, one would have to make a double comparison, between the saints of both religions, and, again, between the average sinners of both. One would require to know whether the average, faulty, largely worldly minded Christian reveals himself to be, at any rate, more sensitive to non-secular influences than the average Moslem, or not, and also whether in the highest and best of the saints of Islam, there may not be something lacking which we find in the saints and heroes of Christianity, and which, so far as we can see, is secured

[1] One might fairly say that the graces manifested, often strikingly enough, in the lives of members of the Society of Friends are mediated by the reception of the Christian sacraments, though not by their own personal reception. The reception by the Christian community at large plays the same part here that the "faith of the Church" does in the baptism of infants.

for them, directly or indirectly, by the Christian sacramental tradition.

To be really fruitful, the inquiry would need to be conducted with anxiety to avoid a further insidious source of misapprehension. If the judgement finally reached is to be worth anything, the effects on which it is based must be themselves quite definitely fruits of the religious life. The question is not at all whether societies honouring and practising sacraments will be found, on appeal to history, to enjoy marked social and economic prosperity, to make striking contributions to art and science, or to acquire and retain political eminence. Macaulay's well-known attempt to decide whether Calvinism or Romanism is the better religion by contrasting the post-Reformation history of Scotland with that of Spain [1] is an obvious example of a bad *ignoratio elenchi*. One cannot simply take advance in wealth, comfort, political prestige, and the industrial arts as unfailing indications of special nearness to God.

But we need equally to remember that a similar, though less obvious, *ignoratio elenchi* would be committed if judgement were based upon "*moral* statistics", unless the word "moral" is to be understood in a sense which would make it impossible to prefix it as an epithet to the noun "statistics". Two societies may exhibit much the same degree of respect for the commonly recognised moral duties of regard for life and property, female honour, and the spoken word, and yet stand on different levels in apprehension of God and the eternal. The commonly recognised and easily constated obligations are of a kind which men find forced upon them as conditions of a tolerable secular civilisation. Their importance may be clearly perceived, and a high average standard in the practice of them attained, by a

[1] In the Essay on Ranke's *History of the Popes*.

society intelligently bent on the pursuit of a worldly and second-rate aim in life, and grossly indifferent to the eternal and transcendent. Even men who are content to aim at nothing more than stable, comfortable existence, if they are clear-sighted, will discover the necessity of being, in the main, honest and humane, faithful husbands, decent parents, loyal observers of their promises, though their whole conception of good may remain thoroughly worldly.

There are, it is true, virtues for which a completely this-world scheme makes no provision, such as the humility which expresses our sense of our creatureliness. But a virtue like humility does not manifest itself in a recognisable distinct group of performances; it is rather an attendant disposition of soul by which all the performances connected with the various "departmental" virtues gain an added beauty. It shows itself not so much in what is done as in the manner of the doing, and thus the sort of moral statistics which may be instructive about the standing of a society in regard, for example, of respect for human life, or for the bond of legal wedlock, will throw no light on the degree of humility present in it. And speaking more generally, the real differences between a highly religious man or society and a man or society with a morality of a worldly minded type will mostly escape the notice of the collector of moral statistics. Both types of society may, for example, respect the bond of marriage; the difference between the two lies not so much in their respect for that bond as in their conceptions of the principal good to be promoted by regard for it. The divergence between the man to whom marriage has a sacramental significance and one in whose eyes it is merely an important social institution of the civil law means that the first will not be satisfied with himself as a husband, if he has succeeded in being what the second understands by a model husband; it need not show itself in the records of the percentages of divorces, or in any similar form recognisable by the moral statistician.

In general, the kind of information provided by such statistics would be inconclusive for the purposes of the sort of inquiry I have in mind for a double reason. All that these statistics can tell us is whether grave transgressions of overt act are relatively many or few in a community. This throws some light on the moral condition of the average man in the community, though not all the light we could desire. But it leaves it quite uncertain whether in a society in which the average moral practice is high, and there are not many who fall below it, there are, or are not, those who rise above it.

It is conceivable that the same society which is shown by statistics to be fertile in gross offenders may also be unusually fertile in great saints. The gross sinners affect the statistics; since the saint cannot be detected by externals, the great saints do not. Again, the sins which will show up in the statistical record—sins of carnality and violence—though grosser, are not so fatal to the soul's life as the highly respectable sins of self-sufficiency, cold egoism, and spiritual pride. But these, not being transgressions of the civil code, do not appear in the records. One society may be more disfigured than a second with offences springing from appetite and anger, and yet more fruitful in examples of spontaneous self-forgetting, kind offices, and little heroisms which go unchronicled, and these are the things which really reveal life of supernatural quality. But they do not stand out visible to the human observer, except where we find them displayed on an exceptional scale in the life of the saint. This is why, as it seems to me, in instituting the appeal to history of which I have spoken, it is imperative to take into account not only the comparative level of average goodness exhibited in two societies, but the comparative fertility of the two societies in the highest types of heroism and sainthood.

VIII

THE ULTIMATE TENSION: TIME AND THE HISTORICAL

Nulla tempora tibi coaeterna sunt, quia tu permanes; et illa si permanerent, non essent tempora. . . . Quid est ergo tempus? si nemo ex me quaerat, scio; si quaerenti explicare velim, nescio.—AUGUSTINE.

τυπωθέντα ἀπ᾽ αὐτῶν τρόπον τινὰ δύσφραστον καὶ θαυμαστόν, ὃν εἰς αὖθις μέτιμεν. —PLATO.

WE have now, only too inadequately, passed under review some of the outstanding characteristics of the great positive religions which might seem, at least on a surface view, least conciliable with the spirit of rational metaphysics, and may, I believe, say that such opposition as we have detected has, under all its varied forms, a single root. The intellectual discomfort of the metaphysician confronted with positive institutional religion is not due to any merely accidental features of the different great faiths and worships of the world; it has a deeper source in the way in which all these faiths apprehend God, the central object of religion. It is not that there is any ultimate *conflict* between the Theism of the great religions and a strictly philosophical Theism, based on a sound metaphysic. We have not to make our choice between a *dieu des savants et des philosophes* and a *dieu des pauvres et des humbles*, as Elijah bade the people make their choice between Baal and the Lord. The "god of the poor and lowly" is no other than the eternal source of all being demanded by the intellect of the metaphysician; neither the "head" nor the "heart" can be contented with less. Historically Christianity, the faith of the *pauperes et humiles*, has proved to be also the religion which has been most successful in assimilating the natural theology of the great philosophical thinkers. The actual tension between natural and revealed religion arises in a different way. Because they are historical, and in proportion as they are historical, all the great positive religions conceive the relation between man and God as itself involving an irreducible element of the historical; hence their insistence on the permanent significance of individual historical persons, incidents with a date and place, membership of definite historical societies, participation in acts and practices which belong to the web of physical becoming. The tendency of the metaphysical mind, on the other hand, is to find in God simply an answer to a problem about the *rationale*, it may be of nature, or of the moral, or of the specifically religious life, but, in any case, an answer to a problem which deals with *universal* features of the realm of becoming, prescinding from reference to the individual quality of this or that becoming. The problem being posed in this non-historical way, the answer given to it inevitably ignores history.

To reduce the element of permanent truth about God contained in actual religions and theologies simply to the contents of a rational "natural theology" involves committing ourselves to the view that though the metaphysical analysis of becoming, as such, may reveal the presence of God as its super-historical ground, the particular *what* of an individual piece of becoming can never disclose anything not already revealed by this general analysis. Hence acceptance of a positive historical religion requires us to ascribe a significance to time and temporal events and processes which is denied to them by that large body of metaphysicians, old and new, who regard temporality as a sort of illusion which must be overcome before we can reach truth. If time is only a dream, it is reasonable to hold that we shall attain truth about God, or indeed about anything else, only in proportion as we avoid attaching significance to the concrete detail of the historical. Our theologians *par excellence* should be metaphysicians as indifferent to history as Spinoza or Schopenhauer, and our chosen watchword should be *Alles vergängliche ist nur ein Gleichnis*, with a particular emphasis on the *nur*. If time is more than an illusion, the irrationality would be precisely in this indifference to the significance of the concrete historical person, or event, as revelatory of the character of the supra-historical source of all real becoming. At the end of our review we are once more thrown back on the same problem of the status of time of which we spoke, almost at the beginning of our discussions, as the most insistent and perplexing of all the questions of metaphysics.

We may illustrate the insistency of the problem, as well as its importance for theology, by a reference to the marked tendency of definitely Christian thinkers of our own day, under the influence of contemporary philosophical speculation, to revolt from the type of doctrine about God so common in the more philosophical of the Fathers, and, I suppose, universal in the great schoolmen, whose minds had been moulded on the study of Plato and Aristotle. Patristic and scholastic divinity is emphatic in its insistence on the kindred thoughts of the absolute unchangeableness and consequent utter "impassibility" of God. To admit becoming, still more to admit suffering of any kind into the divine nature itself is, from the point of view of this theology, on, if not over, the verge of formal blasphemy. Indeed, if we would be rigidly orthodox scholastics, we must not even admit the reality of any reciprocal relation between God and His creatures. When we speak of them as made by Him, as the objects of His love, or of His displeasure, we are at best using language which tells us something about the creatures, viz. that they depend in various ways on God, but nothing about God Himself. There is no "real" relation of God to anything *ab extra*.

As we know, this line of thought led, in the early centuries of the formation of dogma, to grave difficulties even about the reality of the redemptive sufferings of the God-Man. That Christ suffered in reality, not in mere semblance, in the Garden and on the Cross, could not be denied without plain and direct contradiction of the emphatic and repeated declarations of the New Testament Scriptures, and complete surrender to the Docetism which, almost from the first, threatened to evaporate the Gospel into a theosophical fairy-tale. But how difficult the Graeco-Roman mind found it to reconcile its conception of Deity with the conviction that the Passion of Christ is genuine historical fact is proved by the paradoxical phraseology, ἀπαθῶς ἔπαθεν and the like, in which the more metaphysically minded of the Fathers strove to express the thought. Nor are such phrases a mere antiquarian curiosity. Until well on in the last century they continued to flourish in the current language of Christian devotion among ourselves. I can myself well remember a hymn—I do not know whether it may not still be in use—in which it was said of the crucified Christ, in the very terminology of St. Gregory Nyssen, "impassive, he suffers, immortal, he dies".

When we remember the marked contrast between Greek metaphysical speculation and the radically unmetaphysical, frankly anthropomorphic, tone of

Hebrew prophecy, in which the language of human action and passion is unreservedly used about God, it should not be surprising that the last generation has seen a violent reaction, conducted in the name of Christianity itself, against this whole body of conceptions. Whether or not it is good divinity and metaphysics to look for process, suffering, defeat, in the very heart of the divine life itself, there is no doubt that language which implies the real presence of mutability and suffering in the life of God is constantly heard to-day from Christian pulpits—from those of the Roman Church, with all its tenacity of established theological formula, as well as from others—and that everywhere, outside the Roman Church at least, there is a marked tendency on the part of theological writers themselves to attempt an intellectual justification of such language. The late Dr. Fairbairn wrote years ago that "Patripassianism is only half a heresy"; more recent divines of more Churches than one seem ready to go further, and to maintain that Patripassianism is the true Christian orthodoxy, working itself clear at last of entanglement with the errors of Stoicism,[1] that most unhistorical of the major philosophies of antiquity. The late Baron von Hügel has included in his second series of *Essays and Addresses* what to myself seems a wise and timely warning against the dangers of this excessively "Christocentric" theology. But to me the most significant thing about his admirable essay on *Suffering and God* is that the warning should have been felt by the author to be so imperatively needed. It could only be necessary in an age which ascribes to process and temporality a significance very different from that given to them in any Hellenic philosophy. For good or bad, the growth of the sense

[1] I may refer for an account of this tendency in contemporary divinity to the careful study of J. K. Mozley, *The Impassibility of God* (Cambridge, 1926).

of the historical has made what our American friends call the metaphysical "status" of Time the most urgent of our philosophical problems.

It may be instructive to remind ourselves, at this point, that according to a view which has a great deal to say for itself, the permeation of Graeco-Roman civilisation by a great positive religion is actually the cause to which we owe it that European thought, unlike Indian, for example, has become, as a whole, thoroughly historical. The κόσμος of pre-Christian Greek thought only became a really historical world under the influence of Christianity and its ancestor, Judaism. The point is excellently put by a very recent writer on the history of philosophy in a passage which summarises the position of M. Laberthonnière—a position not accepted by the historian himself—in a few admirable sentences. "The κόσμος of the Greeks is, as we might say, a world without a history, an eternal order in which time counts for nothing, whether because it leaves that order always self-identical, or because it produces a series of events which always reverts to the same point through an indefinite repetition of cyclical changes. Is not even the history of mankind, according to Aristotle, a perpetual recurrence of the same civilisation? The antithetic thought that there really are radical changes, absolute beginnings, genuine discoveries, in a word, history and progress in the wide sense—such a thought was impossible until Christianity had swept away the Greek κόσμος. A world created from nothing, a destiny which man does not receive from without, but shapes for himself by his own obedience, or disobedience, to the divine law, a new and unforeseeable divine intervention to save man from sin, redemption purchased by the sufferings of the God-Man—in all this we have a dramatic picture of the universe . . . in which nature is effaced, and everything depends on the intimate spiritual history of man and his relations with God. Man sees before him a possible future of which he may be the author; he is delivered for the first time from Lucretius' melancholy *eadem sunt omnia semper*, from the Fate of Stoicism, from the eternal geometrical scheme in which Plato and Aristotle imprisoned the real. This was the outstanding peculiarity which impressed the first pagans who took the Christians seriously. What is the reproach brought against them by Celsus? . . . That they worship a God who is not *immutable*, since He takes initiatives and decisions to meet circumstances, nor yet *impassible*, since He is touched by pity; that they believe in a kind of myth, that of the Christ, which 'will not permit an allegorical explanation'; in other words, it is presented as genuine history, and cannot be made into a symbol of physical law."

In reproducing Laberthonnière's thought,[1] M. Bréhier rightly warns the reader against the danger of making the antitheses too rigid, but the caution, though necessary if justice is to be done, for example, to the Platonic conception of the relation of Becoming to Being, leaves the substantial truth of the contrast unaffected. It is, in the main, true that all Greek philosophy *au fond* teaches the doctrine *plus ça change, plus c'est la même chose*, exactly as the same thing is taught, with some small variations in the manner of the instruction, by the most illustrious of the modern philosophers who have been markedly in revolt against the traditions of historical Christianity, Spinoza, Schopenhauer, Nietzsche; that the moral consequence of brooding on such doctrines of self-sameness, or of eternal recurrence, has always been *taedium vitae*; that without new beginnings and non-reversible changes there is no

[1] E. Bréhier, *Histoire de la philosophie*, i. 489-90.

genuine history, but only a surface illusion of history; that, in point of fact, the conception of history as a whole with a real significance, and consequently, the idea of a "philosophy of history", makes its first appearance in the great literature of the world with Augustine's *De civitate Dei*, and that its source must be found in the Jewish and Christian Scriptures, with their doctrine of the redemptive purpose of God as the key to history.

These are facts which cannot well be gainsaid, and they have no real counterpart in the pre-Christian Hellenic world, not even in the philosophy which, of all the Hellenic doctrines, comes by far the nearest to a worthy appreciation of the historical, that of Plato. Plato and others might speak of human life as a divine puppet-play,[1] in which God is at once the sole spectator and the manipulator of the marionettes; Thucydides might set himself to compose an accurate narrative of the doings and motives of the two great warring powers, the Athenian "empire" and the Peloponnesian confederacy,[2] as a lesson in statesmanship for future generations, and might incidentally show himself to students who know how to read with understanding the noblest and austerest moralist who has ever written history.[3] But even the "divine" Plato has not yet the clear conviction that the play is working out to an end in which its author-spectator takes a supreme interest, nor does Thucydides see the struggle of which he is the historian as an act in a drama which has significance as a whole, a stage in the "education of humanity". To see things thus, you must understand what is meant by

[1] *Laws*, 803 C *φύσει δὲ εἶναι θεὸν μὲν πάσης μακαρίου σπουδῆς ἄξιον, ἄνθρωπον δέ, ὅπερ εἴπομεν ἔμπροσθεν, θεοῦ τι παίγνιον εἶναι μεμηχανημένον, καὶ ὄντως τοῦτο αὐτοῦ τὸ βέλτιστον γεγονέναι.*

[2] Thuc. i. 22, 4.

[3] Though he has been strangely mistaken for a Machiavellian by Nietzsche, who does not know how to appreciate the great men of the fifth century B.C. historically.

sic Deus dilexit mundum, and that thought is only very faintly adumbrated when Plato makes his Timaeus speak of the delight the Creator took in the perfection of his handiwork.[1]

The modern historian of civilisation, though often enough he may not know it, is what he is because he cannot get away from the influence of convictions born of the belief that human history has a significance which only became transparent in the concrete individual happening of certain events which began with the call of Abraham out of Harran, reached their climax in the procuratorship of one Pontius Pilate, and the opening of their fifth act on the day of Pentecost. It is in the end the Jew, to whom the "oracles" were entrusted, from whom the Christian community, and through them the modern Western world, has learned to think historically, just because Judaism and Christianity are absolutely bound up with convictions about certain historical events as no system of philosophy is. We owe the "historical sense", on which we sometimes pride ourselves, to the very peculiarity of the "Christian myth" which disconcerted Celsus, the impossibility of sublimating it into a symbol of "physical law", its incorrigible and unabashed concreteness.

I believe we may trace a more subtle effect of the same influence of Christian theology in the fundamental distinction which separates our own most abstract "scientific world-view" from that of all Greek philosophers. If there is one thought rather than another about the physical order itself which is specially characteristic of the Hellenic natural philosophers, it is their conviction that all physical processes are reversible;

[1] *Tim.* 37 C ὡς δὲ κινηθὲν αὐτὸ καὶ ζῶν ἐνόησεν . . . ὁ γεννήσας πατήρ, ἠγάσθη. This is an exact counterpart of "God saw his work that it was good"; but even Plato does not know that God loves sinners.

whatever has taken the "way up" may always be expected, in time, to take the "way down" again, and *vice versa*. If vapour condenses into water, and water into earth, earth is once more rarefied into water, and water into vapour. If atoms once come together in an eddy and so form a "world", they must scatter again, and the scattering will unmake the world;[1] but the *débris* will again come together a second time after the scattering, and a "world" will be made over again. So in Aristotle's universe, though it never was made and never is unmade, there is one, and only one, set of motions which are irreversible, the revolutions of the celestial "spheres", and the reason of the irreversibility is precisely that these motions and no others have a direct *supra-mundane* source. In Plato's *Timaeus* we are told, indeed, that the making of the world will not, in fact, be followed hereafter by an antithetic unmaking; but here again the reason for the irreversibility is a theological and supramundane one, the will of its Creator. "Ye are indeed not wholly immortal, nor indissoluble", says the Creator in that dialogue to the "created gods", who are, in fact, the stars, "yet ye shall have no dissolution, nor taste of death, since ye have in my will a greater and stronger bond than those with which ye were compacted in your making".[2]

[1] Cf. Lucretius, v. 243:

quapropter maxima mundi
cum videam membra ac partis consumpta regigni,
scire licet caeli quoque item terraeque fuisse
principiale aliquod tempus clademque futuram;

ii. 1144:

sic igitur magni quoque circum moenia mundi
expugnata dabunt labem putrisque ruinas:
omnia debet enim cibus integrare novando
et fulcire cibus, etc.

The Christians agreed with Lucretius in expecting an "end" of the "world", but they looked forward to this end as the entrance on a better and abiding world, not as a recurrence to the beginning of an old and tedious story.

[2] *Tim.* 41 B.

Our thought about nature, on the other hand, is dominated by the so-called principle of Carnot, the law of the "dissipation" of energy, which, by forbidding us to believe in the complete reversibility of any temporal processes, profoundly modifies our conception of time itself. For us the "world's great age" does not and cannot "begin anew"; the images of the phoenix renewing its youth in its own funeral pyre,[1] or the snake casting its senility with its skin, have lost their cosmic significance. What has happened once does not, and cannot, happen again, and thus the historical event has won for us an absolute and unique individuality which it could not have for any ancient thinker. To us it is not irreversibility but reversibility which would be the *miraculum*, demanding an immediate cause *extra rerum naturam*.

The reluctance of many men of science to accept Carnot's principle as valid for natural processes at large without restriction, their readiness to make heavy draughts on imagination of what may be contained in inaccessible regions of space and time to upset it,[2] are still with us to testify to the difficulty with which physical science accommodates itself to a strictly historical way of conceiving becoming. If, in spite of these protests, the mass of our scientific men look askance at ingenious devices for getting rid of the second law of Thermodynamics, the reason seems to be that they are antecedently prepossessed in favour of irreversibility by the distinctly modern "sense for the historical", itself so largely a creation of Christian theology. It is from the history of human life that they have drawn the conviction that the past does *not* recur, and when they make its non-recurrence into a corner-stone of

[1] The phoenix has its meaning as a Christian symbol too, as when Crashaw writes "the phoenix builds the phoenix' nest," but it does not mean the κόσμος.

[2] Cf. É. Meyerson, *L'Explication dans les sciences*, i. 206, ii. 405-6.

their physics, they are definitely breaking through the old classical Platonic tradition of a purely geometrical natural world. We see exactly the same tendency to make physical science historical, in a way in which it could not be historical under the classical tradition, from Plato to Newton, in the anxiety of Dr. Whitehead to save natural philosophy from becoming flatly "incredible" by making the eminently historical concept of "organism" its foundation.[1] Must we not say, in the light of such considerations, that the peculiarity which Celsus alleged as a reproach against the spirit of Christianity, its insistence on a μῦθος which cannot be allegorised, is in fact its glory? What the complaint really means is that with Christianity there came, for the first time, into the Graeco-Roman world, a really adequate appreciation of individuality.[2] We are still far from having done full justice in our philosophy and science to all the implications of this heightened sense of the reality of the individual, but we are on our way to do so. The historicising, if I may call it so, of the physical sciences, now apparently in process, is but one further step along the same road which has led, in our moral, social, and religious thinking, to the conquest of the great conception, so imperfectly grasped in ancient philosophy, of personality in God and man.

The particular point to which I would ask attention at present, then, is this. All the various tendencies, so familiar to us in the intellectual life of our age, which are most hostile to the recognition of the historical as an indispensable element in religion, the disparagement as merely temporary and accidental of everything in the positive religions which resists reduction to positions

[1] Cf. *Science and the Modern World*, cc. 5, 6.

[2] I suppose the nearest Greek equivalent to "individual" is the Aristotelian τόδε τι. But the equivalence is most imperfect. The most commonplace John Smith is something a great deal more than ἄνθρωπός τις.

of general metaphysics, the hardly concealed desire of some even among our theologians to obliterate the distinctions between a faith like Christianity and the kind of religion possible to a Neo-Platonic philosopher, the anxiety of metaphysicians of various schools to interpret the affirmations of all the positive religions as no more than figurative expressions of some vague principle of "conservation of values", all are, if we come to reflect, only forms of the old protest against the "myth which refuses to be allegorised". And this means that they spring from inability to adjust one's mind to the characteristically modern habit of thinking historically, as one sees, in fact, quite plainly in the efforts of the small minority who "follow the argument wherever it leads" to discard even the bare fact of the actual historical existence of a personal founder of Christianity.

It should be easy to see that the position of these extremists is at variance with sane judgement and common sense, and one takes no great risk in prophesying that their thesis, in its cruder forms, will soon be laughed out of the world. Men who can believe that Christ and the apostles are astral symbols, or Semitic nature-deities, or the creations of pious romancers, deserve to end by believing that Francis Bacon was the heir to the crown of England and the creator of Falstaff, or that the date of the Millennium is built into the Great Pyramid. But it is not so easy, in view of the tardiness with which the full implications of the significance of individuality are making their way from the human into the physical sciences, to guard our own thinking from infection by subtler forms of the same prejudice. We are all still too much, in a great part of our thinking, under the spell of the ancient conception of the unhistorical, purely geometrical, world. If we were not, it would surely strike us as something of a paradox that philosophers should be trying to make religion truer by the elimination of the historical in the same age in which they are trying to make physical science truer by its introduction. If the geometrising of nature, thoroughly carried out, leads to the incredible,[1] is it likely that the geometrising of God will have any other result?

Perhaps I can best illustrate what I mean by the characteristic difference between the ancient geometrical and the modern historical conceptions of time and the temporal, if I start from a well-known and eloquent passage of Plato's *Timaeus*, and consider how the description of time given there differs from that to which our own modern physical science appears to be finding its way. This may look like going a long way back for the purposes of the contrast, but it will, I think, be seen as we proceed that the ideas of Timaeus are in principle those which dominate the seventeenth-century classical mechanics from Galileo and Descartes to Newton. In the passage to which I refer, time is being described as a uniform "measure" of becoming, becoming having already been set in the strongest possible contrast with the stable and selfsame *being* of eternity. We have already been told in a general way that the world which *becomes*, the historical world, was fashioned by its Maker in the likeness of a model which does not *become*, but *is*, the αὐτὸ ὃ ἔστι ζῷον, or intelligible pattern of a supreme living organism embracing all other organisms. The narrative proceeds, "And when the Father who had begotten it beheld it, a created image of the eternal things,[2] moving and quick, he was well-

[1] Whitehead, *Science and the Modern World*, p. 80: "It"—*i.e.* the Newtonian scheme taken as an account of the real world—"is fully worthy of the genius of the century which produced it. . . . It is not only reigning, but it is without a rival. And yet—it is quite unbelievable."

[2] *Tim.* 37 C. The MSS. read τῶν ἀιδίων θεῶν "of the eternal *gods*", but θεῶν is pretty certainly an old corruption.

pleased, and rejoicing devised how to make it yet more like its model. Since, then, that model is, of a truth, a thing living and eternal, he essayed to make this All also such, so far as he might. Now the nature of that living thing was in truth eternal, and this it was impossible to bestow wholly on a creature. But he contrived the making of a moving likeness of eternity; so in his ordering of the heavens, he fashioned an everlasting likeness, proceeding by number, of eternity that abides in unity, even that we have named time."[1]

There are several points in this passage deserving notice. In the first place, time is conceived, as it was to be in the classic mechanics of later days, as something in its nature independent of extension, or volume, and adventitious to it. We have already heard of "becoming", and also of corporeality and its three dimensions as characteristic of "the creature", before it is mentioned that it was endowed with temporality, as an added perfection. Timaeus clearly does not think of "that we have named time" as logically complicated with that which we name *volume*; to him it is manifestly conceivable that there might be volumes, and even movements, without time, though a world of this kind would be less "like its eternal model", and therefore a worse world, than the one which is actual. This means that, like Dr. Whitehead, Timaeus distinguishes between "passage", transitoriness, as a universal character of the physical world throughout its parts, and the *measure* of that passage which we call "time". It is also implied that there is just *one* such measure of passage, one time which, in the well-known phrase of Newton, "flows equably". We may, indeed, use the periodic movements of any of the heavenly bodies we please as our timepiece, and Timaeus is careful, in a

[1] *Tim.* 37 C-D.

later passage,[1] to censure the dullness of mankind in general, who speak of the periods of sun and moon as "time", but do not see that the name is equally applicable to those of any other "planets". But all that he means by this is that the period of any one of these bodies may always be computed in terms of the period of any other, so that if you reckon by periods of Mars, for example, you will speak of a lapse of five such periods where another man, reckoning in the more customary way, would talk of a lapse of ten years. He really means only to complain of the general neglect to determine the periods of all the planets with proper precision.[2] This complaint does not affect his fundamental assumption that any lapse or interval in the universe has an unambiguous measure; in the sense there is a single "universal" or "absolute" time, in which events may be unambiguously located, though we may use different unit-intervals for its computation, just as we may measure a single unambiguous interval of length either by the foot or by the metre.

The "time" of Timaeus is thus precisely the "true, absolute, or mathematical time" of Newton's *Principia*. This explains what is perhaps the most striking feature of the description I have quoted. The *temporality* of "becoming", because it has been thus carefully distinguished from its mere transitoriness, or successiveness, is dwelt upon not as the character which distinguishes what "becomes" from what "is", but as the point of closest resemblance. The world is given the form of time, not to differentiate it from its "intelligible" model, but to make it as like that model as the case will

[1] *Tim.* 39 C.

[2] In fact, his point seems to be simply that mankind at large do not understand that the revolutions of all the planets—the word means literally the "tramps" of the sky—are as much embodiments of "natural law" as those of the sun and moon upon which man depends for his knowledge of times and seasons. The "tramps" are not really vagabonds.

permit. The thought is that by receiving its unambiguous location in the universal time-order, a given piece of becoming is de-individualised; it is taken out of the immediate concrete "flow" of things, and receives a kind of quasi-eternalisation by being made thus abstract. This is why time is said to be not merely an *εἴδωλον* or *ἄγαλμα*, an image, but an *εἰκών*, a true *likeness* of eternity.[1]

If we put all this together, may we not fairly state its implications thus? The temporal as we directly experience it, in all the concreteness of actually lived life, is at the furthest remove from the reality of things; "perceptual time", *durée réelle* as Bergson calls it, with its indefinitely varied pulsations, is mostly according to the estimate suggested by the language of the *Timaeus*, illusion. It is the "abstract" and "conceptional" duration of the Newtonian scheme, divorced from all setting in a framework of individual experience, "clock-time", as fixed by reference to a single flawless ideal time-keeper for the universe at large, and sharply contrasted with the personal and "local" time of a particular observer, which is the *real* time, so far as the epithet "real" is applicable to the temporal. The nearer we get to the locating of events in such a cosmic chronological scheme, the nearer we are getting to the "truth about the facts". The further we are from it, the further from reality. When we speak of the "glorious hour of crowded life" as brief, and the hours of monotonous pain or boredom as intolerably long, we are nearest to concrete experience, but furthest from reality and truth. What is most vivid in the actual experience is also most delusive. If by "rationalisation" of the individual we mean

[1] It is also why "time", like the exact geometrical structure of the corpuscles of Timaeus, is expressly said to be contributed to the physical world by *νοῦς* or God, the intelligent and purposive "cause", not by *ἀνάγκη*.

what rationalists in philosophy have only too often meant, the reduction of it to a featureless uniformity of pattern, succession is all but completely rationalised in Newton's account of "true, mathematical" time, or, what comes to much the same, Kant's account of time as a pure "form of intuition"; the only element of the unrationalised "given" left is that provided by the bald fact that, as Timaeus says, the likeness is not the same thing as the model, that succession itself is irreducibly there, that there *is* "temporal location". All that makes the *tempo* of one succession so recognisably different from that of another has been eliminated, exactly as, to use an arresting phrase of Dr. Whitehead, "the shapiness of shapes"[1] is eliminated from pure geometry. In being thus reduced to uniformity succession has lost its significance for life and become unhistorical, just in proportion as it has lost its character of being mysterious and baffling. Time, thus standardised, becomes what it has been pronounced to be by an eminent philosopher recently lost to us, a form which reveals very little of the true nature of reality.[2]

Let me turn for a moment, by way of contrast, to very different conceptions which have been made widely current in our own day, first by the brilliant polemic of Bergson, and then by the rise among the physicists of the ideas to which we owe the "theory of Relativity", in its various forms. I am speaking, of course, as an utter

[1] *Science and the Modern World*, p. 38: "This fact, that the general conditions transcend any one set of particular entities, is the ground for the entry into mathematics, and into mathematical knowledge, of the notion of the 'variable'. It is by the employment of this notion that general conditions are investigated without any specification of particular entities. This irrelevance of the particular entities has not been generally understood; for example, the shapiness of shapes, *e.g.* circularity and sphericity and cubicality as in actual experience, do not enter into the geometrical reasoning."

[2] Bosanquet, *Logic*[2], i. 258: "Time is real as a condition of the experience of sensitive subjects, but it is not a form which profoundly exhibits the unity of things".

outsider in all matters of physical science, and I am not suggesting that either Bergson or any later *Naturphilosoph* has actually succeeded in working out a final and consistent metaphysic of time. We are, I take it, only at the beginning of a philosophical reinterpretation of nature which will need to be developed further, by men of the highest originality and acumen, before its deepest implications become fully clear to us. Yet both in Bergson and in the later theorists of Relativity we may note certain definite advances in the direction of a sound metaphysic of temporal process, which are bound to affect future "philosophy of history" very deeply.

To begin with Bergson. The permanently valuable feature of his treatment of succession appears to me to be simply his insistence on the real and profound difference between *durée réelle* and the artificial "mathematical" or "clock" time of our scientific manuals. That point, as I venture to think, Bergson made plain once for all in unusually impressive fashion in the three chapters of *Les données immédiates de la conscience*, though his own account of the process by which the second comes to be so easily confused with the first has always seemed to me unsatisfactory, since, so far as I can see, it both involves error of fact and also manifestly never gets to the heart of the problem. It is confusing and mischievous to see in intellect itself, as Bergson professes to do, a faculty inherently deceptive.[1] Reasoned philosophy cannot credit intellect with this inherent deceptiveness without committing suicide. It is not, I should say, true that the intellect is what Bergson seems to think it, essentially a *geometrising* faculty, if by this is

[1] Cf. Whitehead, *Science and the Modern World*, p. 74: "I agree with Bergson in his protest; but I do not agree that such distortion is a vice necessary to the intellectual apprehension of nature."

meant, as Bergson shows by the development of his argument that he means, a *measuring* faculty. If it were true that the fundamental operation of the understanding is to measure, surely metrical geometry ought not to be, as it appears in fact to be, a complex doctrine resting on the application of special metrical axioms and conventions to the simpler system of pure descriptive geometry; it should itself be the whole of the science, and descriptive non-metrical geometry ought to have no existence.[1] And, again, there ought to be no sciences but those of measurement and calculation; there should be no such things as the historical sciences, whose task is not to measure, calculate, and compute, but to interpret; and, again, no branches even of the mathematical sciences in which the fundamental conception is neither magnitude, nor number, but order. Indeed, if the intellect were really limited in its procedure in the way Bergson assumes, it is hard to understand how it could ever have discovered and proclaimed its own defect.

Again, the evolutionary explanation of the alleged limitation offered us, by the suggestion that intelligence has been fashioned under the stress of the practical necessity of finding our way about among the bodies around us, and is therefore naturally only competent for that task, seems to be naught. Even if we accept this speculation about the "origins" of intellect without misgivings, as we are not all prepared to do, it is a dangerous assumption that a power "evolved" to meet a particular practical need, can, when it has been evolved, do nothing but meet that particular need. Consider, for example, our capacity to appreciate beauty. Either this appreciation has come into exist-

[1] On the relation of metrical to projective and descriptive geometry see Russell, *Principles of Mathematics*, cc. xlvii., xlviii.; Couturat, *Les Principes des mathématiques*, pp. 190 ff.

ence by being "evolved" to meet a practical need, or it has not. If it has not, there seems no reason to assume that our capacity of understanding must have its origin in the pressure of practical needs. If it has, then it is at least clear that a "faculty" originally called into existence to meet a practical need continues, in this case, to serve wholly different purposes, and why may not the same thing be true about the "intellectual powers"? Finally, if we agree to leave these questions unraised, even on the double assumption that intelligence has "originated" entirely under the pressure of specific practical needs, and can do nothing, now that it is in existence, but meet those particular needs, it is pertinent, is it not, to remember that ever since living creatures have existed, it has been as much a practical problem for them to understand one another and establish a *modus vivendi* among themselves as to pick their way among their inanimate surroundings. So that, even on Bergson's own assumptions about the way in which intelligence has been developed, there seems to be no particular reason why its capacities should have the limitations he supposes.

Moreover, it seems a subordinate falsification of the facts to say, as Bergson apparently does,[1] that the whole "distortion" effected by the intellect in its attempts to deal with time arises from the dependence of all measurement on the primary measurement of segments of straight lines. All measurement is not measurement of lengths on a straight line; there is a second most important measurement of intervals, independent of such measurement of lengths, the estimation of angles, or, what comes to the same thing, of the ratios of arcs of

[1] At least this seems to be assumed throughout the argument (*op. cit.* c. 2) offered to show that time "as a homogeneous medium" is reducible to space. (E. Tr. *Time and Free Will*, p. 98.) It seems to be forgotten that "spatial" measurement itself has its own problems.

circles to the whole circumferences. In point of fact, it is by angular measurement that we habitually estimate temporal intervals, whenever we appeal to a watch or a clock, and in the prehistoric past, the first rough estimates of intervals within the natural day must presumably have been made, independently of measurement of lengths, by this same method, with the sky for clock-face. Measurement of temporal intervals is thus primarily angular measurement, and angular measurement is, in its origin, independent of measurement of straight lines.

It is true, of course, that when we come to the construction of a complete metrical theory, we find ourselves driven to establish a correlation between these two, originally independent, systems of measurement. For in practice I can only assure myself that two angular measurements are equal by reference to the circle, the one plane curve of constant curvature, and I satisfy myself that my curve of reference is a circle by ascertaining the equality of length of its diameters, and this is done by the rotation of a measuring-rod. This consideration suggests two observations. One is that the problem which has attracted Bergson's special attention is not rightly conceived when it is spoken of as the translation of temporal into spatial magnitude, or the imposing of spatial form on the non-spatial. It is only one case of the more general problem of the "rectification of a circular arc", which, of course, meets us in metrical geometry itself, independently of any application to the estimation of temporal intervals. The only inevitable "deformation" which arises in connection with measurement, so far as I can see, is the element of approximation and error introduced when we attempt to find an expression for the *length* of an arc of a curve, and *this* "deformation", as I say, has no necessary correlation with time. The difference between *durée réelle* and "mathematical" time must therefore be due to some other cause than the alleged artificial establishment of a correlation between temporal intervals and intervals on a straight line. It must come in already in the first attempt to apply *angular* measurement to temporal lapses, if it comes at all.

It should be further observed that the estimation of linear intervals themselves, apparently assumed by Bergson to be the special function of the intellect, and therefore to involve no difficulty or mystery, presents a real problem on its own account. Measurements made with different straight lines as axes can only be compared if we presuppose that the rotation of a measuring-stick, or its transference from one point of application to another, either makes no difference to its length, or affects it in a way which we can precisely determine. If our measuring-rods can change their length as they are turned through an angle, or carried from one place to another, and that to an unknown extent, there is an end of all comparison between segments of different straight lines. We have to postulate that our measuring-stick either remains of constant length during the process of transference from one position to another, or, at any rate, that if it changes its length during the process, it does so in accord with some knowable law of functional dependence. For this reason, some reference to *time* would appear to be involved in any set of postulates of spatial measurement. The complication of space with time is thus more intimate than it would be on Bergson's assumption that measurements primarily form an exclusively spatial framework into which duration is subsequently and, in fact, accidentally inserted, with a good deal of deformation, by the misguided "surface" intellect. This is what I had in mind in saying above that Bergson's doctrine seems to me, after all, not to get to the heart of the real problem.

It is just here, as I think, that the broad philosophical implications of the theory of Relativity come to our aid, and would still be forced upon us as metaphysicians, even if there were not well-known specific difficulties in the details of physical science, which seem to be most readily disposed of by the theory. The general implications of which I am thinking are, so far as I can see, independent of the divergences between the versions of "Relativity" advocated by individual physicists; their value, as I think, is that they enable us to formulate the problem to which Bergson has the eminent merit of making the first approach in a clear and definite way, and to escape what I should call the impossible dualism to which Bergson's own proposed solution commits him. So long as you think, as Bergson does, on the one hand, of an actual experience which is sheer qualitative flux and variety, and on the other, of a geometrical ready-made framework of sheer non-qualitative abidingness, there seems to be no possible answer to the question how *such* a "matter" comes to be forced into the strait-waistcoat of so inappropriate a "form", except to lay the blame on some wilful *culpa originalis* of the intellect. But if the intellect suffers from a *culpa originis*, *all* philosophical or rational thinking, including Bergson's own theorising about the purely qualitative nature of "real duration", is vitiated at its source. If the intellect is so radically corrupted, philosophy or science ought to be as impossible without supernatural revelation as morality must be, if the human will had been *totally* "depraved by the fall of Adam". Yet Bergson puts forward his own philosophy as the product of ordinary rational reflection, not of special supernatural illumination. Moreover, as I have said already, his speculation loses its attractiveness when we reflect that it must always have been as much an intellectual necessity for our ancestors to find a *modus vivendi* among themselves as to explore the topography of their *habitat*. The "social environment" is as old and as insistent a condition of life as the geographical. Hence, even if we feel no difficulty in bisecting our experience into two mutually exclusive domains, an "outer" acquaintance with the bodily environment, and an "inner" experience of social and moral environment—though meditation on Kant's *Refutation of Idealism*[1] ought surely to suggest serious difficulty—it is hard to see what features of the second, if Bergson has described it correctly, can have suggested the systematic deformation of it by the imposition of a radically alien type of structure. We should rather expect to find the whole *given* falling apart into two separate and disjunct fields, the intrinsically geometrical field of an "outer world", devoid of temporal form, and an intrinsically durational "inner world", ungeometrisable, and therefore wholly non-metrical. For it is obvious that not every "matter" is susceptible indifferently of every "form"; the "matter" which is to exhibit, on being subjected to certain operations, the metrical "form" must at least have *dispositionem quandam ad formam*.

I believe we escape this difficulty when we put ourselves at the point of view from which the various formulations of the theory of Relativity agree in taking their departure. In the recognition that the true source of the problem to which Bergson has called attention lies deeper than he supposed, in the impossibility of *locating* an experience temporally without reference to space, or spatially without reference to time, we

[1] *KdrV.*[2] 274 [*Werke*, iii. 197]. Cf. N. Kemp Smith, *Commentary on Critique of Pure Reason*, 298 ff.

reach a standpoint which no longer presupposes the primitive bisection of experience into "outer" and "inner" against which the Kantian refutation of "idealism" protested, and therefore no longer requires us to believe in the transference of metrical structure from one domain, where it is supposed to be wholly adequate, to another, where it is merely inappropriate. We do justice to the patent fact that in life as it is lived the "inner" and the "outer" are given to us inseparably conjoined in every pulse of experience, and that every constituent of the "given" thus has intrinsically, for each experient, its own orientation in an individual "space" and dating in an equally individual personal "time", and the two are given together.

Every one of my concrete "experiences" has its own intrinsic *when* and its own intrinsic *where* in the "fourfold continuum" of my life of personal interaction with my "environment". Our difficulties, the very difficulties which lead in the end to the formulation of the theory of Relativity, arise in the process of "transsubjective" intercourse between persons, because such communication imposes on us the necessity to devise a supra-personal system of reference by which experients at different *wheres* may adjust their statements about the *when* of an event, and experients at different *whens* their statements about its *where*. Thus it becomes necessary to construct a scheme of location in space without reference to "local time", and of location in time without reference to the experient's momentary *where*. This process, described by Bergson as the forcing of an alien geometrical form upon experiences of pure duration, is really something different; it is a process of cutting location in time and location in space, originally given in actual experience together, loose from one another, and the motive for the artificial separation now becomes obvious. It arises from the need of mutual understanding between a plurality of experients. The separation of space and time is thus seen to be no freak of the intellect presuming beyond its proper limits, but an inevitable and justified moment in the execution of its rightful business. We are thus delivered from the view, really fatal to serious thinking, that we can get nearer to understanding reality by merely setting ourselves to undo the results of intelligent reflection, and reverting to a primitive intuition which is only another name for crude apprehension of the unanalysed and *not* understood. At the same time, the discovery that all metrical comparison of spatial magnitudes involves reference to time and date, and all comparison of durational magnitudes reference to place, makes it clear that, necessary as the separation is, it can never be carried completely through.[1]

If there is to be intercommunication, the intercommunication must have a common "timeless space", and a common "spaceless time", which may be used indifferently as frameworks of reference by experients located in different *whens* and *wheres*, but it is inherently impossible to construct a single timeless space, or spaceless time, which could serve as schemes of reference indifferently for *all* experients whatsoever. Thus the most "spaceless" temporal scheme we can construct for the purpose of unambiguous dating is, after all, weighted with an inherent reference to our *ubi*;

[1] The process is necessary, because it is part of that "rationalisation" of experience without which communication between persons would be impossible, and the communication of experience is necessary for the understanding of it. It can never be fully carried through, because no experience is completely communicable in its concreteness. Plato understood this better, perhaps, than any philosopher before or since. *Ep.* vii. 343 E ἡ δὲ διὰ πάντων αὐτῶν (*sc.* names, λόγοι, δόξαι, etc.) διαγωγή, ἄνω καὶ κάτω μεταβαίνουσα ἐφ' ἕκαστον, μόγις ἐπιστήμην ἐνέτεκεν εὖ πεφυκότος εὖ πεφυκότι, and yet none of the indispensable means of communicating ἐπιστήμη can ever communicate it whole and unambiguous. *Ib.* 343 B μυρίος δὲ λόγος αὖ περὶ ἑκάστου τῶν τεττάρων, ὡς ἀσαφές.

it is a "local" time, though independent of the particular *ubi* of the individual experient who uses it, exactly as "Greenwich time" provides a common scheme for unambiguous dating, but a scheme only common to experients who are related by the condition that their particular *wheres* are all on the surface of our planet, and that they thus all partake in the motions of the planet relative to other bodies. There can be no one unambiguous scheme of location in either space or time valid for all experients, independently of *every* restricting condition. And the restricting condition of a common supra-individual scheme of spatial location will always involve reference to time, that of a common impersonal scheme for dating reference to space.[1] The presence of these restricting conditions plainly means that every supra-personal space or time system of reference is artificial, or "conventional", and, to that extent, arbitrary. But the arbitrariness is not the same thing as wilful caprice.

The difference is this. As the exponents of the theory put it, all such schemes involve the making of a "cut" between separation in time and separation in space, and the precise way in which the "cut" is to be made depends on the position of the experient making it in the fourfold "space-time" continuum. This position is arbitrary, in the sense that it is not dictated by the intrinsic character of the continuum itself that *A* should have his position in it here and now, *B* there and then. But it is not capricious; *A* does not assign himself his position "at his own sweet will". That his position is what it is is given fact from which *A* cannot get away. It is thus, to take a simple example, arbitrary that the "common time" of a plurality of human observers should be Greenwich time, or Paris time. But it is not

[1] Cf. Whitehead, *Principles of Natural Knowledge*, cc. 9-12; *Theory of Relativity*, c. 2; Eddington, *Nature of the Physical World*, lecture 3.

a matter of caprice, of "postulation" in what *seems* to be the Pragmatist sense of the word,[1] that the "common time" of human astronomers and cartographers should be based on the selection of a meridian of the earth for reference; this condition is dictated, not indeed by the intrinsic character of temporal reckoning, but by the given fact that these *savants* are human beings, and that the habitat of man is just this particular planet.

The impossibility of working out a single unambiguous scheme which shall make the "cut" between the spatial and the temporal in precisely the same way for all experients, without any cross-reference to their *when* in the one case, or their *where* in the other, once more illustrates the principle on which we have repeatedly insisted, that though "rationalisation" of the given is the rightful and sole function of human intellect, the rationalisation, from the very nature of the problem, can never be carried out to the point of resolving the whole content of the given into completely analysed connections. However far the process may be carried, we are always still left with an unexhausted residue of the simply given and unexplained. In the words of our homely proverb, there are always more fish in the sea than have ever come out of it, and this is why we need never fear that the successive triumphs of intellect will ever have the melancholy consequence that experience will cease to furnish men with mysteries which provoke their curiosity, and so supply the intellect itself with its necessary stimulus.

My point, then, is that Bergson was right in asserting that duration as lived through has a rich individual content, and that when the immediate experience is,

[1] I say "seems", because I have never been able to discover with certainty whether the leading professed "Pragmatists" really mean what their insistence on the "personal factor" ought to imply, or something much more moderate, to which I, for one, should have no objection, or both at once.

for perfectly legitimate purposes, replaced by the concept of monotonous uniform clock-time, this actual content of experienced duration has been artificially eliminated. He is right, again, in holding that it is this wealth of unanalysed content which makes duration as experienced historical and individual, and the elimination of it which explains why chronology is so different from, and inferior to, history. But in his further speculation I should contend that he is doubly wrong: wrong in supposing, as he seems to suppose, that there is not a difference of exactly the same kind between real volume and the qualityless, purely "mathematical" volume of the geometer,[1] and wrong, also, in treating the process of "abstraction" by which we form the concept of clock-time as a sort of wanton blunder of the intellect, which the philosopher is called on simply to undo. The abstractive process, indispensable if the given is to be understood, is as salutary as it is necessary; the only pure error which calls for mere reversal is the error, which there is no logical necessity to commit, of supposing that the result of abstractive analysis has preserved the whole content of the concrete experience, of forgetting the presence of the unexplored remainders, of taking the function of analysis, which is to discriminate features within an unexhausted whole, to be the substitution for the whole of something else. If we are clear on these points, we shall not be tempted to imagine that scientific analysis and persistent thinking are no more than an elaborate process of misunderstanding, or to believe that the way to understand an inexhaustible reality is to stop thinking about it, and surrender ourselves to an undirected impressionism.

The defect of Bergson's method in philosophy has

[1] I am thinking of Prof. Whitehead's happy references to the mathematician's complete neglect of the "shapiness of shapes" already quoted.

always seemed to me to be that, however sound his impressions may be, as they clearly were in his intense appreciation of the variety of *durée réelle*, by his depreciation of logical thinking he deprives himself of all means of convincing us that they are sound. This, I imagine, is why, in spite of what seems to be the ultra-Monism of his metaphysic, he could be so eagerly welcomed as a philosophical Messiah by a professed radical pluralist like William James. It really looks to me as though James was more anxious that a philosophy should be *un*reasoned than that it should be true. Whatever else the philosophical exponents of the "theory of Relativity" have done, or failed to do, they have at least succeeded in showing that the distinction between real "becoming" and the de-individualised events of an abstract kinematical scheme can be reached as surely (and more intelligently) by exceptionally resolute hard thinking as by surrender to first impressions.

The main point for which I am contending, then, is this. We have at last learned to think of the simplest processes of "becoming", or "happening", as historical in a sense to which none of the familiar classical philosophies of ancient or modern times does justice, unless we are to make an exception in favour of Leibniz. We can think of all such processes as individual to the core, as intrinsically irreducible to any mere kinematical scheme. None of them, it seems, can any longer be thought of as no more than a mere translation through a temporal interval of an object which is what it is, and all that it is, "at a mathematical instant", so that the time through which the object "lasts" is external to its specific nature.

I may illustrate the point from an analogous difference remarked upon by M. Meyerson,[1] between our

[1] É. Meyerson, *L'Explication dans les sciences*, i. 273 ff.

view of the spatial character of events and that which reigned until yesterday. M. Meyerson observes that we find a difficulty to-day in conceiving the adventures of Gulliver in Lilliput and Brobdingnag which could not have been felt by a reader of the eighteenth century. To the men of that, and indeed of the greater part of the nineteenth century, there was no inherent incredibility in the fiction that there are somewhere on our planet creatures precisely like human beings in every respect but their "absolute size", English and French, like the English and French we know, except for the single fact that they are constructed on a much smaller or larger physical scale.[1] For such a supposition was in keeping with the standing assumption of the science of the period that the only difference between the "molar" and the "molecular", or "sub-molecular" worlds is one of scale, groups of molecules or atoms, for example, behaving exactly after the fashion of reduced solar systems. Even after the rise of modern chemistry, as we know, the physics of the early nineteenth century was still dominated by this analogy; physicists and physical chemists were looking everywhere for explanations of natural processes based on the transference of the Newtonian conceptions of attraction and the law of the "inverse square" to molecules or atoms. To-day Swift's fiction is incredible to us for a much more serious reason than the absence of Lilliput and Brobdingnag from the map. We are satisfied that size is not a purely external and accidental character; molecules do not simply behave after the fashion of big visible lumps of stuff, nor atoms or electrons after the fashion of molecules. The molecular world is not a

[1] Johnson, who was prejudiced against Swift, it may be remembered, denied that his fiction showed any real invention. "When once you have thought of big men and little men", he said at the Club on Friday, March 24, 1775, "it is very easy to do all the rest."

reduced replica of the molar, nor the sub-molecular of the molecular.

No one, it appears, has so far succeeded in devising a wholly satisfactory account of the behaviour of the electrons which constitute an atom, but one thing, at least, seems clear, that they behave in ways to which the deportment of members of a solar system offers no analogy. Thus, our conviction is that, in some unexplained way, there is an intrinsic connection between the scale on which a thing is built and its qualitative behaviour. In the same way I should anticipate that the philosophy and science of the future will probably come to recognise an intrinsic connection between the quality of real "happenings" and their temporal scale. (Indeed, I presume it follows from the mutual implication of space and time by each other that the connection cannot show itself in the one without showing itself in the other as well.) We may, I think, take it that a piece of real becoming regularly has its own distinctive *tempo*, intrinsic to it in the same way in which the *tempo* of a musical "movement" may be said to be intrinsic. If one changes the *tempo* of a funeral march, what one gets is not a funeral march with the pace of a polka, but something which is not a funeral march at all. So, I feel confident, if we could cut down the duration of the rhythmic cycle of our daily physical existence from twenty-four hours to twelve, we should not have left the quality of the life standing. A being who got through two of his periods to our one would not be a man living twice as fast as the rest of us, but a creature with a new type and quality of life.

Now this, if it is true, means that every different type of "continuant" involved in the cosmic "becoming" has quite literally its own "biography": the translation of the historical succession of its phases into events in an abstract scientific "absolute time" demands the same sort, though not necessarily the same degree, of artificial reconstruction and schematisation as does the transcription of a piece of living human experience, in which, as lived, time has now raced, now ambled, now crawled, into a succession of chronological dates. The differences between the *tempi* of various "becomings" in the infra-conscious world will not, of course, reveal themselves to the continuants involved as such differences disclose themselves in our human sense of the contrast between "swift-footed" and "slow-pacing" time, but, for all that, they will show themselves in the qualitative character of the contribution made by each continuant to the whole "becoming" of the world. And this should make a very real difference to a philosophy of history. The more thoroughly we are convinced that the course of events is a complex of patterns of which the ingredients are individual "lives", or, if the suggestions of that word are thought unduly biological, individual "adventures", with a bewildering maze of *tempi*, the more completely shall we be emancipated from the tendency to look on history as a mere transcription into temporal succession of some general "law", capable of being formulated in advance of the facts, just as we are the more emancipated from the confusion of history with such disciplines as economics, the more vividly we apprehend the truth that human history is not made by "economic forces", but by countless individual men and women, not one of whom is an "economic man". To be aware that history, the course of the actual, is made by individual creatures, and therefore by agents saturated with contingency, is to be delivered from that *a-priorism* which has beset philosophies of history in the past just because the philosophers who have constructed them have not sufficiently understood the difference between the historical and the merely chronological.

I do not, of course, mean that, like too many who have fallen under the spell of Bergson's admirable rhetoric, we should see in history nothing but sheer contingency, confused and meaningless flux, any more than we are condemned to see nothing but meaningless flux in the succession of the themes of a symphony, or the scenes of a drama, though both are typical examples of a *durée réelle* very different from the "time" of text-books of kinematics. The symphony, or the drama, can exhibit a wide range of different *tempi*, but the differences and their order are prescribed by the unitary purpose of the composer or dramatist, present to all, transcending all, and *freely* expressing itself through all. I mean that the artist's purpose is at once really in control of the "flux", and itself—apart from incidental conditions which hamper it, such as the need to make a living by pleasing the fancy of a particular patron or audience—subject to no overriding "law". One cannot presume, for example, to say that the supremely significant passages which most definitely disclose the artist's purpose, and have to be taken as the clues for our understanding of his work as a whole, *must* be looked for in such and such a place (at the beginning, let us say, or in the middle, or near the end), nor exactly what contrasts we may expect to find in his work, and where we may expect to find them. These things are the artist's "secret"; they may come to us quite unexpectedly as daring surprises, though, when we have read the whole in the light of them, we may end by finding them as much "in place" as they are surprising. If we found that we had a formula which would, of itself, tell us where we must anticipate the peculiarly revelatory passages of a man's work, or just what contrasts it had in store for us, we should judge at once that our artist was not at his best, that his mind had been working, as we say, "mechanically". It is the capable tradesman in the arts, not the great artist, who works with a formula.

Similarly it is the second-rate critic who comes to the study of a genius like Shakespeare with a philosophical formula out of Aristotle or Hegel which determines for him in advance what a great tragedy must be like, and proceeds to estimate works like *Macbeth* or *Othello* by their conformity to the formula. The truly intelligent method in criticism, as I take it, is inductive and tentative. It is to discover what the tragedian, for example, can do and should do for us by attentive study of what the supreme tragedies actually have done. Of course, such a method is hard to apply, because the fruitful application of it presupposes the soundness of our initial immediate aesthetic response to the work of art. If our "taste" is initially wrong, so that we begin, for instance, by founding our induction on Seneca's plays rather than Shakespeare's, this initial want of perception will vitiate our whole consequent theory. To say this is only to say, with Aristotle, that where there is absence of some form of αἴσθησις, direct apprehension of an aspect of the immediately given, there must also be corresponding absence of the "science", the reflective analysis, which presupposes *that* aspect of the given as its foundation.

All this applies to the philosophy of History as much as to Aesthetics. The conviction that history is a drama with a meaning, and with a divine author of the play, does not mean that we can hope to invent any general formula on the strength of which we could anticipate the actual march of events, or tell just where to look for the particular episodes in which the purport of the drama is most plainly unveiled. History would be much more mechanical than it is, if we could say, for example, that it is dominated by a definite law of progression (or retrogression) on such and such specific lines. This is, in fact, what writers like Spencer and Comte, and, to a minor degree, Hegel, have tried to do, with the result that though their influence has often supplied a potent stimulus to interest in historical studies, adherence to their dogmas has generally ended in the distortion of historical actuality to make it fit some preconceived scheme, usually one which flatters our own vanity. It is manifestly preposterous, for instance, to maintain that Proclus or Damascius, rather than Plato or Aristotle, *must* be the "high-water mark" of Greek philosophical development, merely because the fifth and sixth centuries of our era are so much later than the fourth century before Christ, or that, for a similar reason, "industrialism" *must* be a sounder basis for the organisation of society than "militarism". The facts may be as alleged, but the point has to be established by examination of them on their merits, not by appeal to an assumed law of the order of historical development. Reliance on such laws is only possible for us, if we lose sight of the all-important consideration that the rhythm of history is a very complex one, built up out of a multitude of intensely individual processes, each with its own characteristic rhythm. A truly historically minded philosophy of history has, for this reason, to recognise contingency, the possibility of "being otherwise", as something much more deeply ingrained in the character of all historical fact than most philosophies of history hitherto attempted have been willing to allow.

As for the old bold programme of contemplating the world of fact not as *suggestive* of that which transcends time, but as *itself* transcendent of time, "under a form of eternity", is it not really a proposal to contemplate that which is in grain historical as unhistorical; in plainer words, to contemplate it as though it were just what it is not? Along those lines there seems to be only one goal for thought, the Indian denial that finite individuality is more than an illusion, and, I suppose, an illusion which deceives the very finite individual who is declared not to be there. We might, indeed, have reached these conclusions independently of the particular reflections which have occupied the greater part of this discourse, but it was necessary to my purpose to take the route we have taken, since it seems to be conscious or unconscious preoccupation with the de-individualised spatial framework, or system of reference, mistakenly assumed to be given reality, which commonly does more than anything else to create the prejudice against finite individuality, at least in our Western world.

Spinoza's *Deus sive natura*, for instance, is plainly simply "Euclidean space", assumed to be conscious of itself and of all its possible geömetrical configurations. The *intellectus* of this "god", for that reason, consists of awarenesses of all these configurations in their various interrelations, in Spinoza's own phraseology, of "ideas" corresponding one to one with all the "modes" of the attribute "extension". The "finitude" of *my* mind means the fact that my mind has as its correlate only one small selection out of this system of geometrical determinations, the successive configurations of *my* body (my body being conceived simply as so much figured extension). Since, in such a purely geometrical world of uniform spatial relations, there are no real boundaries between one region and adjacent regions, my individuality is, *of course*, an illusion. But so also, though Spinoza seems not aware of this, is the individuality of "God". An infinite "Euclidean" space is not a whole, nor a unity, and a mind which is by definition simply awareness of the possible determinations of such a space is not a unity either. So far as I can see, the only way in which personal individuality can get recognition as even an apparent fact, in such a system, is through consideration of the body. The finite body may perhaps be regarded as at least *quasi*-individual, on the ground that it is capable of being displaced relatively to other finite bodies, while retaining unchanged the geometrical relations between its sub-regions; *i.e.* it *moves* as a whole. But to urge this, as the explanation of the fact that I seem to myself to have an individuality, is to make the unity and individuality of my body depend on its character as a continuant through an interval of time, and time thus becomes an ultimate of the system, an "attribute of God" on exactly the same footing as space. The proposition that *deus est res extensa*[1] ought to apply to extension through time exactly as it does to extension over space; duration should belong to God in the same way in which volume does.

"Adequate" knowledge, therefore, ought to involve knowledge of a "mode" under an "attribute" of duration, exactly as it does knowledge of it under an "attribute" of extension. Or, alternatively, if reference to duration is, as Spinoza maintains,[2] characteristic of *imaginatio*, *in*adequate thinking, the same thing must be true of reference to extension. But this is just what Spinoza will not admit. He wants us to think of volume as real in some sense in which temporal continuance is not real. At the end of his short life, indeed, he seems to have become aware of the immense difficulty of his position, as we see from his significant admission to Tschirnhaus that "Descartes was wrong in defining matter by extension, whereas it must and ought to be

[1] *Ethics*, ii. 2.

[2] *Ib.* ii. 30, 31, 44, cor. 2.

explained by an attribute which expresses an infinite and eternal essence".[1] Now this is precisely what extension does "express", according to the *Ethics*.[2]

Apparently, then, if Spinoza had lived to the normal term of man's life, he would have reconstructed his doctrine on lines which require the disappearance of "extension" from the divine "attributes". Such a reconstruction from the foundations might or might not have led him to an agnosticism as complete as that in which Parmenides in Plato tries to entangle the youthful Socrates;[3] in either case it would have been completely destructive of the "double-aspect" metaphysic of mind and body which recommends Spinoza to so many of our contemporaries. In view of the thoroughly unhistorical character of Spinoza's ideal of knowledge, complete agnosticism would seem to be the reconstruction requiring the minimum amount of transformation in the system, since it would follow naturally from the combination of two positions—the elementary one that kinematics can no more dispense with the notion of duration than with that of configuration, and the familiar Spinozistic rejection of duration from "adequate cognition". This would bring us back to the doctrine, with which Greek philosophy ended in the hands of Damascius, that the historical "phenomenal world" is throughout dependent upon a supra-historical principle, but a principle which is strictly "ineffable", since we have, and can have, not even so much as an "analogical" knowledge of its nature. Metaphysics would have uttered its last word in formulating the doctrine of absolute nescience. This is, in fact, the goal which has been historically reached by all those theologies, within and without Christendom, which, starting from the

[1] *Ep.* 73 (V.V.L.). [2] I. 15 Schol., ii. 2.
[3] Plato, *Parm.* 133 A ff.

sharp and absolute antithesis between the eternal and the temporal, foreclose all avenues to knowledge of God except that of the *via remotionis*, the rejection on principle of all propositions which characterise the divine by definite predicates.

How we are to escape from such a conclusion has, I think, been already indicated. If we look a little closely, we may see that, as I have suggested, what all philosophers of the Spinozistic type really resent in their experience of life is not so much its successiveness as its individuality. It is individuality they are trying to strip from the real when they bid us conceive it under what they call a "form of eternity"; they would like to get the *hoc aliquid* with no *haecceitas* about it. But in fact, to preserve reality as real, without its individuality as the given and *this*, is as impossible as it is to divest a man of his skin without killing him. The supra-historical, if sought along these lines, turns out to be nothing but the mere abstract forms of Newtonian uniform space and time themselves. Whatever is "in" them has a history and individuality of its own, and must therefore be relegated to the level of the merely contingent, the "passing" show. When we are in earnest with this way of thinking, we readily find that nothing is left of which we can say that it is not "in" time and space, beyond the time and space of the Newtonian kinematics themselves; they, and only they, are left standing as the "eternal" reality. And of them, as distinct from configurations and patterns within them, there is really nothing significant to be said; they are the merely formless, and consequently ineffable.[1]

It is this, I suppose, which explains the lifelong

[1] Cf. Plato, *Tim.* 50 E *πάντων ἐκτὸς εἰδῶν εἶναι χρεὼν τὸ τὰ πάντα ἐκδεξόμενον ἐν αὑτῷ γένη*, 51 A *ἀνόρατον εἶδός τι καὶ ἄμορφον, πανδεχές, μεταλαμβάνον δὲ ἀπορώτατά πῃ τοῦ νοητοῦ καὶ δυσαλωτότατον.*

furious crusade of that half-educated man of genius, William Blake, against the work and name of Newton, a hatred springing from Blake's intensely vivid sense of individual historical reality, the "minute particular", as he repeatedly calls it. Like William Morris after him, Blake "looked on science as the enemy"—you may remember that his chosen name for the Aristotelian logic which he supposed to be its characteristic method was "the mills of Satan"[1]—because to him also science seemed to aim on principle at depriving things of the individual character which gives them their interest for the artist. It is suggestive, in this connection, to take note of the support Blake has incidentally received at the moment at which I am writing these words from a recent public utterance of one of our most distinguished mathematicians, who certainly intended no reflection on the fame or genius of Newton. In his address to the mathematical section of the British Association, delivered in the summer of 1927, Professor E. T. Whittaker contrasts the attitude of the "modern" physicist to geometry with that of the classical physicists of the seventeenth century, and, in doing so, makes striking use of a simile we have ourselves employed in an earlier passage. Geometry, he says, was formerly imagined to set the stage for the play in which the physicist's atoms and molecules are the *dramatis personae*; now we have come to think of the characters of the play as making their own stage, as they move about. That is, I take it, we think of our protons and electrons historically, as genuine individuals, with real characters of their own, which determine the situations in

[1] When Blake asks

> "And was Jerusalem builded here
> Among these dark Satanic Mills?"

he must not be supposed to be making a prophetic attack on factories and "industrialism".

which they find themselves, much as the personalities of men and women determine the situations to which they are called on to respond; on the older, classical view, the physicist's atom could hardly be said to have an intrinsic character of its own; its adventures were prescribed for it by a situation it did nothing to make, and this was why it could be called a "manufactured article".

It is true, indeed, that the simplest and minutest corpuscles with which the classical physicist could actually work were supposed to have at least one intrinsic endowment which contributed to determine their adventures, their *mass*, and that the masses of the atoms of different chemical elements had to be taken as differing. But in theory the hope was persistently cherished that the chemist's atoms might still some day be resolved into complexes of still more primitive "prime atoms", all indistinguishably alike even in mass. To-day, I understand, we are told that even the mass of the atom is not strictly invariable, but undergoes modification in the course of its adventures. To say that for the physicist of the future the personages of the play will be envisaged as creating their own stage is definitely to say that they must henceforth be thought of as genuine historical individuals, whose adventures will at once determine and be determined by their intrinsic characters, not be prescribed for them by the restrictions imposed by an external framework. Geometry will, in fact, apparently stand to physics much as "sociology", if there really is such a study, stands to history.

If this is really so, we seem to be on the verge of a new and fruitful conception of the relation between the eternal and the temporal. Everywhere in the world which science appears to be opening to us we are dealing with the adventures and reactions on one another of genuinely historical individuals. Nowhere do we come on anything which has no more individuality than that of being located *here* and *now*, rather than *there* and *then*, in an external framework. It looks as though the conception of a "matter" which is no more than a name for the *here* and *now* as a sufficient "principle of individuation" had received a death-blow. But within the world of historic individuals there are indefinitely numerous conceivable degrees of wealth of individual character. A man has a richer individuality of his own than a terrier, and a terrier than a cabbage. And below the level of the animate there may well be a whole complicated hierarchy of types of individual, all lower than the cabbage, yet all graded among themselves. If so, the richer the type of an individual's individuality, the more will his adventures on his course through history be seen to be determined by his own intrinsic character and his relations with individuals of his own or a higher type; the less will they appear to be prescribed for him by anything which can be plausibly mistaken for an indifferent and homogeneous framework. One might suggest (and I presume this is the significance for metaphysics of Professor Whittaker's statement that in future the starting-point for the physicist's construction of space will be the Riemannian geometry of infinitesimal regions) that what wears the look of such an indifferent framework, in reference to the adventures of creatures among their equals and superiors, is in truth itself a complex of adventures of individuals of poorer types among *their* equals.

Thus, to make my meaning clear by an example, since a man has a richer type of individuality than a beast, or a lifeless thing, it is the man's relations with his fellowmen, much more than his relations with the brutes, or with inanimate nature, that determine his course through life; for they, in the main, make his *personality* what it is, and personality counts increasingly as shaping a man's destiny, as we advance from the life of the savage "child of nature" to that of the civilised man who has an organised and conscious "personal" code of duties and rights. Similarly, among the beasts themselves, it is just those which have been admitted to some degree of intimate fellowship with men, such as our household dogs, among whom we most readily detect something analogous to an individual, not a merely specific, character as a determinant of the course of the creature's life.

In practice the inanimate and the merely animate world are here for us as something to be increasingly overcome and moulded to our own characteristic human purposes, not as a source of fixed and final checks and limitations. Man, as we read in *Genesis*, was placed among the beasts "to have *domination* over the fish of the sea, and the fowls of heaven, and all living creatures which move on the earth". Even the apparent indifference of inanimate nature to human purposes, the apparent ruthlessness which caused searchings of heart to Tennyson and his contemporaries, may most truly be read as an indication that this nature is there to be subdued increasingly to the real dominant interest of a fully human life, the establishment of right relations between a man and his fellows, or his God. Our main business in life is not that of the electron, to come to an understanding, if I may so express myself, with an environment of electrons; it is to "follow God", and to be *Mensch mit Menschen*. It is the electron, not the man, for which the principal thing is to steer its way in the whirl of electrons. And yet this very complex of individuals of poorer content, which for us wears the *prima facie* appearance of an external framework of limitation to human individuality, is itself seen on closer inspection to be a complex of individuals with their own histories of adventure. Neither do we seem to come upon a reality which is, like the space and time of the classical kinematics, wholly de-individualised; that is a useful fiction constructed by selective abstraction, and nothing more.

It should follow that, with a strictly historical interpretation of individuality, we are forced to recognise that the ideal type of individuality, perfect and complete personality, can only be actual in an individual whose own inner character is not only the dominant and principal, but the complete and sole, determinant of the individual life, and such an individual could be no other than the *ens realissimum*, God. Here, with the complete disappearance of "outside", or background, we should at last have transcended the historical, and risen from "becoming" or "process" to a life which is all activity of self-expression. And this, I believe, is the right way in which to understand the antithesis between the temporal and the eternal. When we say of God that He, and He only, is strictly and fully the eternal being who knows "no change, nor shadow of turning", but is *immotus in se permanens*, we do not mean that there is nothing in this life in any way answering to what we experience as movement and process; we mean that the experience is there, but that in Him it is not, as it is in varying degree with all His creatures, one of being, more or less, "at the mercy" of circumstance; there is nothing in Him like what we experience as movement to an unknown or half-known, goal. He cannot say, as all of us have to say, "we know not what to-morrow will bring forth", "we know not yet what we shall be". For Him there is neither "*unborn* to-morrow," nor "*dead* yesterday". We are temporal, not because there is a foreign element in our being which does not come from God, but because what there is in us is not the whole plenitude of the riches of God's being. That is withheld from us, not because "deity is jealous", or is subjected in its generosity to some external limitation, but because full and perfect personality is unique in its very nature. And *for us* the meaning of this is that God always has in reserve more to give than we can either "deserve or desire".

The bearing of all this on the problem to which we find ourselves once more recurring, of the relation of time as experienced, *durée réelle*, to eternity, would be briefly this. "Becoming" and time, as we know them by actual acquaintance, should be thought of not as the logical "contraries" of being and eternity, but as depotentialised, imperfectly communicated, being and eternity. Even at the lowest level of individuality to be met with in the actual world, what I have called the "adventures" of the humblest individual are not *mere* "becoming", mere *absolutes Werden*, incessant "turning into something else", such as Plato has in mind when he speaks of a γιγνόμενον ἀεί, ὂν δὲ οὐδέποτε. A real becoming is rather what the *Philebus* calls a γένεσις εἰς οὐσίαν, change, or process, tending to the establishment of self-maintaining activity of self-expression,

> Still as while Saturn whirls, his luminous shade
> Sleeps on his steadfast ring.

In the degree to which there is such self-expression on the part of the individual, its formal character is, *so far*, abidingness, not successiveness, eternity, not time; it does not become, but is. In the case of individuality which has reached the level of conscious personality in proportion as personality is realised, it is always possible to say

relation stands,
And what I was, I am,

and this is to possess a communicated and imperfect, but still a conscious, "form of eternity". In our moral life, the word *moral* being taken in its widest sense to cover the whole of specifically human endeavour, our one omnipresent task is to convert mere *γένεσις*, transition, into *γένεσις εἰς οὐσίαν*, transition into abiding being, a task only completed as, in theological language, grace, the supernatural, comes to and crowns the achievement of effort, the natural. In so far as what has been said in our earlier discussion of eternity and temporality may seem, for expository purposes, to have treated the conversion of succession into abidingness almost as though it *began*, without any "natural" preparation, with a sudden passage from nature to supernature—though I doubt whether anything we said really implied so much—it calls for rectification in the light of this subsequent reconsideration, and in virtue of the sound and familiar principle that the work of grace is not to undo nature, but to complete it.

Now this has a direct bearing, both on the claims of institutional religion, with all its apparent contingency and externality, on our allegiance, and on the more speculative difficulties connected with the conception of divine immobility and impassivity. If abiding being is not the mere contrary opposite of becoming, but the end to which all real becoming strives, and which all, in varying degrees of fullness, achieves, we shall not be acting advisedly in trying to attain the "form of eternity" within our own souls by simply cutting ourselves off from participation in and profit by the ordinances of an institutional religion, on the ground that they are full of contingency as to their origin and suffer strange vicissitudes in their historical development. It will be an entirely invalid reason for denying that these ordinances may be for us eminently precious ways of access to God to urge that their worth could never have been discovered *ante eventum* by speculative metaphysics or "philosophy of religion", that they are possibly historically continuous with practices which had at first no such spiritual value, or that their significance has undergone traceable modifications within historical times. For they, also, are γενέσεις, but γενέσεις εἰς οὐσίαν, and the question which really concerns us in practice is not how they began, or what transitions they have passed through, but what they succeed in being. If eternity does not simply stand outside time and opposed to it, but permeates it, contingency of origins and fortunes is compatible with abiding significance and value, and there is an end at once of two great prejudices which have done much to impoverish the spiritual life of serious aspirants after the eternal in all ages; the prejudice which is perpetually trying to create a fatal divorce between the "intellectual"—a phrase only too often virtually equivalent to the "conceited and half-educated"—and the "common people" in matters of religion (as though there were some special route to Heaven for the graduates of Universities), and the rival prejudice which sets up the real or supposed practice of some one age, the age of the Councils, or of the apostles, or of the little Galilean community of the years or months before the "giving of the Spirit", as a stereotyped model for the spiritual worship of all mankind in all times, and at all places.

It ought, indeed, to be evident that the presence of contingency throughout the historical domain makes the establishment of such a fixed model once for all impossible. We know so little of what the future may hold for us, that we cannot say, for example, that Europe will hereafter continue to be, as it has been for so many centuries, the main home of the Christian tradition of worship. If it should ever happen, and we do not know that it may not, that the living centre of the Christian religion should be in India or China—or even in the younger of the United States—we may safely predict that the effects of such a change may be even more marked than the known past effects of the transplantation of that centre from Jerusalem to Rome.

Let us suppose, merely for the sake of illustration, that the existing dissipation of Christians into a plurality of conflicting Churches and sects should end in a general submission to the Papal See, with a full acknowledgement of the claims advanced for the Roman Pontiff. Even were that to happen, it is at least fairly certain that a Catholicism in which Popes and Cardinals were regularly Chinese, or Indian, or even Western Americans, steeped in the general national traditions of China, India, or, if the suggestion is thought too fantastic, even of the Pacific States, would be something very different in all sorts of unpredictable ways from a Catholicism such as we see to-day, with its long established traditions of exclusively Italian Popes and a preponderantly Italian Cardinalate. The "deposit" might be retained substantially intact through the transmigration, but the experience of the transmigration would certainly entail interesting discoveries about the precise nature and limits of this unchanging deposit.

And, again, with reference to the speculative problems of the meaning of divine immutability and impassivity, and the difficulties these conceptions suggest about the attitude of God to human folly, perversity, and wickedness. If we conceive the relation of time to eternity rightly, it will hardly be possible for us to interpret immutability and impassivity as though they meant that there is nothing at all in the divine life corresponding to the experiences we know as sorrow, disappointment, distress due to the disloyalty of those who profess to love us, and the ingratitude of those for whom we have done much, honest indignation at wrong. We shall hardly be satisfied to explain away the strongly anthropomorphic language of the Old Testament prophets on all these topics, after a fashion too prevalent among some older divines, as though it all meant nothing very much in particular, or to think of our Maker as a martinet schoolmaster, who makes a hollow pretence of prefacing his flagellations with the formula, never seriously believed by the victims, that "it hurts me more than it hurts you". Nor, again, shall we be likely to take the "easy way out" adopted by many, really ditheistic, pietists of our own early days, who transferred all the real feeling to the human Christ, and at heart thought of the Father as looking on at the Passion from the outside, much as Edward III. is said to have looked on at the Black Prince's struggle at Creçy from his safe observation-post in the windmill. If we have once understood that eternity is the characteristic form not of inaction, but of activity of self-expression, we shall hardly be likely to retain the prejudice that emotion has no place in a strictly eternal life, or the fancy that any such phrase as Aristotle's "thinking upon thinking" can be adequate as a description of the abiding self-expression of Deity. There will be as good reason for believing that emotion has its place in the divine life as for holding the same thing of intellectual apprehension.

In neither case, indeed, can we possibly think of the

divine activity as merely identical with the poor human counterpart we know in ourselves. Emotion in God *must* be of a different tonality from emotion in ourselves, since there it cannot have the special characters which tinge even our richest emotional life, derived as it is from the experiences of aspiration to an unattained self-expression, of baffled endeavour, endurance of final impoverishment or defeat. But we may learn something from those richest of emotional experiences which in us accompany patient conflict with opposition and acceptance of wounds, when there is also serene and confident faith in the victory which is to crown the conflict. These experiences we should rightly refuse to describe by the superficial name of pleasures, but we should hardly hesitate to say that they are experiences of a joy which is all the richer for its costliness.

Imagine the experience Shelley has in mind when he tells us

> To love and bear; to hope till Hope creates
> From its own wreck the thing it contemplates;
> Neither to change, nor falter, nor repent,

as it would be if vision took the place of hope. Would not that be to "enter into the joy of the Lord"? It is along such lines, I should say, that we must try to find a real meaning in the traditional language about the "impassivity" of the Supreme. Nor is it really harder to conceive of an emotional life which transcends our own in this fashion, in virtue of its freedom from *transition*, whether from a less to a more perfect, or from a more perfect to a less perfect, activity, than it is to conceive of an intellectual life free from our human need of crawling, hardly and slowly, from truth to truth by groping and inference. Neither in our own experience of knowing nor in our own experience of feeling do we ever reach the point at which there is actual achieved and complete saturation of subject by object, full and final possession of object by subject. Yet we may be sure that this point is always reached and rested in in God's perfect possession of His own being. Our joy, and our self-apprehension, at their highest, can only be distant analogues of such an experience; but it is as true that the analogy is real as it is that it is distant.

IX

FAITH AND KNOWLEDGE. REVIEW AND CONCLUSION

Ex divinorum et humanorum malesana admistione non solum educitur philosophia phantastica, sed etiam religio haeretica. Itaque salutare admodum est, si mente sobria fidei tantum dentur quae fidei sunt.—F. BACON.

WE have now, very rapidly and imperfectly, tried to consider some of the outstanding characteristics which distinguish an historical, or revelational religion from a purely philosophical. We must finally attempt to deal directly with the issue which has been long enough in my own mind, as I do not doubt that it has been in yours. Have we anywhere, by anything we have said, compromised the rightful claims of either living religion or reasoned science and philosophy to independence and freedom from alien interference, each within its own sphere? In particular, have we advanced anything which can prejudice the demand of a rational philosophy to pursue its own problems, by its own methods, in a strictly disinterested spirit, without apprehension of being arbitrarily arrested by dictation from the priest, or the dogmatic theologian? Or have we, in all good faith, anywhere played into the hand of the "obscurantist" who, in the famous image of St. Peter Damiani,[1] would confine the critical intellect to the

[1] *De divin. omnipotent.* v. (Migne, *Patrolog. Latin.* cxlv. 603), "quae tamen artis humanae peritia, si quando tractandis sacris eloquiis adhibetur, non debet ius magisterii sibimet arroganter arripere, sed velut ancilla dominae quodam famulatus obsequio subservire." On this conception of the strictly "ancillary" functions of human knowledge see É. Gilson, *Études de philosophie médiévale,*

functions of an *ancilla*, a handmaid, and in fact a slave, to a purely authoritarian and supra-rational theology? A sense can be put on the familiar formula, "philosophy the handmaid of divinity", in which its adoption would be a formal treason against rationality in God or man, and a surrender to the intellectual indolence which is itself a capital spiritual sin. To such a sin I trust I may plead not guilty with a good confidence. Yet it may be that this same metaphor of the mistress and the servant, rightly interpreted, may yield a valuable lesson. This is the point on which I could wish, in conclusion, to be a little explicit. I must therefore crave your indulgence if I raise, quite briefly, by way of conclusion, the general question what sort of autonomy or independence may, and what sort may not, be legitimately demanded for any intelligent activity of the human mind.

When does the reasonable demand for freedom pass, as it so easily may do, into the unreasonable and arrogant claim to play the dictator? Universal history has taught us how light-heartedly the transition is made in practical mundane affairs; how imperceptibly, for instance, the "patriot", with his passion for national independence, becomes the aggressive "imperialist", proudly conscious of a mission *parcere subiectis et debellare superbos*. There is also an imperialism of the speculative intellect against which we need no less to be on our guard. Nor is it only the theologian who requires the warning; metaphysicians, physicists, biologists are all only too apt, in the hour of their dominance, to assert the same right *regere imperio populos*

---

essay ii., "La servante de la théologie ". Presumably the image is connected by some obscure link of derivation with the *mot* attributed in antiquity to Aristippus that those who give themselves to the *ἐγκύκλια παιδεύματα*, but neglect philosophy, are like the suitors in the *Odyssey* who consoled themselves for their ill-success with Penelope in the embraces of the "handmaids" (Diog. Laert. ii. 79) (or is the allusion simply to the domestic arrangements of Abraham and Jacob?).

pacisque imponere morem. There was only too much truth in the complaint once made by a brilliant living writer against the science of thirty years ago, that "science appears to be developing the vices of theology without any of its virtues—the dogmatism, the 'index expurgatorius', and the whole machinery for suppressing speculation, without any of the capacity to impose upon the conscience a clear and well-defined scheme of life".[1] And though our most eminent professed metaphysicians of the same period were conspicuously modest men, and expressed themselves more decorously, I think it would be true to say that they were not without some touch of the same temper. They often tended to assume that a general metaphysic, and that a metaphysic which is at bottom an epistemology, can prescribe in advance the ground-plan of a rational universe so completely that the epistemologist is in a position to say definitely just what is the permanent truth embodied in the great religions, and that everything in their divinity or their devotions which cannot be covered by his formulae is no more than imaginative fable, often actually, and always potentially, mischievous.

Towards natural science the attitude of these metaphysicians was often formally deferential; yet it was made politely clear that knowledge of nature was not rated very high as a possible source of valuable contribution to the philosophical interpretation of the world. Since epistemology, either alone or, at most, in conjunction with ethics, was widely supposed to be able to indicate the ground-plan of a rational world, there was a tendency to assume that, in all essentials, the work of philosophical interpretation had already been done by Aristotle, and might, indeed, have been equally

[1] G. Lowes Dickinson, *The Meaning of Good*, p. 193.

well done by the Milesians in the sixth century, if they had only possessed Aristotle's capacity for logical analysis, in spite of their inevitable ignorance of the detail of natural processes. Perhaps no other view could have been expected from philosophers who derived so much of their inspiration from Kant. For Kant seriously believed himself to have drawn the ground-plan of a rational world once and for all in the *Critique of Pure Reason*, in a way admitting of no serious modification or improvement; his successors were to do no more than build up the fabric of positive knowledge on the foundations so well and surely laid in 1781.[1] It is in making this assumption that Kant gives the supreme proof of the radically unhistorical character of his thinking. The world in which a philosophy of this type moves, just because it is, in principle, a completely comprehended world, is a dead world. If our philosophical thought is to keep its contact with the living world of the historical, it will have to reckon everywhere with the contingent and surprising, and will have therefore to be empirical, in a sense in which the best thought of the last century was not empirical, even when it was loudest in its repudiation of *a-priorism*. And this unavoidable empiricism will be reflected in our interpretation of the claims of the various activities of the mind to autonomy.

True empiricism cannot mean, as has sometimes been supposed, that it is the business of the philosophical interpreter of nature to jump at the first impressions conveyed by the observation of sequences in nature, make sweeping generalisations from them by "simple induction", and canonise the results as dogmas. A metaphysic of first impressions would be no better than an intellectual house of cards. But to be truly and sanely

[1] *KdrV.*[2] xxiii-xxiv. (*Werke*[2], iii. 21).

empirical, which is the same thing as to think historically, must mean that we are to be in earnest with the conviction that in our metaphysic, our science, our art, our divinity alike, we are "moving about in worlds not realised". It must mean that the conviction of the rationality of the world, on which all pursuit of truth is founded, is strictly a postulate of the "practical" reason. An historical world is not rational in the sense that it ever has been, or ever will be, actually rationalised, made self-explanatory and self-justifying, by the labours of philosophers, even to the extent of successfully mapping out its ground-plan with finality. It is our unending task to divine the supreme pattern of the real, and so to rationalise it, to the best of our power, knowing well that the element of the disconcerting and perplexing will never be eliminated.[1]

For our intelligence, which is not "intuitive", but works by painfully piecing fragments of reality together, a world in which time and contingency are more than illusions must always remain in large part unfamiliar and "uncanny". Since this is so, one thing at least seems certain; whatever the ultimate structure of the real may be, it cannot be discovered by any mere consideration of an abstract scheme of logical categories. Epistemology, *Kategorienlehre*, analysis of the methods of the sciences, taken by themselves, cannot furnish the sole and complete clue to the character of the historical reality in which our thought and action are embedded, for the obvious reason that we are not related to the real as spectators to a picture. The world,

[1] Cf. Jeans, *The Universe Around Us*, p. 330: "There is no need to worry overmuch about apparent contradictions. The higher unity of ultimate reality must no doubt reconcile them all, although it remains to be seen whether this higher unity is within our comprehension or not. In the meantime a contradiction worries us about as much as an unexplained fact, but hardly more; it may or may not disappear in the progress of science."

indeed, sets us questions and provokes our curiosity. If it did no more than this, it would be conceivable that in constructing a critical theory of knowledge we should *eo ipso* arrive at a true metaphysic. The reason why this is not so is that we are not in the position of the spectator before the picture; our "picture" is a *tableau vivant* in which we are ourselves actors.

So much has often been said before with an eloquence which I cannot aspire to rival. I do not know whether the inference I would draw has always been made as explicitly as I would make it. It seems to follow that it is a grave mistake to assume, as I think must be assumed by anyone who accepts the full claims made by Kant for criticism, or by Hegel for his logic, that a theory of knowledge is, by itself, a sufficient basis for a metaphysical philosophy. For is it not perfectly possible that epistemology may only present us with an account of reality which is systematically ambiguous? With what right can we assume that unhistorical analysis, such as is the business of the logician and the critical student of scientific method, must conduct us to a single and determinate conception of the pattern of a historical reality? Might it not prove that these inquiries, pursued with the utmost vigour and subtlety, end by offering us a scheme in which there are ambiguities, just as the attempt to solve a numerical problem in which there are more unknowns than known independent relations between them leads to a system of indeterminate equations?

There might prove to be alternative metaphysical interpretations of the given historical reality, all equally consistent with the only condition which the epistemologist can legitimately insist on, the condition that, on any interpretation, the real world must be capable of being progressively known as intelligence is steadily brought to bear upon it. I do not see that a critical theory of knowledge entitles us to presuppose more about the character of the real world than that it must be such that an intelligible question about it is capable of receiving an intelligent answer, if investigation is patiently pursued far enough, though that answer may sometimes be only that data such as would lead to a determinate solution of the problem are not available. If this is so, it is obvious that the last word about the structure of reality cannot be uttered by the epistemologist. Where the critical theory of knowledge has left open alternatives, it will be permissible to ask whether other than purely speculative considerations may not properly have weight as closing some of the apparently open alternatives, and to admit such a claim will involve no disloyalty to reason. It would be disloyalty to reason to deny that the real world is one in which the prosecution of science is possible; it is not disloyalty to hold that the world is something other and more than a mere field for the elaboration of science.

As we all know, Kant himself definitely held that there are alternative interpretations of the pattern of reality, equally providing for all the legitimate claims of the sciences, and the choice between them has to be made on other than purely speculative grounds. So far as the sciences are concerned, the real world might equally well be an assemblage of mindless and purposeless automata, or a commonwealth of free and purposive agents under the moral government of God; only the extra-scientific consideration that if the first account is the true one genuine moral responsibility must be an illusion justifies our acceptance of the second, and the justification has no force except for the man who accepts the fact of moral responsibility, and accepts it, not because there would be a demonstrable absurdity in denying it, but because he is personally a man of high inward morality, whose *life* would become purposeless if morality were dismissed as an illusion. So far, as it seems to me, Kant's procedure is thoroughly sound, and his philosophy, whatever other defects it may have, is sounder in principle than that of Spinoza or Hegel, precisely because it is not a *panlogism* ; it does not try to stand on logic alone; but if it has one foot planted, so to say, on logic, it has the other securely planted on life. But Kant, I would submit, is not sufficiently alive to the full possibilities of what I have called the systematic ambiguity of epistemology. The places left open in the metaphysical interpretation of reality, when epistemology has "done her do", are, according to him, very few; we know exactly where to find them, and the possible alternatives left open are, in each case, just two and no more. Since he only finds room for this limited amount of ambiguity, it is possible for him to hold, as he does, that what ambiguities there are are completely removed by the appeal to ethics.

If the possibilities of such ambiguity are greater than Kant was willing to allow, it may be in principle impossible to say exhaustively beforehand just where we shall find them, or how many alternative readings of the facts they permit, and, again, it will be premature to assume that it is only to ethics that we may look for guidance in these cases. It may be, for example, that the specifically religious life has the same right to unprejudiced consideration by the metaphysician as the specifically moral life. There may be alternatives which ethics leaves still open, and, if so, some may be closed when we take into account experiences which are neither those of the man of science, nor of the morally virtuous man as such, but belong specifically to the personally religious man, and to no one else. If this should prove to be the case, religion will have its claims to a real autonomy, no less than science or morality, and we have no right to determine in advance of examination that it is not the case.

There is at least a fair *prima facie* reason for thinking that the state of matters I have just described as possible is actually the fact. I would adapt here to my own purpose a line of argument which has been forcibly employed by Dr. E. R. Bevan against the type of "rationalist" who regards reason as identical with secularistic natural science, and religion as a mere widespread popular delusion. As Dr. Bevan has urged,[1] the "appearances" are very strongly against this kind of rationalist, much more decidedly than they are, for example, against the average, more or less orthodox, Christian. For it is no part of the orthodox Christian's case that the articles of his creed are all capable of being shown by demonstration, or by probable reasoning, to be either certainly true, or, at least, possessed of a high degree of probability. Such a claim is excluded by his belief in an actual historical revelation, and his acceptance, in some form, of the principle of authority. He does not assume that, with sufficient native intelligence and adequate education, every man must necessarily come into his own convictions, since they are admittedly inspired by a "faith" which, unlike the assurance won by proof, involves a "free assent" of the will. On his own theory it is no paradox that there should be men of the highest intelligence and the best education who reject his convictions as false. But it is part of the militant "rationalist's" case that the orthodox Christian belief can be proved to be false, or unfounded, to anyone of high intelligence and good education. It ought therefore to be a serious paradox to him, as it is not to

[1] See the acute essay "Christianity in the Modern World" in *Hellenism and Christianity*, pp. 249 ff.

his orthodox opponent, that in actual fact the line of division between the orthodox and the "infidel" is not lateral, but vertical, so that, at all levels of intelligence and education, from the lowest to the highest, we find the believer and the "unbeliever" side by side. Among the most ignorant and least intelligent you will find both the devoutly orthodox and the scornfully anti-religious, and you will meet the same situation at the very top of the pyramid, or at any intervening level. This of itself is good reason for holding that, whether orthodoxy is true or not, it is at least not a mere product of dullness or ignorance.

The same line of argument may fairly be used to vindicate the autonomy of religion as a specific apprehension of features of reality, against attempts, like those of Kant in his work on *Religion within the Limits of Mere Reason*, to deny the serious value of everything in the historical religions which is not strictly ethical. If it were really true that everything in a great religion which is not directly ethical—in other words, the great body of its theology and cultus—is no more than superfluous "survival", to be explained by the conservatism of human emotion, but not to be justified, we might fairly expect to find that the influences which make for such survival are regularly most potent where intelligence and education are at their lowest level; they should be weakest at the top of the pyramid. It ought to be the rule that, though I may attach value to these elements in the tradition in which I have been brought up, and persons of feebler intelligence and fewer "educational advantages" than myself may value them more highly still, when I look upwards to those whom I recognise to be more acute and better informed than myself, I should see them sitting more loosely to all these things than I do, and more generally agreed than myself and my intellectual equals in a "religion of all men of sense" which amounts to little more than the "morality touched with emotion" of Matthew Arnold's unhappy definition.

Whether this state of things is what we do in fact see, each of us must judge for himself. For my own part, I have to confess, that I do not see the facts so, though I might have been predisposed in that direction by some of the educational influences to which I have been subject in earlier manhood. Among the dull or ill-informed I do, indeed, often see vehement confessional and theological attachments which I cannot share, but I often also see among them marked confessional and theological indifferentism which I cannot share either. And when I consider those whom I am constrained to regard as my superiors in mental acumen, or solid education, or both, in some of these again I find indifferentism, but in others very marked attachments with which I do not always personally sympathise. Consequently, for my own part, I discover no connection between intellectual eminence and any one particular attitude to Christian or other "orthodoxy", certainly no connection between such eminence and agnosticism or scepticism about the possibility of knowledge concerning God.[1]

There is, indeed, one particular mental attitude which, so far as my observation goes, is commonly an accompaniment of recognisable intellectual inferiority of some kind, the contemptuous and rancorous self-satisfaction which springs from inability either to see

[1] And, in the same way, among those whom I cannot but recognise as morally better than myself I find a similar disagreement. Some of them are devoted adherents of a Church and a creed, some are indifferent in the matter, some decidedly "anti-confessional". Moral purity and elevation of character thus seem to be no adequate guarantee for agreement in "religion" any more than for agreement in aesthetic appreciation.

any difficulties in one's own position, or any advantages in that of one's opponents; but this moral defect seems to show itself among inferior adherents of all the possible points of view. There are rancorous militants of all varieties of possible belief, contemptuous and angry deniers of everything, even bitter and scornful indifferentists. The men of unmistakable mental distinction, again, are to be found alike among believers in a positive theology, convinced disbelievers, sceptics. Only they, in whichever of these classes they are found, regularly combine the power to hold their own position with confidence with the ability to appreciate the difficulties it involves; they know the "weak side" of their own case better than most of their opponents do, just as in political life a man of real statesmanlike insight usually knows better than any critic from outside the vulnerable spots in the programme of his own party. We must all have learned long ago that it is a delusion to imagine that the "infidel"—the man who denies the convictions which make up our own "faith", whatever it is—*must* be "wicked"; it is an equal delusion to fancy that the "orthodox" of an orthodoxy which is not our own must be stupid, or insincere. Behind the orthodoxy of a really great historical religion—and this is peculiarly true of our own religion—there is safe to be a great philosophy. It is not the only philosophy tenable as an interpretation of the actualities so far disclosed by everyday practical life and the prosecution of the natural sciences—this is what I meant by speaking of the systematic ambiguity of a metaphysic based on mere epistemology, or on a mere combination of ethics with epistemology—and, like all philosophies, it is sure to have its difficulties: there are sure to be some "appearances" which are intractable to it, but it is a great philosophy, not to be spoken of except with respect, and no man is entitled to presume lightly that it may not prove to be the true philosophy. To understand this is the first condition of approaching the problem in the right spirit.

The case, then, as it seems to me, stands thus. Theologies arise, in the first instance, not from the indulgence of an idle curiosity, but from the attempt to take as a clue to the interpretation of the historical world certain experiences, or phases of experience, which, to those who are sensitive to them, come stamped with a significance that marks them as authoritative self-disclosures of the supreme reality, and, moreover, are not self-contained, but at least appear to throw light on the whole pattern of historical reality. As we have said before, the claim that these experiences have this significance is not refuted by the objection that, in their full intensity, they are confined to the few. For, as we remarked, the same thing may be said of the appeal of art to those who are sensitive to it. Thus, to take a definite example, and one which I choose with a great deal of trepidation, to a very large number of men Beethoven's *Third Symphony* probably conveys no impression whatever beyond that of being a vast volume of pleasing or unpleasing sounds. Many more, I suppose, find such a work vaguely suggestive of something which impresses them as fine and great, but would be incapable, if left to themselves, to give any more precise account of the impression made on them. But there are some hearers to whom the composition has a much more precise significance. Rightly or wrongly, they find in it a "meaning" which is of importance for the appreciation of the whole of human life, and perhaps of something more. It suggests to them a specific attitude of the human soul to the vicissitudes of human fortunes, or even to the entire rhythm of the cosmic process. I suppose it would not be exaggerating to say that to such hearers the *Eroica* is something of a "revelation" of the meaning of life and death, though not a revelation which can be digested into propositional form.[1]

Now a philosopher who is also a wise man, if he happens to be one of the many to whom the work says nothing of all this, will not argue that what he cannot find for himself was never meant to be found, and in fact is not there to be discovered. Nor, again, if he is truly wise, would he take the line of admitting that there is "something" there, but denying that the "something" can be what the more "suggestible" auditor supposes it to be, on the ground that, if this is so, there must be something in the world of which his own analyses have taken no account. He would not, for instance, argue that it *must* be a delusion to find there a disclosure of the meaning of life and death, because there can be no truth except truth capable of expression in the form of propositions. He will rather reckon with the fact that there are those who agree in finding some such disclosure there, and note the fact as suggesting a possibility that there may be "truth", apprehension of reality, which is not "propositional",[2] however difficult he may find it to make a place for such "truth" in his metaphysical scheme. He may find himself incapable of making the necessary reconstruction of his scheme, and have to be content with recording an outstanding and unexplained fact which he does not know how to rationalise. But, if

[1] Cf. the words of Romain Rolland, *Vie de Beethoven*[15], p. 75: "il est bien davantage que le premier des musiciens. Il est la force la plus héroïque de l'art moderne . . . et quand la fatigue nous prend de l'éternel combat inutilement livré contre la médiocrité des vices et des vertus, c'est un bien indicible de se retremper dans cet océan de volonté et de foi." Romanticism perhaps; but, then, Beethoven *was* a "romantic", and the greatest of them, and we are not likely to understand him as he meant to be understood if we forget the fact.

[2] On this whole much-neglected subject of "non-propositional truth" see the instructive and too brief chapter 9 of L. A. Reid's *Knowledge and Truth*.

he does so, he will recognise that the inability shows that his own intellectual scheme is an inadequate instrument of rationalisation and calls for amendment, though he may be quite unable to say what precise form the amendment should take. He will note not only the presence of an outstanding and perplexing fact, but the presence of a definite problem raised by that fact for the philosophy of the future. He will avoid, if he is wise, both the temptation to pretend that there is no problem to be solved, and the temptation to produce a premature solution.

It is this second temptation to which philosophers appear to be peculiarly ready to succumb. They are too ready to assume that to say that an intelligent question must be capable of receiving an intelligible answer is equivalent to saying that it must be capable of being answered in terms of the "categories" with which their own thought habitually works. They forget that in speculation, as in practice, the obviousness and reasonableness of a solution to a problem is often apparent only *après coup*. The rationalising of the given, we must remember, is an "inverse" problem; the solution of it is comparable not with differentiation, where we have a simple universal rule for procedure, but with integration, a procedure just as "rational",[1] for which no general rule can be given, and where success depends on the combination of original "divination" with a well-stored memory of the devices which have proved serviceable in the past.

[1] "Just as rational." I mean that though the integration may only be achieved by a stroke of ingenuity for which no rule can be given, when it has been obtained, we can reverse the process. One can differentiate the integral now found, and so recover the expression from which one started as the datum to be "integrated", and for this "verificatory" procedure there is a precise and definite rule. Similarly there is no rule for the solution of an equation of a higher degree than the fourth, but if one has, by some ingenious manipulation, hit upon the roots of a particular "higher equation", one can verify one's result by reconstructing the original equation from the roots, and for this there is a simple rule.

I trust I am not dwelling with too wearisome an iteration on a type of illustration of which I have already made some considerable use. My special reason for reintroducing it at the present moment is this. If great music, or great art of any kind, is something more than a clever sporting with geometrical or quasi-geometrical patterns—and the great artists, I think, have regularly believed that it is something much more than this—it seems undeniable that it makes a real contribution to the understanding of the world, and has a profound metaphysical signification. At the same time, this signification cannot make its appearance anywhere among the categories of a logic, or the principles of an epistemology; we cannot call it irrational, but it is certainly extra-logical. When it has been grasped by those to whom immediate apprehension of it has been granted it can be reasoned upon, and attempts can be made, as they so often are made, to transcribe it into a language created by the analytical understanding. But such transcriptions are notoriously unsatisfactory, and, what is more, they are only intelligible to those who already possess in some measure the immediate apprehension itself.

We all, perhaps, remember the famous declaration of Hegel,[1] that the categories of his logic describe "God as He is in His eternal being before the creation of nature or any finite spirit". I would not deny that there is an intelligible meaning in Hegel's boast. No "true worshipper", of course, can concede that a system of logical categories describes the "eternal being of God", but there is something which the system should elucidate, the "intelligible" ground-plan of the historical world, and if Hegel's own *Wissenschaft der Logik* does not fully realise this ideal, it might be fairly said that

[1] *Logik*, Einl. (*Werke*[1], iii. 36).

it is, at any rate, the ideal which a perfect logic would embody. But my point is that Beethoven would have had the same right to make the claim for his symphonies. They too declare to us something about the ground-plan of the historical world, and it is something which could not be disclosed by any system of logical categories, the most flawless that could be devised. It might be asked, indeed, how we know that the claim is substantiated. But the answer would be simple. It would be, in the first place, that the witness of those who are sensitive to the disclosure is concordant; they are in a story together, to a degree which makes it incredible that their story should be fiction, and, further, that many of us who do not belong to their number can at least learn, with their story before us, to see for ourselves that they are telling us of no wholly strange country, but of one of which we have ourselves had our more perplexed and uncertain glimpses. And the case, as I have argued at some length before, appears to be typical.

My purpose in recurring to all this is to urge that, if it be true, we shall be led to recognise a genuine autonomy, for both religion and its intellectual elaboration in the form of theology, against all over-confident metaphysical short-cuts to a final "synthetic" interpretation of the world. For it will follow that no metaphysical system, working, as all such systems must, with the implements of the analytical understanding, can give a final account of that ground-plan of the real which the metaphysician is seeking to formulate. An intelligence before which the whole plan lay bare would be the intelligence not of a metaphysician, but of God. Philosophy, as Diotima is made to teach in Plato's *Symposium*, is not the fruition of such a vision, but the always unfinished and partly baffled aspiration to it.[1] If we think thus of the functions of philosophy, we shall be careful not to make the mistake of requiring the theologian, any more than we require the interpreter of literature or art, to work under the control of a body of "categories" prescribed to him from without, whether they are "categories" dictated by reflection upon the natural, or by reflection upon the moral sciences. What we have a right to demand of the theologian, as of the workers with whom I have compared him, is that the matter upon which his thought works shall be something genuinely *given*, and that in his reflective elaboration of it he shall be true to *it*. I do not see that we have a right to demand more.

We have no more right to expect that the theologian as such shall be himself a super-metaphysician than we have to expect the same qualifications in the interpreter of art, the moralist, or the scientific specialist. I may find it beyond my powers to fit in the convictions of any of the four with the scheme which guides my own thinking in metaphysics, but this difficulty need not require me to censure any of them. What would be fatal to the claims of any of the four is not that *I* should not see where he is going, but that he should have no definite goal before him. His reality need be none the less real, nor his own account of it any the less true, that *I* do not know what to make of it. He, presumably, in such a case, will say with equal justice that he does not know what to make of me and my metaphysic. All that is necessarily proved by our misunderstanding is that neither of us has done what no man ever will do, rationalised the whole of "possible experience". Neither of us, so far as I can see, has any right to dismiss the other as "under an illusion", because he himself does

[1] Plato, *Sympos.* 204 A *θεῶν οὐδεὶς φιλοσοφεῖ οὐδ' ἐπιθυμεῖ σοφὸς γενέσθαι· ἔστι γάρ· οὐδ' εἴ τις ἄλλος σοφός, οὐ φιλοσοφεῖ κτλ.*

not see just what to make of the other's work. If either of us did adopt this attitude to the other, he might profitably be admonished to attend more to the beam in his own eye than to a mote—or even a beam—in his brother's eye.

The claim, too often advanced by eager metaphysicians, to prescribe with finality to all the rest of the world what "categories" may be employed in the attempt to understand experiences of specific type is, after all, only a form of the dangerous spiritual sin of pride, the very fault justly charged by the metaphysicians of to-day upon so many of the constructive theologians of the past. A contemporary divine may fairly retort, as Plato is fabled to have retorted on Diogenes, when he set his muddy feet on the carpet with the brag, "Thus I trample the pride of Plato", *Yes, with an equal pride of your own.*[1] There is a sense in which there can be no metaphysic which is final, even relatively. If the last word could ever be said even on the world of man—itself no more than a fragment of the whole world—the speaker who should utter it would need to be furnished with the experiences of all men as his matter, to be, in his own person, at once St. Paul and Newton, Caesar and Columbus and Keats (and how many more besides!), and also to be Plato, or Aristotle, or Hegel into the bargain, and "there is no such man". He who lives one life intensely cannot live all. It is just conceivable that it might lie in a man's choice, for example, to be St. Paul, to be Caesar, or to be Newton. But in choosing to be St. Paul he would be cutting himself off from effective possibility of being either of the others.

Again, those whose mental vision is most habitually

[1] Diog. Laert. vi. 26 *οἱ δέ φασι τὸν Διογένην εἰπεῖν, "πατῶ τὸν Πλάτωνος τῦφον"· τὸν δὲ φάναι, "ἑτέρῳ γε τύφῳ, Διόγενες."*

limpid do not commonly live any life with the richest intensity; like Browning's *Grammarian*, they determine "not to be, but know", and the quality of the knowing itself is affected by the choice. Systematic all-round clarity is hardly possible except for a vision content to remain on the surface. The system-maker in metaphysics—and it is the system-makers who prescribe dogmatically for the human mind—is a man who has made it his special business to see what he does see with exceptional clearness, but he commonly does not see so deep as some other men. It is not to the great systematisers who supply us with admirable "bird's-eye views" of the *omne scibile* that we naturally turn, if we want to sound the depths of a specific sphere of human experiences, if, for instance, we would know the heart of the lover, the adventurer, the sinner. When a man is, like Plato, a great metaphysician, and also has, like Plato, an eye for the depths, he refuses, as Plato did,[1] to make a system. But I think it is the common experience that, when all is said that there is to say in the way of a *sed contra*, we get the most penetrating and convincing glimpses of a tremendous reality less often from the most illustrious of the great systematisers, an Aristotle, a St. Thomas, a Hegel, than from the intense unsystematic thinkers, the Pascals and the Schopenhauers.

I would seriously urge, then, that the systematic, methodical metaphysician is going outside his province

[1] *Ep.* vii. 341 C *τοσόνδε γε μὴν περὶ πάντων ἔχω φράζειν τῶν γεγραφότων καὶ γραψόντων, ὅσοι φασὶν εἰδέναι περὶ ὧν ἐγὼ σπουδάζω . . . τούτους οὐκ ἔστιν κατά γε τὴν ἐμὴν δόξαν περὶ τοῦ πράγματος ἐπαΐειν οὐδέν. οὔκουν ἐμόν γε περὶ αὐτῶν ἔστι σύγγραμμα οὐδὲ μήποτε γένηται.* This is clearly meant as Plato's refusal to put the substance of his famous discourse on "the Good" into writing, and I believe we may add that it is also meant to dissociate himself from responsibility for the versions of the discourse which we know to have been circulated by some of those who heard it. It was one of his grievances against Dionysius II. that he had composed, or at least circulated, such a professed exposition of "Platonism".

if he undertakes to prescribe to religion, to morality, to art, limits beyond which they must not expatiate, on pain of losing contact with reality. It is not for him to declare with authority what religion, or art, or morality must be if they are to be capable of a rational justification. Their legitimate bounds are set to them, not from without, but from within, by the character of the specific living experiences which are their matter, and by nothing else. The "irrationality" which would be fatal to any one of them is not some failure of adjustment to a preconceived epistemological scheme, but absence of internal unifying principle. And what is true of morality, religion, art, as ways of life will hold good equally for the intellectual reflective interpretation of them in the disciplines of ethics, theology, "aesthetics". It would be fatal to the claims of an ethical or theological body of doctrine if it were found to contradict itself, or if, again, there were an unremoved and unremovable conflict between the ethical or theological interpretation and those very facts of the moral or religious life which it professes to interpret. But mere inability to see how the presuppositions of the religious life can be harmoniously adjusted to those of the moral, or both, again, to the presuppositions of our natural knowledge, seems no valid reason for disputing the rights of ethics or theology to be genuine knowledge of a genuine reality, or to deal autonomously and independently with its own specific "matter", any more than the acknowledged difficulty of adjusting biology with physics is a reason for disputing the character of biology as a genuine field of knowledge, with a right to its own presuppositions and methods.

When we bear in mind that all our knowledge is always *in fieri*, in the process of making, not finally made, it is manifest that this lack of complete adjustment is no more than a consequence of the fact that everywhere "we know in part and we prophesy in part". It is our business to do all we can to effect a completer adjustment and to wait patiently for its arrival, not arbitrarily to suppress one part of a necessarily imperfect apprehension of an infinitely rich whole, because we are puzzled about its precise links of contact with other apprehensions which are equally partial. Indeed, I think we may fairly say that an apparently flawless synthesis, for example, of natural knowledge and theology must be a *false* synthesis, since its very faultlessness—when we remember how fragmentary and confused is our knowledge of nature, and much more our knowledge of God—would be proof that it had been obtained by the mutilation of one, and probably of both constituents. (Just as the once fashionable "reconciliations" of physics with the opening chapters of *Genesis* ought to have been seen to be condemned as vain in principle by the single consideration that a complete agreement between *Genesis* and the physical text-books of the current year must inevitably lead to contradiction between *Genesis* and the text-books of twenty years later—unless, indeed, the interpretations of the supposedly infallible narrative of *Genesis* should prove to be just as much perpetually *in fieri* as the doctrines of the physical text-books, in which case each successive conciliator's labour is once more in vain.)[1]

It seems to me, then, that in the matter of the claim to autonomy, theology, ethics, and natural knowledge stand all on one footing. All have a right to exist, and each has the right to deal with its own problems without

[1] Thus I have read works of the last generation in which "religion" was reconciled with "science" by a proof that Scripture teaches the doctrines of Herbert Spencer's *First Principles*. If this could really be proved, where would Scripture be to-day?

dictation from either of the others. We have a right, and a duty, to be satisfied, in the case of each, that we are being presented with real problems, not with senseless conundrums excogitated by our own vanity, and, so far as theology is concerned, the whole of what we have said throughout these discussions, may be regarded as a continued attempt to plead that its problems are real problems, forced on us by life, whether we will or no. We have also the right to demand everywhere that the problems thus forced upon us shall be met by strenuous thinking, that there shall be none of the idle mystification which, in fact, has, in different ages, infected men's attitude towards all the problems set us by life, no substitution of acquiescence in an accepted formula for honest thinking, whether in natural science, in moral science, or in divinity. But if, as we have urged is the case, theology itself has inevitably arisen in the honest attempt to think out the implications of genuine experiences, which are other than, or at least more than, the experiences intellectually elaborated by the natural and moral sciences, it is as vain to dismiss theology as illegitimate on the strength of the acknowledged difficulty of fitting its presuppositions into a metaphysical scheme based on the assumption that the course of physical nature and the history of our social relations with our fellowmen, between them, disclose all the reality there is to be known, as it would be to deny some adequately established position in natural science for the like reason that it is hard to adjust it to a metaphysical scheme inspired by exclusive attention to experiences of a distinctively religious kind.

We may all of us probably remember Pascal's incisive comment on the attempt to subject natural science to theological dictation: "The Jesuits have procured a decree from Rome that the earth does not revolve, but, if it really revolves, no decrees can alter the fact".[1] In our own day we more commonly, perhaps, see the process reversed: we see the invoking of something like a "decree" from the Royal Society in condemnation of the doctrines of theology. But here also we may comment, in the spirit of Pascal, that if the life of which theology attempts to give us the theory is real fact, no decree of anyone can make it unreal. If, for example, sin and the remission of sins are real facts of life—and the physicist or biologist assuredly cannot pretend to settle *that* question by his physics or biology—it is idle to dismiss the theologian's doctrines of sin and grace on the plea that the biologist, for the purposes of his biology, can dispense with the notions. Both theologian and biologist are dealing with a restricted selection from our experiences of a rich and bewildering reality; it is preposterous to dispute the worth of the special view into that reality disclosed by either on the plea that we are at a loss how to combine the two views into one.

In principle the difficulty is the same, though in degree it may be less, when we try to understand how the living organism can be at once what the pure physicist says it is and what the biologist declares it must be. It is not the least of Prof. Whitehead's services to clear thinking that he has made it so apparent that the "conflict of theology with science", so much talked of in the nineteenth century, has its counterpart, on a smaller scale, in a similar conflict between the biology of the century and its physics. It may be that the remoulding of scientific concepts which is so busily prosecuted from

[1] *Lettres écrites à un provincial*, xviii: "Ce fut aussi en vain que vous obtîntes contre Galilée un décret de Rome, qui condamnoit son opinion touchant le mouvement de la terre. Ce ne sera pas cela qui prouvera qu'elle demeure en repos; et si l'on avoit des observations constantes qui prouvassent que c'est elle qui tourne, tous les hommes ensemble ne l'empêcheroient pas de tourner, et ne s'empêcheroient pas de tourner aussi avec elle."

within at the present moment may bring us, in the course of a generation or two, to a fairly complete solution of this lesser problem. It would be too much to hope for any final solution of the graver problem, but at least we may learn the lesson that difficulties of this kind are not to be removed by the facile device of refusing to see those features of the reality on which we live which conflict with our natural preference for a simplified and unified view of the world.

It is our duty as rational beings to aim at the unified view, but it is surely an illusion to imagine that the unified view will ever be within the grasp of finite intelligences, condemned by their finitude to get at truth piecemeal. Any account of the real which is to do justice to all the features it presents to us is bound to be untidy in places, to be scored with seams and ridges. What we can do is to note where the gaps are found and to try our best, with hope, but also with patience and a fixed resolve to avoid premature syntheses, towards filling them up. So we shall best make our own contribution to the only true *philosophia perennis*, a philosophy which is, as Francis Bacon said,[1] the work, not of some single superman, but of Time, and of which, just because it is always in the making, we might use the phrase of Tennyson, that it is

> never built at all,
> And therefore built for ever.

Of course, to defend the claim of theology, or any other discipline, to autonomy on these lines is, at the same time, to recognise that the right to autonomy is never merely unilateral. Theology, we have urged, is

[1] *N.O.* i. 84 "summae pusillanimitatis est authoribus infinita tribuere, authori autem authorum atque adeo omnis authoritatis, Tempori, ius suum denegare. Recte enim Veritas Temporis filia dicitur."

entitled to deal with its own very real problems without suffering either its procedure or its conclusions to be clipped and curtailed to the pattern presupposed in the natural sciences, and no less entitled to refuse to let itself be made into a mere instrument of morality. For the very same reasons there must be no well-meant edificatory interfering with the unfettered and single-minded investigation of natural fact in the supposed interests of a sound social morality, nor any shirking or wresting of the results of either natural or moral science for the convenience of the divine. If we would be intellectually honest, as it is no easy task to be, it must be our rule, whether our particular work is done in the field of natural science, of ethics, or of theology, to "follow the argument wherever it leads". To force the "argument" to a conclusion dictated in advance, to cut it arbitrarily short in its progress, when the goal to which it is tending is an unwelcome one, to avoid so much as entering on a legitimate investigation because we are afraid of the conclusions to which it might conduct, all these devices, so often illustrated by the history of both divinity and science, are but so many ways of "offering to the God of truth the unclean sacrifice of a lie". In the realm of thought, as in the sphere of political relations, independence is something very different from a right to domineer over a neighbour who has an equal right to an independence of his own, though it is the lamentable fact that sciences, like nations, are always apt to overstep the boundary which divides independence within one's own borders from domineering outside them.

At the same time, it needs equally to be said that, however fully natural science, moral science, divinity, are justified in asserting their several rights to pursue their own tasks without interference, no one of the three can be indifferent to the conclusions asserted by the others. The conclusions of natural science cannot be wholly irrelevant to those of moral science, nor the conclusions of either to divinity, since all alike deal with elements in the same *given*. Life and the world are, in the end, one and not many, and therefore any version of the doctrine of the "double truth" must, in the long run, be destructive of the ideal of truth itself. Hence it is only as a rule of method that we can unreservedly accept the principle of what has been called "ethical neutrality", and the analogous principle of "theological neutrality". It is perfectly true that in pursuing any line of inquiry we have a duty, as well as a right, to refuse to be diverted by considerations which, however important, are strictly irrelevant to the question what conclusions are indicated by the evidence before us. To urge that, as may perfectly well be the case, the moral practice, or the devotion of a given community is likely to suffer from the general admission of certain inferences in natural science or in history is strictly irrelevant to the question whether the available evidence justifies or supports those inferences. So far[1] it is our business, in pursuing any special branch of knowledge, to be consistently "neutral" towards all considerations which fall outside the purview of that branch of knowledge itself. What cannot be true is that there should be one "truth" of physical science, another of moral science, and possibly a third of divinity, all incompatible with one another and irrelevant to one another.

[1] But no further. If, for example, biological investigations should provide evidence that it is possible, by various artifices, to control the fertility of marriages, or the sex of the resulting offspring, the moralist may not deny the possibility because he thinks that the practice of the artifices is morally deleterious. So far he is bound to be "ethically neutral", and the obligation is itself a moral one. But if the biologist goes on to advocate the practice of these artifices, he has himself ventured into the field of morals, and the moralist is not *free*, but actually bound, to judge the recommendation from the moral point of view. Here he has no right to be "neutral".

The moralist cannot afford to be indifferent to an alleged scientific account of the world which would make it a system with no place for genuine effort, real freedom and causality, true responsibility and desert, or the divine to a scientific or ethical reading of life which leaves no room for God. In view of the ultimately practical character of our concern as individuals with the ordering of our lives, this may at least explain, though it does not follow that it justifies, the attempts which have been made at various times to arrest the advance of scientific and historical inquiry in the real or supposed interests of morality and religion.

Without subscribing to Newman's unqualified assertion of the inherent right of ecclesiastical authority to prohibit further pursuit of investigations in every department at its discretion, we may at least be able to understand that such interference has not necessarily always been prompted simply by arrogance and meddlesomeness, or by the criminal and impious concern of a powerful order for its own prestige. Human nature being what it is, it is not surprising that these unworthy motives have played only too prominent a part in history, but it would be the blindness of the mere partisan to deny that behind the "obscurantism" of ecclesiastical authority there has often been a genuine, I do not say an unadulterated, concern to safeguard the interests of practical good living, and that the quality of the practical morality advocated by the so-called "advanced scientific thinkers" of the past and the present has often shown this concern to be well founded. Some part, at least, of the "domineering" of the divine and moralist has been provoked by a correct perception that the autonomy of religion and morality has been challenged from the other side and needs to be defended.[1] The pity is that so often the defence has been conducted on the wrong lines.

By way of illustration we need only remind ourselves of the attitude taken up, often for quite honourable reasons, by moralists as well as divines, in the last century towards Darwin's researches into the origin of species. The legitimate procedure for a divine or moralist who anticipated, correctly enough, that the actual consequences of general acceptance of the doctrine of our physical kinship with the brutes might be, in various ways, injurious to morality, would have been twofold. It should have been argued that the scrutiny of the available evidence and the full interpretation of it must necessarily be the work of years; what *precise* conclusions would in the end emerge under patient examination could not have been said at the time, and, I suppose, cannot be said even now, except in a very general way, and with a good deal of reserve on all points of detail. And, further, and this is, of course, the important point, it should have been persistently repeated that even if the facts on which Darwin's speculations were based were absolutely certain, and known to be the whole of the relevant facts, they could not be, and still less could his, or any man's, speculative inferences from them be, more certain than the certainties on which morality and religion are based, the certainty of absolute moral obligation, of human responsibility and

[1] Cf. the remarks of Lord Acton on the suppression of the Albigenses: "There was a practice which the clergy desired to restrain, and which they attempted to organise. We see by their writings that they believed in many horrible imputations. As time went on, it appeared that much of this was fable. But it also became known that it was not all fabulous, and that the Albigensian creed culminated in what was known as the Endura, which was in reality suicide. It was the object of the Inquisition that such people should not indeed be spared, but should not perish without a trial and without opportunity of resipiscence, so that they might save their souls if not their lives. Its founders could claim to act from motives both of mercy and of justice against members of a Satanic association" (*Lectures on Modern History*, p. 111). The words are the more weighty from the writer's notorious hatred of "persecution".

freedom of choice, and of the reality of the saint's "life in God, and union there". The facts in this order are as certainly facts as those of the breeder of plants and animals, or the palaeontologist, and inferences about what men are which are really guaranteed by them are at least as trustworthy as inferences about what their remote ancestors once were which are guaranteed by the others. We may therefore rest assured of one thing, and it is the only thing which matters very much, that whatever the newly discovered facts of the natural order really prove, they cannot prove anything incompatible with what is really proved by the already familiar fundamental facts of the moral and religious order. They may seem for a time to do so, and we may not at present see how this apparent contradiction is to be avoided, but we may also be assured that it cannot be more than apparent, and may therefore be content to confess our perplexity, without concealment, but also without dismay. There should really have been none of the unedifying eagerness which was shown, and not by professed theologians only, to get rid of inconvenient facts by hasty denials, or to disguise the conclusions to which they, *pro tanto*, pointed, by ingenious special pleading and forced interpretations. The appeal to certainties of one order should have been met by a counter-appeal to equal certainties of a different order, not by disingenuous or irrelevant rhetoric, nor by the superfluous invocation of official custodians of faith and morals to cut investigation short by the *fiat* of authority.

I should not, however, like to maintain that there are not circumstances in which this last procedure may be justified as a temporary and purely *administrative* act, since the prosecution of scientific research is neither the only interest of mankind, nor necessarily the principal interest of all human societies in all circumstances. We can all think of researches in course of eager prosecution at the present time which it might be for the immense gain of humanity to arrest, if the thing could be done, on precisely the grounds on which, by general consent, it is also desirable, if we can, to "call a halt all round" to naval construction, and I have sometimes been inclined to wonder whether, in the absence of some authority capable of enforcing such a general arrest, civilisation is not in some danger of being destroyed by its own men of science. It does not seem quite impossible that "divine philosophy" may yet fulfil Tennyson's mournful prophecy,[1] and become "procuress to the Lords of Hell" in a fashion undreamed of by sober, decent "mid-Victorians", who had never heard of "poison-gas", "death-rays", "rejuvenation", or artificial birth-control. Indeed the possibility is, I fear, something more than a bare possibility, unless the world can be won to take the poet's warning to "hold the *good*" in a degree of earnest of which, at present, it shows no sufficient signs. It may even be that society will only, in fact, save itself at the eleventh hour by desperately reverting to an iron authoritarianism more rigorous than any claimed by a Hildebrand, or a Boniface VIII. But if that should prove to be the price of holding fast the good, it will only be a mutilated good which will have been preserved from the general wreck; for an unforeseeable time, philosophy and science will once more have retired, like Astraea, from the earth, as once long ago in the midnight between the age of Justinian and that of Charlemagne, and the recovery from the new "dark

[1] *In Memoriam* liii.:

"Hold thou the good: define it well:
For fear divine Philosophy
Should push beyond her mark, and be
Procuress to the Lords of Hell."

age" may be more painful and slower than the recovery from the old. One must at least hope that mankind will find a more excellent way while there is still time, and the Avar and Vandal are not as yet actually within the gates.

If we are to find that more excellent way, we must, I should say, safeguard ourselves in all our thinking, alike as theologians, as metaphysicians, as workers in the various sciences, by a real and frank confession of a sane agnosticism, unwelcome to the temper of a self-confident age. We inheritors of such an age—for I cannot, of course, speak for a younger generation—are all too prone to exaggerate the amount of our certain knowledge. Theologians have often been specifically derided, as by Matthew Arnold, for their alleged tendency to take it for granted that they know all about God, and with respect to all but the greatest theologians there is too much truth in the charge. But metaphysicians are no less apt to assume that they know so well what "ultimate reality" is as to be able to say with some confidence what can happen and what cannot possibly have happened; men of science, at least when they are addressing the public at large, frequently speak with a great deal of assurance about the lines on which "nature" has been laid down. It is true that, as a matter of form, all these classes are ready enough to make a "general confession". In words, the men of science will readily admit that "nature" is, after all, in the main a still unexplored field, and the metaphysician that "the absolute" is very much of a mystery; the theologians even adopt it as a truth of their science that though we know *that* God is, in this life, at least, we do not know, except in the most distant fashion, *what* God is. Yet when we come to the application of the admission in practice, we only too often find that each party uses it mainly to keep his rivals in their place. If you are an average divine, you dwell on the limitations of human knowledge chiefly by way of rebuke to the over-confident assertions of metaphysicians, or men of science, who do not accept your theology; if you are a metaphysician, you labour the same theme to confute the rashness of the divine, or the scientific specialist; if you are yourself a scientific specialist, you apply the whip to repress the self-confidence of everyone who has not cultivated your own particular specialism.

A genuine agnosticism, which is neither that of indolent indifference nor that of despair, means something different. It means the repression not of another man's self-confidence, but of my own. Nor does repression of my own self-confidence mean treating my most assured convictions as quite probably mere illusions. It means taking care to avoid the assumption that "what *I* don't know isn't knowledge"; in other words, scrupulous conscientiousness in distinguishing what is really forced upon me by the given from what may be personal and arbitrary in my interpretation of the given, and capable of being shown to be so by comparison with the attempts of others to say what they find given to them. We need always to remember that there is a double source of fallibility in our personal interpretation of the common given. Our personal intellectual interpretation of our most familiar experiences may be vitiated by want of thoroughness, or by reliance on uncriticised categories of thought; and, again, not all of us are equally responsive to every element in the common given. On both grounds we can only hope for approximation to a true understanding of the "common" in which our life is set on the condition that we are willing to learn the lessons of an experience which is not our own, in a spirit of docility. None of us can escape from intellectual disaster, unless he is ready to walk somewhere in life by the faith which comes by hearing; no man's soul can successfully walk by its own private light alone.

The particular danger against which such a sane and hopeful agnosticism is most needed as a prophylactic in our own day does not seem to me to be undue confidence in dogmatic theologies or metaphysical systems. These have been dangers in the past, but our present peril is rather that of being too confident in science, or what we take for science. We commonly do not realise as fully as we need to do that there is so much in life, so much, too, which is of the first moment to us, which is not knowledge, and yet must imperatively be acted on, and that very much which is knowledge is not science. Science is not the whole of life; it is not even the whole of knowledge, but one rather curious and restricted department of knowledge. Life would be a poor affair if there were not many things which each of us knew with much more certainty than the scientific man knows any of the theorems of his own science. And, again, as our philosophically-minded scientific men seem almost unnecessarily eager to convince us at the present moment, the more scientific we make our science, the nearer we bring its conclusions to being demonstrations, the more remote they appear to be from all contact with actuality, and the more completely do they take on the character of hypothetical inference from assumed postulates, which are themselves declared to be no more than hypothetical. If the day has gone by for ever when science could be treated, in the fashion of some of the older apologists, as a short cut to the establishment of a particular theology, no less has the day gone by, though this is not always equally recognised, when theology could be treated as though it had been rendered absurd or superfluous by the existence of natural science. The very fact of our own existence and the existence of our world sets us problems, and thereby imposes on us the moral obligation of dealing with problems, not all of which can be treated by the special methods of natural science, nor yet all by the special methods of theology, and thus justifies the existence of both studies, while the necessarily tentative character of all our human thinking makes it impossible that either should ever be simply absorbed into metaphysics. That consummation would only be possible if the actual could be completely rationalised without ceasing to be a *given* actual. And if we were in possession of a completely rationalised actual, we should no longer have either science or theology; both would have given place to something better than either—vision. "ἀλλ' οὔτ' ἀπολέσθαι τὰ κακὰ δυνατόν, ὦ Θεόδωρε· ὑπεναντίον γάρ τι τῷ ἀγαθῷ ἀεὶ εἶναι ἀνάγκη· οὔτ' ἐν θεοῖς αὐτὰ ἱδρῦσθαι, τὴν δὲ θνητὴν φύσιν καὶ τόνδε τὸν τόπον περιπολεῖ ἐξ ἀνάγκης. διὸ καὶ πειρᾶσθαι χρὴ ἐνθένδε ἐκεῖσε φεύγειν ὅτι τάχιστα. φυγὴ δὲ ὁμοίωσις θεῷ κατὰ τὸ δυνατόν. . . ." [1]

[1] Plato, *Theaetetus*, 176 A, B.

APPENDIX

It may be advisable to add here one or two observations on certain important topics which present themselves at more than one stage in the argument of these lectures, and could not therefore be disposed of in footnotes. I select, in particular, three such topics, because I think it possible I may be thought to have treated them, in different places, in inconsistent ways. I do not believe there has been serious real inconsistency, and I would ask the reader who suspects it at least to suspend his judgement until he has weighed the remarks now to be made.

A. *The Rationality of the Universe*

In some places I have spoken of the conviction that reality is a rational whole as the fundamental postulate alike of true science, true philosophy, and true religion; in other places I have spoken of the "rationalisation" of the universe as a task which, from the nature of the case, can never be finally achieved. The apparent consequence might be stated epigrammatically by saying that I maintain, in effect, that there are "irrationalities" which are not unreasonable. If this sounds like paradox, the paradox, I believe, is only apparent and arises from what Plato calls[1] τὸ τῶν λόγων ἀσθενές, the inadequacy of language to convey the whole of a speaker's meaning and nothing beyond that meaning.

[1] *Ep.* vii. 343 A.

By the "irrational" we may mean (1) that which is in conflict with the first principles of coherent thinking, the inherently *unreasonable*, as I should prefer to call it. It would be irrational in *this* sense to maintain that there are integers which are at once odd and even, are not, and yet also are, divisible by 2 without a remainder. To say that the real, or the universe, may be irrational in this sense would be to say that it is not only a riddle, but a riddle to which there can be no answer, because it is a question with no genuine meaning. A riddle which has no answer is not even a riddle. If reality were a pseudo-enigma of this sort, manifestly science, philosophy, religion would be alike worthless; all would be vain attempts to solve a conundrum which, *ex hypothesi*, has no solution, to translate "gibberish" into sense. But "gibberish" which could be rendered into sense would not be "gibberish".

But we also speak of the "irrational" in a very different sense to mean (2) that to which we can find an approximate answer, or even a series of ever more closely approximate answers, but not a complete answer. "Irrationality" in this sense means only that we are dealing with a problem which we are always on the way to solving, but never *have* solved and never *shall have* solved. This is what we mean when we speak, in the language of the discipline from which the very word "irrational" has been borrowed, of an "irrational" magnitude or number. When we say that $\sqrt{2}$ is an "irrational", we do not mean that the question "What number, multiplied by itself, will give the product 2?" is insoluble in the sense in which Lewis Carroll's conundrum "Why is a raven like a writing-desk?" is presumably insoluble. For, as we know, we can readily find an unending series of fractions such that the product of any term of the series by itself is more nearly equal to 2 than that of any of its precursors by itself. We have a simple rule for constructing this series, and by travelling far enough along it, we can find a number of which the product by itself differs from 2 by a fraction smaller than any we please to assign. What we cannot do is to get to the end of this unending series, or, again, when we "extract the square root of 2" by the more rough-and-ready familiar arithmetical method, to come to a last "decimal figure", or a group of recurring "decimal figures". That is, we cannot answer our question "What number, when multiplied by itself, gives the product 2", by pro ducing a fraction which has finite integers for its numerator and denominator. If $x^2/y^2 = 2$, x has not to y the λόγος or *ratio* of an integer to an integer, and this is why $\sqrt{2}$ has been called an ἄλογον, or "irrational". But there is nothing *unreasonable* in the statement that some integers have "irrational square roots"; the unreasonableness would lie in denying this. For by denying it we should be asserting one or other of two propositions, (*a*) that there are actually pairs of integers which satisfy such equations as $x^2 = 2y^2$, $x^2 = 5y^2$, or (*b*) that if we consider the pairs of values of x and y yielded by the integral solutions of the equations $x^2 = 2y^2 \pm 1$, $x^2 = 5y^2 \pm 1$, though the "absolute difference" between 2 or 5 and the fraction x^2/y^2 steadily diminishes as we consider higher and higher values of x and y, it always remains greater than some assignable rational fraction σ. And both these propositions are at variance with the foundations of coherent thinking. The example will explain what I mean by a reasonable irrationality.

I hold, then, that because our intellect is not creative of the universe, but receptive of a reality which it has to understand but does not freely create, our problem of interpreting that reality by theory is in principle like the evaluation of a "surd". We may, and should, make persistent efforts to carry our valuation a "place" further than any we have actually reached, but we can never expect to write down the "last decimal figure", or the "last convergent", if I may so express myself. This is what the rationalist *pur sang*, whether he is confessionally as orthodox as Descartes at least meant to be, or as fanatically anti-orthodox as the contributors to the "Rationalist Press", assumes that we can do, and this is why rationalism of that kind is inherently unreasonable. On that point, at least, I may claim to be loyal to the central thought of Kant. I would add that, so far as I can see, the case would be the same with a "separated intelligence", supposing that intelligence not to be itself the Creator of the world. Even for the angels, the "works of the six days" remain the "*unbegreiflich* hohen Werke".

B. *Freedom and Contingency*

To prevent misunderstandings I should like to state briefly what I take to be the essentials of such a doctrine of "choice and avoidance" as seems to me indispensable if our moral accountability for our voluntary actions is to be regarded as more than illusory.

(1) It is a fact that we, sometimes at least, really choose between alternative courses of action. It is not true that when we think we are choosing, the real fact is *always* that we are discovering that there is no choice open to us. (Whether there are *some* occasions when we fancy ourselves to be choosing, but are mistaken, I am not called upon to decide, but I am not concerned to deny that it may be so. My only concern is to maintain that sometimes at least all of us really do choose, and that the fact must not be explained away. *All* our choices are not "Hobson's choice".)

(2) Again deliberation is a real process, not a mere illusion. Sometimes, at any rate, we really weigh the goodness whether of alternative acts, *A* and *B* themselves, or of their consequences, before making our choice, and the weighing, sometimes at least, affects the choice. Deliberation is neither, as Hobbes thought it was, a mere oscillation between conflicting "appetites"[1] nor yet a pretence of looking for reasons for an act which we are already "determined" to do. It is genuine "practical" *thinking*.

(3) Further, there is no reason to doubt that we can, and sometimes do, come to this process of practical thinking with minds not already prejudiced for or against either of the alternatives under examination, just as we sometimes consider the evidence for or against a statement of alleged matter of fact without secret prepossession either way. A man may come to the estimation of evidence with an "open mind", devoid of any antecedent bias other than a desire to reach the truth about the matter under examination.[2] Similarly he may weigh the alternative courses of action *A* and *B* with no prepossession beyond the intention to adopt the course which shall, on examination, approve itself to him as the "right", or the "better". If many men mistakenly suppose themselves to be impartial in deliberation when they are not really so, men also often suppose themselves to be weighing testimony or arguments with an open mind, when this is not actually the fact. Yet a man can be, and ought to be, candid and open with himself

[1] *Elements of Law*, pt. i. c. 12: "This alternate succession of appetite and fear during all the time the action is in our power to do, or not to do, is that we call DELIBERATION". *Leviathan*, c. 6: "When in the mind of man, Appetites and Aversions, Hopes and Fears, concerning one and the same thing, arise alternately . . . the whole summe of Desires, Aversions, Hopes and Feares, continued till the thing be either done, or thought impossible, is that we call DELIBERATION".

[2] *E.g.* Did Virgil write (*Ecl.* iv. 62) "*qui* non risere *parenti*," or "*quoi* non risere *parentes*"? Surely it is ludicrous to suggest that I cannot consider the question without a secret antecedent bias.

in deliberation, as he can be, and ought to be, candid and open in the balancing of testimonies, or the scrutiny of arguments.

(4) When the conditions thus laid down are fulfilled, it is strictly true to say that during the process of deliberating a man is "indetermined" *ad utrumque*: in fact, it is the deliberation itself which puts an end to this "freedom", and "determines" him to one of the alternatives. Until he has deliberated he is "free" to take either course, to do a proposed act, say *A*, or not to do it.

(5) Such "freedom" does not mean that a man is ever "free" to take just any course he pleases. The alternatives between which I am effectively "free" to choose in a given case will always be limited in number, partly by my present situation, partly by my "past". I am not "free", at the moment of writing these lines, to choose whether I will go on with my writing in Edinburgh or spend the evening with a friend in Westminster, since I cannot transport myself forthwith to Westminster. Nor am I "free" to lay down my writing and read the Chinese classics; I have not in the past learned the Chinese language and so could not read a Chinese book, even if I had one at command. But I *can* choose either of the alternatives to go on with my writing or not to go on with it. If I could not, it would be equally futile to express moral approbation of my conduct if I stick to my work, in spite of the temptation to lay it aside for a diverting romance, and to express disapproval if I abandon my work for the story. Life would not be an education into morally stable character for us if it did not present situations in which we are confronted with the real alternative of doing the act *A* or not doing it, both courses being really open to us until one of them is blocked by our deliberation itself. Genuine morality would be impossible if it were true that when we take

a decision, or suppose ourselves to do so, we are in a position like that of an engine-driver at the point of divergence of two sets of tracks, one of which is already closed against him by an invisible pointsman. I am my own pointsman, as well as the driver of my own engine.

(6) It follows that when I really deliberate and decide, my decision and the ensuing act, though largely *conditioned* by the past, which restricts the range of effective alternatives open to me (as in the supposed example, it excluded the dropping of my work to read a Chinese classic, though not the dropping of it ἁπλῶς), are not wholly *determined* by it. And therefore, when we prescind from the question of the range of effective alternatives, and consider simply the choice "to do *A* or not", the "past" leaves the issue truly undetermined. To put the point in quasi-mathematical language, if my act is to be considered as a *function* of my "past", it must be regarded as a *many*-valued, not as a *one*-valued, function of it. This, not the mere difficulty of obtaining sufficiently minute information about the events of another man's past history, is the reason why it must always be impossible to calculate a man's future unambiguously from knowledge of his past, and why there could never be such a science as the "ethology" contemplated by J. S. Mill (*Logic*, bk. vi. c. 5).

(7) It does not follow from these positions that it must always be open to a "free" rational agent who is not the Creator to make a morally *evil* choice (so that we should have to say that if men, or angels, are free agents, any man, or any angel, may at any moment commit any conceivable sin). For the discipline of the past closes many paths, though it may not close all. Our choice is not always between a morally right and a morally wrong, not necessarily always between a good

and a better; it may perfectly well sometimes be between two courses equally good, but different.[1] There is thus no inconsistency between such "freedom" as is implied in moral responsibility and the attainment of a stable character from which the discipline of the past has eliminated all possibility of effectively preferring the morally evil, or even the morally less good, alternative. It would even be possible, humanly speaking, that God Himself should always have open "alternatives", though, if He has, they cannot differ as a morally better and a morally less good. But it is not *necessary* to make this assertion about God, since always to see the absolute best and to follow it because it is best is to enjoy a "freedom" far transcending our human "freedom of choice" between a bad and a good, a best and a less good. A man who loves his wife is not the less free because his *love* forecloses any effective possibility of deserting her.[2]

I think it will be apparent that these positions do not involve any unreasonable version of Indeterminism, and that they are fully consistent with the acceptance of the Socratic and Platonic *dictum* that to be in assured and unclouded apprehension of the "best" would always entail following it. And, so far as I can see, such "freedom of the will" as I am here maintaining is equally in harmony with the teaching, *e.g.*, of St. Thomas

[1] As, for example, when a man considers whether he will spend his holiday in the Scottish Highlands, seeing lochs and mountains, or in Italy, seeing cities and pictures. It may be that, for a given man, either course is as good as the other, though the two goods are different. Or one might have to choose between two different careers without being able to say that one could serve God or man better in the one than in the other.

[2] Thus *God's* freedom should probably not be called "freedom of *choice*". (Kant, it will be remembered, denies that we can properly speak of *Triebfeder* in connection with the divine activity.) "We must not conceive God to be the *freest* agent, because he can doe and prescribe what he pleaseth, and so set up an Absolute will which shall make both Law and Reason, as some imagine. For as God cannot *know* himself to be any other than what indeed he is; so neither can he *will* himself to be anything else than what he is. For this were to make God free to dethrone himself" (John Smith, *Of the Existence and Nature of God.* c. ii. § 6).

Aquinas. If a man likes to say that he means something more than this by "freedom", and therefore regards Plato and St. Thomas as "determinists", I can, of course, have no objection to his saying the same of myself. But the doctrine here laid down is so different from anything which was taught by the inventors of the word "determinism", or the scientific men who have adopted it as a badge of their profession, that I believe nothing but confusion can come of such a careless use of terminology. I may add a remark or two about "contingency" to make the position adopted still clearer.

C. *Contingency in Nature?*

There are writers for whom I have a deep respect who would, I believe, on consideration, accept all, or most, of the foregoing seven propositions, but would, at the same time, reject the whole conception of any real "contingency" in the course of events.[1] As will have been visible from more than one passage in these volumes, I am compelled to take a different view, and to agree with James Ward that any interpretation of the world which is to make room for real history, real morality, real religion, must "let contingency into the heart of things".[2] Accordingly, though I do not appeal to the return of so many eminent physicists at the moment to the assertion of a "principle of Indeterminacy" in the physical at large as an *argument* for our moral freedom, I believe it to be an important step in the direction of a sounder metaphysic and cosmology. The opposing

[1] I am thinking particularly of the avowed "determinism" of such moralists as Dr. Rashdall and Dr. McTaggart, and, again, of the position taken by the Rev. C. J. Shebbeare in his recent *Problems of Providence*. To judge from the incidental remarks on the subject in *Five Types of Ethical Theory*, Dr. Broad would probably agree still more closely with the general view I have tried to set forth.

[2] *Naturalism and Agnosticism*, ii. 280.

view, which regards contingency as an illusion begotten of our ignorance of the details of becoming, seems to me to rest in the end upon a misunderstanding of the meaning of the "contingent". It is taken to mean the capricious occurrence of events which have no sufficient "why and wherefore" in the plan of reality, and might "just as well never have occurred at all"; such meaningless "random" occurrences are then truly said to be incompatible with a genuine theistic faith in the divine *government* of the world. Or it is also said that they are excluded by the divine *omniscience*; "if God eternally knows the whole course of history, how can any of the events so known be contingent?" And yet an intelligence which does not know the whole course of history cannot be the God demanded by religious men, for of it it could not be said without reserve, "Trust in the Lord with *all* thy heart, and lean not to thine own understanding".

Now here there is, I believe, a bad confusion of thought. It is antecedently most unlikely that such philosophers as Plato and St. Thomas—if I do not add Aristotle, my reason is that the famous αὑτὸν ἄρα νοεῖ seems intended to exclude the course of *events* from God's knowledge—should have believed with equal conviction in divine omniscience and divine government of the world, and also in contingency (the πλανωμένη αἰτία of the *Timaeus*), without seeing the glaring contradiction, if it really does "glare". And I think it not hard to satisfy one's self that the contradiction is no more than apparent. As St. Thomas is careful to explain,[1] a *contingent* event does not mean an event which

[1] Cf. *S.C.G.* i. 85 "requirit autem ordo universalis aliquas causas esse variabiles, cum corpora sint de perfectione universi, quae non movent nisi mota . . . unde videmus quamvis causa remota sit necessaria, si tamen causa proxima sit contingens, effectum contingentem esse." *S. Th.* i.ª q. 19, art. 8 resp. "cum igitur voluntas divina sit efficacissima, non solum sequitur quod fiant ea quae Deus vult fieri, sed

has no cause, or is not "determined" relatively to the supreme (in the older terminology the "superessential")[1] cause, the divine purpose, but one which is not unambiguously determined by its more "proximate" causes. (Thus, to take the standing example, it was held that the motions of the heavenly bodies are "necessary" causes of certain effects, *e.g.* of the alternation of day and night. But among the effects of the motion of these bodies we have also to include the growth and ripening of crops on earth. Now in this particular case the effect of a "necessary" cause is a *contingent* event, because there may be some *debilitas* in the seed which has been sown, and in that case the effect, the ripening of the harvest, does not follow. In fact, in this case, the revolutions in the heavens are not the proximate, but a remote (though not the ultimate and "superessential") cause of the result considered, and it is therefore not fully "determined" by them.)

It would, no doubt, be hard to defend this doctrine of contingency to-day in the precise form in which it was used by the great schoolmen, who inherited Aristotle's unfortunate and perverse crotchet of a radical distinction between terrestrial and celestial "matter" and their respective dynamics.[2] We tend at once to meet the Thomist example of the harvest which is "contingent"

et quod eo modo fiant quo Deus ea fieri vult. Vult autem quaedam fieri Deus necessario, quaedam contingenter, ut sit ordo in rebus ad complementum universi." Professed Thomists, I observe, commonly speak of *three* kinds of effects—"necessary, contingent, and *free*". But I presume that "free effects" are not meant to be "contra-divided against" the other two as a third species, but to be understood as a sub-class of the contingent, "contra-divided against" the contingent but unfree.

[1] Thus R. Bacon in his Commentary on Aristotle, *Physics*, i.-iv. (Oxford, 1928, p. 249), speaking of the succession of the seasons, distinguishes (1) the *superessential* cause, the divine *dispositio* of the universe; (2) the remoter cause (*causa longinqua*), the revolution of the *primum mobile*; (3) the *proximate* cause, "the movement of the sun in his proper circle", viz. that of the Ecliptic.

[2] It cannot be too carefully remembered that the distinction was *introduced* into cosmology by Aristotle, and that it is, in particular, anti-Platonic.

because it is sometimes abundant and sometimes fails, by saying that the presence or absence of a *debilitas* in the seed is itself a part of the whole cause of the effect—so far, of course, the scholastic could concur—and that it is a neither more nor less "necessary" cause than the *motus solis*; if the scholastic thinks otherwise on this last point, that, we say, is because by a cause he means an *agent*, and he mistakenly supposes the "seed" *not* to be an agent in its own growth, but to be simply and purely passive, a view made impossible to us by our conception of reciprocal interaction in physics. And, as already said, he is also unfortunately imbued with the Aristotelian fancy of the contrast between the immutability of the "heavens" and the mutability of the sub-lunary region of the universe. If we are to retain the distinction between necessary and contingent causation, we shall be driven to say that the "superessential" cause, God, is the *only* cause which causes with complete necessity, *all* other causes, remote or proximate, "celestial" or "terrene", being infected with contingency.

If we make this modification, the doctrine seems to me to be perfectly intelligible. It means, in effect, that while everything that happens in cosmic history happens as God ordains or permits, no event is a perfectly determinate "one-valued function" of other specific events, and that when we say that the occurrence of *X* may certainly be inferred from the occurrence of *A*, *B*, *C*, . . . there is always an understood *Deo volente*. It may be that the ultimate "pattern of the whole" demands a divergence from the most uniformly exhibited "routine of sequence", and if it does, the sequence will not occur; the sun will, at need, "stand still upon Gibeon". But whether the sun stands still or "hastes to go down", it is certain that there is a "pattern of the whole" and that *it* will not be violated. No "innovation" will be a capricious departure from it. But it is impossible in principle to calculate from data already in our possession whether and when an "innovation" will take place, because the "pattern of the whole" is not and cannot be a *datum*. (Or, to take an illustration from human action, it would be manifestly fallacious to argue that a phrase found in the published work of a writer must be an "error of the press" because the same writer has published many thousands of lines, but has nowhere else used that particular phrase. If it is the specially right and appropriate expression of the thought in his mind at the moment of writing he may use it, though he never used it before and will never use it again. A man's habits of speech have a great deal of influence on his choice of phraseology, but they never absolutely dictate it.)

It would thus be wholly consistent with theistic belief in the government of the world by God to recognise a genuine element of contingency in all historical events. You may in a sense resolve this contingency into defect of knowledge on our part, but only if you mean that we are not fully acquainted with the divine *purpose*. The defect could not be removed by any extension of our acquaintance with the details of past cosmic history, since the fullest acquaintance with them would not put us in possession of the "whole counsel of God." There is thus, so far, no reason to take up *a priori* an attitude of opposition to physicists who tell us they are led by their own special studies to admit a "principle of Indeterminacy" pervading the whole physical order. They may be right, or they may be wrong, but they are not saying anything which conflicts either with the inherent reasonableness of the universe, or with theistic faith. Professor Eddington, for example, is not maintaining that Δῖνος βασιλεύει, τὸν Δί' ἐξεληλακώς.

Nor do I see that the admission of contingency conflicts with belief in the divine *omniscience*, as is often supposed. It would do so, if we impiously thought of God as inferring our future from our past much as an astronomer calculates the future positions of a planet from a record of positions it has occupied in the past. But no theologian, I take it, ever thought of God's knowledge in this fashion. To quote James Ward, "How God knows, or even what knowledge means when attributed to the Supreme Being, few of us will pretend to understand".[1] But, as Ward is arguing in the context of the remark, at least it will not be imagined that He calculates the course of events, like a "Laplacean demon", from a multitude of differential equations. Whatever omniscience is, it is not this.[2]

These observations leave it still an open question whether it is *requisite* for human freedom of choice that there should be "contingency" in nature at large. May we not accept all the seven theses we began our discussion of choice by formulating, and at the same time deny that any natural event really is contingent ? (Perhaps nature, at all events, really is bound "fast in fate"?) Clearly, of course, the denial of contingency, if it is to leave human moral freedom unaffected, must not be extended to those physical events which are the expressions of our responsible choices, the *actus imperati* which carry the *actus elicitus* which is my decision over into the physical order. If it is true that the movement of my

[1] *Naturalism and Agnosticism*[1], i. 42.

[2] Cf. the remark of St. Thomas (*S.Th.* ii.ae ii.ae, art. 171, q. 6 ad. sec.) that "divina praescientia respicit futura secundum duo: scilicet secundum quod sunt in seipsis, in quantum scilicet ipsa praesentialiter intuetur; et secundum quod sunt in suis causis, in quantum scilicet videt ordinem causarum ad effectus. Et quamvis contingentia futura, *prout sunt in seipsis*, sint determinata ad unum, tamen *prout sunt in suis causis*, non sunt determinata quin possint aliter evenire." That is, it is eternally part of the divine providential plan that a certain event shall happen: also, it is not the case that this event is what I have called a "one-valued function" of preceding events. *Both* these truths are known to the divine Mind.

hand is ever the result of my choice, then *that* movement cannot be a determinate one-valued function of previous events of the physical order; these events must leave it an open issue whether my hand is to move or not. Consequently, the same consideration must apply to all events of the physical order which depend causally, no matter at how many removes, on the choice of a moral agent. And of how many actual events, if of any, could we say that no actual choice by *any* moral agent is conceivably to be found among their causal antecedents? Theoretically, however, we might, I conceive, say that events of the physical order which have no acts of choice by moral agents among their causal antecedents, *if there are any such events*, might be regarded as wholly non-contingent without any compromise of the positions upon which the reality of man's moral freedom depends. Even *if* God be needlessly assumed to have bound "nature" fast in fate, *our* moral freedom may be none the less real, provided that by "nature" we only mean whatever in the actual physical order is entirely independent of causation by the choice of a moral agent, if anything is so independent. To assert moral freedom, one *need* not assume the omnipresence of an element of "indeterminacy" in physical processes as *such*. There are apparently good grounds for this assumption, but they are of a different order. (I should perhaps add that I should regard it as very rash to assume that there is a single physical event which is wholly independent of the causality of *some* moral agent, since I see no reason to suppose that men are the only such beings in the universe. And in this context, when I speak of "moral agents", I am, of course, intending *created* moral agents, whether human or otherwise.)

I suspect that the reason why some excellent writers who seem to assert freedom of choice in express terms yet describe themselves as "determinists" is that they assume that Libertarianism is *necessarily* committed to this admission of contingency as a *cosmic* principle; and that they regard such a conception as "unscientific". I would urge on any reader of my own who takes this point of view, two considerations: (1) In point of fact there is apparently reason to believe that contingency is actually making its way back into scientific thinking on strictly theoretical grounds, as forced upon us in the interpretation of experimental results[1]; (2) in any case, this is not the issue really at stake between Libertarian moralists and the "scientific determinists". It is not contingency in "nature", but *choice* which the determinists of the nineteenth century were anxious to explode as a superstition, and they have left their representatives behind them. If anyone doubts this, I recommend to his notice an address on "The Nature of Life", delivered by Professor L. Hogben to the British Association at Cape Town on July 25, 1929. Mr. Hogben, at least, makes no attempt to disguise his conviction that all human moral purpose is an illusion; the whole social and moral life of man consists of "conditioned reflexes" which have no purpose, and a "new school of psychologists", with whom the speaker clearly sympathises, "has come into being with the express object of . . . relieving Man, the celestial pilgrim, of his burden of soul".[2] It is surely

[1] On this see, *e.g.*, Eddington, *Nature of the Physical World*, pp. 220 ff.; Whitehead, *Process and Reality*, p. 30.

[2] "The modern mechanist", says Mr. Hogben in the next paragraph of his discourse, "does not say that thought and love and heroism do not exist; he says, show me behaviour to which you apply the adjectives thoughtful or loving or heroic, and we will, one fine day, endeavour to arrive at predictable conclusions with reference to it by following the only method of enquiry which we have learned by experience to trust". But if the "endeavour" is to be successful, if we are, "one fine day", to discover that all the acts we call thoughtful, loving, heroic, can be predicted without taking the existence of thought, love, heroism, into account (and not one of the three can be discovered as a "laboratory" fact), how does the position Mr. Hogben accepts on behalf of his "mechanist" differ from the position he disclaims? What is meant by saying that "love exists", but

a pity that moralists who would regard this reduction of the spiritual life to "conditioned reflexes" as the death of all morality should mark their dissent, where it exists, from those of us who believe in contingency in "nature" at large, by adopting a label which confounds them with the "scientific" enemies of responsibility and practical reason.

It is hardly necessary to add that the "Libertarian" is left by his theory perfectly free to recognise that the full character of human "free" action is only to be found in acts of conscious deliberate choice. How far impulsive acts can be said to be done with freedom, and, again, how far my choice is free when my own past misconduct or negligence has closed alternatives which would otherwise remain open, is another question.

D. *Free Will of Indifference*

A reader of the preceding paragraphs may conceivably ask whether I mean to assert or to deny the reality of what has been called "free will of indifference". Do I, or do I not, mean that we can, and sometimes do, choose between alternatives without a "motive" for our preference? I should reply (1) that if there are such "unmotived" choices, they must surely have no significance for our moral life, since they do not express the *character* of the agent supposed to be making the choice. It is just the choices which are rooted in our personal moral *quality* and give expression to it with which the moralist is concerned. If "motiveless choice" occurs at

that there are acts which *cannot* be predicted without knowing that the agent *loves* someone, or something? And does Mr. Hogben never count on the good behaviour of his banker, or his servants? If, like other men, he sometimes does so, will he say he has studied banker or servant "by the only method of enquiry" he has "learned by experience to trust?" (My references are to the report of the discussion published by the *Cape Times* as "revised by the authors".)

all, it may fairly be taken to occur only in connection with the kind of insignificant movements regularly treated by the schoolmen as their standing examples in discussing the possibility of morally indifferent acts (*barbam vellere, festucam de terra tollere*, and the like). Or, to put the point differently, "motiveless choice", if really possible at all, would be a grave abuse of our liberty in any matter of the slightest moment, because it would mean refusing to deliberate in a case where we ought to deliberate.

Further, it is not clear that there is, even in these apparently trivial cases, anything we can properly call *unmotived* preference. This becomes clear, I think, if we define our terms with a little care. A *motive*, we must remember, is not the same thing as a mere impulse which releases, or discharges, an act. To act with a motive is not merely to be impelled to act in a certain way, but also to regard one's act as *justified* by a certain consideration. When I say that I act thus and with this motive, I mean both that the considerations I allege are truly those which impel me to act as I do, and also that they make my acting as I do the right and reasonable thing for me to do. A motive is always something which, at the time of acting, the agent regards as a *reasonable* incentive. It is a "reason" in the double sense that it explains why the agent does what he does, and that, so long as he does not repent, it is held by him to justify his behaviour. It follows that a man's "motives" are rarely, if ever, present to his own mind at the moment of action in "clear and distinct" apprehension; they are usually very largely "subconscious", or "habitual". But this does not detract from their rationality. A driver who has learned the British rule of the road "drives to the left", because he has learned that this is the established rule, and that it is dangerous to disregard it. He does not actually recall these considerations—if he has really "learned how to drive"—as he steers himself through the traffic. If he is at all practised, he regulates himself "automatically" by the rule. But it is a *rule*, and it is because he has *knowledge* of the rule so deeply ingrained in him that his "secondary automatic responses" are what they are. His whole conduct is an example of *rational* choice; it does not issue from what some writers are fond of calling the *passional* nature, but from intelligence. In the vast majority of those voluntary acts which are not preceded and conditioned by explicit deliberation, scrutiny will, I believe, reveal "motives" as rational as the driver's preference for the recognised rule of the road. In most cases there is intelligent "justification" for the course adopted, and the agent would not have taken that course if he had not been acquainted with that justification, though he was not actually thinking about it at the moment of acting. (I do not, of course, mean that the "justification" will always bear strict investigation; in the case of our morally wrong acts it will not. I mean that there are considerations which the agent regards as justification, and to which he will sincerely appeal, if the morality of his act is disputed. The man who has taken a human life will at once plead, if his act is impugned, that "it was his life or mine", and this is meant, and is felt by the homicide to be a rational justification of the fatal shot or blow, though it is another question whether the plea will satisfy the "impartial spectator".[1])

[1] Or, to take a standing example from St. Thomas, fornication is *malum in se*, and therefore has no real justification. But it is true that the fornicator—unless he is actually deliberately sinning "in contempt of God"—is taking the means to a *delectatio carnalis* which is, considered simply as such a delectation, *bonum quoddam temporale*. He is not wrong in thinking that this *bonum* is a *bonum* so far as it goes; but there is a superior *bonum* with which it is incompatible. The sinner is not alive to the superiority of this other *bonum*, and hence, from his point of view, his conduct *appears* to be rationally justified. (This is, of course, why Aristotle says that it συμβαίνει πως ὑπὸ λόγου ἀκρατεύεσθαι.)

I believe this analysis applicable to almost all the normal acts of human beings, when free from external constraint. There are grounds which, in the opinion of the agent at the time of acting, make his act the reasonable one to be done. Those grounds are not commonly *before* his mind, since most of his acts are done without explicit deliberation between alternatives. But they are *in* his mind, as is shown by the readiness with which they are produced in reply to any suggestion that his conduct has been unreasonable. I am, therefore, convinced that it is a mistake to attack the standing doctrine of Greek moralists, that the sinner does wrong because he is misled by a false judgement of good, on the ground that it over-rationalises human action. If unmotived, or unreasonable, choice occurs at all, it only occurs, I would submit, in connection with alternatives which are taken to be morally indifferent. It might be alleged that it occurs *here*. "Where you can take either of two courses, A_1 or A_2", it may be urged, "and there is no reason for regarding either as in any way more or less good than the other, clearly the fact that you take the course A_1 shows that you are making a choice, and yet, *ex hypothesi*, you know of no reason why A_1 should be chosen rather than A_2. Here, then, there must be unmotived choice".

But will the argument really stand examination? A typical example would be that of a man who is about to play a game of chess and is "offered his choice" of taking the white pieces (and attacking) or the black (and defending). In discussing such a case we need to draw distinctions. It may be that the player to whom the option is given knows himself to be stronger and more practised in attack than in defence, or *vice versa*, and chooses accordingly. He may do this with clear and full consciousness of the reason for his choice. Or he may not be consciously thinking about the matter, and yet it may be what really decides his option, as is shown by his reply, when asked, *e.g.*, why he chose white, that "I am more accustomed to the white pieces and more at home with them".[1] In neither case can it fairly be said that there is not a rational motive for his choice, though it may be a "subconscious" one.

But what of the case of the man who is *equally* expert in the attack and the defence, and knows this? He also may be offered his option, and he must make it, or there will be no game. Is not this a clear case of making a choice which *must* be unmotived? It does not seem to me that it is so. The man in question has, indeed, no motive for choosing White rather than Black, or Black rather than White. But he *has* a motive for making either option rather than declining to opt, since if both players are equally expert, and both know it, and therefore refuse to make any option, the game, which is what both desire to have, will never begin. I think, therefore, that what really happens in such a case is that the player who is "offered his choice" makes a real choice which has a motive, and a sound one, the choice to foreclose one of the alternatives, but does not *really* choose as between White and Black. He simply says the word which happens to "come to the tip of his tongue". In practice we commonly avoid this situation of having to make what appears to be a choice between equally desirable alternatives by enacting a rule that the point shall be decided by "tossing up". That is, we voluntarily remove the particular decision from the sphere of the voluntary. So again, when I, who am not much interested in such things, am offered a choice between two

[1] Or, as might be the case, "I am more accustomed to Black, and so wish to take this opportunity of practice in handling White". Greater familiarity with the pieces of one colour may lead to either choice, according as the chooser cares more about winning on this particular occasion, or about "improving his game".

dishes or two wines, I feel sure that I often make no real option; I say the word which "comes handiest", merely because I want to get the point decided one way or the other. This is making a real and rational choice between settling the question and leaving it open, but not, as it seems to me, a real choice for one alternative as against the other.

On these grounds I feel very doubtful whether any genuine choice is really without a rational motive, *i.e.* without what the chooser, at the moment of choosing, regards as a reasonable ground for preference. Even when, to take the old example of the schools, I pick up a straw from the ground, I should probably not do so consciously unless I disliked the look of "litter", or wanted to exercise a group of muscles, or something of the kind, and these are rational grounds for choice. The nearest approach we make in actual life to "indifferent" choice, I should say, is made in the cases when we rationally will to eliminate one of two alternatives, but do not care which is eliminated. This is not a typical case of morally significant "free choice", but rather, in the words of Descartes,[1] *infimus gradus libertatis.* It is not in our "indifference" in such a case that we show our freedom, but in our resolution to bring the indifference to an end.

A final word may perhaps find its place here, as a *Rechtfertigung* against the charge, urged more than once in private correspondence against the present writer by Dr. Rashdall, of clinging to an "unintelligible" Libertarianism. If I have no desire to find the source of responsible moral freedom in a liberty of caprice, why am I not content to treat moral freedom,

[1] *Meditat.* iv. "indifferentia autem illa quam experior cum nulla me ratio in unam partem magis quam in alteram impellit, est infimus gradus libertatis, et nullam in ea perfectionem, sed tantummodo defectum sive negationem quandam in cognitione testatur".

after the fashion of Leibniz, as spontaneity *along with the consciousness of spontaneity*?[1] Why do I hold that a free man is not adequately described as *automaton spirituale*? I would reply by reminding my reader of a striking passage in Kant's second *Critique*.[2] Kant is there admitting the existence of moral "incurables", on whom *all* education and discipline is wasted. They manifest utter moral depravity in early childhood, and grow only the more depraved as they grow older. But we are justified, he says, in treating them morally and juristically as no less responsible and accountable than others, and they themselves admit the justice of this attitude, "in spite of the desperate native mental constitution thus imputed to them". This, Kant pleads, is an argument for his rigid distinction between temporal appearance and eternal reality. The depravity displayed through life by the "incurables" is itself merely the consequence of the "free causality" of their morally evil wills.

What does this amount to, if we have once rejected Kant's identification of the temporal with mere appearance, but to the doctrine that the "incurable" is *created* incurable, and then held accountable by his "dark Maker" for the flaw in the *Naturbeschaffenheit seines Gemüths*? It is the horrible Augustinian notion of the *massa perditionis* reduced to its simplest terms. The "incurable" is imagined to be sent into the world already "damned", with a will already and unalterably "wholly averse from God". And we are expected to acquiesce in the justice of this situation. (I do not dwell on the difficulty of the *quaestio facti* whether there *are* such "incurables". If our failure to strike the right note

[1] Though possibly this is an unduly minimising interpretation of Leibniz's own phrase, "spontaneity along with intelligence" (spontanéité qui devient liberté dans les substances intelligentes), *Discours de métaphysique* xxxii.

[2] *KdprV*. I. Th. i. B. iii. *Hptst*. (*Werke*, v. 104).

with some transgressors could be taken as evidence of their incurability, I am afraid, when I consider how helpless candid self-scrutiny seems to prove us all to be against some of our weaknesses, that we may fairly suspect ourselves and all mankind of belonging to the *massa*.) If we seriously believe in the theory, can our moral theology be anything better than a dishonest attempt to curry favour with a malevolent Maker by flatteries we know to be undeserved? If there were no Creator, or an evil Creator, the difficulty would not arise. But since there is a Creator, and a righteous and merciful Creator, we cannot reconcile determinism with an ethical Theism by assuming that some men have been created already "damned". And we must not shirk the issue, as Kant tries to do, by saying that the "incurable" is not created "damned", but damns himself once and for all by a primal free act of wrong choice which is not "in time".[1] *This* is a rank "unintelligibility". For a "first act" of the series of my transgressions must have a place in the temporal series to which the rest of my transgressions belong, and thus, on Kant's own theory, it should be part of the "pheno-

[1] I put the matter as Kant himself puts it in *Religion innerhalb d. Grenzen d. blossen Vernunft*. In the *KdprV*. (*Werke*, v. 106-7) he speaks less pictorially. We are there told that if space and time were more than "appearances", it would follow that the moral responsibility for the conduct of creatures rests with their Creator, and not with themselves. But a Creator creates only realities, and space and time are merely phenomenal. God is therefore the cause of my existence as a free agent in the intelligible world, but not of my actions in time and space. Surely we must say that *this* way of relieving my Creator from responsibility for my sins reduces the whole moral life to an illusion. Kant apparently wants to reproduce the scholastic reasoning which argues that God is not the author of my misdeeds, since God created me free, and I freely choose to do wrong. But he ruins the force of the argument by trying to make it turn on the "ideality" of time and space. If that were part of the argument, it should also follow that God is not the cause of any of the observed events of the natural order. The "argument from design" must not only cease to be probative; it must also lose all that right to our respect which Kant himself claimed for it. And it then becomes very hard to understand how Kant's virtuous man can be entitled to a rational faith that the natural order is controlled by God in the interests of a moral end,—the crowning of virtue with happiness.

menal series" of consequences, not the "intelligible" cause of the whole series. If Kant's language is to have a tolerable meaning, the primal free wrong choice should be taken merely as an imaginative *symbol* of the character exhibited by all our temporal wrong choices, and in becoming such a symbol it ceases to be an explanation. If it is more than such a symbol, our actual moral life is deprived of the significance Kant in particular is anxious to ascribe to it as a discipline into goodness of will; in the case of the "incurables", the discipline and struggle must be no more than illusion, and none of us can be sure that he is not himself one of their number.

I see no way out but to strike at the root of the whole conception by insisting on the utter "creatureliness" of all finite agents. Nowhere in them is there any element of character which is unmade, an eternal and unalterable datum. Their being is always a *γένεσις εἰς οὐσίαν*, never simply *οὐσία*. And the admission destroys in principle the foundation of all determinism, "hard" or "soft". The real "unintelligibility" seems to me to be with the determinist who is, consciously or unconsciously, transferring to the creature, or to some ingredient in its composition, the "once-for-allness" incommunicably proper to the Creator. And for that reason I cannot feel certain that there are actually any "incurables"; the notion may have its uses, as a check on moral presumption, but it may be only a "limiting concept".

[illegible]

ment[illegible] ... cause[illegible] ... A [illegible] ... should[illegible] ... has [illegible] ... an[illegible] ... exp[illegible] ... unc[illegible] ... occ[illegible] ... goo[illegible] ... de[illegible] ... and [illegible] ... than [illegible]

[illegible] com[illegible] ... all [illegible] aspects. [illegible] of character which [illegible] able [illegible] never simply [illegible] principle [illegible] "[illegible]" [illegible] with [illegible] ... [illegible] concept.

INDEX OF PROPER NAMES

Printed in Great Britain by R. & R. Clark, Limited, *Edinburgh.*